SMALL INDUSTRY DEVELOPMENT IN INDIA

SMALL INDUSTRY DEVELOPMENT IN INDIA

The Outlook

Edited by

Prof. C. Suryanarayana

Ph.D.

Coordinator, UGC-SAP

Dept. of Commerce & Management Studies

Andhra University

Dr. V. Krishna Mohan

Dy. Coordinator, UGC-SAP

Associate Professor

Dept. of Commerce & Management Studies

Andhra University

ANMOL PUBLICATIONS PVT. LTD.

NEW DELHI - 110 002 (INDIA)

ANMOL PUBLICATIONS PVT. LTD.
4374/4B, Ansari Road, Daryaganj
New Delhi - 110 002
Ph.: 23261597, 23278000
Visit us at: www.anmolpublications.com

Small Industry Development in India: The Outlook

First Published, 2005

ISBN 81-261-1441-X

PRINTED IN INDIA

Published by J.L. Kumar for Anmol Publications Pvt. Ltd., New Delhi - 110 002 and Printed at Mehra Offset Press, Delhi.

Contents

Foreword ix

Preface xi

Acknowledgements xv

Prolegomena xvii

List of Contributors xxxiii

SECTION – I: Policy Perspective and Implications

1. Policy Regime and Legal Framework for SMES: The Global Perspective 14
   —Dr. B. Yerram Raju & Mrs Sarah Varkki

2. SSI Challenges and Strategies in the Liberalization Period 31
   —D. Nagayya & K.V. Rao

3. SSI Policy with Special Reference to Identification and Product Reservation 41
   —Dr. P.B. Appa Rao

4. Reforms in the Industrial Sector with Focus on Small Scale Industries 55
   —Prof. C. Suryanarayana & Dr. D. Nagayya

5. Liberalisation and Exports of Small Scale Industries in India 66
   —Prof. B. Appa Rao

6. Small Scale Industries Sector in India: Emerging Trends and Implications 76
   —Dr.. A.D. Madhavi, Dr. M. Vijayalakshmi & Dr. S. Vijay Raju

7. Topsy-Turvy Policy of the Government on Small-Scale Industry 86
—Dr. S.V. Pulla Reddy & Dr. M. Mutyala Naidu

SECTION – II: WTO and Small Industry

8. SME's in the Era of Globalization—WTO Implications 102
—M S Bhagawatgita

9. Globalisation: Challenges of Small-Scale Industries 110
—Prof. C. Suryanarayana

10. WTO and Its Implications to Small-Scale Industries 119
—Dr. G. Tulasi Rao & Dr. T. Kama Raju

11. Challenges of WTO Agreements for Small Industry Development 122
—Dr. J. Revathy & Prof. K.V. Rao

12. WTO Scenario: Strategies for Small Industry Development 138
—Prof. C. Suryanarayana & Dr. V. Krishna Mohan

13. Quantitative Restriction: Some Insights 144
—Dr. A.V. Shukla, Ms. V. Prabhu & Mr. V. Varshney

14. The Impact of WTO on Indian Industries 151
—Prof. M. Chandrasekhar

15. WTO Agreement: A Boon or a Bane to the SSI Sector 159
—Mr. Israel Raju Vuram

16. Challenges of Small Industry in the Post Liberalization Period 165
—Dr. V. Krishna Mohan

17. Development of SSI Sector in the Context of WTO: A Focus on Financial Implications 174
—S. Prabhakar Reddy

SECTION - III: DIC and Small Industry Development

18. Impact of District Industries Centres on Rural Industrialization 194
—Prof. L. Venugopala Reddy, Prof. P.B. Appa Rao & Dr. T. Suresh Kumar

19. Changing Role of District Industries Centres 248
—D. Nagayya

20. Performance of DIC: A Case Study of Nellore District 259
—K. Lavanya Latha & Prof. BEVVN Murthy

21. District Industries Centres (DICs): Future Perspectives 270
—Dr. T.V. Rao

22. SSI Sector in East Godavari District–Role of District Industries Centre 277
—Dr. J. Chandra Prasad & K. Nageswara Rao

23. District Industries Centres— The Outlook 286
—Er. H. Shivaji Rao

24. DICs – Role in Changing Scenario 293
—B. Suresh Babu

25. Working of District Industries Centres: A Case Study of Visakhapatnam District 297
—Prof. C. Suryanarayana & Mrs. M. Meher Karuna

SECTION – IV: Infrastructure Development

26. Infrastructure for Small Industry Development in A.P.: A Study of APIIC 309
—Ch. Venkateswara Rao

27. Strategies of Academic Institutions to Promote Entrepreneurship 330
—Prof. BEVVN Murthy

28. Maintenance of Industrial Estates in Andhra Pradesh: Role of Industries Associations 337
—Ch. Venkateswara Rao

29. Study of Managerial Aspects of Small-Scale Industries in Rayalaseema and Nellore Districts of Andhra Pradesh 351
—M.Chandrasekar & P. Balaji Prasad

30. Role of Government in Revitalizing Sick SSI Units 362
—Prof. K. Seshaiah & Dr. B. Ramachandra Reddy

31. Technological Development in Small Manufacturing Enterprises: Some Insights 372
—Dr. M.Usha

Appendices 381

Index 391

Foreword

I am delighted to write this foreword to the volume of selected papers of important **National Seminars on Small Scale Industries** held under the aegis of the **UGC Special Assistance Programme** (Phase-III) of the **Department of Commerce & Management Studies of Andhra University**, Visakhapatnam. It is a compilation of a large number of Research Papers presented by a cross section of delegates from various Universities, SMEs, Small Industry Associations, SSI promoting agencies of the Government, Banking Sectors, Trade & Business, Consultants, Research Institutes and others.

These seminars have been organized at a time when the small scale industries are facing fierce challenge and keen competition from China, Japan, Taiwan, South Korea and other developed and more advanced countries, especially in the Post-WTO business environment. A platform has been created to experts to deliberate upon important themes and crucial issues pertaining to SSI sector. The papers reflect analytical and empirical evidences, experiences and views of experts about the Government initiatives, during the last five decades for development of small scale industry and the threats and opportunities for the small scale sector consequent to the onset of economic reforms and the advent of WTO. The consensus emerged at the seminars are offered as recommendations to the Government, SSI Promoting Agencies, Associations and entrepreneurs.

I trust that in this way University has been able to play a vital and useful role not only by taking-up research in the identified thrust areas but also creating ample opportunities for other institutions to interface with the University and share their experiences and contribute for knowledge building, curriculum development and policy making.

I sincerely believe that many more such seminars and workshops on emerging issues of SSI sector will be held so that the University will help generate innovative ideas that will be useful to the economy and society at large.

I congratulate Prof. C. Suryanarayana, Co-ordinator of UGC SAP for his efforts in successfully bringing out the compilation of the papers which will be of immense benefit to various sections of people in the realm of industrial development.

Prof. Y.C. SIMHADRI
Vice Chancellor

Andhra University
Visakhapatnam

Preface

The small-scale sector is an effective instrument of social change and economic growth in a number of countries. The small and medium scale industries represent 80 per cent, of industrial base of most of the developed countries. In Japan about 99 per cent of the units are SMEs contributing 52 per cent, of the total exports revenue. In Italy approximately 94 per cent of the Italian firms are SMEs contributing about 43 per cent of the total GDP. In USA, SMEs have generated about 54 per cent of the sales revenue.

In modern India the Small-scale industries have been a success story. They have emerged vibrantly in the face of rising threats from large-scale sectors inside the country and of multinationals from abroad. At the micro-level the small-scale sector has succeeded in diffusing entrepreneurship culture and played a prominent role in converting the physical, material and human resources into productive assets.

The Small scale units constitute about 95 percent of the total industrial units and produce more than 7,500 products. The production from this sector has reached an impressive level of Rs.5,784 billions in 1999-2000. This represents 40 percent of manufacturing output and 35 percent of total exports. About 18.6 million people are provided employment by this sector.

The post-liberalization business environment has turned harsh for the small scale sector due to increased internal and external competition. The far reaching impact of various WTO norms have also posed a threat to the future of small scale sector in India. Unfortunately, inspite of sufficient advanced information and growing awareness of the impending threats, the SSI sector has not been able to adequately prepare to face the new challenges. Even after several committees and study groups recommendations over the past decade the WTO compatible policy for this sector is yet to be enunciated. Much confusion prevails over a number of issues such as the cap on capital investment, foreign direct investment ceiling, interest subsidy, dereservation of items and creation of technology up gradation fund.

Even after the creation of the new Ministry of small scale industry and agro and rural industries in 1999 many of the problems of the SSI sector have remained unsolved. Though this sector has grown at a rapid pace, during the last three decades, the incidence of sickness is on the increase. While the official figures registered only 10 percent of over 32 lakhs of SSI units as sick , the unofficial figures of sickness is 40 percent. In view of the crucial importance of SSI sector to the economy, it deserves all the policy support of the Government. This Small entrepreneurs need, at present not protection but institutional support for modernization and technology upgradation, better infrastructure facilities, adequate working capital finance from the banking and other financial institutions.

There is also need for small enterprises to keep pace with the structural and technological changes taking place in large scale industries and improve their competitiveness by converting their threats into opportunities in the global economic scenario.

The Global challenge is looming large with the entry of almost all the industrialized countries for instance, Japan, Germany, France, Korea as well as other Asian countries. Excellence in manufacturing can only provide competitive weapon to compete in the sophisticated worldwide markets. The small enterprises need to continually redesign their products and also shorten the time to take the new product to marketplace. The economies of scale have been replaced by the concept of economies of scope, which means flexibility or ability of a firm to adjust its operations at any moment in accordance with the rise and fall of demand or change in the mix of the product. Quality must be built in production at every stage of design and manufacture. All the players in the industrial field, namely the Government, the large industrial houses, small industries, village and cottage industries have been contributing their mite to the growth of the economy. What is required is a proactive and participative synergy, instead of decimated hostile stance among the various players, to gain mutual benefit and progress.

In view of the prominent role being played by SSI sector in the growth and development of the national economy and also the challenges and opportunities of this sector in the present global environment, a convergence of views and opinions of experts from various quarters has been felt necessary. Accordingly a series of two national seminars, a workshop and a symposium on SSI sector were organized under the aegis of UGC Special Assistance Programme of Department of Commerce and Management Studies, Andhra University, each with specific objectives and focus. Some select papers presented at the seminars are given in this book.

The first workshop was held on 28th February 1999 on the theme 'Economic Reforms – Small Industry Development'.

The National seminar on 'WTO – Challenges and Opportunities for Small Industry Development in India' was organized on the 18-19 March, 2001.

The next seminar was held on 17th February 2002 on the theme 'DICs, Role Dynamics and Strategies for Industrial Development in the Changing Global Economic Scenario'.

This book is presented in four sections. Each section contains an introduction about the theme of the seminar, the seminar proceedings , brief summary followed by full text of the select papers presented at the seminar.

Section-I deals with an overview of the SSI policy perspectives during the era of planning and the growth of the sector. It contains papers, which focus on legal framework of SME in global context, small industry in liberalized scenario, identification and product reservation, policy reforms, emerging trends and implications for SSI sector and Topsy -Turvey policy of the Government.

Section-II presents a brief account of WTO and Small industry development in India. The papers incorporated in this segment includes Globalization-WTO implications for SMEs, Globalization challenges and opportunities for SSI, WTO implications, Quantitative restrictions, impact of WTO on Indian Industry, post-liberalization challenges and focus on financial implications.

Section-III analyses the genesis, scope and role of District Industries Centres and various issues confronting them. It also contains papers on changing role of DICs, performance of DICs, perspectives and role dynamics in changing scenario and case studies.

Section-IV provides an insight into the role of Government institutions in the development of infrastructure to motivate and encourage small entrepreneurs with special reference to Andhra Pradesh. Industrial estates in Andhra Pradesh, Strategies of Academic Institutions for Entrepreneurship Development, Role of Industrial Associations, Industrial Infrastructure Corporation and its catalystic role and marketing and financial management of SMEs are some of the papers that are dealt with in this section.

—**Prof. C. Suryanarayana**

Acknowledgements

The faculty, scholars and students of the Department of Commerce and Management studies express their grateful thanks to University Grants Commission for sanctioning the III Phase of Special Assistance Programme with a substantial financial assistance. We are extremely thankful to the University administration particularly Prof. R. Radhakrishna, respectable former Vice-Chancellor of Andhra University for his invaluable advice in preparation of the project proposal.

My profound thanks are due to our esteemed Vice-Chancellor Prof. Y.C. Simhadri, for his able guidance, encouragement and all the support to us in taking up various activities under the SAP.

My heartfelt thanks are due to Sri K. Vidhyadher Rao, Hon'ble Minister for Major Industries, and Sri. B. Gopala Krishna Reddy, Hon'ble Minister for Small Industry for sparing their valuable time to inaugurate the two National Seminars and for their invaluable messages.

I am greatly indebted to Sri T. Gopala Rao, IAS (Retd.) former Principal Secretary of Industries, and Sri. T.S. Appa Rao, IAS, Commissioner of Industries for their cooperation and encouragement in our research and other activities relating SSI sector under the Special Assistance Programme.

Prof. A. Sankaraiah of Kakatiya University and Prof. V. Surendar of Osmania University, who are the external members of the Advisory Board have been a source of inspiration, help and their rich counsel at different stages of the SAP are immensely acknowledged with grateful thanks.

I also acknowledge the cooperation of the present Head of the Department Prof. U. Babaji and former Head of the

Department Prof. B. Parvathiswara Rao, Prof. J.V. Prabhakara Rao, Chairman, PG Board of Studies, Prof. B. Appa Rao former Chairman, PG Board of Studies for rendering good and timely support.

I also thank Dr. D. Nagayya, Consultant on Small Enterprises, Guntur, Prof. P.B. Appa Rao of Sri Krishnadevaraya University for their expert counsel.

The valuable services of the former coordinators of Special Assistance Programme, Prof. M. Gangadhara Rao, Prof. V. Balamohandas, Prof. G. Subrahmanyam and Prof. D. Panduranga Rao deserve all appreciation and special mention as they have strengthened the base for the development of SAP. We are grateful to them for their ceaseless cooperation and contribution to SAP.

Thanks are due to our faculty colleagues of the Department, who have extended their affectionate and learned support in our successful accomplishment of different tasks under SAP. My colleague Dr. V. Krishna Mohan, Associate Professor and Dy. Co-ordinator, SAP deserves all appreciation and thanks for his unstinting involvement and also contribution.

Indeed the Special Assistance Programme helped in a great measure to networking and collaboration with Department of Industries and other Government SSI Promoting agencies, SIDBI, APSFCs, DICs, SISI, Small Industry Associations, Consultants, Faculty of affiliated colleges. I may be failing in my duty if I do not express my heartfelt thanks to all these players including the paper presentors, resource persons, student organizers.

Thanks are also due to our research scholars especially Mr. Israel Raju Vuram, Mr KVRNS Kondayya Rao, Mrs. N. Mehar Karuna and Mr. V. Sudhakar Rao for their active involvement in field surveys and also organizing various activities under SAP.

Mr. K. Durga Prasada Rao, Stenographer is an asset to the Co-coordinator, his services with commitment and patience have really helped in making things to happen on time under the SAP.

(Prof. C. SURYANARAYANA)

Prolegomena

SECTION - I

Dr. Yerram Raju in his article ***'Policy Regime and Legal Framework for SME's : Need for a Global perspective'*** outlines that Laws and regulation for SMEs have been put in place in countries throughout the world under a variety of policy regimes. Whether in the USA or Korea, the Philippines or Poland, legal intervention have been found to be necessary to regulate markets, ensure fair competition and provide an environment for SME development. These policy thrusts are articulated in the Seoul Declaration of SMEs(1992) and Bologna Charter for SMEs (2000). The biggest democracy with the most complex multi-party system, viz, India, offers interesting insights into the balancing act of attaining reforms with a human face.

A study of India's policy and regulatory frame work for SMEs raises issues which are of wider relevance in the current debates on re-structures State intervention. In India, the new approaches to regulation will need to be based on simplified procedures, transparency, and stronger partnerships between government and business through greater public -private participation (PPP). The main task for the next decade is to put in place a new legal system and the corresponding institutional mechanisms to facilitate the development of SMEs and enable them to fulfil their economic potential. This required a global understanding and perspective, the paper attempted to explore.

Dr. Nagayya and Dr. Rao in their paper ***'Small Scale Industries Challenges and strategies in the liberalization period'*** highlighted that an important element of the globalisation process is the growth of intra-firm trade, which creates barriers to entry for developing countries. The design of reform policies which facilitates India's participation in the global network of production needs greater attention. "I will make what you need" and not "I will sell what I make" should be the attitude of manufacturers in the global environment. Quality infrastructure and productive manpower are the basic necessities to participate in the global production network. These are critical problem areas. Two special economic zones (SEZs) are planned to be established in Gujarat and Tamil Nadu on the Chinese model. Special attraction in these zones will be applicability of flexible economic environment, flexible labour laws, and improved high quality infrastructure, apart from removal of bureaucratic hurdles.

The SSI units should be given incentives to enable them to graduate into medium size. Technological upgradation and modernisation, adoption of cluster approach for quick and effective delivery of inputs to SSI units, review of labour laws are some of the factors that need utmost attention to make the sector competitive in the LPG environment. Through simplification of rule s and regulations and creation of friendly environment the is sector will benefit more than by making small concessions.

Prof. Appa Rao in his paper ***'Small-scale Industrial policy with special reference to Identification and Product Reservation'*** says that de-reservation of the items reserved for exclusive manufacture by the small-scale industrial sector has now become important because many de-reserved items could be freely imported under Open General License (OGL), giving rise to an anomalous situation. Also, the emergence of a common market for SAARC, and phasing out of qualitative restrictions under the WTO commitment has rendered such reservation irrelevant.

De-reservation of the products reserved for exclusive production be the small industry is in accordance with the wish of he World Trade Organisation and objectives of Globalisation. The effect of its is exposure of the small industry to the rigors of competition from the economically strong large scale industry and both economically and technologically strong foreign industry. The changes in the policy have been introduced anticipating something good but whether it causes good or bad has to be awaited and seen.

Prof. Suryanarayana and Dr. Nagayya's paper ***'Reforms in the Industrial Sector with focus on SSIs'*** examined that debureaucratisation, deregulation and simplification of rules and regulations and procedures were emphasized in the SSI policy. Some of the steps need approval from the Parliament/State Legislature, and some others need to be followed up by executive actions. Careful analysis and study should precede these actions.

A significant aspect of economic reforms launched since 1991 related to deregulation and liberalization in the field of industrial development. For achieving the objective of reforms, the role of the Government needed to change from that of only exercising control to one of providing help and guidance by making essential procedures fully transparent and eliminating delays. The SSI sector need to pursue measures such as using of innovative technology, positive and right attitudinal change in promoting agencies, institutional credit flow to tiny sector units, improvement of Delayed Payment Act, strict implementation of Single Window System etc.

Prof. Appa Rao, in his paper ***'Liberalization and Exports of SSIs in India'*** expressed the view that in the light of the importance of exports to the national economy, product groups which have export potential need to be given adequate support and encouragement, in the form of incentives and infrastructural support. A sharp decline in the growth of world trade, appreciation of the rupee vis-à-vis the currencies of India's major trading partners and competitors, and the dramatic depreciation of some East Asian Currencies during 1997 have all contributed to export sluggishness. India needs to initiate measures to protect her SSI sector from international competition by imposing non-tariff barriers such as social clauses, environmental regulations, and quality standards for products and processes.

Dr. Madhavi and others highlighted in their paper ***'SSIs in Inida : Emerging Trends and Implications***' that the agreement on TRIPS, it would be difficult for the SSI sector to continue with reverse engineering and manufacture many items without having to pay royalty to the patent holders. In terms of sanitary and phytosanitary measures, SSI's will have to adopt international standards with regard to quality, health and hygiene. In this scenario, there is an urgent need to sensitize the entrepreneurs on all issues and agreements relating to WTO -- the Agreement on Agriculture, the Competition Policy, The General Agreement on Trade in Services (GATS), and Trade Related Intellectual Property Rights (TRIPS). It is imperative to dovetail the latest technological advancements into the production process. These measures would provide the necessary cutting edge for the SSI sector to boost exports.

Dr. Pulla Reddy and Dr. Mutyala Naidu in their paper ***'Toposy-Turvey Policy of the Government on SSI'*** opined that there is a need to bring these changes in the small-scale industry. But these changes should be brought after informed debate and discussion. The consensus arrived at on the most crucial part of the reforms should be used to improve the efficiency of small sector for the benefit its consumer.

SECTION - II

Dr. Bhagwatgita in his paper ***'SMEs in the era of Globalization - WTO implications'*** discussed that the threat to the SSIs is the growing competition from overseas and the challenges lie in the new opportunities opened for them. The competition and Cooperation should be the new strategies of SMEs as they need more sophisticated and professional support mechanism. Investment, technology, infrastructure and human resources are more important than subsidies in order to produce on cost effective lines and offer the product at competitive price. In the WTO environment SSIs will have to gear up to the market trends and changing consumer behaviour. Small entrepreneurs should acquaint themselves with WTO provisions and procedures and voluntary intervention of NGO's and others as facilitators and solicitors of SSIs is worth while.

The paper on '***Globalization : Challenges of SSIs***', Prof. Suryanrayana focused that Indian small entrepreneurs have to absorb, adopt and assimilate new technology to improve their operational efficiency and to meet the global quality standards of goods and services. The SSI sector in our country will have greater export potential in this decade especially in electronics and computer components, automobile components, food products etc. consumer goods. The service sector also offers great potential for small scale industry particularly in the areas of communication, information technology, internet, e-commerce and e-business. The SSI sector should come out of the protective environment and develop and compete on their own through innovation and production and improvement in product attributes and tapping of potential markets world over.

Dr. Tulasi Rao and Dr. Kama Raju explained in their paper ***'WTO and its implications for SSIs'*** that the Indian trade-both domestic and foreign -- is under severe pressure due to the impact of the WTO. Technology, credit, raw materials and price have often been identified as the problems. Several public sector institutions have stressed on problem solving rather than as active agents of change. The phasing out of Quantitative Restrictions (QR's) on 715 items effective 1st April, 2001 has resulted in instances of large scale dumping of cheap products. Majority of these 715 items are reserved for production by the SSI. A little over 52% of the items freely importable over the year 2000-2001 fall into two broad sectors of food and textiles.

The MNCs has an advantage of global branding is use of latest technology and competitive price structure. The removal of QR's lead to an anomalous situation in the case of products reserved for the SSI sector as these items are freely importable now. The Government's decision to reduce customs duties on list of inputs of the SSI combined with the enhancement in the exemption limit on excise duty will improve the price competitiveness of the domestic SSI sector and help the industry to compete with cheap imports.

Dr. Revathy and Prof .KV Rao in their paper ***'Challenges of WTO Agreements for Small Industry Development'*** discussed that in the era of globalization, protection to SSI sector could be given through multilateral process. The Government's intention to keep tariff levels (customs duties) at not higher than 35% is a misleading because the total tariff, after 10% surcharge, would be 38.5%. Tariff levels might even be brought down further in the coming years. There are now four slabs of duties, 35%, 25%, 15% and 5%, with surcharge of 10% continued.

The Export-Import Policy 2000-2001 has placed 58 items that are reserved for SSIs on the Open General License (OGL) list, and 198 more items from the reserved list will be freed on April 1, 2001. At present, 624 out of 812 items of the reserved SSI list can be imported freely. As a result the Imports will enjoy a clear edge over products produced within the country. Removal of QRs has not so far resulted in significant rise in imports. The New Export and Import Policy will provide focussed fillip to export of gem and jewelry, software, pharma, agro chemicals and bio-technology.

Dismantling of QRs, lowering of tariffs, opening of reserved categories, reduction in subsidies for exports, legislation on Trade Related Intellectual Property Rights (TRIPs), etc. are some of the challenges placed before the SSI sector. Government should act as a facilitating agency for SSI sector by providing subsidy on R&D projects, ensuring protection through WTO - friendly measures, and creating a level playing ground for SSI sector.

The paper '***Small Industry Development: Challenges and Opportunities under WTO scenario***' presented by Prof. Suryanarayana and Dr. Krishna Mohan emphasizes that liberalization, privatization and globalizations alerted Indian industries to produce quality products at competitive prices. Organizations, big or small, are compelled to upgrade technology, cut costs, improve quality and adopt innovative management strategies.

With the emergence of World Trade Organization (WTO) and its conditionalities, Small-scale Industries will have to compete on their own to find a place for themselves in the domestic as well as international markets. They will have to improve the quality of products and be efficient and competitive in order to survive and grow. While technology up-gradation is inevitable for SSIs, the size of investment, as per the recent definition, is considered a severe credit crunch. inadequate knowledge of markets, infrastructure poor R& D facilities, tradition bound outlook of entrepreneurs, low productivity of labour are some of the weaknesses of SSI sector.

The WTO agreement does not discriminate on the basis of size of industry or its nature. There is no single agreement of

WTO, which directly deals with SSIs. The Indian SSIs will have to face competition both from MNC's and from Indian large-scale industries. The ethical and moral value of the Indian small entrepreneurs also influence their competitiveness in the domestic and international market. Quality consciousness should be ingrain in the entrepreneurs and employees to gain competitive advantage in the liberalised business environment.

Dr Shukla and others presented the paper on '***Quantitative Restrictions: Some Insights***'. It highlighted that with the removal of Quantitative Restrictions (Qs), the domestic industry including the Small industry (SSI) sector will be affected by the on slots of imports and virtual flooding of markets with cheap imports particularly from countries like China. However, the removal of QRs will bring in some benefits such as 1) consumers will get wider choice of goods and services at a lower price, 2) free trade is likely to bring down prices and keep the level of inflation low, 3) Govt. may benefit from higher customs duty on imports, 4) easier access to import raw material and capital goods for the domestic manufacturers leading to foster industrial groups. Removal of QRs therefore, can be viewed as a challenge and an opportunity to Indian SSIs to initiate steps to enhance competitiveness. It will trigger off a number of effects as, a new class of customers will emerge who will exercise a kind of choice that peers across the world, the new class of entrepreneurs who will focus on distributing imported items and a major shift in brand perception and so on.

Prof. Chandra Sekhar discussed in his paper '***The impact of WTO on Indian industries***' that according to WTO the trading nations are required to adhere to uniform rules of trade and the trade procedures are based on the principles of transparency, predictability and certainty. The main functions of WTO include administering and impelling the multilateral trade agreements, acting as a forum for multilateral trade negotiations, resolving trade disputes, overseeing national trade polices etc. the protection enjoyed by Indian industries for more than 45 years resulted in low productivity, lack of research and development, unplanned growth, and above all lack of competency.

Awareness in Indian industries is spreading fast to

restructure and concentrate on core competencies. Many enterprises are expanding the areas of competence to reap the benefits of economies of scale. Indian companies have to shake off the lethargy to improve performance on aspects of cost, quality, lead-time, and service to customers. They have to change their corporate culture ,management styles and structure, marketing strategies etc. for growth. Globalization, if it has any meaning for the developing countries, should help to improve the lot of 85 percent of the world population living in these countries. Ironically, globalization is helping 15 percent of the population of the industrially advanced countries. They are able to take advantage of WTO by forcing the developing countries to open up their potentially huge markets to foreign goods and services and capital.

Mr. Israel Raju's paper on '***WTO Agreement : A boon or A bane to the SSI sector*** ' elaborated that the economic boundaries of nations for all practical purposes have expanded enormously much beyond the geographical limits and the rules of the trade are no longer different for domestic zone and international zones. The Govt. may have to do away with the criteria of local area content and dividend balancing which may prove to be a jolt to the development of subcontracting and result in loss of domestic market of SMEs. The impact is severely felt especially in automobiles, consumer electronics, electronic appliances etc. It is essential that the fruits of R&D should be adequately protected throughout the world under the harmonized potential system. In the event of multilateral agreement, the market constituted by the governments may have to be opened up for foreign competition and the system will have to be made more transparent.

Dr. Krishna Mohan in his paper on '***Challenges of Small Industry in the post liberalization period***' examined that the process of economic liberalization and globalization has been an effective instrument in promoting efficiency, new capital investment and faster economic growth in many nations. It has also created keen competition among Indian SSI sector which was virtually non-existent in the earlier era of protectionism and planned development. it is now imperative for companies as well as global managers to understand what globalization is, in terms of product quality technologies, marketing strategies, investment decisions and so on.

The development of small-scale enterprises is generally believed to contribute substantially to employment creation and generation of income, particularly for low -income population groups. Small-scale sector with strong basics, is now caught up in winds of change, which are ushering in a contemporary industrial culture, business ethics. Small-scale industry opened their frontiers by absorbing new technology to sharpen their artistic skills and deepening their creativity to be competitive in the global market.

Sri Prabhakara Reddy in his paper on '***Development of SSI Sector in the context of WTO: A focus on Financial Implications***' mentioned that the bureaucratic intervention in SSIs should be curtailed. The Industry Associations have been demanding that the procedures need to be simplified and the stamp duty registration charges, instruments of mortgage have to be rationalized to make the financial instruments viable and catalystic in the flow of credit to SSI sector. The tax structure should be changed to have three tiers system namely federal tax, sales tax, and local tax which is in vogue in some countries. It is also suggested that the RBI may consider advising banks to reply at least 25% of their net bank credit to SSI sector. The Govt. might consider setting up of private industrial estates so that there will be some element of competition in providing industrial infrastructure services.

SECTION – III

The paper on '***The Impact of District Industries Centre on Rural Industrialization***' jointly authored by Prof. Venu Gopala Reddy, Prof. Rao and Dr. Suresh Kumar analyzed the performance of DIC of Ananthapur District. A pivotal role has been played by the DIC by promoting 5948 SSI units during 1988-89 to 1997-98 and generated employment opportunities to 54,316 persons. Credit facility to the tune of Rs.932,206 thousands, was arranged to SSI units by various financial institutions and other banks. During the same period 38,245 artisans were assisted in setting up of village and cottage industries and also through credit sanctions. Training was imparted to 11,467 rural artisans. In many years the DIC's actual achievements exceeded the targets, which could be considered an outstanding performance.

The coefficient of correlation between number of agro based units setup in rural and urban areas is 0.1475, which is positively insignificant. The average number of units setup in rural areas per annum is more than the average of urban units per year in this district. A positive significant correlation is observed between the number of engineering units setup in rural and urban areas. The average number of units set up in rural areas, per annum is more than the average number of units set up in urban areas per annum in this district. The employment generated was 5 persons on an average per unit and the investment made worked out to Rs.345.75 on average per person. It is observed that Category wise-distribution of entrepreneurs benefited is unequal. Since there is a lot of scope for developing and assisting SC and ST entrepreneurs, efforts should be made to motivate them and assist them on much more priority basis.

Dr. D. Nagayya, in his paper, 'Changing Role of DICs' observed that the single window concept envisaged at the district level through District Industries Centres (DICs) has been implemented all over the country from 1978, with varying degrees of success in different states and union territories. Along with the institutional frame, change in policies and programmes in tune with the changing economic environment, and delegation of powers by various organizations to the field level functionaries, and simplification of the process of setting up small enterprise, upgradation/diversification and sustained growth of the enterprises becomes highly necessary to accelerate the process of industrialization and decentralized pattern of development. Role played by DICs so far, and assessment of their performance of various studies and all India committees have been attempted in this paper. A few suggestions are presented for revitalizing decentralized industrial strategy through the DICs, as a result-oriented field level institution providing an effective link for all institutions associated with the industrial sector.

Dr. K. Lavanya Latha & Prof. BEVVN Murthy, in their paper, 'Performance of DIC; A case Study of Nellore District' emphasized that the concept of industrial estates has gained importance in India from 1955 when the Hadapsar Industrial Estate's experience was impressive and found to be an effective tool of industrialization. The District Industries Centres, which are nodal agencies, were considered to take up development of SSI sector through industrial estates. Due to their economic significance, the DICs have been given the task of motivating young and talented persons to start tiny and micro ventures through PMRY and CMEY programmes. The study revealed that the demand for plots in industrial estates situated in urban areas is more than rural areas, which indicates the entrepreneurs' preference to locate their enterprises in urban areas. In Nellore district, development of industrial estates helped for a gradual increase in number of SSI units from 1,131 to 1,772 during 1995-96 to 1999-2000. However, the artisans are unaware of modern marketing techniques and their utility in business. The DICs need to take the mantle of the entrepreneurship to every corner of the district to meet the twin challenges of unemployment and under-utilization of the resources to accelerate the pace of industrialization of the district.

The paper on '***DICs : The Future Perspectives***' by Dr. T.V. Rao, dealt with the supposed role of the DICs and the actual role being played by them. After the establishment of DICs, there has been a substantial growth in the SSI units from the point of view of their number, investment, production and employment generation. However, the DICs suffered from drawbacks, such as, lack of proper coordination with different SSI promoting agencies, lack of relevance and objective criteria in the projects and product profiles prepared by DICs, lack of necessary zeal and initiative among young professionals of DICs, and so on. The artisans were not given enough assistance from any agency at the district level in respect of supply of raw-material, credit, modernization of machinery and marketing. They should become district development centres rather than district information centres. The DICs need to work with vision and mission to make single window concept a virtual reality.

Dr. Chandra Prasad & Dr. K. Nageswara Rao, in their paper '***SSI Sector in East Godavari District : the Role of DIC***' observed that the District Industries Centre has promoted 9,544

SSI units comprising of 33 per cent of food and agro-based industries, 18.8 per cent engineering units, 13.1 per cent polyester-based units and 8 per cent mineral-based units. These units have generated employment to 83,170 persons and the highest employment of 35.55 per cent is registered in food and agro-based units. The operation efficiency of the units is not very impressive due to low and weak investment position. The internal resources of the units are so meagre that they were not left any surplus to sustain themselves during the periods of business strain. It is suggested that the SSI units should have promotional agencies, which could assist them in the initial stages. More and more infrastructural facilities need to be created, especially in the rural areas to motivate rural entrepreneurs. Mini industrial estates may be developed near mandal headquarters and major panchayats and DICs need to establish a workable nexus with other SSI promoting agencies and service institutions.

Mr. H. Shivaji Rao's paper on '***District Industries : The Outlook***' examined that the District Industries Centres have not been taking necessary initiatives to obtain the approvals and clearance from different establishments to enable the entrepreneurs to start the industry. These Centres are more engaged in processing the registration and subsidy allotment rather than giving the necessary technical support. The DICs need to maintain library of technical, industrial projects that are essential in the district of Srikakulam, in order to assist new entrepreneurs. After the units are grounded, follow-up action need to be taken to render necessary counseling and assistance. Programmes, such as, PMRY, CMEY can also be handled by DICs but it should not engross completely in these activities. In spite of some of weaknesses, the DIC of Srikakulam district could contribute substantially for the growth and development of SSI sector.

Mr. B. Suresh Babu, in his paper, entitled '***DICs' Role in the Changing Scenario***' made a critical assessment of the strengths and weaknesses of the DICs. The entrepreneurs are compelled to approach different agencies to get clearances to start a SSI unit and in the process they are getting frustrated and disappointed. The single window system is considered not effective. To overcome this difficulty, an industry facilitation cell may be created at DIC to enable all connected departments to meet periodically and provide for speedy clearance and implementation of projects. The DIC may act as an arbitrating agency to resolve differences between SSI units and ancillary, large-scale enterprises. All statutory procedures should be dealt with through single window system. A Centre of Marketing Intelligence needs to be developed by DICs by providing facility of information technology. The SSI Associations are required to play a positive role as they constitute more as a source of strength rather than conflict breeding bodies. DICs may be made as nodal centres for ISO certification of SSIs.

A paper on "***Working of District Industries Centres: A case study of Visakhaptnam Dt.***" by Porf. Suryanarayana and Mrs. Karuna dealt with the working of DIC, Visakhaptanam. During the 1993-94 to 2001-2002 the DIC promoted 24,786 SSI and tiny units with a total investment of Rs.21,330 lakhs providing an employment to.2.43 laksh persons. Most of these units (68percent) are tiny units with an average investment of less than Rs. 1 lakh. Among the units promoted, engineering and forest based constituted 46 percent. More emphasis was given to promotion of industries in urban mandals. DIC could not achieve the objective of industrialization of rural areas as rural mandals were thoroughly neglected. The achievement under PMRY was impressive. However, it was not uniform through the period of 1993 to 2002.

SECTION - IV

The paper on '***Role of APIIC in Industrialization through Industrial Estates***' by Dr. Ch. Venkateswara Rao deals with the genesis and working of Andhra Pradesh Industrial Infrastructure Corporation (APIIC). Before the advent of the corporation, development of industrial estates and industrial area activity was conducted by the Department of Industries. The APIIC, which came into existence in 1973 performs the functions of identification, acquisition of suitable land for construction of factory sheds, getting power and water supply and allotment of plots and sheds to the entrepreneurs. Fixation of price of the built-up sheds, plots in industrial estates promoting effluent treatment schemes also come under the purview of the Corporation. During 1973-1976, 48 industrial estates, 15 industrial development areas have been developed by the Department of Industries and were handed over to the Corporation. The APIIC acquired 25,357 acres of land and developed 13,271 acres. In this area, it had promoted 226 industrial estates of different kinds, 20 commercial and 17 industrial housing complexes in the state. In the estates and the industrial area, the Corporation developed 17,911 plots, out of which 14,001 were allotted. At the same time, 3,258 sheds were allotted as against 3,514 sheds constructed.

Another important dimension is that 17 housing complexes were developed in 10 districts and constructed 4,678 houses in an area of 330 acres of land. Thus the APIIC has made a remarkable contribution for development of mostly medium and small-scale industries in the state of Andhra Pradesh.

Prof. BEVVN Murthy, in his paper, on '***Strategies for Promoting Entrepreneurship by Academic Institutions***' emphasizes that the development of entrepreneurs and entrepreneurship is necessary in developing countries to meet the challenges posed by population growth and unemployment. Academic institutions, especially management schools can play a vital role in development of entrepreneurship by undertaking research on topics, such as, entrpreneurship development among different communities, professions and regions; training and development of entrepreneurs, and transfer of technology to different areas, which offer scope for development of backward areas. Development of entrepreneurial talent in the youth from the very early age through socialization in the family and in the years of schooling, evaluating the performance of various agencies in entrepreneurship development and problems of small entrepreneurs are some of the issues that need to be examined through empirical information. Many governmental and non-governmental agencies have committed themselves for entrepreneurship development. Academic institutions should also lay focus on entrepreneurship development and join hands with other institutions engaged in similar activities to gain mutual benefits.

Dr. Ch.V. Rao, in his paper on '***Maintenance of Industrial***

Estates in Andhra Pradesh: Role of Industrial Associations' pinpoints that maintenance of facilities created in the industrial estates and areas should be the responsibility of local bodies, wherever the APIIC transferred these estates and areas to such bodies, as property tax and other taxes are collected by these bodies. Since the maintenance has not been virtually taken up by these agencies, the entrepreneurs and the APIIC have resorted to alternatives for maintenance of infrastructure facility on the lines being followed in states like Gujarat and Maharashtra. In these states, the notified area committees play a greater role in maintenance of the estates. The specially constituted committees are vested with the powers to collect taxes and use the same for maintenance of facilities in the respective belts. The part of the revenue is transferred to local bodies. It is suggested that the entrepreneurs need to realize that the property tax collected from them will be utilized for maintenance of the industrial estates and the process of collecting advertising tax in the notified industrial areas may be initiated without any delay in order to increase revenues of the societies. The APIIC should extend cooperation to service societies in preparing work estimates, finalizing tenders, issuing work orders, work measurements, supervision and payment of bills.

Prof. M. Chandrasekhar and Dr. Balaji Prasad, in their paper on '***Managerial practices relating to finance and marketing of SSIs in Rayalaseema and Nellore district'*** analyzed that the small-scale industries are promoted with an objective of better utilization of local resources for achievement of local self-sufficiency. It is revealed by the study that majority of the small enterprises in the 5 districts of Rayalaseema have insufficient technical and managerial background. Out of the 629 units covered by the study 50 units were employing 5 to 10 workers while 48 units employing 10 to 20 workforce. Regarding investment, the highest number of 67 units has made investment of Rs.5 to Rs.10 lakhs. In terms of investment, the granite and ceramic units made investment to the tune of Rs.50 lakhs, which is more than any other units in the manufacturing sector. There are some capital intensive SSI units which are found to be working well. On the whole, performance of SSI units in these districts is impressive though not to the expected level.

The paper on '***Role of Government in Revitalizing Sick SSI Units***', by Prof. K. Seshayya and Dr. B. Ramachandra Reddy, analyzes that the symptoms of sickness are gradual in nature, and the entrepreneurs therefore need to be alert to initiate preventive measures in order to maintain the health of the units. Profit fluctuations, rejection of goods, failure to face statutory liabilities, longer period of credit, non-submission of periodical financial data, decrease in working capital, etc., are some of the critical issues, among other things, that send signals of sickness. There has been a gradual increase in the number of SSI sick units from 2.35 lakhs in 1997 to 2.49 lakhs in 2001. The total bank credit blocked up in these sick units increased from Rs.13,787 crores from 31st March 1997 to Rs.19,646 crores on 31st March 1999. Of this, the SSI sector has Rs. 4,314 crores, i.e., 22.2 per cent blocked up in its units. It is suggested that governments initiative and priority allocation of raw material, extending marketing facilities, granting some privileges and concessions, penal action for delayed payment to SSI units would helps salvage of the SSI sector. The government policy should gradually shift from protection to development of SSI on competitive lines.

List of Contributors

1. Prof. B. Yerram Raju and Dr. Sarah Varkki - Administrative Staff College of India(ASCI, Yusuf Nagar, Hyderabad
2. Dr. D. Nagayya - Consultant on Small Enterprises, Former Director (Industrial Dev.) NISIET, Hyderabad

   Prof. KV Rao - Dept. of Commerce & Business Admn., Nagarjuna University Guntur
3. Prof. P.B. Appa Rao - School of Business Mgt. Sri Krishna Devaraya University, Ananthapur.
4. Prof. C. Suryanaryana - Dept. of Commerce & Mgt. Studies, Andhra University, Visakhapatnam
5. Prof. B. Appa Rao - Dept. of Commerce & Mgt. Studies, Andhra University Visakhapatnam
6. Dr. S. V. Pulla Reddy & Dr. M. Mutyala Naidu - School of Business Management, Sri Krishna Devaraya University, Ananthapur
7. Sri M.S. Bhagawatgita - Convener, Academic Council NISIET, Yousufguda, Hyderabad

8. Dr. G.Tulasi Rao & Dr T. Kama Raju	-	Dept. of Commerce & Mgt. Studs., AU Dr BR Ambedkar PG Centre Etcherla, Srikakulam
9. Dr. J. Revathy	-	PG Dept. of Commerce & Mgt. VRS & YRN College, Chirala.
10. Dr.V. Krishna Mohan	-	Dept. of Commerce & Mgt. Stds., Andhra University, Visakhapatnam.
11. Dr. A.V. Shukla; Ms. Prabhu; & Mr. Varshney.V	-	Dept. of Business Admn. & Mgt., Amaravati University Amaravathi
12. Prof. M. Chandra Sekhar	-	School of Business Management, SV University, Tirupati
13. Mr. Israel Raju Vuram	-	ACTS Degree College MVP Colony, Visakhapatnam
14. Sri S. Prabhakara Reddy	-	Andhra Bank Zonal Office Visakhapatnam
15. Prof. L. Venu Gopal Reddy; Prof. P.B. Appa Rao; & Dr. T. Suresh Kumar	-	School of Business Management, Sri Krishna Devaraya University, Ananthpur
16. Prof. BEVVN Murthy & K. Lavanya Latha	-	School of Business Mgt. Sri Venkateswara University Tirupati
17. Dr. T.V. Rao	-	Pragati Mahavidyalaya Post Graduate College Hyderabad.
18. Dr. J. Chandra Prasad	-	PG Dept. of Commerce DNR College, Bhimavaram
Mr. K. Nageswra Rao	-	Dept. of Commerce SVSS Arts & Sci. College, Attili.

19. Er. H. Shivaji Rao	-	Small Industry Consultant Srikakulam
20. Sri B. Suresh Babu	-	General Manager, District Industries Centre Visakhapatnam.
21. Sri Ch. Venkateswara Rao	-	Dy. Registrar University of Hyderabad Hyderabad
22. Prof. BEVVN Murthy	-	School of Business Management Sri Venkateswara University Tirupati
23. Prof. M. Chandra Sekhar; and Dr. B. Ramachandra Reddy	-	School of Business Management Sri Venkateswara University Tirupati
24. Prof. K. Seshaiah; Dr. B. Ramachandra Reddy	-	School of Business Management Sri Venkateswara University Tirupati
25. Dr. A.D. Madhavi; Dr. M. Vijayalakshmi and Dr. S. Vijay Raju	-	Gitam Institute of Foreign Trade (GIFT), Visakhapatnam.
26. Mrs. N. Mehar Karuna	-	Dept. of Management Studies Visakha Institute of Professional Studies, Visakhapatnam.
27. Dr. M. Usha	-	Department of Commerce Osmania University, Hyderabad.

SECTION – I
Policy Perspective and Implications

Introduction

The goals and objectives set out for the nation on the eve of Independence, include, the rapid development of agricultural and industrial sectors of our country, rapid expansion of opportunities for gainful employment, progressive reduction of social and economic disparities. Removal of poverty and attainment of self-reliance, remain as valid today as at the time when Pandit Jawaharlal Nehru first set them out before the nation. Any industrial policy must contribute to the realisation of these goals and objectives at an accelerated pace. The present statement of industrial policy is inspired by these very concerns, and represents a renewed initiative towards consolidating the gains of national reconstruction at this crucial stage.

Characteristics of SSI Sector

Ever since the country obtained independence in 1947, the small-scale industries (SSI) are given a special emphasis as they are the vehicles of generating additional employment through low capital investment. In the national economy this sector offers scope for individual, village or cooperative enterprise development and means for rehabilitation of displaced persons. SSIs are particularly suited for the better utilisation of local resources and for the achievement of local self-sufficiency in respect of certain essential consumer goods. Another significant role of these industries is that they are a means to ensuring more equitable distinction of national income and facilitate effective mobilisation of resources of capital and skill, which might otherwise remain dormant.

In view of the pivotal role played by SSIs in industrializing, the neglected backward and rural areas and in generating employment on a mass scale, the govt. has been supporting the small-scale industries by restricting the volume of production in the large-scale sector, by differential taxation and by direct subsidies. The prime aim of the State Policy is to ensure that the decentralised sector acquires sufficient vitality to be self-supporting and its development is integrated with that of the large-scale industry. During the era of planning, the Government has formulated and introduced a large number of schemes to promote and strengthen the small-scale industries in the country.

Policy Initiatives

Industrial policies over the years have promoted SSIs through various incentives in order to fulfill socio-economic objectives. These incentives related to financial, fiscal and infrastructural measures and were targeted at achieving the growth of the sector during the Plan periods. Incentives were provided either on a "one time" basis (initial support for setting up of units) or in the form of sustained support for a specific period (protectionist measures, subsidies, etc.). While some incentives were made applicable to all industrial units including the large-scale sector, others were available exclusively for the SSIs.

Industrial Policy Resolution, 1948 envisaged that some basic and strategic industries to be established by the State in addition to those, in which the private sector could be permitted to play a role, subject to controls and regulations. The Policy aimed at balanced growth of different manufacturing sectors and focused on the co-existence of large, cottage and small industries. An emphasis was laid on the promotion of cottage and small-scale industries as these could play a crucial role in the rehabilitation of displaced persons through the establishment of individual/cooperative enterprises.

Industrial Policy Resolution, 1956 endorsed the philosophy of initiating measures to improve the competitive strength of the small enterprises while recognizing the role of SSI sector in providing employment opportunities, mobilizing local skills and capital resources, and integration with the large sector. Emphasis was placed on the creation of facilities such as industrial Estates and rural community workshops to provide the required production technologies, other amenities and incentives.

Industrial Policy Statement, 1977 stressed the wider dispersal of cottage and small industries into rural areas and small towns. It emphasized the "whatever could be produced by small and cottage industries must only be so produced". Accordingly, there was an expansion of the list of reserved items for exclusive production by the SSI sector. The concept of the Tiny Sector was introduced within the SSIs giving special consideration and extending help by way of provision for margin money assistance. The concept of District Industries Centres (DICs) was also mooted so that in each district a single agency could meet all the requirements of village and small industries under one roof.

Industrial Policy Statement, 1980 focused on integrated industrial development and suggested the setting up of nucleus plants in the districts, which were identified as industrially backward. It is expected that these would help spatial dispersal of small and ancillary units and the existing network of SSI units would grow faster. SSI units were redefined by raising the ceiling of investment in plant and machinery.

Industrial Policy, 1990 introduced important measures like raising the investment ceilings in plant and machinery for SSIs, export oriented and tiny units, creating a central investment subsidy exclusively for the SSI sector in rural and backward areas, assisting women entrepreneurs with an objective of widening the entrepreneurial base.

Industrial Policy, 1991 announced "New Policy Measures for Small, Tiny and Village Enterprises" with the objective of imparting a vitality and growth impetus to the sector. These measures were announced subsequent to the policy of delicensing, decontrol, deregulation, overall liberalization and structural reform of the economy in general and industrial and trade policies in particular that were initiated in July 1991.

Small-scale and ancillary undertakings were exempted from licensing for all articles of manufacture, which were not covered by the reserved list for Public Sector, and those kept under compulsory licensing. The investment limit for tiny enterprises was raised to Re. 0.5 million and locational conditions were withdrawn. All industry related service and business enterprises (with an investment ceiling as those of tiny enterprises) irrespective of location, were recognized as SSIs. Equity participation by other industrial undertakings was permitted up to a limit of 24 per cent of shareholding in SSIs to boost ancillarisation and a strengthening of the capital base. A new scheme of Integrated Infrastructural Development (including technological back up services) for SSIs was provided for with the participation of State Governments and financial institutions.

The Industrial Policy measures announced in 1991 laid special thrust on promotion and strengthening of small, tiny and village industries. Besides effecting changes in investment limits, equity participation, etc., a new scheme of Integrated Infrastructure Development for SSIs with the participation of State Governments and Financial Institutions was initiated and a pro-active role for NGO sector was mooted.

In order to protect their interest and facilitate their rapid development, the Government in pursuance of its policies, have initiated a number of support measures from time to time which include policy of reservation, revision of investment ceilings, modernisation, technology upgradation, marketing assistance, etc. The emerging economic scenario in the changed liberalised and competitive economic environment, has necessitated structural and fundamental changes in the policy framework put into place for the development of this vital sector of the economy. Accordingly, there has been a shift in focus from "protection" to "promotion". In the post-reform period, a number of steps including partial dereservation, change in investment limits, facilitating foreign participation, establishment of growth centres, export promotion, marketing assistance and incentives for quality improvement, etc. have been taken by the government for strengthening of SSI sector.

In order to enable the government to place more focussed

attention on the problems of the SSI sector, a new Ministry of Small Scale Industries and Agro and Rural Industries has been created on 14th October 1999, under the Independent Charge of a Minister of State. To give a direction and perspective to the development strategy, the Minister in-charge of Small Scale Industries and Agro & Rural Industries announced an *"Agenda for the Millennium"* which places special emphasis upon improved supply of credit, better infrastructural facilities and impetus for modernisation and technology upgradation in small scale industries. The Agenda takes cognizance of the special role to be played by Information Technology, sunrise industries, hi-tech industries, export potent industries, and at the same time stipulates all possible steps to meet the requirements of the tiny and micro-enterprises which constitute over 9 per cent of total small scale industrial units in the country.

Contribution of SSI Sector

The small industry sector, as an important segment of the Indian economy, accounts for around 95 per cent of the industrial units, contributes 40 per cent of output of manufacturing sector, 26 per cent of exports and provides direct employment to 18 million persons in around 3.2 million registered SSI units in the country. The sector enjoys the pride of being second largest employer in the country and offers a wide spectrum of products. This sector serves as a greenfield for the nurturing of entrepreneurial talent enabling the small-scale units to graduate into medium scale. The SSI sector has been receiving attention from the policy makers by way of support and incentives, infrastructural facilities, technology, marketing and other similar measures. For providing financial assistance, a "priority sector" treatment was accorded to SSIs by the financial institutions. With the onset of economic reforms and globalization, a number of challenges and opportunities have emerged for the sector. The development strategies that were put in place during the fifties and pursued till the initiation of reforms in 1991 are in the process of restructuring in order to increase the role of market forces in economic decision-making. The control measures for a majority of industries and import licensing have been liberalized and fiscal policy reforms initiated. Efforts have been made to attract Foreign Direct Investment and transfer to technology into the country. These measures are designed to put the Indian economy on a sustainable growth path.

The Present Scenario

In order to give a boost to the development of small-scale industries sector in India, the Government announced a Millennium Mission in December 1999. The main features of the Mission include, amongst others, the creation of a sound policy environment to enable the SSI sector to cope with the emerging challenges of globalization. The inflow of Foreign Direct Investment has been taken as a means to infuse additional resources, technology and modern management practices to make the SSI sector internationally competitive. In the direction of simplification of complex rules and regulations, it has been proposed to set up a High Power Committee for recommending a single comprehensive legislation for the SSI units. To create an appropriate fiscal environment conducive to the growth of the SSI sector, rationalization of taxes and tariffs has been considered essential. In addition, the rationalization of subsidies has become necessary to make them WTO compatible looking into the broader interests of the SSI sector.

Prospects and Outlook

The industrial policy initiatives taken by the Government over a period of time had a favourable impact in the process of growth of SSI sector in terms of increase in production, employment and exports. Initiatives have fostered a well-set structure of institutions that meet varying requirements of the sector. The promotion policy measures have, by and large, covered the basic requirements of the SSIs. However, in the changed environment, with the onset of economic reforms there is a need for the building of the competitive strengths of the sector. Operational efficiency and sustainability in openness are strategic to ensure continued growth and better prospects.

The year 1991 marked the dawn of a new era for the Indian economy. Major structural and economic reforms were initiated with the objective of transforming the centrally managed economy to a market-driven one. The reforms were aimed at easing the ambit of direct controls by the Government, thereby increasing the role of market forces in economic decision making, which would accelerate the process of growth.

The process of liberalization, while providing tremendous opportunities, has thrown up new challenges for the Indian small-scale industries sector. Having been hitherto nurtured in a sort of protective environment, with industrial globalization, it now finds itself vulnerable to cross-border enterprise activities, which include free international movement of goods, investment, strategic alliances for product development, production, sourcing and marketing.

For SSIs, the globalization of economic activities has two interfaces. For some, the process opens new opportunities to expand and grow; for others, a much larger group, the process poses a fresh gauntlet or threat, from abroad. Two aspects of globalization, i.e., inward and outward refer to (i) SSIs seeking to compete beyond national boundaries, and (ii) domestic SSIs being subjected to impending competition from across the border, respectively. The structure and ownership pattern of Indian manufacturing enterprises, where more than 97 per cent of the units are proprietary concerns, suggests that a large number of SSIs subsumed in the second category would need to converge their technical capabilities, integrate with the capital markets and assimilate limited foreign ownership to turn threats into opportunities and achieve self-generating expansion. To satisfactorily proceed on the growth path, the domestic policies and programmes for the SSI sector would have to be effective and growth oriented.

General problems faced by SSIs, certain sector groups, such as, tiny sectors, micro enterprises, women entrepreneurs etc., require special attention. Undertaking continuous reviews of the credit policies and evolving new ones in the changing economic scenario for meeting emerging conditions has been the corner stone of the credit policy so far.

1. Nayak Committee – 1991

The Nayak Committee, 1991 of the Reserve Bank of India mainly dealt with the question of adequacy and timeliness of credit made available to SSIs. It recommended that the SSI sector should obtain 20% of its annual projected turnover by way of working capital.

As a follow up of the Nayak Committee recommendations, the Government announced in 1995-96 a Seven Point Action Plan for improving the flow of credit to small scale sector. This included-setting up of specialized SSI bank branches; adequate delegation of powers at branch and regional levels; conducting sample surveys of the banks performing SSI accounts; sanction of composite loans as far as possible; regular meetings with SSI entrepreneurs; sensitisation of bank managers towards working of SSI sector; and simplification of procedural formalities by banks. The banks have initiated necessary steps for effective implementation of the points of the Action Plan.

Report of the Study Group on Development of Small Enterprises

There were about 20 lakhs SSI units in 1990-91, producing goods worth Rs.1,55,340 crore, exports of the order of Rs.9,661 crores and providing employment to about 125 lakh persons. Achievements of the SSI sector in 1998-99 were 31 lakh units, production of Rs.5,27,515 crore, exports at Rs.48,979 crore and providing employment to 171 lakh persons.

Though this sector has shown substantial progress, its major problems like inadequate credit flow from banks and financial institutions (FIs), inadequate infrastructure facilities, low quality standards of products, use of obsolete technology, plant, machinery and equipment, inefficient management techniques, etc. are still inhibiting the sector. Besides, this sector has to face challenges of competition from the opening up of economy to globalisation, need for increasing exports and meet WTO commitments.

The policy support provided so far has acted as a catalyst in promoting this sector. However, the Planning Commission felt an urgent need to review the policy measures so as to make this sector more growth oriented and enable it to withstand the pressure from global competition.

At the instance of the Deputy Chairman, Planning

Commission, a Study Group on Development of Small Enterprises (hereafter expressed as Study Group) was set up vide OM No. VSI/8(10)/99, dated 20th May 1999 under the Chairmanship of Dr. S.P. Gupta, Member, Planning Commission. While constituting the Study Group, wide representation was given to SSI associations, economists, Management Institute, Ahmedabad, SSI entrepreneurs, Secretaries of various Departments like SSI & ARI and Banking, RBI, SIDBI, FICCI, etc.

The major and important recommendations of the Study Group are listed in the following:

The Small Scale Enterprise (SSE) sector has emerged as an engine of growth in most of the developed and newly industrialized countries. India's vision of emerging as an economic power in the 21st century can be realised through the promotion and development of the Small and Medium Enterprises (SMEs). In fact, the SME is the sector of the Millennium. The role that small scale enterprise sector has to play in the next ten years must be viewed in the dynamic context of a changing world. It must address to the requirements of the time and the changes which are taking place both within and outside the country.

Liberalisation and globalisation are the order of the day. Market forces will determine the system and manner of production. The allocation or resources within the sector must be governed by the criteria of efficiency, productivity and competitiveness. The SSEs will have to move from a regime of a protective environment to a competitive environment. The role of Government is to be that of a facilitator.

A three tier definition is recommended for Tiny sector, SSI sector and Medium sector separately which is as under:

Tiny Unit	:	Up to Rs. 10 lakh investment in plant and machinery
SSI Unit	:	Above Rs.10 lakh to Rs.100 lakh in plant and machinery
Medium Unit	:	Rs.1 crore to Rs.10 crore in plant and machinery

The supportive measure to be made available to the three sectors will have to be decided by the Government from time to time. The endeavour will be to provide maximum support and protection to tiny units, somewhat lesser support to the SSI units and still lesser facilities/support to the Medium Enterprises. Medium Enterprises would not be supported through reservation, fiscal concessions or credit from banks and Financial Institutions (FIs) under priority lending sector, etc., which is normally made available to tiny and SSI units. However, medium enterprises could be helped for technology upgradation and modernisation through a separate fund.

The investment ceiling indicated above should be revised upwards every three years, to account for inflation. For this purpose, the wholesale price index of the Government of India should be used.

Industry related services and business enterprises up to investment of Rs.10 lakh in fixed capital including land and building should also be included, and should be treated at par with tiny industries for priority sector lending excepting for financing of truck operators, cars, heavy vehicles, taxis, auto-rickshaws and tempos.

The term 'small scale industry' should be replaced by 'Small Enterprises' which will consist of the following segments:

(i) Tiny Industrial Units

(ii) Small Scale Industrial Units, and

(iii) Service and Business Enterprises.

Regulatory Law for SSIs

The vision for the 21st century cannot be realised with a plethora of laws, rules and regulations governing the SSE sector and there is need for a Single Unified Act governing the promotion and development of Small Scale Enterprises in the country. There should be a separate Small Enterprises Development Act for SSEs as the Industrial Development and Regulation (IDR) Act which regulates SSI units covers the industries as a whole.

The SSE units should be free from laws/procedures, which

cause under harassment. Inspection should be generally replaced by self-certification. Procedures should be transparent and hassle free. There is need for similar simplifications in other fields as well. Inspections could be prescribed under three conditions: (i) on receipt of complaint; (ii) selection of unit for sample check (10% of total units); and (iii) for audit purposes.

It is suggested by the Study Group that for new units, single window clearances should be arranged irrespective of whether they relate to clearances from Central Authorities or State Authorities or Local Authorities.

Reservation

The reservation of products for exclusive manufacture in the SSI sector should continue for the present because the reserved items of the SSI sector are making significant contribution to employment, output and exports. The position may be reviewed from time to time, taking into account the developments and strength of the concerned sector and the market situation and implications of GOI agreements with WTO.

Dereservation of some selected export thrust items could also be considered since the country is losing valuable foreign exchange by production of low value added items by using traditional or low-grade technology. Production of reserved items could be allowed to be taken up by non-SSI units, subject to minimum export obligation of 30 per cent to be achieved in the first three years. Thereon 30 per cent export each year is to be achieved. Presently it is 50 per cent.

Consequent to removal of quantitative restrictions, which may affect the manufacturers of SSI reserved products, the endeavour of the governments should be to make the sector WTO competent and more competitive during the transition period by way of sensitization to WTO provisions, keeping import duty at bound rates, maintenance of duty differential on raw materials and finished goods, providing interest support for technology upgradation and easy access of credit to them.

In order to make SSI products competitive in both the internal and international markets, it is necessary to adopt State of the Art technology. Hence the investment ceiling of those items which are important from the angle of exports and also play an important role in employment generation, could be suitably enhanced to Rs. 5 crores, e.g. leather products, ready-made garments, hosiery, hand tools, toys, packaging material, auto components, pharmaceuticals, food processing, etc.

The Industrial Estates need to be managed by levying charges to the user industries so that these could become self-sustainable in the long run. Maintenance of these industrial estates should be done by the associations of user industries and paying charges for utilities, services, facilities, roads, etc. These industrial estates should be self-sufficient in maintenance.

Human Resource Development and Training

Training should cover both the entrepreneurs as well as the workers (labour) and future programmes should be built up at the Central and State Government levels through the Entrepreneurship Development Institutes (EDIs) and Industry Association. Training has to be forward looking in order to be compatible with the fast changing economic, technological and global scenario. Training for self-employed persons should be encouraged. It should also address to the requirements of the 'service sector'.

Various institutes providing training for small scale entrepreneurs must be brought under the umbrella of the National Entrepreneurship Board to provide uniformity in training and to avoid duplication of efforts. Adequate funds should be provided for upgrading the training equipment particularly the latest machines being used by the industry.

The syllabus of various training courses/modules should be regularly updated. For this purpose, Standing Committees should be constituted by the institutes in which industry associations should be given a role. Efforts should be made by the Government to avail of external sources of funding for Training and Entrepreneurship Development programmes. National Renewal Fund should be used for training and skill development.

Limited Partnership Act

The Study Group recommends that the government should expedite the enactment of the Limited Partnership Act for injecting equity into the SSI sector. The Bhat Committee (1972) had recommended limited liability for SSI entrepreneurs so that more persons could be persuaded to invest in new small enterprises. This would also ensure a greater flow of risk capital, bring in the concept of partnership with limited liability. The Nayak Committee (1992) and Abid Hussain Committee (1997) have also recommended enactment of Limited Partnership Act.

Women Entrepreneurs

The Study Group recommends that a separate division should be created in the Office of DC(SSI) for women entrepreneurs. Special programmes for women entrepreneurs should be formulated for credit and marketing and for export promotion of their products.

REFERENCES

1. Krishnamurthy, S, *Small Scale Industries: policy, Rules and Regulations*, Orient Publishing Co., New Delhi, 2002.
2. SIDBI, *Technology for Small Scale Industries: Current Status and Emerging Trends*, Tata McGraw Hill Pub.Co. Ltd, New Delhi, 2001.
3. *Entrepreneurship in the New Millennium: Challenges and Prospects*, Chukka Kondaiah, NISIET, Tata Mc-Graw Hill Publishing Co., Ltd, New Delhi, 2002.
4. Bajpai A.D.N and others (Ed), *Emerging Trends in Indian Economy,* Atlantic Publishers & Distributors, New Delhi, 1995.
5. *Small Industries Development Bank of India (SIDBI) (2000),* SIDBI Report on Small Scale Industries Sector 2000, Lucknow.

1

Policy Regime and Legal Framework for SMES: The Global Perspective

Dr. B. Yerram Raju & Mrs Sarah Varkki

The Seoul Declaration on Global Cooperation for Small and Medium Enterprises, adopted at the Sixth International Conference on SMEs (ICSME) on 25th April, 1992, emphasizes "the emergence of new perceptions and strategies to respond to the fast-changing world scenario and to meet social and economic needs of peoples of developing countries and those in transition to market economy. The baffling dimensions of inadequacies of political social and economic structures in many economies are manifesting themselves. Structural changes in all sectors of human endeavour will call for total mobilization of global support to stem the accelerating movement towards poverty and unemployment. Such a movement, if unabated, will threaten world peace and endanger prosperity even of the most industrialized nations. The Sixth ICSME believes that "...: developing countries and nations in transition to market economy, owe a special responsibility to create the most favourable environment for the creation of a vibrant, healthy, self-reliant small and medium enterprise sector, which alone could make a meaningful contribution in alleviating poverty, unemployment and meeting the need for essential goods and services".

The Changing Focus of State Intervention

The role of the State has been structurally redefined in economics throughout the world over the last two decades. The shift towards free market-oriented approaches to development which occurred in the 1980s in response to "over-regulation" by States proved unsustainable. Within a decade, the problems arisen from unregulated markets and attempts to "roll back" the State were revealed in the economic and social costs of market failure. Changes in the framework of international trade through new international agreements, the increased pace of technology, capital and information flows in an integrating global economy, and concerns over issues such as intellectual property rights and the environment, demanded intervention by national governments. The question at the end of the 1990s was no longer whether the State should intervene, but how it could effectively do so, and through what mechanisms and agencies, in order to achieve positive development outcomes. These developments have led to dramatic changes in the framework, focus and forms of State intervention in countries throughout the world.

The interface between government and industry is changing in countries across the globe as a result of the State re-inventing itself on the one hand, and intense international competition on the other. Institutional change has moved to top of the policy agenda calling for new approaches to development. The search is, therefore, now on for policy interventions, legal systems, and regulatory framework that are more attuned to public private participation to achieve policy goals in the emerging global setting.

The future growth of SMEs in developing countries, raises policy and regulatory issues which are of wider relevance in the current debates on deregulation and the need to develop appropriate institutions for markets to work more effectively. SMEs are a strategic component of the industrial structure in most developing countries and their promotion is closely linked to development goals such as employment-generation, and the promotion of exports, inter-sectoral linkages and regional dispersal. The emerging global economic environment calls for flexible and focused state interventions, to ensure fair competition and build institutional foundations in the transition towards market-oriented economics. The choice of regulatory mechanisms to achieve these objectives is the area where policy focus will be directed in the next decade.

The broad themes of this paper are: the importance of State intervention to enhance the capability of SMEs, the range of interventions/laws/regulations for **SMEs in India** as a case study. India has one of the longest histories of State support to the small towards deregulation. The first part of the paper, sets out the conceptual issues, and then gives a broad overview of the policies and legal framework for SMEs in some of the developed, developing and transition economies around the world. The policy and regulatory environment for SMEs in India is the subject of the second part of the paper.

Conceptual Issues

The question of scale is extremely crucial today, in political, social and economic affairs, just as in almost everything else because we seem to be suffering from what Schumacher calls as "universal idolatry of giantism". (F. Schumacher; 1973). Prof. Walter Heller once said- and most modern economics echo the same voice – "In a fully employed, high-growth economy you have a better chance to free public and private resources to fight the battle of land, air, water and noise pollution than in a low-growth economy".

How do we then get into the virtuous cycle of higher employment and high growth economy? While many realize that small industries are employment-intensive and need to be encouraged, the policies are sometimes caught in a web of conflict between producers interests and those of consumers. However, whether it is USA, or China, Germany, U.K. or Japan, South Korea or Malaysia, Taiwan or Turkey – all have a deliberate policy for helping small firms both through protective legislation and fiscal concessions.

The philosophy of 'smallness" has one disadvantage. The individualism, the privacy – rather, the attitude of non-sharing – act as antidotes for their growth. The second, and the most important, the access to resources is either denied or kept at a reasonable distance. The third, the economic philosophy of the nation should get embedded in a deliberate policy towards their promotion. Once this policy is clear, then a law to preserve and promote the smallness makes a lot of sense and quickly we should strive towards it.

Definition

Small and medium enterprises, both in size and shape, are not uniform across the globe. The way they are defined depends on the stage of economic development and the broad policy purposes for which the definition is used. There are said to be more than 60 definitions of small and medium industries used in 75 countries surveyed (Kim Seung Jin and Suh Jan-Won, 1992; 9). The most commonly used definitions relate to either size of employment and/or quantum of capital investment/fixed assets. In the European Union, small and medium enterprises are defined as enterprises with less than 500 employees. In Poland, a small enterprise is defined in terms of employment (less than 50 workers) and net revenues from sales of goods, products, services and financial operations (not exceeding 7 million ECU). In most countries of the East Asian region, the cut-off point for small industries varies between 50 to 100 workers. In India, the definition of small-scale industries is in terms of historical costs of plant and machinery, which is set at Rs.10 million at present. (See Annexure 1 for a comparative picture of definitions of SMEs in selected countries).

Staley and Morse used a five-type classification to identify small enterprises, which includes : subsistence manufacturers, artisans working at home, artisans with workshops, and industrial home-workers paid wages, or paid by piece (putting-out system). UNIDO categorizes manufacturers into: modern (largest enterprises, modern technology, mainly urban); modernizing (mainly small-medium, intermediate technology, mainly urban but also rural); and non-modern (small firms and artisan workshops, traditional and upgraded technology, mainly rural but also urban). Thus UNIDO's definition uses size, technology and location, while Staley and Morse consider where work is done, how workers are paid and whether they are artisans or industrial labour (Namet Ilahi: 1999). Even in India, the policy makers provided for a similar distinction when they separated out the Khadi, village and cottage industries, tiny industries, and artisans with a view to providing special dispensation.

SMALL-SCALE INDUSTRTIAL SECTOR IN INDIA

Policy Framework

Pre-independent Indian economy had a widespread presence of rural and cottage industries and artisans. These were dependent mostly on local resources and local markets. The skills in most cases were inherited. It was only during the 1950-70 period that the growth of small industry sector occurred.

There were at least three policy shifts in India's development strategy: from the Nehruvian phase of the 1950s to the social-justice oriented phase of the 1970s and again a more open, market-oriented approach in the mid-1980s. the main thrusts in each of these periods were, sequentially, heavy industrialization, poverty-alleviation and redistribution, and high –technology driven economic growth.

The focus of policy concern towards the SME sector changed with the priorities of each five year plan and the six Industrial Policy Resolutions, which have been framed since 1948. The Industries Development and Regulation Act of 1951, provided the basic framework for the post-independence industrialization strategy, regulatory policies were laid down for the regulation of licensing, location, production, pricing, imports, exports, foreign exchange controls, inter-state movement of commodities and several other areas of industrial operation. For small scale industries, there were regulations with regard to definition which was in terms of ownership – i.e. a small scale unit had to be an entrepreneur-directed concern and not a subsidiary to another industrial undertaking. The Karve Committee Report (1955) was one of the earliest of the exercises which recommended a protective environment for the growth of small; industries in India. Supportive policies through the 1960s, 70s and 80s took for m of reservation of products exclusively for the SSI sector, grant of fiscal concessions and government procurement of supplies from the sector. For increased credit flow to the SSI sector, a policy of priority sector lending through nationalized banks has been followed, through this has not been adequate for the growth requirements of the sector. This is perhaps the most compelling reason for the Expert committee on Small enterprises to state that: "Small enterprises will continue to need exceptional support in terms of financial resources, technological development and infrastructure". (Expert Committee on Small Enterprises; 1997:21).

Economic Profile

The small-scale industry (SSI) sector in India comprises of around 3 million units dispersed throughout the contrary (Table 1). The sector employs 17 million persons and accounts for 40% of total industrial production. Around 35% of the country's total exports come from the small industries sector. (Table 2). Small-scale units are engaged in the production of more than 7,500 products.

The SSI sector in India is at present in the phase of increasing returns to scale which leads to increases in factor productivity (H. Sidhu, 1998; 264). Further, the value added per unit of product is almost comparable for all size groups of industry. This implies that the products produced by the SSI units are comparable with the products of the larger sized units, inspite of the fact that most of the large firms enjoy economies of scale (Ibid; 265). Structural change in the SSI sector in the 1970s; and 1980s brought five industry groups to prominence: food products, chemicals, non-metallic mineral products, metal products and machine tools. Ownership-wise, proprietary concerns constitute 87%; partnership firms, 11% private limited companies 1% and others 1%. The equity base small-scale units constituting 87% under proprietorships could not be enlarged due to insecurity for introducing fresh capital. Resultantly, competitiveness also suffered. This major structural weakness has to be combated through appropriate legal facilitation.

Finance

The claim for easy access to finance from SSIs is unfulfilled. Several committees have gone into simplification of systems and procedures, relaxations in the collaterals and guarantees, setting out debt equity norms on a preferential scale etc. Most of them have remained on paper as the Reserve Bank of India(RBI) could not enforce any of the accepted recommendations. It was also not able to monitor several of the directives issued in regard to facilitation to SSIs. Even an exclusive institution like the Small Industries Development Bank of India (SIDBI), set up in 1990, has eluded the small enterprises. Lately there have been some interventions in the fields of technology upgradation and market promotion, which are also yet to crystallize and reach the targeted small enterprises. The gap between the expectation and the actuals for working capital disbursements is of a huge order of 70,000 to 80,000 crores of rupees. The travails of the small industries in accessing finance can best be seen by the case study on Risk Aversion.

Regulatory Framework

India's choice of regulatory mechanisms and their form is a product of her own specific history and development priorities at the time of independence. The origins of India's industrial regulation policy can be traced to specific context of the 1950s. the model, which strongly influenced the choices made at the time were the British practices which favoured authoritarian provisions to protect the ruler from the ruled, along with an excessive reliance on bureaucratic structures for policy implementation. Therefore, they turned out to be impractical and redundant. They provided scope for needless harassment and the only escape route for such harassment was corruption.

The quasi-federal system of Centre-State relations has a major influence on the implementation of industrial policy in India; distribution of powers has to conform to the Constitutional demarcation of subjects found in the union, state and concurrent lists. Though small industries are basically State subject, there are many areas where the subjects on the concurrent list have a bearing on industrial development. Industrial policy is formulated by the Centre but the States have flexibility to pursue their own policies within the broad framework of the Centre's norms. (see Chart in Annexures for the existing legal framework).

Either the regulatory mechanisms initiated by the Central Government or the flexibility in their implementation resting with the State Governments or both, have not prevented many an entrepreneur bee-lining for a particular activity (acquaculture, slag cement, edible oil, etc.). Such bee-lining rendered all of them to collapse simultaneously due to too many goods chasing too few markets.

The New Industrial Policy of 1991 has brought about several changes in the regulatory framework for industry. All industries – except those in the public sector and some specified industries subject to compulsory licensing, and industries in the small scale sector – are exempt from industrial licensing (with some provisos relation to location). The thrust of industrial policy has been towards deregulation and privatization with a dismantling of controls over industry. This can be evidenced from the policy statement of 1991:

"All statutes, regulations and procedures would be reviewed and modified, wherever necessary to ensure that their operations do not militate against the interests of the small and village enterprises".(para 1.3).

"Procedures would be simplified, bureaucratic controls effectively reduced, unnecessary interference eliminated and paper work cut down to the minimum to enable the entrepreneurs to concentrate on production and marketing functions". (para 8.2).

One of the issues that has emerged in the era of liberalization is the diminution in transaction costs for the large industry right from the start to running the industry. Their access to resources has vastly expanded. The small industry, on the other hand, has come to bear the increased transaction costs: right from registration to accessing credit for setting up and running the enterprise. Increased interest rate burden, enhanced collateral or widened guarantees, increased costs of remittance have contributed to raising the cost of production. Many small industries, unable to bear this tortuous change, are folding up. But the exit is not so easy. The exist carries sometimes more costs than entry. The small industry even while running on loss or after folding up too, has to pay up the provident fund bills, bonuses, minimum power consumption charges, security expenses etc. (see case study 'Rubber melts under Feet' for problems leading to sickness).

Procedures for SSIs

There are a number of procedures to be followed by an SSI at different points in the life cycle of al unit. At the entry stage, a small scale unit is expected to get clearance in principal for allocation of land, water, electricity, etc. and , in some cases only, an approval that the product proposed can be manufactured in that quantity. (e.g. defence equipment). The project implementation stage involves the conversion of the application after clearance into actual supply of the commodity or the service. The operational stage in the cycle of an SSI unit relates to the maintenance of a large number of registers whose number, nature and use are not clear to the entrepreneur. There is also a plethora of returns to be filed with different agencies.

The areas of focus which need to be addressed while re-designing the legal framework for small industries are as follows:

- **Complexity of the laws:** Apart from the multiplicity of the laws, there are complexities with regard to legislative powers and regulatory authority. Under the laws Constitution of India, several items of production are on the concurrent list, where both the Centre and States have legislative powers. In these areas, the Central Acts are supplemented by the State Rules and may later be followed with Government Notifications and ad hoc instructions. Further, there are different definitions of SSI used by different agencies/authorities for specific purposes which further complicated the situation. There are also different definitions of certain terms under various Acts. For example, the pivotal definition of an "industry" or "industrial undertaking" varies according to The Industrial Dispute Act and the Industries (Development and Regulation) Act. (ASCI Study Report 1, June 1998:2)
- **Enforcement** of the Laws and Procedures: The enforcement of laws is the most important test of the

effectiveness of a regulatory system. But this stage is found to be highly flawed in the present context where corruption, lack of transparency and of accountability are characteristic features of the system. There are 64 inspectors who visit SSI units for inspection from State and Central and Government Departments. The lack of any adequate system of monitoring at the field level is also one of the problems at this stage of regulation. Other problems in this area are: clearance/approvals required on the same issues from several distinct authorities; inadequate communication among related departments/functionaries and inadequate training to officers and staff. (Report of the Task Force on Administrative Procedures,1996)

- Compliance with the Regulatory Mechanisms. The existing regulatory framework falls short of ensuring compliance for effective functioning. This is mainly due to lack of awareness by the entrepreneur of the complex system of laws and regulations within which h/she has to function. Poor dissemination of information regarding rules and procedures contribute to a situation where non-compliances becomes easy. This points to the need for realistic evaluations of the ability to comply with regulations to be built into the legal system at the time of framing laws. The limitations of the implementing agencies, administrative structures and the interventions themselves need to be recognized.

New Approach to Regulation

The changing scope of governance in a rapidly-changing world requires changes in the law. The existing laws do not provide for the altered economic realities in the domestic and international spheres. A regulatory system which would be "ideal" or, at least, more appropriate for the present economic environment, would have to be transparent, easy to comply with, participatory, and built on an updated industrial information database. There would need to be a role for advocacy and a greater presence of business representatives in implementing bodies. The aim of self-regulation is of immense relevance in changing the environment for industry.

In a model structure of law, registration would be voluntary, but benefits of law would be made available only on registration. The measures, which an ideal legal structure would provide are as follows: measures against undue regulatory burdens (special considerations, provision for Ombudsman and grievance redressal mechanisms); measures to support marketing and competitiveness (protection against undue bundling of contracts by the State, and against restrictive and monopolistic trade practices); measures for funding and financing (loan guarantees right to reasonable credit) and measures relating to organizational set up.

Several promising initiatives have been taken up by different states. The main thrust is to enhance the capability of small-scale industries to achieve their full potential as a dynamic segment of the country's industrial structure.

Single Window Clearance

The concept of Single Window through Commissionerate/ Directorate of Industries at the state level and District Industries Centre (DICs) at the district level, for getting all the clearances at one place was initiated and encouraged by the Government of India. The objective was to reduce the burden of getting clearances under the plethora of Acts.

One of the problems with the Single Window system is that the legal framework, as it exists today, does not support the single window concept as it does not empower the Industries department with overriding powers on others departments to implement its decisions.

Andhra Pradesh

Illustratively, the initiatives of Government of Andhra Pradesh deserve special mention. A policy for SSI has been evolved and, on the basis of interactions with Federation of Andhra Pradesh Small Scale Industries Association (FAPSSIA), the following changes in the regulatory framework, have been introduced:

The setting up of a Central Documentation Clearance Centre(CDCC) is aimed at simplifying the procedures involved in obtaining multiple registrations and certifications. An Escorts service is provided as well as a system by which information updates are provided to the entrepreneurs on the status of their applications. However, since information and awareness of the functioning of these initiatives is inadequate, the response by entrepreneurs has not been as expected. The government has now made it mandatory for all new applications to be routed through the CDCC.

An Industrial Commission has also been set up to explore possibilities of allowing inspection by accredited private agencies.

Inspections by government officials are to be reduced to an annual inspection. Other changes proposed are for licenses for selected categories of SSIs to be renewed once in five years.

The promotion of small-scale industries in the state is being facilitated by a focus on critical infrastructure. The critical Infrastructure Balancing Scheme would provide funds to industrial estates or to SSI clusters as identified under the SSI Cluster Development Programme. The development of industrial estates is to be promoted through a policy whereby APIIC spends 65% of the taxes collected from industrial estates on such development.

There are plans to develop an organisation called Andhra Pradesh Small Scale Industries Development Authority (APSSIDA) – with similar authorities at the District level – to provide infrastructure and coordinate the activities of all agencies involved in small industry development.

Gujarat State

Gujarat is another state where the District Industries Centres have been empowered to grant provisional registration across the counter and in any case, not beyond 24 hours. The Centre for Entrepreneurship Development has been implementing a program to upgrade the enterprise status gradually, enabling modernization and technology upgradation. The State Government has also strengthened the machinery for rehabilitation of sick industries by modifying the definition of sickness. The revised definition recognizes sickness when there is erosion in the net worth of the industry by 30 per cent (as against the RBI norm of 50 per cent) and considers a package of rehabilitation subject to unit agreeing to repay all outstanding dues to the extent of 25 per cent from its own private sources. While the approach may not be perfect in itself, it has helped many genuinely sick industries turning the corner(according to the statistics put out by the Government, 27 per cent of the sick units have been helped out during the last one year). The national average of such rehabilitation effort is barely one to two percent.

Tamil Nadu is also contemplating rehabilitation of sick industries in the SSI sector on similar lines.

In fine, the regulatory framework would depend on (a) a clear policy for the SSI sector (b) unambiguous definition of a small industry (c) the domain of law we propose (d) self-regulation followed by heavy penalties for deviant behaviour and (e) effective grievance redressal mechanism.

Future Outlook

India's economic policies are in the process of being restructured through the second generation of reforms to adjust to the emerging challenges. The emphasis of future policy will be on focused, sustained and wide-ranging interventions to promote the growth of the SSI sector which has , so far, been insulated from pressures of competition both domestically and internationally. One of the challenges is to come through the impact of the WTO Agreement to which India is a signatory, along with 134 member countries. The WTO-stipulated requirements – reduction of subsidies, greater market access, removal of non-tariff barriers and reduction of tariffs – will have an impact on industrial and economic policy and call for suitable responses.

The forms of State intervention may change but the role of the State is unlikely to be reduced. The WTO Agreements, contrary to some perceptions, do not call for the removal of all subsidies. There are distinctions between actionable (i.e. permissible) and non-actionable subsidies. The former, which are also referred to as "amber" subsidies, are permissible "if they do not hurt the interests of other members". Such subsidies may include, for example, a subsidy specific to an enterprise, group of enterprises, or designated geographical location. The non-actionable or "green" subsidies are granted on the basis of objective criteria that are " economic in nature and horizontal in application and do not favour certain enterprises over others, are not specific". Subsidies given by governments to SMEs identified on the basis of their size of number of employees would be non-actionable.

A Mismatch between what SSE Seek and what they Need

Sathguru Merchant Consultants do quarter of their business with SSE. They work with a clear strategy that their revenues have to be telescoped – the fee grows as the ability of the SSE to pay grows. However they are very choosy about their clients. Till now they have worked with around 40 SSE of which 20 no longer remain small. Sathguru would to taken on clients only if they are willing to be a part of the core strategy. Though they have capabilities of transaction related services by virtue of having audit firm- they never use this an entry strategy. Sathguru never accepts a one time consulting assignment. Sathguru thinks that there is a very large mismatch between what SSE seeks and what they need. This is a classic problem of in mindset. For instance, for the Pharma industry around Hyderabad, there is no sense of worry about the patent regime. All the small units are still bogged down by how to get the drug inspector off their back.

"They are in a sense like the fisherman of Orissa before the Cyclone. They are blissfully unaware of what is going to hit them!"

Enhancing global competitiveness of SSIs holds the key to their future development. This requires identifying industries exposed to different degrees of risk from international competition based on their competitiveness.(see box on 'Mismatch between what SSE seek and what they need'). Support to low-risk industries by way of promotional measures would differ from longer-term interventions for high-risk industries (such as those facing stiff competition from TNCs for example). A study by World Association of Small and Medium Enterprises (WASME) has examined selected sub-sectors within the SSI sector, which are worth watching, which need active encouragement from government and institutions for SSI development. These sub-sectors are : ready-made garments, leather footwear and goods, electronic components, processed foods, and automotive components (WASME, Vol.1). Tiny industries (with fixed investment below Rs.25 lakhs) are likely to emerge as the dynamic segment within the small industries category. Their flexibility will prove to the an advantage at a time of rapid economic change bringing about changes in demand patterns.

The future outlook will also provide an impetus to women entrepreneurial activity and the development of entrepreneurial centers targeted specifically for women (SIDBI Report, 1999).

New Generation Small Industries

Information technology has given birth to a host of new enterprises in the small industry sector initially. The volumes of turnover, mergers, amalgamations, and joint ventures, the market capitalization of the outbound IT companies, the emergence of dot com companies and their quick retreat has brought to fore new issues of (1) integration with the existing small industry sector and (2) structural issues. The competition policy of the country in its draft stage, and the IT policy would also require to be absorbed in the emerging small industry policy and the law that supports it.

Linkages between Large and Small Industries

Usually seen as competitors, large and small industries can complement each other to mutual benefit, if institutional arrangements are put in place. When small industries coexist with large, prices are likely to be lower, and innovation and efficiency greater (N.Ilahi, 1998). The earlier the small firm occupies its position in the supply chain, better would be its capacity to influence future market directions. Small industries serve as seeds for the growth of large-scale industries using modern technology. In 1990, the Economist predicted that the "incredibly shrinking firm" is the wave of the future.

In a member of sectors, e.g., automobile, electronic, leather, manufacture of bicycles, toys, etc., there is a demonstrated evidence of mutual cooperation between the large and the small. There are a number of ways: franchising, co-branding, ancillarization, manufacture of intermediary goods, technology sharing and up-gradation etc. there is a need to provide an institutional umbrella for such processes to flourish.

The policy measures announced by the Government on 6th August 1991 for promoting linkages between large and small industries include:

- Encouraging for production in a techno-economically viable manner through small and ancillary enterprises of parts, components and sub-assemblies required by large public and private sector undertakings.
- Encouraging industry associations to establish sub-contracting exchanges in addition to strengthening the existing ones under SIDO.
- Amendments to the Prompt Payment Act.
- Allowing equity participation up to 24 per cent by large scale units in SSI/ancillary units (sub-group on Policy set up by the Planning Commission, Government of India recommends an increase to 49 per cent).

There is clearly immense scope for framing policies for SMEs which would help them to re-position themselves for the economic challenges ahead.

Conclusion

The promotion of SMEs in the changing global economic environment is a major focus of State interventions in countries throughout the world. Laws and regulatory frameworks have been put in place for the achievement of policy goals pertaining to SME development. The Seoul Declaration and the Bologna Charter for SMEs, stress the need to provide a competitive environment for these industries and enhance their capabilities in developed, developing and transition economics.

The success of State interventions in these efforts depends on changing the whole framework of regulations and procedures for SMEs. There is a need for clear and simplified regulatory structures which facilitate entry and competition, lower transaction costs, enforce contracts, provide stability to financial markets and provide an enabling business environment. The aim is to move from rule-based regulatory systems to self-regulation.

This requires dismantling dysfunctional regulatory systems and designing legal systems which are attuned to institutional capabilities. As stand in the World Development Report, "Government are learning that market reforms and fast-changing technology pose their own regulatory challenges" (1997:45) and that States cannot abandon regulation. Putting in place a new legal system and the corresponding institutional mechanisms based on transparency, accountability, fairness and greater participation of all stakeholders, is the main task for the next decade. It is important that these mechanisms act as effective delivery systems by ensuring compliance. Wherever the supporting institutions are found to be functioning, there is tremendous overlap in their functions and responsibilities. It is necessary to look at all these institutions from the point of view of the objectives in their respective statutes and see whether we can restructure/re-engineer them to meet the future of the small-scale Industry sector.

All the branded products in the consumer goods category imported after removing the tariff barriers do not confirm to the agreed/approved quality standards. But they cannot be prevented from entry. Many developing economies like India, unlike their counterparts in developed economies, do not have testing laboratories at the landing points.

Exchange of information on technologies, products, packaging standards, prices, markets will take place only when a global understanding emerges on the need for protecting any country's SMEs from hostile international competition and promoting them aggressively through public-private partnership. Employment intensity, low factor costs, and even spreads will be the best balancing factors in the reform agenda of the transition economies.

2

SSI Challenges and Strategies in the Liberalization Period

D. Nagayya* & K.V. Rao **

Implications of liberalization for the small scale sector have been analysed, and directions suggested for strengthening the sector in two recent reports: (i) *Report of the Expert Committee on Small Enterprises* (Abid Hussain Committee) submitted to the Union Ministry of Industry in January 1997, and (ii) *Report of the High Level Committee on Credit to Small Scale Industries* (S.L. Kapur Committee) submitted to the Reserve Bank of India in June 1998. Subsequently, Planning Commission, Government of India has set up a **Study Group on the Development of Small Enterprises** in May 1999 under the chairmanship of Dr. S.P. Gupta, Member, Planning Commission.

The Study Group in turn constituted four sub-groups : (i) Policy and Legal Framework, (ii) Financial and Fiscal Measures, (iii) Marketing and Exports, and (iv) Technology and Modernisation. An attempt is made in this paper to bring together major areas of discussion in the Small Enterprises sector in the context of liberalisation in terms of challenges and strategies. The viewpoints of the documents referred to above

* **D. NAGAYYA** :Former Director (Industrial Development), National Institute of Small Industry Extension Training (NISIET), Hyderabad, and currently Consultant on Small Enterprises at Guntur.

** **K.V. RAO** : Professor and Head, Department of Commerce and Business Administration, Nagarjuna University, Nagarjuna Nagar, Guntur District - 522 510.

including the discussions of the Study Group currently in session are drawn upon to highlight the major approaches. Key areas covered for discussion are: macro economic parameters, deregulation and debureaucratisation, cluster approach, reservation policy, trade policy and WTO compatibility, export promotion, export competitiveness, technology up gradation and technology transfer, improving the credit flow to the SSI sector, revival of sick SSI units, and role of industry associations.

Apart from the recent Major Industrial Policy and Small Enterprises Policy statements of Government of India (1991), a few of the State Governments have also been releasing policy documents on Small Enterprises. Government of Andhra Pradesh released the policy paper in November 1998, and Federation of Karnataka Chambers of Commerce and Industry released a policy paper on Small Enterprises in May 2000. These documents also refer to experiences of a few countries, and models that can be considered for adoption in India.

A few observations from the recent Karnataka paper are recalled here. Lack of access to institutional credit, marketing bottlenecks, compliance with cumbersome procedures, technological obsolescence, harassment by inspecting functionaries, outdated labour laws and operational inflexibility are some of the major problems faced by small scale industries. One of the key recommendations is that the **policy shift should be in favour of self regulation rather than control mechanism.** It has recommended a single legislation for the SSI sector. Another recommendation is **cluster approach** by locating a group of SSIs in specific industrial belts to enable them to obtain technological upgradation, supportive infrastructure, bank branch network, market share and personnel. Common facility centres should be established for a cluster of SSIs to enable individual units to have access to specialised facilities such as input quality control, in-process and end product quality check, tool room facilities, quality certification, packaging, and labelling. It has favoured their establishment in the private sector and functioning on commercial lines with the support of the Government. They can also have common warehousing facility. Such an approach is considered highly desirable for industries such as electronics, automobiles, textiles, and defence - related industries.

Complying with cumbersome statutory requirements is another major hurdle; hence simplification of laws, rules and procedures is suggested. The paper also recommended that SSIs should have easy access to institutional credit and working capital at reasonable interest rates, and pleaded that SIDBI should charge interest rates less than two per cent above the primary lending rate (PLR). The bank credit system should be transparent so that entrepreneurs with good track record can secure greater benefits.

Future direction of reforms for the Central and State Governments is envisaged as follows:

(a) Further deregulation and decontrol for simplifying procedures including labour legislation and environmental clearances

(b) Need for greater transparency at all levels

(c) Comprehensive review of delegation of powers

Simplification of registration and regulation of industries, both large and small, involves three areas of operation at the state level: (a) policies and procedures for regulation and registration, (b) legal structures, and (c) institutional arrangements.

Through the introduction of innovative approaches, action needs to be initiated on the following aspects:

(a) Follow up action in terms of sensitizing officials at different levels to meet the needs of industry-friendly procedures and regulations;

(b) Increased awareness of policies of industry, urban development and employment;

(c) Drawing up a training module for this purpose;

(d) The operational guidelines for adoption at the Central and State levels in terms of the expected output.

Cluster Approach

Clusters of small firms, their use of flexible manufacturing systems, inter-firm co-operation and provision of services, enable them to derive benefits of collective agglomeration and external economies of scale. A study of 138 clusters in the country revealed that only 13 of them were induced by public policy. The others have grown spontaneously on the initiative of entrepreneurs. Such clusters can stagnate in their later stages of development unless they are supported by institutions keeping in mind the vision for the industry in the national and international scenario. These clusters are appropriate units for focussed development of a large number of enterprises. Since these clusters usually specialise in a single area of activity, it is possible to design composite programmes meeting inter-related needs.

It is suggested that the cluster industry associations should take the lead, and act as nodal points for the constituent units, and draw upon the support of various agencies by maintaining necessary documentation on market trends at home and abroad. Research and development, quality assurance, skill enhancement, information dissemination, entrepreneurial competency development, and networking among themselves, and with specialised agencies in the country and abroad can facilitate upgradation and quality improvement of the products of the clusters. There is a strong case for the government to take the initiative in the matter with the active collaboration of the stakeholders themselves. Stakeholders' model for all institutions is recommended as that is a desirable direction to ensure maximum interaction between institutions and entrepreneurs giving priority to the interests of each other. Existing public institutions should be made to perform more efficiently by involving the beneficiaries in their activities. The emergence of private institutions to provide services alongside the stakeholders' institutions may create a healthy competitive environment. SIDBI has so far selected 22 small industry clusters for technology upgradation. The cluster level interaction of the Bank has brought out mixed results as success depended very much on external environment prevailing in the cluster, positive response of entrepreneurs in effecting such technology changes, etc. Thus, while the Bank was successful in a number of its endeavours; in a few cases, success was moderate. This programme of cluster development needs to be pursued vigorously for tiny, artisan, and SSI units in every state in different locations.

Reservation Policy

The Expert Committee advocated total abolition of reservation policy for exclusive manufacture in SSI sector. For meeting the transitional arrangements, the Committee recommended that a financial package of Rs. 2500 crore be provided by the Government for a five-year period to industrial units affected by dereservation. This can be used to leverage greater resources from SIDBI, banks and other financial institutions to provide concessional funding for expansion, technology up gradation, modernisation and training, and fiscal concessions. Among the reserved items, 68 products which account for more than 80 per cent of the total value of production of reserved products need to be paid special attention by identifying geographical areas state-wise where such affected units are concentrated. Government has already dereserved 15 items out of this list.

In the context of liberalisation, opening of reserved product lines through open general license (OGL) removal of quantitative restrictions, and in the light of the performance of SSI sector in the reserved list of product lines, dereservation is an imperative. Perhaps phased dereservation at a fast pace could be attempted. Any dereservation without financial package of support to the affected units would be harmful to the overall interests of the SSI sector. For 24 items dereserved during the recent two years, bringing down the reserved list from 836 to 812, no financial package has been provided to the affected units. There is no feedback so far available on the impact of such dereservation. Studies need to be carried out for assessing the impact of dereservation. It should be borne in mind that reservation is not the only measure, but one of the important measures to promote small scale industries. There is need to strengthen other measures for the growth of the SSI sector. Product lines which can be manufactured equally efficiently in SSI sector could be continued to be reserved, and those which are beyond the scope of SSI should be dereserved.

Another category is the list of items reserved for SSI sector for government purchases. The number stands at present at 358 items (including 8 items from the handicrafts sector). Up to end-March 1999, nearly 35,500 SSI units were registered with NSIC under the single point registration programme. Orders secured by SSI sector from various central organisations for 1998-99 accounted for Rs. 1670 crore. Concentration of SSI units which have secured orders under this provision continue to be largely from the Western and Northern states. About half a dozen states account for the major share. It is important to popularise this marketing outlet of the Central Government, and corresponding provision of the State Governments among SSI units in a large number of states to strengthen the marketing programme.

Trade Policy and WTO Compatibility

In the era of globalisation, protection to SSI sector could be given through multilateral process. Government intends to keep tariff levels (customs duties) at not higher than 35%; and with 10% surcharge, the tariff would be 38.5%. Tariff levels might even be brought down further in the coming years. There are now four slabs of duties, 35%, 25%, 15%, and 5%, with surcharge of 10% continued.

The Export-Import Policy 2000-2001 has placed 58 items that are reserved for SSIs on the Open General License (OGL) list, and 198 more items from the reserved list will be freed on April 1, 2001. Thus at present, 624 out of 812 items that figure in the reserved SSI list can be imported freely under OGL. On April 1 2001 more items will become freely importable. Imports will enjoy a clear edge over products produced within the country. Quantitative Restrictions (QRs) on 1429 items would be lifted by April 1, 2001; on 714 of them, restrictions have already been removed from April 1, 2000. Earlier, during 1996-99, on as many as 1914 items, QRs have been lifted. Many of these items are consumer goods including domestic appliances and food items. Union Commerce Ministry is of the opinion that withdrawal of QRs would not affect SSI sector adversely as sufficient safeguards such as tariffs and anti-dumping measures would be available. Besides, it is time to remove QRs as these exist at present only in six countries. Removal of QRs has not so far resulted in significant rise in imports. The new Policy will provide focussed fillip to export of gem and jewellery, software, pharma, agro chemicals and bio-technology, rationalise a raft of export promotion schemes, and simplify procedures to cut down transaction cost. State Governments will be assisted based on their export performance for granting assistance for export-related infrastructure development.

Very soon, other benefits like post-export Duty Entitlement Pass Book (DEPB), and Export Promotion Capital Goods (EPCG), and other schemes are also likely to be axed or substantially modified. With that our Export-Import Policy will be WTO compatible, but our exports may become uncompetitive in the process. Dismantling of QRs, lowering of tariffs, opening of reserved categories, reduction in subsidies for exports, legislation on Trade Related Intellectual Property Rights (TRIPs), etc. need to be taken into account to analyse the challenges placed before the SSI sector. Government should act as a facilitating agency for SSI sector by providing subsidy on R & D projects, ensure protection through WTO-friendly measures, providing focussed policy treatment, and level playing ground for SSI sector. There is an urgent need to strengthen SSI sector to face the challenges of WTO.

Safeguards in WTO Rules

WTO system has created certain rights in favour of Small and Medium Enterprises (SMEs) to protect themselves from cheap imports through Articles 6, 12, 20 and 21. Some of these are:

- Right to enterprises to request their governments to take action to restrict imports in the face of increased competition resulting from liberalisation measures.
- Right to enterprises to request for levy of anti-dumping duties on imports that are being dumped, and for imposition of countervailing duties on products that are entering the country at extremely low prices because of the subsidies they are receiving.

The invocation of these rights is subject to certain conditions. The request for such action can be made if it is supported by enterprises which account for a substantial proportion of domestic production, and it is possible for them to demonstrate that increased imports are injuring the industry by bringing about reduction in production, employment and profits.

The WTO agreements would be a continuous process, and regular monitoring / study would be required to assess their impact on the SSI sector. SSI associations would have to be taken into confidence, and made aware of the implications of WTO agreements.

Export Promotion

Problems of export-oriented units need attention on a priority basis. These include finance, technology upgradation, raw materials, quality assurance, packaging, marketing intelligence, infrastructure, etc. The governmental mechanism should be geared for this task. Industry associations should play a leading role in studying the requirement of member units, and share responsibilities with governmental agencies. Consortia of export units are being encouraged to assume greater responsibilities. Participation in international exhibitions, gathering marketing intelligence, and facilitating tie-up with importers in other countries will speed up the process. As globalisation process gets incorporated into the Indian scene, industry has to reorient its production and marketing strategies. Our effort should be not only to produce goods and services at competitive cost but to carve out a niche for Indian products in the export market.

At present, in some of the items, the share of SSI sector in total exports of the respective groups ranges between 60 and 100 per cent. Sports goods and readymade garments contribute nearly 100 per cent, finished leather and leather products are around 90 per cent, processed food, rayon and synthetic products are around 60 per cent. The emerging thrust areas for export are electronics, computer software, textiles, leather goods, food processing industries, and a wide range of consultancy and technology services. Setting up of joint ventures and technology tie-ups in developing countries is a recent activity which needs to be pursued vigorously in view of its high potential.

In respect of auto parts industry, a cross-country study of export competitiveness was carried out by the Administrative Staff College of India, Hyderabad covering China, Taiwan, South Korea and India. Comparative advantage indices are indicative of the relative advantage of nations. In the case of auto parts and accessories, and motorcycle parts, India seems to enjoy an advantage. This is particularly high in the case of the latter. The changing nature of the motorcycle industry must be kept in mind. In the case of auto electrical equipment, Korea is naturally ahead, with China and India, practically non-existent in exports in this field. China is making conscious efforts to make the automobile industry a pillar industry. The cross-country assessment has brought out the relative strengths and weaknesses of different countries in selected categories of auto components in the complexity of global development, home country policies, and state of the industry. Technology is, thus, a critical factor in this field, and its enhancement would depend on the joint initiative of government and industry in a country. While this is happening to a significant extent in Taiwan, South Korea and China, in India such partnership measures between government and industry are yet to emerge. The sooner such measures emerge, the greater the industry would stand to gain. Such efforts should be focussed on areas having a comparative advantage for higher returns to the nation.

Individual companies in India in auto component manufacturing should clearly understand their areas of core strength as also weaknesses. While weaknesses have to be overcome, the companies must evolve strategies to grow around their core strength. Every company should acquire the latest technology, and work for technological advancement and excellence. Marketing strategies adopted by the industry play a crucial role in the development and creation of a brand image.

Conclusion

SSI units should become competitive to face the challenges of liberalisation and globalisation, and also there should be no restrictions on SSI units to grow. Incentives should be made available for small units to graduate into medium size. There is need for technological upgradation and modernisation, adoption of cluster approach for quick and effective delivery of inputs to SSI sector, need to study tariff / non-tariff barriers under WTO, review of labour laws and steps for enhancing capacity utilisation of SSI units. There is need to increase employment and productivity per employee in the SSI sector to make it more competitive.

3

SSI Policy with Special Reference to Identification and Product Reservation

-Dr. P.B.Appa Rao

India's small industry Policy owes its origin to the industrial policy resolution of 1948 and 1956, subsequently India's policy was formed mainly on the basis of the recommendations of (i) Ford foundation experts (2) the village and small Industries committee (known as Karv committee). The former led to the evolution of a countrywide institutional network headed by SIDO. The latter resulted in a comprehensive framework of protection of small industry.

Though small industry grew significantly in terms of units, employment, and production and exports. The impact of institutional network and protective framework as its performance in terms of productivity and efficiency has been debated deeply by analysts, academicians and policy makers particularly, in the late 80s and early 90s.

The definition of small-scale industry, in terms of investment in the units, underwent significant change in our country over the past three and half decades. The investment ceiling in plant and machinery, imposed by the Government, has been shown in Table 1.1.

In 1960, the ceiling limit of investment in plant and machinery of any small-scale industrial unit was fixed at Rs.0.5 million later this unit was raised to one million rupees in 1977, to Rs.2 millions in 1980, and to Rs. 3.5 millions in 1985. Keeping in view the inflationary tendency in the prices of capital goods and in order to make small-scale units more competitive in the wake of liberalized policy measures, the Government reviewed and raised the investment limit in plant and machinery of small-scale industrial units to Rs. 6 millions in 1991. In the second week of December 1997 to bring in a wide range of industrial units of relatively bigger size into the gambit of the term "Small-scale Industry". The investment limit was further increased to thirty million rupees. It is felt that the small-scale industrial unit is an "Industrial undertaking in which the investment in plant and machinery, whether held on ownership terms or on lese or on ohire purchase, does not exceed Rs. 3 crores (Rs.30 millions)"[1].

1.2 Ancillary Unit

As is evident form Table 1.1 the investment limit in plant and machinery of an ancillary unit ever remained higher than that of the small-scale unit. The most prominent reason for fixing a higher investment limit is relatively wider coverage of activities by ancillary units.

Table 1.1 Ceiling on Investment in Plant and Machinery

Month and Year of Implementation	*Investment in Plant and Machinery (Gross Value in Rs. Millions)*			*Difference in Investment between SSI and Ancillary Unkits*	*Percentage of difference in Investment*
	SSI Unit	*Ancillary Unit*	*Export-oriented Unit*		
Jan 1960	00.50	01.00	-	00.50	100.00
Dec 1977	01.00	01.50	-	00.50	50.00
July 1980	02.00	02.50	-	00.50	25.00
Mar 1985	03.50	04.50	-	01.00	28.57
April 1991	06.00	07.50	07.50	01.50	25.00
Dec 1997	30.00	30.00	30.00	00.00	000.00

* *Source: The Hindu (Daily) 5 January 1998, p.18.*

1. Special Correspondent, "New Norms for SSI Investment Limit", *The Hindu* (daily), 5 Jan 1998,p18.

The investment limit in plant and machinery of an ancillary unit was fixed at Rs. 1 million in January 1960, Rs. 1.5 million in December 1977, Rs. 2.5 million in July 1980, Rs. 4.5 million in March 1985, Rs. 7.5 million in April 1991 and Rs. 30 million in December 1997.

The difference in the maximum investment limit in plant and machinery between an ordinary small-scale industrial unit and an ancillary small-scale industrial unit was Rs.0.5 million from January 1960 to July 1980, Rs.1million from March1985 to April 1991 and Rs.1.5 million from April 1991 to December 1997.

In relative terms the difference was 100 per cent unit December 1977, 50 per cent from December 1977 to July 1980, 25 percent from July 1980 to March 1985, 28.57 per cent from March 1985 to April 1991 and 25 per cent from April 1991 to December 1997. The difference was reduced to cipher in December 1997. Maintenance of the difference between the maximum investment limit in the ordinary small-scale unit and the ancillary small scale unit, at different levels, at different times does not look to have depended on scientific reasoning.

As the importance of ancillary units increased along with significant growth of their number, the favorable policies of the Government led to raise ceiling of investment to Rs.7.5 million in April 1991. In December 1997, an ancillary unit was defined as "an industrial undertaking, which is engaged in the manufacturing or production of intermediates, or the rendering of services and an undertaking which supplies or proposes to supply or renders or proposes to render not less than 50 per cent of its production or services, as the case may be, to one or more other industrial undertakings and whose investment in fixed assets in plant and machinery (whether held on ownership terms or on lease or on hire purchase) does not exceed Rs. 3 crores (Rs. 30 million)"[1].

In calculating the value of plant and machinery for the purpose of definition of SSI/Ancillary unit, "the original price thereof, irrespective of whether the plant and machinery are new or second hand, shall be taken into account"[2]. Costs to be

1. Special Correspondent, "New Norms for SSI Investment Limit", *The Hindu* (daily), 5 Jan 1998, p18.
2. Ibid., p. 18.

excluded, while calculating the value of plant and machinery are:

- Cost of equipment like tools, jigs, dies, moulds;
- Cost of spare parts and consumable stores;
- Cost of installation of plant and machinery;
- Cost of R and D and pollution control equipment, power generation sets and extra transformer installed as per regulations of the State Electricty Board;
- Bank charges and service charges paid to the National Small Industries Corporation or the State industries Corporation;
- Cost of procurement and installation of cables, wires, bus bars, electrical control panels (not those mounted on machines), oil circuit breakers, or miniature circuit breakers needed for producing electrical power and for safety;
- Cost of gas producing plants;
- Cost of transporting (excluding sales tax and excise0 indigenous machinery to site;
- Technical know-how charges for erection of plant and machinery;
- Cold storage of raw materials and finished products (not linked with the manufacturing process); and
- Cost of fire fighting equipment.
- In the case of imported machinery, costs to be included in calculating the value of plant and machinery are import duty, shipping charges, customs clearance charges and sales tax.

Export Oriented Small-Scale Industrial Units

The concept of export-oriented small-scale units was introduced for the first time in April 1991. The investment limit was fixed on par with an ancillary unit, but later in December 1997 it was equated not only with ancillary but also with an ordinary small-scale industrial unit.

A unit, which undertakes to export at least 30 per cent of its annual production by the third year form the date of commencement of production was referred to as a small-scale export-oriented unit. The limit on investment in plant and machinery was R. 7.5 million (from 1991). The investment limit was raised to Rs. 30 million from February 1997.

Prior to 1960 a small-scale unit was defined in terms of number of employees. From January 1955 to 1959 a small-scale industrial unit was defined as the unit employing less than 50 persons if using power and less than 100 persons without the use of power and with capital assists not exceeding Rs. 0.5 million. Since March 1959 until January 1960 also, undertakings, which employed less than 50 persons when using power and less than 100 persons when not using power, were considered as small-scale units.

Efficacy of small industry in solving the problems of unemployment, scarcity of capital[1], concentration of economic power and imbalance in the development of different regions was recognized by the economist, planners and policy makers, increasing emphasis has been laid on the development of small industry in the successive five-year plans (Table 1).

Importance of the development of small industry and the steps enunciated for that purpose could be made clear by referring to the industrial policy resolutions and statements. The policy promulgations of the Government from time to time

Cf. "Large industry is very often capital-intensive, and accumulation of capital takes time. During intervening period, small industry, which is very often labour intensive would, therefore, be able to stay on". Also "The number of persons unemployed, disguisedly as well as openly, is truly large. A welfare state is expected to provide relief to the unemployed. In view of the paucity of resources, however, this is ruled out. Creation of employment opportunities on a large scale is therefore, a way out. Here in view of the facts of capital scarcity and capital intensive nature of large industry, the organized sector can play only a limited role. The hope is then pinned on small industry because of its labour intensive character, especially where it is technologically feasible and economically tolerable. Sandesara, J.C., 'Small Industry in India: Evidence and Interpretation', Sardar Patel Institute of Economic and Social Research, Ahmedabad, November 1980, pp.2,3, & 5.

reflect the care, concern and commitment for the nurture, growth and development of the small-scale industries, which playa vital role in the Indian economy. The policy initiatives and procedures ever sine the first Industrial Policy Resolution 1948 and until the New Industrial Policy of 1991 encompass several aspects, which assumed much significance at various points of time. It is worthwhile to present here the policy of the Government on small-scale industries from time to time.

The Industrial Policy Resolution 1948: Cottage and small-scale Industrial units have very important role to play in the national economy. They give scope for the development of individual, village and cooperative enterprises.

They are the means for the rehabilitation of displaced persons. These industries are particularly suited fr the better utilization of local resources and for the achievement of local self-sufficiency in respect of certain types of essential consumer goods like food, clothing and agricultural implements. Healthy expansion of cottage and small-scale industrial units depends upon a number of factors like the provision of raw material, cheap power, technical advice and organized marketing. Sometimes it also requires safeguards against intensive competition from large-scale industry and education to the workers in the use of the best available technique.

The Industrial Policy Resolution 1956: "The Government of India would, in this context, stress the role of cottage and village and small-scale industries in the development of the national economy. In relation to some of the problems that need urgent solution, they offer some distinct advantages. They provide immediate large-scale employment; they offer a method of ensuring a more equitable distribution of the national income and they facilitate an effective mobilizations of resources of capital and skill which might otherwise remain unutilized. Some of the problems that unplanned urbanization tends to create will be avoided by the establishment of small centres of industrial production all over the country.

The State has been following a policy of supporting cottage and village and small-scale industries by restricting the volume of production in the large-scale sector, by differential taxation, or by direct subsidies. While such measures will continue to be taken, whenever necessary, the aim of the State Policy will be to ensure that the decentralized sector acquires sufficient vitality to be seff-supporting and its development is integrated with that of large-scale industry".

Industrial Policy Statement 1977: The Industrial Policy announced on December 23, 1977 by the Governemnt emphasized the need for strengthening the small-scale industries and the tiny sector. " The proposed nucleus plants in industrialist backward districts would generate a spread-out network of small-scale units or the existing network of small-scale units would acquire a faster growth by the coming up of a nucleus plants in the area".

Government is determined to promote such a form of industrialization in the country as can generate economic viability in the villages. Promotion of suitable industries in rural areas will be accelerated to generate higher employment and higher per capita income for the villagers in the country without disturbing the ecological balance. Handlooms, handicrafts, Khadi and Village industries will receive greater attention to achieve a faster rate of growth in the villages".

Industrial Policy Resolution 1980: "In order to boost the development of small-scale industries and to ensure their rapid growth" Governemnt has redefined the term small-scale units. "The enhancement of the limit in terms of investment opinion plants and machinery will also help genuine small-scale units particularly these being set up by young and technically qualified entrepreneurs, to come up. This measure will also facilitate long over due modernization of many of the existing small scale units".

"One of the major constraints to the growth of decentralized sector has been the difficulties of finance experienced particularly by industrial entrepreneurs in small, cottage and rural sector. Although there is adequate network of institutional finances, yet there is need of coordination the flow of capital, both short term and long term. Government would evolve a system of coordination to ensure the flow of credit to the growing units in the decentralisd sector at the right time and on appropriate terms. Government proposes to strengthen the existing arrangements and make such changes as may be necessary to facilitate the availability of credit to the growing units in the small-scale sector.

"In order to assist the growth of small-scale industries it is proposed to introduce a scheme for building up of buffer stocks of essential material which are often difficult to obtain". "Policies regarding marketing support to the decentralized sectors and reservation of items for small-scale industries".

In spite of provision of raw material, cheap power, technical advice organized marketing facilities, safeguards against intensive competition form large-scale units, restrictions on the volume of production in the large-scale sector by differential taxation and subsidies etc., the progress and performance of small-scale sector is not commendable. This may be due to lack of entrepreneurship[1]. Entrepreneurship is scarce in many parts of our country and among the vast sections of our population[2]. Entrepreneurship is a vital input for the success of any venture. This is more so in case of small industry. Because a large-scale unit can employ professional managers but a small-scale unit cannot do so due to economic constraints.

Entrepreneur for a venture is like salt for sea water[3]. Entrepreneurs are the engineers of industrial progress and the chief agents of products. Development of entrepreneurship is directly linked with industrial development[4]. Hence there is need to know the meanings of the terms 'Entrepreneur' and 'Entrepreneurship'.

The new policy document for small enterprises titled "policy measures for strengthening small, tiny and village enterprises" brought out in 1991. The following are some important features of the new policy[5].

1. Sandesara J. C. , Cit., p. 30.
2. IDBI, Entrepreneurship Development Programmes, Proceedings of Seminar, March 3, 1980. p. 1.
3. Ram K. Vepa, How to Succeed in Small Industry, Vikas Publishing House Pvt. Ltd., New Delhi, 1984, p. 5.
4. IDBI, Op. Cit., p. 64.
5. Kashyap, S.P., "Emerging Industrial Policy Reforms: Implications for Small Size Enterprises", Productivity, April-June 1995, Vol.36, No.1, pp.17-18.

For the first time the policy differentiated explicitly the 'small' from the 'tiny' units. It was noted that small-sized enterprises, other than 'tiny' enterprises, would be entitled to one time benefit (preference in land allocation/power connection, skill and technology up gradation) where as the 'tiny' enterprises would be sustained on a continuous basis in terms of easier access to institutional finance, priority in the Governemnt purchase programme and relaxation in the provisions of labour laws.

The new policy document for small enterprises titled "policy measures for strengthening small, tiny and village enterprises" was brought out in 1991. The following are some important features of the new policy.

1. For the first time the policy differentiated explicitly the 'small' from the 'tiny' units. It was also noted that small-sized enterprises, other than 'tiny' enterprises, would be entitled to one time benefits (preference in land allocation/power connection, skill and technology upgradation) where as the 'tiny' enterprises would be sustained on a continuous basis in terms of easier access to institutional finance, priority in the Government purchase programme and relaxation in the provisions of labour laws.
2. The other definitional change relates to industry-related services and business enterprises which, irrespective of location and having investment ceiling would be treated as tiny units.
3. Another important feature of the new policy relates to equity participation. The new policy provides for equity participation by other (presumably large) industrial units in the small units not exceeding 24 per cent of the share holding. The measure is expected to boost ancilliarisation.
4. The other special features the introduction of anew legal form of organisation of business, i. e restricted or limited partnership. In this form, the liability of at least one partner is unlimited whereas other partners have their liability limited to invested capital. The measure

was excepted to attract equity capital in the small-scale sector particularly form fiends and relatives.

5. The new policy recognized that the small units require timely credit rather than cheap credit. The Governemnt expect that by speeding up procedures through am enlargement of the scope of thee single window clearance ot cove projects upto Rs. 20 lakhs and working capital upto Rs.10 laksh, investment in this sector would be facilitated.
6. The new policy also envisages an important role for non-governmental agencies, such as industry/trade associations. The village industries, as in earlier policy document are expects to promote rural industrialization and provide employment, particularly to weaker sections of the people. A number of measures – supply of raw material, sale of products, up gradation of production methods and improvement in the quality of products, strengthening the existing support organisation, expansion of training facilities and so on- are suggested to enable healthy growth of village industries. The product reservation for small-scale sector was yet another policy measure initiate in the direction of protection the small-scale sector.

Reservation Policy for Small Sector

Small-scale sector is contributing immensely for the growth of the economy. It accounts for 80 per cent of the country's industrial employment employing 16 million people employment growth in the small scale sector has been around 5.8 per cent as against 2 per cent growth in the large industrial sector. Production from the small-scale sector is valued at over Rs.1,10,500 crores per annum. Out that 35 per cent is exported.

The product reservation for small scale sector was yet another policy measure initiated in the direction of protecting the small-scale sector. Initially in 1967, 47 products were placed on the reserved list, which was expanded to include 800 products during the Janata regime. Such an expansion, which was to some extent a disaggregation of established product divisions, reflected the government policy at that time, which categorically declared that "It is the policy of the government that whatever can be produced by small and village industries must only be so produced".

It can be observed from the above policy that the small scale industry in India was expected to grow under the protection. The policy to protect and promote small firms encouraged the entry of opportunities or those who do not possess the required skill to run a small enterprise thus leading to a widespread malaise in the small-scale sector.

About 6000 items are presently being manufactured by SSIs out of which only about 836 are from the reserved category. Out of them 143 items continue to be protected under qualitative restrictions. Products, which involve high technology and production facilities for which are set up in backward areas fall outside the purview of the reservation policy. Also, the big business houses, which have facilities to produce goods reserved for small-scale sector, have been allowed to do so without expanding their capacity. Obviously, notwithstanding the reservation policy, initiated in 1967, a large number of big units are in a position to encroach on the domain reserved for the small sector. Though many items are reserved for exclusive production by the industrial units in the small-scale units in the small-scale sector, various forces are working towards de-reservation of a number of them in the wake of the new liberalization policy.

Dereservation of the items reserved for exclusive manufacture by the small-scale industrial sector has now become important because many reserved items could be imported under Open General License (OGL), giving rise o an anomalous situation. Also, the emergence of a common market for SAARC, and phasing out of qualitative restrictions under the WTO commitment has rendered such reservation irrelevant.

The Abid Hussain Committee in 1997 recommended for total dereservation of the small sector and opening it to competition. The Committee advocated that the government protection in the form of reservation of products, for exclusive manufacture by the small-scale sector, should be abolished and thrown open to foreign investors as well. However, the issue of dereservation has failed to make any headway.

The government has initiated the dereservation, as a partial response to the Abid Hussain Committee Report, by dereserving 14 items. The Finance Minister in his Budget Speech said that government will examine carefully other recommendations of the Abid Hussain Committee on the small-scale industries sector. With a view to reduce wastage in agricultural commodities, improve quality and hygiene and promote exports, the Advisory Committee on reservation and dereservation recommended that 14 items, then reserved for production in the SSI sector. The dereserved items include rice milling, dall milling, poultry feed, vinegar, synthetic syrups, biscuits, ice-cream, a variety of automobile parts and corrugated paper and boards. It is expected that new investment and improved technology will flow into these businesses.

The industry is divided over the issue of dereservation of items. Large-scale industries allege that many items reserved for small industry are not being manufactured by small industry. As small-scale units are not able to manufacture and supply those items the exports being restricted. The Chambers of Commerce want a fresh review of the reservation policy as nearly 233 items of the reserved list is not being manufactured by the small-scale industry at all. Over 300 items under the revised list are imported but non-SSI units are not permitted to manufacture them.

It can be said that in the post-liberalization era where one is not even required to take a license to set up an industrial unit, no purpose is served by the reservation of certain items for small industry. Just like in certain developed countries, small industry should become complementary to the medium and large industry rather than treating them as competitors.

Spokesmen for the small-scale sector fear that with dereservation of the items hitherto reserved for exclusive manufacture by the small industry, financially and technically strong, medium and large-scale industry, both Indian and foreign, would definitely take advantage and cause damage to the small industry. But the Abid Hussain Committee Report says that a large number of reserved items are either not manufactured by the small industry or their sales turnover is insignificant.

A recent report of the Parliamentary Standing Committee says, reservation is not the solution to the various ills of the small-scale units. Anyhow, the Committee has also suggested not yielding the pressures of multinationals regarding dereservation. Yielding to the pressures of multinationals and large industry regarding dereservation would amount on ruining the small industry. The recommendations of the Abid Hussain Committee should not be implemented into and the protection given to small industry should continue, says the Report.

It is said that the policy of reservation has put an end to the spirit of competition, which is against the philosophy of the new economic reforms. At the same time, SSIs want to retain their identity and not to be over-shadowed by large enterprises.

The Union Government has now mooted a proposal seeking to dereserve all items currently under the exclusive domain of the small-scale industrial units (SSIs). As such, total dereservation is sought to be achieved by April 1, 2001, when quantitative restrictions on most items are also expected to be lifted in accordance with India's commitments before the World Trade Organization.

In the first phase, the targeted items for dereservation would be those which are not produced by small-scale industrial units but continue to be in the domain of the small-scale units.

In the next phase, the items on open general license (OGL) and that are freely important from Sri Lanka under the free trade agreement are sought to be taken out of the reservation list.

In the final phase, labour intensive goods with export potential for Indian products are expected to be opened up for big corporates and foreign investors. This will coincide with proposed total elimination of licensing imports from April 1, 2001.

Interestingly, the government is seeking to push ahead the dereservation and increase foreign investment in SSI areas at a time when even the big Indian corporates unnerved by dumping from countries like China, Taiwan and Philippines using the Nepal route. For the purpose along with phasing out reservation for SSIs, foreign equity capital is raised from the existing level of 24 to 49 per cent.

The above discussion reveals that the move is towards widening of the horizon of the term small-scale industry and dereservation. Dereservation of the products reserved for exclusive production be the small industry is in accordance with the wish of the World Trade Organization and objectives of globalization. The effect of it is exposure of the small industry to the rigors of competition from the economically strong large-scale industry and both economically and technologically strong foreign industries. The changes in the policy have been introduced anticipating something good but whether it causes good or bad has to be wait and seen.

4

Reforms in the Industrial Sector with Focus on Small Scale Industries

*Prof. C. Suryanarayana & ** Dr. D. Nagayya

Introduction

Liberalization of the economy as a package startod with reforms in the industrial sector in 1991 with the announcement of the Major Industrial Policy and a separate Small Enterprise Sector Policy. The policy directions and prescriptions announced in these two statements continue to be pursued even today. Implementation of what was envisaged in these two statements so far has been a modest effort; a lot more remains to be implemented. This speaks of the heavy economic legislation awaiting clearance from the Parliament in the near future.

The paper reviews the overall macro economic trends of recent years; indicates the importance of exports and services sector; and then plunges into reforms in the Industrial Sector, with focus on Small Scale Industries. The effort is to identify the areas in economic reforms where action has not been initiated so far or where action has been initiated but progress continues to be modest. The unfinished agenda is analyzed in depth on

* Professor of Management, Department of Commerce and Management Studies, Andhra University, Visakhapatnam.

** Former Director (Industrial Development), National Institute of Small Industry Extension Training (NISIET), Hyderabad, and currently Consultant on Small Enterprises at Guntur (Andhra Pradesh).

select aspects. Deregulation and liberalization are emphasized in a few of the specialized studies carried out recently which suggest strategies for future direction of reforms. These include institutional framework, procedural simplification, and support systems. Simplification of registration and regulation of industries, both large and small, has been analyzed and According to the preliminary estimate of the Central Statistical Organisation(CSO), the Gross Domestic Product (GDP) during the first quarter (April-June 1999) of the current year (1999-2000) has increased at 5.5 per cent against 3.6 per cent in the previous year. Assuming that the recovery in industrial production witnessed in the first half of the year will gather further momentum during the rest of the year, and there is no unexpected setback on the agricultural front, growth in GDP in the current year is projected to be in the range of 6.0 to 6.5 per cent, as against 6.0 to 7.0 per cent visualized earlier, as per indications given by the Reserve Bank of India (RBI) in its Monetary and Credit Policy announced at the end of October 1999. GDP growth rate at constant prices in the earlier years ranged from 7.6 to 7.8 per cent during the three years 1994-95 to 1996-97. During 1997-98, it was as low as 5.0 per cent, and in 1998-99 only 6.0 per cent.

Macro Economic Parameters

In the industrial sector, after a period of deceleration, there are now welcome signs of recovery. The Index of Industrial Production (IIP) registered a growth of 6.9 per cent during April-October 1999 as compared with 3.4 per cent during the corresponding period of the previous year. The increase in the IIP was mainly due to revival of growth in demand for manufactured products, and is reflected in the significant improvement in the manufacturing output growth by 7.5 per cent as against 3.5 per cent in the comparable period of the previous year. Signs of recovery were observed in steel, cement and certain other sectors. This is reflected also in the turnaround in the demand for non-food-bank credit, and in the buoyancy noticed in the stock and fixed income securities. The industrial recovery which is under way has been led by the consumer durables sector which posted a growth rate of 12.3 per cent during April-October 1999. Although the capital goods sector registered a growth rate of 8.6 per cent during this period, the transport sector, on the whole, did not put up commensurate performance. The intermediate goods sector which is dependent on construction and infrastructure development activities, has posted only a moderate growth at 9.8 per cent. The cement industry with an output growth of 20 per cent clearly points to a rising level of construction activity in the economy. The overall index of industrial output and of manufacturing output recorded growth of 12.7 per cent and 13.8 per cent respectively during 1995-96. Thereafter, for three consecutive years, the growth rate was very low. For industrial output, it was 5.6 per cent, 6.6 per cent, and 4.0 per cent respectively during the three years 1996-97, 1997-98 and 1998-99. For manufacturing output, the growth rate was also low at 6.7 per cent, 6.7 per cent, and 4.4 per cent respectively for these three years.

Performance of the modern small scale sector has emerged to be much better than the manufacturing sector or industry as a whole in the post-liberalisation period. It continued to record steady growth up to 1996-97. However in 1997-98, there was a decline. Growth in real terms of production of SSI sector was 7.1 per cent in 1993-94, 10.1 per cent in 1994-95, 11.4 per cent in 1995-96, and 11.3 per cent in 1996-97. It declined to 8.4 per cent in 1997-98. Liberalization has thus given fillip to the growth of small industries.

An important area of concern for the management of the Balance of Payments position continues to be that of exports. Partly because of the slowdown in the world economy, and also the East Asian economic crisis, exports in 1998-99 declined by 3.9 per cent in US dollar terms. There is some evidence of pickup in exports during the first seven months (April-October 1999) of the current year (1999-2000), when exports grew by 10.0 per cent in US dollar terms, in relation to the corresponding period of the previous year. It is necessary that this momentum is kept up. During 1996-97 and 1997-98, export growth in US dollar terms was 5.3 per cent and 4.6 per cent respectively. During the earlier three years 1993-94 to 1995-96, it ranged from 18.4 per cent to 20.8 per cent. Growth of exports from small scale industries in US dollar terms was 39 per cent in 1993-94 and

27.1 per cent in 1995-96. In the other recent years, it was very low ranging from 1.4 per cent to 7.2 per cent.

Some measures were announced by the RBI in April 1999 in order to ensure timely availability of export credit and remove procedural hassles. Improvements have been made in the procedure for handling of export documents and fast track clearance of export credit at specialised branches of banks. In August 1998, RBI issued simplified guidelines for sanction of credit facilities for software services, project services, and software products and packages.

A notable feature of the dynamics of structural transformation of the economy in recent years has been the rising contribution of the services sector which includes substantial value added and skill-intensive services, such as software, to the overall output in the economy. It is important to note that the growth of the services sector has imparted much of the resilience to the overall growth of the economy, particularly in times of adverse agricultural shocks and industrial slowdown. More importantly this sector has emerged as the fastest expanding sector, with implications for productivity, employment, trade, and fiscal prospects of the economy. Between 1990-91 and 1998-99, the share of services (inclusive of construction) in the real GDP increased from 43.7 per cent to 51.2 per cent. The contribution of growth of the services sector to the overall growth of GDP has also increased significantly from 47.5 per cent in 1990-91 to 49.8 per cent in 1998-99. The recent trends in the services sector point to several implications. Relatively high growth of the services sector would be generally suggestive of gains in productivity in agricultural and industrial sectors, induced by technological progress and other innovations, which result in moving employment away from the non-services sector to services producing sector. It also indicates a shift of real expenditure from manufacturing to value added services, which is generally associated with the process of economic development. On the current economic environment, the 1998-99 Annual Report of the RBI concludes as follows: " The gains at the turn of the new century need to be strengthened by persevering with structural measures that reduce institutional rigidities and further economic activity. Such a forward looking approach alone will give the requisite added strength to meet the unexpected situations that may develop at home and abroad."

(a) All statutes, regulations and procedures would be reviewed, and modified wherever necessary, to ensure that their operations do not militate against the interests of small and village industries.

(b) Tiny enterprises would be eligible for additional support on a continuing basis.

(c) Equity participation by other industrial undertakings in the SSI sector to be increased from 24 to 49 per cent.

(d) A limited Partnership Act will be introduced to enhance the supply of risk capital to the SSI sector. Such an act would limit the financial liability of the new and non-active partners / entrepreneurs to the capital invested.

Deregulation and Liberalization

A significant aspect of economic reforms launched since 1991 related to deregulation and liberalization in the field of industrial development. For achieving the objective of reforms, the role of the Government needed to change from that of only exercising control to one of providing help and guidance by making essential procedures fully transparent and eliminating delays.

In the above background, the Department of Personnel and Training, Government of India, and the United Nations Development Programme (UNDP) have jointly undertaken a project titled "Capacity Building for Civil Service, Administrative Reforms and Training in Centre and States". Under this project, a Task Force has been set up in the Ministry of Industry to recommend administrative reforms and other measures for increasing the efficiency of civil services to promote industrial development. The Task Force studied the regulations, policies and procedures, governing the setting up of industries, both for small scale and other sectors, the functioning of key agencies involved in the process of setting up industrial projects, and the attitudinal aspects mainly from the point of view of the functionaries involved. The Task Force felt that the process of economic reforms initiated and continued by the Centre and the State Governments during the recent years has resulted in a major shift from a regulated and protected regime to a deregulated and competitive system. However, the feeling persists that there still exists an administrative regime of clearances, approvals, etc. which is somewhat cumbersome.

After examining the problems faced and suggestions offered by entrepreneurs from different parts of the country, the Task Force made a number of recommendations, which are summarized as under.

Future Direction of Reforms

(a) Greater transparency at all levels to eliminate possibilities of discretionary controls, involving notifying details, fixing time limits for decision making, delegating powers and providing for greater accountability.

(b) the Central and State Governments could undertake a comprehensive review of delegation of powers. The financial limits for various approvals could be factored through an inflation index.

(c) Sate Government may consider to establish and develop an inter-departmental State level mechanism, involving Trade and Industry Associations to periodically review policies and procedures, and to have a look at various regulations.

(d) for faster implementation of projects at the state level, a State Level Committee for Industrial Approvals, suitably empowered to clear investment proposals in a time bound manner could be set up.

(e) A District Industry Promotion Agency either on the lines of the District Rural Development Agency or as part of the District Industries Centre for providing a single point service for clearances / approvals / registrations, providing information, monitoring and coordination could be set up. A proper harmonization with the district administration would be necessary, and the Block Development Office could also be considered as a block level agency for industrial promotion. The existing staff could function as the Secretariat for this agency, and support services could continue to be provided through various channels. Specialized agencies would provide their assistance and promotional support through this agency.

(f) For land allotment and location, the State Level Committee for Industrial Approvals could consider and clear proposals for allotment of government land, and for this purpose, the body may be empowered under the land revenue legislation. The State Governments should statutorily notify industrial zones where requirements such as conversion of agricultural land to non-agricultural use, permission under Tenancy Act, etc. should not be necessary. Further, general exemption from prior clearances could be restricted to a notified set of specific non-polluting industries. A notified negative list of polluting industries could also be drawn up for whom general exemption would not be applicable. Setting up of industrial estates and development of basic infrastructure facilities with private sector participation could be encouraged.

(g) For power connection, the requirement of obtaining NOC from State Electricity Board for setting up captive power generation capacity could be dispensed with. Adequate delegation of authority should be made to field levels for given power loads. The load availability in the jurisdiction of the official responsible to decide the power connection applications should be publicized and updated on a periodic basis.

(h) System of grant of approval for environmental clearances should be made transparent and objective. A positive list of industries could be considered for which certain clearances would not be required but the authorities would have powers to inspect the pollution control measures at the post-production stage. There could be a Nodal Authority for single window environmental clearance at the state level.

Central Government should consider delegation of some of the authority under Environment Protection Act to the State Governments. The limit of Rs.1 crore for small scale reserved industries for exemption under the Environment Notification of January 1994 needs to be revised to at least Rs.5 crore. Similarly, the industry-specific parameters should be reviewed with reference to benchmark studies on a periodic basis for increasing the threshold limit for industries specified in Schedule 1 and deletion from the Schedule. Such review may be done through industry-specific panels including industry representatives, scientists and non-governmental organizations (NGOs).

(i) The industry should be encouraged to promote a system of self inspection and normative standards in lieu of approvals. Some of the approvals could have presumed automatically while others could have a provision of post facto approvals or disclosure norms.

(j) Viability of projects should be assessed in a time bound manner for speedy sanction of loans by banks and financial institutions.

(k) The procedures for customs clearance could be simplified through electronic filing facility, as also introducing a system of Advance Ruling for Customs Duty for capital goods on the lines of Advance Ruling for Income Tax.

(l) There must be emphasis on the need for regular and effective monitoring of industrial projects at Central, State and District levels.

(m) There should be Facilitation Cells to help and guide entrepreneurs at District, State and Central levels.

(n) District Industries Centres may be modernized in terms of computer facilities and connected to NICNET. NICNET terminals should be extended to all departments and agencies concerned with industrial approvals at the state level. The harmonized ITC classification should be adopted also at the state level..

The task of management of information and data should be assigned to a specialized agency which may be totally autonomous or semi-autonomous as per the requirement of the Government. Such an agency could be created initially with Government support but could be managed through private initiative. Information dissemination could be done on commercial lines in consultation with the Government. Industry Associations, in particular, should progressively assume greater responsibility for management and dissemination of information.

(o) A Training Scheme should be evolved for catering to various levels of functionaries. The programmes and packages for training could be devised by the Centre in consultation with the States, and suggested for adoption by the States. Specialized institutions could be identified for imparting such training.

(p) The Ministry of Industry at the Central Government level should attempt a greater role and involvement in such coordination as may be necessary in matters of policy, systems rationalization, monitoring, implementation of sanctioned projects, and assisting entrepreneurs. An Inter-Ministerial Body at the official level could provide a forum for regular interaction between Government and Industry. A similar arrangement could be considered at the State level.

Simplification of Registration and Regulation of Industries

The Administrative Staff College of India, Hyderabad worked on this project and brought out recommendations on patterns to be adopted by a few States. These are presented here in a generalized form.

Policies can be categorized as: (a) Revenue policies, (b) Uniformity in definitions and applicability of acts, and (c) Exemptions to be streamlined.

For the purpose of clearances, industries may be categorized as:

(a) Scheduled Industries, (b) Unscheduled Industries, and (c) Tiny and Micro Industries.

Procedural stages are : (a) Entry stage, (b) Implementation stage, and (c) Operational stage.

Permanent registration certificates should contain the following details:

(a) List of registers to be maintained

(b) Details of columns in the CAR / CQR form and filing time

(c) Details of inspection: Time and the laws under which the unit is subject to inspection.

Conclusion

Review attempted of reforms in the industrial sector, with special reference to small scale industries, brings out the need to pursue the following directions in the near future through greater intensity of the reforms package.

* Precise knowledge information using innovative technologies
* To bring about overall attitudinal changes to promotional efforts
* Delivery system for institutional credit flow to tiny sector units
* Enforcement of Delayed Payments Act in letter and spirit
* Widening the network of Factoring Services and use of Venture Capital Fund
* Operationalisation of the Single Window Concept
* Institutionalizing a mechanism for continuous monitoring of the impact of policy changes
* Simplification of rules, regulations and procedures to make them more entrepreneur-friendly; greater transparency at all levels; greater delegation of powers;

and streamlining of the institutional structure in the liberalization context.

REFERENCES

Administrative Staff College of India, Centre for Infrastructure Management (1998), *Towards Simplification of Registration and Regulation of Industries, Study Report 1 - Andhra Pradesh*, Hyderabad.

Government of Andhra Pradesh, Industries and Commerce Department (1998), *Policy for Small Enterprises - A Small Step by the Government a Giant Leap for Small Enterprises,* Hyderabad.

Government of India, Ministry of Industry, Department of Industrial Policy and Promotion (1996), *Report of the Task Force on Administrative Reforms to help Liberalise Procedures to Attract Investment,* New Delhi.

Nagayya, D. (1998), *Impact of Economic Liberalization on Small Industry,* Hyderabad, National Institute of Small Industry Extension Training (a study sponsored by the National Small Industries Corporation, New Delhi).

5

Liberalisation and Exports of Small Scale Industries in India

Prof. B. Appa Rao*

The process of liberalization, privatization and globalization was initiated in a comprehensive manner from July 1991 with the announcement of the new industrial policy statement, followed by the policy statement for small, tiny and village enterprises in August 1991. Reform process in a number of sectors, which included industry, trade, finance, banking, capital markets, fiscal policies and some segments of infrastructure, etc. was initiated in sectors such as insurance and some of the infrastructure and resource sectors. With the opening up of the economy in a phased manner, there was apprehension in various quarters, particularly among entrepreneurs in the small, medium and large scale industrial sectors that the reforms might hit domestic industry and trade adversely, some of the enterprises might even face closure in due course. In view of this, at various stages, it was felt necessary to gather feedback from entrepreneurs, institutions and associations to enable the policy and decision makers to decide on the direction and extent of reforms that could be introduced in various sectors of different points of time. In this paper, an over-view of the impact of liberalization has been attempted through the review of the macro economic trends for post-reform era of seven years from 1991-92 to 1997-98. Review is attempted is through the following parameters at the national level, growth of GDP and individual sectors, growth of

* Professor, Department of Commerce and Management Studies, Andhra University, Visakhapatnam.

industry, village and small industries sector and growth of exports. Other parameters covered age, gross fiscal deficit as per cent of GDP, imports and exports as per cent of GDP, foreign reserves, current account deficit as per cent of GDP, short-term external debt as per cent of total external debt as per cent of total external debt, inflation etc. This is attempted from the data and tends gathered from a number of secondary published and unpublished sources.

Growth of GDP and Industry, Agriculture and Other Sectors

The overall economic activity of the Indian economy has responded very well to the macro economic and structural reforms of the last seven years, from 1991-92. Liberalization has accelerated the process of development in different sectors during the eighth-plan period (1992-97). Following the initial down turn in the early phases of stabilization and reform characteristic occurrence in respect of countries undergoing reforms, the recovery of the Indian economy was comparatively faster, rapid and above all robust. The average real gross domestic product growth during the eighth five-year plan estimated to be 6.8% was distinctly higher than the targeted growth rate of 5.6%. It is distinctly higher than the average growth rates achieved earlier of 6% for the 7th plan and 5.1% for the 6th plan. More importantly, the real GDP growth rate during the last three years of the 8th plan period averaged 7.5% which was not only unprecedented for the economy, but also impressive in terms of cross country comparisons. It was 7.3%, 7.3% and 7.8% during 1994-95, 1995-96 and 1996-97 respectively. In the earlier years, it was 5.3% in 1992-93 and 5.9% in 1993-94. Growth during the six years of post-reform period 1991-97 (including the year of 1991-92 the year of stabilization) has been an average of 5.6%. This is just about the same as in the six years of the pre-reform period (1984-85 to 1988-89) of 10.6% raised the average in the pre-reform period, just as the performance in 1991-92 of 0.8% pulled down the average in the post-reform era.

The central statistical organization's GDP figures for 1997-98 confirm that the economy has experienced substantial deceleration during 1997-98. The 4.8% growth in the latest year indicates deceleration by 38% from 7.8% recorded in the previous year. The deceleration has been on account of sharp fall in the growth rate in agriculture (-2.4% compared to 9.6% in the previous year), and deceleration growth rate of the industry (4.3% compared to 7.1% with the previous year), while services sector recorded growth of 9.8% compared to 7.2% of the previous year. Increase in the services sector due to growth rate in financial and business services and community, social and personal services. For the manufacturing sector, growth rate was 9.7% in 1996-97and 1.5% in 1997-98. There is a growth recognition that it is possible to achieve during the ninth plan period. In the light of the growth rate realized during 1997-98, the effort involved to attain the targeted growth rate for the ninth five-year plan period is quite substantial.

Coming to the prospects for 1998-99, provisional growth rate of 6.6% is indicated with a pick up in the agricultural growth rate (7.1) which projected normal rainfall, an industrial growth rate of 3.4% and the services sector growing between 8.9% as it has been doing in the past several years.

Over the medium-term, the broad economic parameters do point to the feasibility of the economy growing around 7%. With the domestic saving rate ranging between 25% and 26%, and even with a modest current account deficit of 2% of GDP. The growth rate of 7% is feasible, with ICOR (Incremental Capital-Output Ratio) remaining more or less at 4% with an improvement in the saving rate better efficiency in the use of capital, it may be possible even to improve on this growth rate.

Utilizing the trends in the index of industrial production with 1980-81 as the base year, growth rate for the industrial sector aw a whole, for manufacturing sector and also for the small-scale industrial sector can be observed. Recently, central statistical organization realized the index of industrial production with 1993-94 base years as 100. Growth rates for industry and manufacturing from 1994-95 to 1997-98 are based on the revised index sense.

The share of agriculture, industry and service sector in GDP in 1996-97 was 26%, 31% and 43% respectively compared to 25%, 31% and 44% in 1997-98. The service sector now accounts for

44% of GDP. Increase in the service sector has been because of the rapid pace of expansion in the sub-sector of community, social and personal services. This in turn is reflected in government administration, defense and household services. The acceleration of growth in these areas is hardly a sign of the soundness of the economy. Growth of service sector in India still does not represent any movement to a post-industrial sector. Opportunities available in the service sector need to be exploited to improve the contribution of thus sector to GDP.

Adequate availability of agricultural produce was the significant feature of the English plan period. Growth slow down can be traced to a combination of underlying supply factors and temporary demand factors. On the demand side, the deceleration in consumer demand especially from agriculture, domestic invest demand from private sector, export demand as well as government demand contributed from private sector, export demand as well as government demand contributed to the slowdown, while on the supply side, infrastructure bottlenecks acted as a constraining influence. These are with reference to power, railways, road (and to a lesser extent ports, airports and telecom) the deceleration was evident in all segments of the sector and was particularly sharp in the consumer durable industry.

Industrial sector acquired itself creditably during the three years 1993-96, and performance in the subsequent two years (1996-98) was moderate. Investment pace slowed down subsequently during 1995-96 due to difficulties in mobilizing rupee resources. Growth rate of industry moved up to a maximum of 13% in 1995-96 from 9.1% in 1994-95 and 6.7% in 1997-98 as per the revised index series of 1993-94. The growth rate in manufacturing touched 14.1% during 1995-96 and declined to 7.3% and 6.7% in the subsequent two years as per the revised series. During 1999-2000, the industrial sector picked up with overall growth rate of 6.6% and for manufacturing it was 7.1%.

Trend of Other Macro-Economic Indicators

Trends of other macro-economic indicators refer to gross

fiscal deficit, imports and exports as a per cent of GDP, and foreign exchange reserves. Foreign exchange reserves position has been quite comfortable in the recent years though it has been fluctuating from time to time. The foreign currency assets rising to US $ 22.4 billion by end of March 1997, and $ 26 billion by end of March 1998 and $ 26.4 billion by 17th April 1998 equivalent of about 25 months of debt service taken together. Gross fiscal deficit as per cent of GDP slided down from 7.5% in 1993-94 to 5% in 1996-97 and moved up to 6.1% during 1998-99. Exports as per cent of GDP ranged from 8.2% to 9.2% in the recent 4 years, it was 8% and 8.5% during 1991-92 and 1992-93 respectively. Imports, as per cent of GDP ranged around 10% during the three years 1992-95 and were slightly above 12% during 1995-96 and 1996-97. It was 8.7% in 1991-92.

The current account deficit as a proportion of GDP had demand low. In 1995-96 it was 1.8% of GDP, in 1996-97 it was 1%, and in 1997-98 it was 1.5%. During this period, foreign exchange reserves continued to rise. Short-term external debt as a percentage of total external debt was 5.5% in 1995-96, 7.2% in 1996-97 and estimated to be 6.3% in 1997-98. The management of the external sector in the country has been guided by certain forces. A modest level of current account deficit and a calibrated composition of capital flows including a low level of short-term debt have always been the guiding factors.

The annual rate of inflation, which was 6.7% at the start of 1997-98, had fallen to an eleven-year low of 3.4% by the end of August 1997. The low inflation rate of less than 4% was maintained up to end-November 1997. Thereafter, there was a slight upward drift in the growth rate to over 5% in December 1997 and close to 6% in January 1998. It reached 5% at the end of March 1998. The average inflation for 1997-98 was 1.4% points less than the average inflation in 1996-97.

Maintaining a reasonable degree of price stability will achieve the twin purposes of domestic stability and avoiding disruptive adjustments to the exchange rate. Efforts to contain the fiscal deficit in the short and medium terms must receive adequate attention. By all indications, the current account deficit will not exceed 2% of GDP during 1998-99. The funding of that level of deficit should pose no difficulty even though it should be admitted that some elements of the capital account would come under strain.

The sharp slow down in GDP, industrial, export and import growth following three years of high growth in each case, are central areas of concern. Lower off take of bank credit is another major concern. Export growth decelerated sharply in 1996-97 and 1997-98, accompanied by a marked deceleration in industrial growth. It is imperative to put back the economy on a higher growth path of the order of 7 to 8% per annum in the remaining years of the ninth plan period.

Growth of Industry, Village and Small Industry Sectors

The upward shift of the industrial production during 1997-98 has come about mainly because of the revised growth rate of the manufacturing and mining sectors. The manufacturing sector, now turns out, actually grew by 6.67% and not 3.6% as had been estimated earlier. The mining sector similarly registered a growth rate of 6.9% put out earlier. Electricity generation remained stationary at 6.6%.

With the shifting of the index of industrial production (IIP) base, it also turns out that the growth of industrial sector was moderate at 6.7% in 1997-98, compared to 6.1% in 1996-97 and 3% in 1995-96. For 1996-97, the revised estimate placed the growth rate at 6.1% compared to 7.1% mentioned earlier. Significantly, the high record growth figure stands reduced to 9.1% against as the earlier figure of 9.4%. Average growth rate of the industrial sector during 1993-96 was 9.5%. Within the industrial sector, an average growth rate of manufacturing was 10.66%.

Analysis of the contributions of various segments to the growth of the industrial sector reveals that manufacturing segment's contribution has been steadily going up in the recent years, with decline in the contribution of mining, quarrying and electricity. Manufacturing has contributed as high a level as 98.7% in 1996-97, with electricity contributing 7% and mining and quarrying 3.64%. In 1997-98, contribution to growth of manufacturing was 81.2%, of electricity 9.9% and of mining 8%.

Deceleration in industrial growth during 1996-97 and 1997-98 was partly due to the slackening of demand for different products as well as keen competition from imports for some products. In 1997-98, sharp decline in the capital goods sector was noticed.

Performance of the modern small-scale sector has emerged to be much better than the manufacturing sector of the industry as a whole in the post-liberalization period. It continues to record a steady growth. In fact, growth in real terms of production of modern small-scale sector was 7.1% in 1993-94, 10.1% in 1994-95, 11.4% in 1995-96 and 11.3% in 1996-97. Liberalization has given the fillip to the growth of small industries. There are nearly 29 lakh small industries by the end of 1996-97, with the production at current prices of Rs.412,636 crore, employment of 160 lakh and exports of Rs.39,249 crore. Production at 1990-91 prices works out to Rs.247,311 crore. Growth of production for 1997-98 is estimated at 167.2 lakh for 1997-98 (growth rate at 4.5% in 1997-98 as against 4.84% in 1996-97). Number of SSI units in the latest year is estimated as 30.14 lakh, compared to 28.57 lakh in the previous year. Contribution of direct exports from SSI sector amounted to 33% of total exports of the country and 40% of the total manufacturing sector's exports.

Performance of village and small industries (VSI) sector for 1995-96 (achievement) and 1996-97 (achievement for SSI and anticipated for other sub-sectors) is presented here. During 1996-97, production of VSI sector increased to an estimated level of Rs.490,278 crore from Rs.426,145 crore recorded during previous years, of which the share of SSI sector was a little over 84%.

The traditional industries sub-sector affected by the slow growth in the export-oriented segments, particularly gems and jewelry, handicrafts and handlooms, recorded a rise of 8.8% in real output. Therefore, there has been a slow down in the overall growth of the sector to about 9.1% during 1996-97, compared with the growth of 11.4% during 1995-96.

Employment in VSI sector increased to 575 lakh persons at the end of March 1997, as against 554 lakh persons as at the end of March 1996. The sector has generated an incremental employment of nearly 20 lakh persons, thereby registering growth of 3.6% in employment during 1996-97.

Growth of Exports

Exports from modern small industries was Rs.39,249 crore in 1996-97, modest increase of 7.6% during the year in relation to the overall growth of the country's exports of 11.7%. In dollar term, in 1996-97, export growth rate for the country was 5.3% and for the SSI sector 1.4%. The export performance of VSI sector has been influenced largely by the near stagnation in exports of handicrafts. Gems and jewelry, a major constituent of handicrafts, registered a decline of exports in dollar terms during 1996-97. Performance of power looms, which are part of the modern sector, has been moderate. Nevertheless, the VSI sector's aggregate exports at Rs.70,628 crore for 1996-97, accounting for a share of 59.4% in the country's exports have shown a marginal increase in absolute terms (7.3% growth). In dollar terms, the increase was only 1.1%.

For 1997-98, the country's total exports are provisionally indicated as Rs.126,286 crore (US $ 33980); growth rate of 6.3% in rupees term and 1.5% in dollaı terms. Analysis of growth of exports from 1991-92 reveals that growth rate in dollar terms was close to or around 20% during the three years 1993-96; in all the other four years, it was very low slightly above or less than 5%. It was negative in 1991-92. For the SSI sector, growth of exports in dollar terms was high in 1993-94 (39%) and 1995-96 (27%) in all other years, it was very low. The deceleration of export growth particularly during the two years 1996-98 has been a cause for concern, because a low export rate places some of the parameters such as debt –service ratio under strain. One aspect of the external sectors, which needs immediate attention in export growth.

Position of exports of SSI sector for the period 1991-97 (6 years) is presented by major product groups. It also presents the share of export of small-scale industries to the total manufacture exports of each product group. A few significant aspects emerging are recalled shard of non-traditional exports to total SSI exports has been close to or above 96% during these years.

In sports goods, readymade garments, cashew kernel and cashew nutshell liquid, and Lac, SSI sector accounted for 100 per unit manufactured exports. Readymade garments alone accounted for 42.6% of SSI sector during 1996-97 (Rs.16,729 crores). With the inclusion of other three categories contributing to 100% exports, the contribution of the four groups to SSI export worked out to 46.7%. The contribution of finished leather and leather products was next importance in relation to total exports of that group (ranging from 80% to 90% though only 58% in 1996-97). Engineering goods, basic chemicals, pharmaceuticals and cosmetics, finished leather and leather products, processed foods; rayon and synthetic products 44.3%. All other categories to growth have been very high in the recent years together accounted for 9%. Some of the product group where growth has been very high in the recent years are; readymade garments, basic chemicals, pharmaceuticals and cosmetics, processed foods. In view of the importance of exports to the national economy, product groups, which have potential for further development for stepping up exports, need to be given adequate importance. Incentives and infrastructure support to overcome bottlenecks will go a long way in improving the import position of SSI and of traditional village industries.

The slow down in export performance reflects a range of factors of foreign and growth origins, the two most important factors were probably the sharp decline in the growth of the value (US $) in world trade in the year 1996-97, and the appreciation of the rupee vis-à-vis the currencies of India's major trading partners and competitors. The real effective exchange rate of the rupee has shown a gradually appreciating trend over the last few years, because of the appreciation of the US dollar against other major currencies and the low international inflation rates relative to ours. Dramatic depreciation of some East Asian currencies during 1997 has also been a contributory factor to our export sluggishness.

Domestic factors responsible are slow down in growth of power, tight supply conditions in the domestic market for agriculture items especially rice and wheat, tightening of domestic environmental regulations and infrastructure bottlenecks. Developed countries have started signs of protectionism in various forms of non-tariff barriers such as social clauses, environmental regulations, and quality and process standards introduced or discussed for possible adoption in future. These are disturbing signals for Indian exports. Efforts needed to comply with these stipulations of developed countries such as quality standards, testing and labeling are very large. Average annual rate of growth of 12% is envisaged for exports in dollar terms for the ninth plan period.

6

Small Scale Industries Sector in India : Emerging Trends and Implications

Dr.. A.D. Madhavi*, Dr. M. Vijayalakshmi**, & Dr. S. Vijay Raju***

Introduction

The small-scale industry sector is an important segment of the Indian economy, which accounts for around 95 per cent of the industrial units, 40 per cent of the manufacturing sector output and 36 per cent of exports. Moreover, it provides direct employment to 18 million persons in around 3.2 million registered SSI units in the country. This sector, until now, enjoys the pride of being second largest employer in the country and offers a wide spectrum of products. The process of liberalization and globalization under the WTO regime has wide ranging implications for the SSI sector, which needs to be addressed in a proper perspective.

Evaluation of Policy for SSI

The contribution that the small industries make was recognized in the Industrial Policy Resolution of 1948. It was

* Associate Professor, GITAM Institute of Foreign Trade, Visakhapatnam

** Asst. Professor, GITAM Institute of Foreign Trade, Visakhapatnam.

*** Associate Professor, Dept. of Commerce and Mgt. Studies, Nagarjuna University, Guntur.

Mahatma Gandhi's clarion call for protecting handicrafts against the onslaught of imports of factory-made products that gave the impetus to develop small industry. The specific role of SSIs was recognized by the Industrial Policy Statement of 1948, which stated that cottage, and small-scale industries are particularly suited for better utilization of local resources and achievement of local self-sufficiency in certain essential goods.

The thrust areas of India's policy for the development of small industry have been reservations, fiscal concessions by way of lower excise duties, extension of business services by the Government and preferential procurement by government. Small industry was sought to be protected from the competition of big companies by earmarking a large number of products for exclusive manufacture by them. Fiscal concessions offer support to take care of cost disadvantages arising out of the non-availability of the economies of scale.

The basic purpose of the policy, institutional and legal framework governing small industry's employment generation so as to spread the benefits of growth to the maximum number of people. While large capital-intensive enterprises reward only a small group of promoters and skilled-primarily urban-labour, small enterprises manufacturing labour-intensive products make economical use of capital and draw on the abundant labour.

Policy Framework

The foundation of SSI policy was laid in the Second Five Year Plan. The 1956 industrial policy chose equity as the guiding principle for SSI development. It said : "Small-scale industries provide immediate large-scale employment, offer a method of ensuring a more equitable distribution of national income and facilitate an effective mobilization of resources of capital and skill, which might otherwise remain unutilized".

1977 policy statement : This watershed policy provided for a heightened role for this sector, by considerably expanding the list of products reserved for manufacture by small industry, a facility launched in 1967.

1980 policy statement : The policy recognized the

importance of ancillary industry and accelerated the development of rural and backward area.

1985 policy statement : Taking into account the impact of inflation, this raised the investment ceiling for SSI to Rs.35 lakh and for ancillaries to Rs.45 lakh.

1991 policy reforms : The Industrial Policy of 1991 was accompanies by a special Policy Statement for Small Scale Industries.

Policy for Reservation of Items for Exclusive Manufacture in the Small-Scale Sector

The policy of reservation was primarily initiated in 1967 as a promotional and protective measure for the small-scale sector vis-à-vis the large-scale sector. Selected products have been identified for exclusive production in the small-scale sector. Those items that went into the consideration for reservation are based on is economical viability and technical feasibility for manufacture in the small-scale sector. For these items, the manufacturing process is of a simple nature, i.e., is essentially labour-intensive, where the small-scale units can meet the requirements of the consumers both in terms of quantity and quality. The rationale for reservation is thus based on small-scale advantages like labour intensity and adaptability to semi-urban and rural environment as well as to make their products competitive with those of the large-scale which have access to mass scale production, economies of scale, wider marketing network, better credit availability and publicity through the mass media. The Industrial Policy Resolution, 1956 had stressed the role of the small-scale sector in the development of the national economy: large-scale employment opportunities at lower capital cost, the establishment of a wider entrepreneurial base and an equitable distribution of national income and wealth.

Performance of the SSI Sector

The small-scale sector had emerged as a dynamic and vibrant sector of the Indian economy. It has contributed significantly to the realization of the socio-economic objectives of growth in employment and exports, fostering entrepreneurship and ensuring industrial dispersal. This sector is producing a vast range of more than 7500 products. During 1999-2000, the production from SSI's was estimated at Rs.5,78,470 crores and provided employment to more than 177 lakh persons in the 32 lakh SSI units spread throughout the country. Exports from SSIs have been estimated at Rs.48,979 crores in 1998-99. The small-scale sector has been contributing about 40% of industrial production and 36% of total direct exports. This sector has been maintaining, by and large, a higher growth than the industrial sector as a whole. The share of this sector in employment generation is next only to agriculture. The growth of employment in sectors like agriculture and large industries has either been declining or stagnant. It is the SSI sector apart from the service sector, which has been consistently recording steady growth and which has the vast potential to generating more employment. It is this sector, which has proved to be an engine of growth for the Indian economy. The small-scale industries (SSI sector in India over the past 50 years has contributed significantly towards building a stable and sound national economy. At present, the SSI sector is one of the largest employers in the country and has thus emerged as a means for fulfilling the national objectives of providing valuable employment opportunities. The linkages between the small-scale and large-scale industries get strengthened through ancillarization and sub-contracting. The sector will continue to play an important role in the industrial development of the country through a sustained process of technology upgradation and quality improvement in future.

Exports from the small-scale sector have over a period of time acquired greater significance in India's foreign trade. What was considered to be the activity exclusively belonging to large-scale or monopoly units has assumed more challenging proportions requiring greater contribution from all sectors of the economy including small-scale sector. The small-scale sector today is one of the large contributors to the foreign exchange of the foreign exchange reserves of the country. In India, in the early years, the small-scale units were mainly catering to domestic requirements and playing an important role in import substitution. With the expansion and diversification in the small-scale as well as the development of favourable international trading environment, the contribution of small-scale industries in exports has been increasing significantly. The SSI sector currently accounts for about 36 per cent of national exports and the growth rate has been impressive particularly after 1971-72. It is worth noting that the share of the SSI sector is very high in the fast growing areas of software/information technology. The share of SSI in this field is also assessed to be around 40% Indian Sector exports a large variety of non-traditional and traditional items covering engineering goods, basic chemicals, chemical and allied products, plastic products, processed foods, woolen garments and knitwear, sports goods, readymade garments, etc. There are apprehensions whether the performance of the SSI will be affected by the emerging trends in international competition.

Economic Liberalization – Implications for the SSI Sector

India started its process of integration with the global economy in July 1991. The government has pursued far-reaching economic and structural reforms in all sectors of economic policy. The thrust of these measures has been to make the Indian economy internationally competitive. The liberalized policy of the government has thrown open most of the industrial sector.

The new environment for SSIs consists of changes emerging from the ongoing process of economic reforms conforming to the WTO Agreement and to the fast changing economic, technological and information environment. In the process, the liberalized policy has posed certain challenges and provided opportunities to the small-scale sector. The challenges are in the form of increased competition, reduced protection due to lowering of tariffs and market determined rates of interest. On the other hand, opportunities have come in the form of access to better technology, availability of variety of raw materials and components, impetus to quality, efficiency and opportunity to restructure and diversify.

Dr. Abid Hussain observed in his introduction to the Report

of the Expert Committee on Small Enterprises that the small-scale sector occupies an important place in the country's economy. The existence of small units is essential to encourage the spread of industrial entrepreneurship throughout the country. It is therefore necessary for the small-scale sector to be provided a proper environment for growth and efficiency. The objective of policy for Small-Scale Enterprises (SSEs) must be to nurture such an environment. He states, "We now have to recognize that government over time has become more bureaucratic and rule-bound and can no longer be characterized as mission-oriented. The basic accent of India's small-scale industry policy has been defensive, aiming to insulate the sector from the dynamics of competitive growth. **Today such insulation is not practicable.** The new policy framework must recognize this new economic environment and should be designed to be much more promotional rather protective. Small-scale enterprises will continue to need exceptional support in terms of financial resources, technological development and infrastructure. It is much easier to organize such support systems in clusters where industries of similar characteristics exist together to reap the benefits of agglomeration economies.

It is also pertinent to note the Dr. Abid Hussain's conclusion in the Report. He states that the policies, programmes, schemes and institutions that provide support to SSIs have two characteristics. First, many of them are designed to protect SSIs from large industries, primarily through reservation. This protection is strengthened by other concessional credit and fiscal measures. Second, progammes and institutions are designed to provide government support to selected sectors and directly to small units. The support structure has reflected well the needs of 1950s and 1960s-the beginning of industrialization in India, and the controlled economic regime characterized by license and quotas. As a result, the government has attempted to intervene directly in its support programmes. But in view of the vast growth of small units over the years, the existing institutional network will not be adequate to serve well the needs of all. Secondly, it is better to provide overall support to small units rather than selecting some sectors or units. Third, with the opening up of the economy and the needs of industrial growth, the continuation of the reservation policy can be questioned. Fourth, the support structure has focused on industries rather than units. He observes, that considering the immense potential in growth of business and technical support services, both in terms of entrepreneurship and employment, the policy framework for the sector should support all enterprises equally. The Expert Group, therefore, he said, stresses the need to review the approach to policy support to the sector and reconfirm the need for providing special support to small units. **However, the support must be much more promotional than protective.**

Emerging Trends and Implications for the SSI Sector

India's share in world trade is at present about 0.7 per cent, which is by any yardstick very low. In order to make India a global player, all efforts should be made at the national level not only to improve domestic marketing but also the international marketing to enable the SSI's to face the challenges and t enable the SSIs to face the challenges and tough competition the world over. In dollar terms, our exports are about 35 billion dollars. If SSI accounts for 1/3rd of this then SSI accounts for 11 to 12 billion dollars of exports. Even to maintain its share of 36 per cent, it is essential that SSI sector must raise its exports to 20 billion dollars in three to four years and about 50 billion dollars in the next ten years. SSI sector has vast potential and with its distinct advantages of flexibility, dynamist and innovativeness, it would be in a position to come up to the expectations. Several initiatives need to be taken to meet the challenges of the highly competitive business environment as suggested by several studies.

1. Improvement in the flow of export finance including a special line of credit.
2. Introducing innovative finance such as Venture Capital Fund, Export Factoring and Export Development Fund.
3. Infrastructural support to cluster of industries.
4. Setting up commercial centers in state capitals in the form of export parks.

5. Linking industrial areas to ports with good roads and communication networks.
6. Recognizing the area of information technology and E-Commerce.
7. Encouraging participation in exhibitions and trade fairs by SSI entrepreneurs and providing necessary facilities for the same.
8. Promoting sub-contracting relationship between small-scale and large exporters.
9. Setting up display facilities in India and abroad.
10. Programmes for encouraging WTO awareness.
11. Evolving a sound system of data collected and accessibility on SSI statistics.
12. Improving Brand Image of SSI products.

Coping with the Emerging Environment under the WTO Regime

The World Trade Agreement and negotiations have a direct impact on all economic activities including the development and promotion of the small-scale sector. WTO Agreements are likely to affect the SSI sector in the following ways:

Removal of QRs will allow free and cheap imports and will result in stiff competition to the SSIs.

De-reservation of the SSI sector: The policy for de-reservation suggests first, the removal from the reserved list those items, which are not even being produced in the small sector. The second is on those items, which are already on the Open General License for import and those that are included in the free trade agreement with Sri Lanka, which provides easy access to Sri Lankan goods into India. The third category relates to those items, which involve labour intensive production and have a good export potential and finally, the recommendation is that the small-scale reservation should be completely eliminated by April 1, 2001. The small-scale sector is already under pressure from import of Chinese goods, which have practically driven out Indian products from the market. There has been widespread apprehension that the small-scale sector would be severely affected by foreign competition once import restrictions are removed. The thinking in the Government, therefore, is that it would be better to de-reserve the small-scale sector instead of allowing it to be squashed in which case Indian presence in the production of these items would disappear.

In view of the Agreement of TRIPS, it would be difficult for the SSI sector to continue with the reverse engineering and manufacture many items without paying royalty to the patent holders. In terms of Sanitary and Phytosanitary measures, SSIs will have to adopt international standards with regard to quality, health and hygiene.

The SSI sector is not without tools to counter the international competitors take undue advantage. If there is a surge in imports and domestic industries are adversely affected, the Government can take safeguard measures to protect the interests of the SSI sector. The safeguard measures, which can be taken include: Reimposition of QRs, imposition of duty up to bound rates or in specific cases even beyond bound rates, imposition of anti-dumping duty, and imposition of countervailing duty.

While these initiatives have begun, there is an urgent need to sensitize the entrepreneurs on all issues and agreements relating to the WTO regime -- The Agreement on Agriculture, the Competition Policy, The General Agreement on Trade in Services (GATS) and Trade Related Aspects on Intellectual Property Rights (TRIPS) and the preparation for trade environment with the removal of quantitative restrictions, which is scheduled for 1 April 2001.

Along with this, measures should be taken for maintaining the track record for price competitiveness, quality and delivery within time; it is imperative to dovetail latest technological advancement and effective applications of information technology resources in the production process. These measures would provide the necessary cutting edge for SSI sector to boost the exports from the sector.

REFERENCES

1. Report of the Committee on Small Enterprises (The Ministry of Industry, Government of India), 1997.

2. *Laghu Udyog Samachar*, April-September 2000.

3. SIDBI Report, 2000.

4. Business Dailies: *Business Line, The Economic Times.*

7

Topsy-Turvy Policy of the Government on Small-Scale Industry

Dr. S.V. Pulla Reddy* & Dr. M. Mutyala Naidu**

From the 1950s onwards, India followed the policy of protectionism in respect of small-scale industry. This was manifested by the policies of restrictions on imports, reservations in production, exemptions on taxation, subsidies in supply of raw materials and financial assistance. Those who supported protectionism are known as 'dependency theorists'. They argued for more protection.

The modernization theories emphasized innovation and argued that development spreads if the existing barriers on trade are removed. They see free trade as engine of growth. Marx was a modernization theorist. For him capitalism meant not simply exploitation, which has existed in all pre-capitalist class societies. It meant specifically the rapid advancement of the forces of production, the over turning of old ways of life and the increasing integration of the world. He saw all these factors not as negative but as laying the basis for socialism. While those speaking in his name today are taking opposition to liberalization and globalization as their slogans. We have to look to the ways the new developments in the process of globalization provide opportunities for growth in welfare and liberation of masses of working people and see in it a basis for using the contradictions they represent for moving towards new and better form of society.

* Department of Law, S.K. University, Anantapur.
** SKIM, S.K. University, Anantapur.

According to Karl Marx, capitalism revolutionizes the means of production and social relations. It smashes the barriers of feudalism and mercantilism everywhere destroying old feudal bondages and old medieval certainties and antiquated dreams. Capitalism is ever-moving, ever-changing and forces humans to face the reality of change. Marx saw capitalism with open eyes.

He could have certainly preferred capitalism if it came to a choice between capitalism and feudalism. He was a proponent of progress and development. To him, free trade meant growth. Today capitalism is represented by globalization. Marxists in India are staunch supporters of Protectionism. Marxists in India are depicting globalization as a demon and are trying to erect 'Great wall' against its threat. They apprehend that the globalization is destructive and enhances unevenness, exploitation and misery. But Marxists should not fail to see human being as a tremendous potential development, a creator of new productive forces and intellectual achievements. Globalization is, thus, a process necessary through which humanity must pass with as little cost as possible. Hence, we have to recognize what was new and transformative in capitalist realm of production.

Gone are the days when our policy was driven by the concepts of 'self-sufficiency' and the sentiments of 'Swadeshi'. The present awareness is that there is little sense in making everything we need by using huge amounts of resources and time for setting up indigenous production units when there was a world market, which could meet our needs more quickly and at a very acceptable cost. It is true that there was a mental resistance to imports at one point of time in the history when India was a British colony when it was treated as a supplier of raw materials to the British Industry and consumer of finished goods to Indians.

The policy of the government on small-scale industry (SSI) is linked to the international trade policy. The government policy towards small sector has undermined its competitiveness and that of the economy as a whole. Today, the government while framing the policy stands in the shadow of WTO. It suffers from a complex. Its freedom to plan and develop the economy is inhibited. It is unable to evolve equitable world trade relations. It is unable to allay the fears of small-scale industry as well as its consumer.

The small-scale sector was conceived some 35 years ago as a means to generate substantial employment opportunities over a wide geographical area apart from promoting entrepreneurial skills among general population. It was thought that this would prevent people from migrating to large towns in search of jobs either in large industries or with the government. To protect this nascent industry, certain limitations were specified in terms of investment in land and machinery so that large industries did not creep into the sector, which was offered a host of excise and other concessions. Some 47 items were initially reserved for exclusive manufacture by small-scale sector so that it did not have to face competition from established units. This list was progressively expanded to reach a peak of 873 in 1983.

Today, in spite of all the protection that was given to it, the small-scale industry is plagued by large-scale sickness, poor quality of products. There are companies that have operated under a system of the government-administered prices, quotas and controls, which they were always able to manipulate for their profits. The alcohol based chemical producers, producers of sugar, edible oils and fertilizers are some examples of industries, which survive only because government helps them by manipulating market prices. Why should Indian people continue to be at the mercy of inefficient industries and their pampered employees? Why should the Indian consumer be deprived of better products for the sake of abnormal profits for the local producers? Will it be worthwhile to face all these hurdles for the sake of few inefficient small-scale industries? Reasons attributed by the industry for their inefficiency are low investment limits, which inhibits technological up gradation, in adequate marketing facilities, the rigid labour laws and complicated procedures in financing it.

Attempts to marry the small and large industries so that some sort of capital and technological support was provided to the former appeared to have borne no fruit. Though the government allowed 24% of investment by large industries in small sector, till date no significant investment has materialized.

The ministry of small-scale industry has mooted a proposal to hike the investment limit selectively for certain sector reserved for the small-scale sector to rs.5 crore from Rs.1 crore. The government is also expected to discuss the issue of raising the foreign investment limit in the sector from the present 24% to 49%. The above changes are likely to be implemented soon so that SSI sector in the country can brace itself for meeting the situation arising out of the total removal of Quantitative Restrictions (QTs) on imports of all items by April 1, 2001.

Abid Hussain Committee of 1997 has recommended for de-reservation accompanied by the suggestion for credible support package for the SSI. This package includes equity support, interest rate concessions and technology assistance. The committee also recommend that funds to the tune of Rs.500 crores per year, i.e., Rs.2500 crores over the next five years be provided. Accordingly, any move for de-reservation should therefore have the accompanying packages as well. He government can meet its obligations of nurturing SSEs more effectively if its aid should be largely restricted to activities at the time of formation of Small Enterprises. District Industry Centres need to be more promotional than regulatory. They should be replaced by flexible broad based District Enterprise Promotion Boards. Another committee by name S.P. Gupta Committee also recommended several support measures in terms of low cost and timely credit, an export assistance package, improvement in infrastructure and comprehensive package to face import competition.

India and US signed a mutual agreement under WTO on December 28, 1999, which has ended the dispute between the two countries on an earlier phase out of quantitative restrictions. In this agreement, India has agreed to advance the date by two years to March 31, 2002 on lifting of quantitative restrictions for all the items. Once quantitative restrictions on imports are lifted, reservation of items for SSI sector would become meaningless. Another apprehension of the SSI is that if the lifting of the quantitative restrictions is accompanied by de-reservation, the competition to it will not only be from foreign companies but also from domestic large units. In addition to this, they argue that, the competition from large industries, which have better access to finance, professional management, marketing out fits and better technological backup would be almost fatal to the small-scale sector. Recommendations to reduce the subsidies, according to them, would also hit the SSI in many respects.

Fears that de-reservation will lead to the extinction of the small-scale units is based on wrong presumptions. For example, countries such as China and Malaysia have no reservations for the garment industry yet they are thriving. The large units specialize in executing large orders of institutional garments while the small units take on small orders of high fashion and seasonal garments. Collaborative relations between the large, the medium and small units through subcontracting, arrangements are well established. Why can this not happen in India? Government policies should seek to strengthen and promote such collaborative efforts rather than keep them apart through protectionism.

SSI further argues that the present rigid labour laws and complicated procedures for getting government's prior approvals for lay-offs and retrenchments are contributing substantially to the spread of industrial sickness. They are forcing industrialists to adopt illegal methods to downsize their operations and encouraging them to opt for capital-intensive technologies. They apprehend that present labour laws, in trying to protect existing jobs, are in effect hampering the creation of new jobs. Flexibility in operations for the industry combined with adequate compensation for the temporary loss of jobs for the workers could be easily achieved by judiciously amending the existing laws and rules.

Majority of labour laws are Central laws though the subject falls in the Concurrent List. Industrial Disputes Act now mandates that an industrial establishment employing more than 100 workers should seek the government's nod prior to closure. The government is proposing to increase this limit to 1000 workers. This will imply that industrial establishments with a workforce of up to 1000 employees can resort to lay-offs without seeking government's clearance. To discourage indiscriminate closures, government proposed to increase the separation package from the present 15 days wages for every year worked to 45 days. The sweeping changes are to be brought in Contract

Labour (Regulation and Abolition) act. The crucial change to be effected in the contract labour law is doing away with the distinction of core and non-core activities as basis for the country's manpower scenario as it will lift checks on industrial establishments that employ less than 1000 workers from having to seek government's sanction before announcing layoffs. As between 70 to 85% of the country's organized sector workforce are in establishment that employ less than 1000 people, the proposed amendments will affect a large sections of workforce.

There is a need to bring these changes in the small-scale industry. But these changes should be brought after informed debate and discussion. The consensus arrived at on the most crucial part of the reforms should be used to improve the efficiency of small sector for the benefit its consumer.

REFERENCES

1. Abid Hussain Committee Report 1997.
2. Alok Mukherjee, "Small Industry Needs Large Aid", *The Hindu*, February 24, 2001, p.14.
3. The Report of Economic Survey 2000-2001. It recommended for complete de-reservation of small-scale sector to make it more competitive. Also see for details of the report *The Hindu*, February 24, 2001, p.1.
4. S.L. Rao, "Indian Companies in an open economy", *Economic and Political Weekly,* February 3 and February 10, 2001, pp. 257-260.
5. Sheela Bhide, "Development of small-scale industries: A collaborative approach", *Economic and Political Weekly,* December 9, 2000, p. 4389.
6. V.S.Sambandan, "Labouring with reforms", *The Hindu,* Business Section I, March 8, 2000.
7. P.K. Vasudeva, "Is small industry ready for a QR-Free regime?" *Economic and Political Weekly,* January 6, 2001, pp.22-24.
8. C.V. Gopalakrishnan, "The road to globalization", *The Hindu,* March 8, 2001.
9. Gail Omvedt, "Marx and globalisation", *The Hindu,* March 1, 2001.

SECTION – II

WTO and Small Industry

INTRODUCTION

Changing World Scenario : The world today is more closely knit, through different means of organization, communication and production than ever before. It is poised for a rapid change. Patterns of international trade, capital and competition have been changing dramatically with serious consequences for business strategy. With change has come increasing complexity, and international managers today find themselves dealing with new issues ranging from cross border alliances responding to competitors backed by powerful governments. There has been striking – and growing – differences between countries in their ability to compete and grow.

The global economy has set in. Global markets are characterized by competition. A dramatically increasing number of firms are going international, and a growing percentage of their overall sales is coming from overseas markets. The opening of markets have created new geographical space for TNCs to expand and access tangible and intangible resources. Also wider choices are created in the methods that firms can use (i.e., licensing, subcontracting, franchising, partnering and so on) to operate in different locations. At the same time, advances in information, communication and transportation technologies, as well as in managerial and organizational methods have facilitated the transnationalisation of many firms, including small and medium enterprises.

Globalisation is praised for the new opportunities it brings, such as access to markets and technology transfer – opportunities that hold out the promise of increased productivity and higher living standards. However, TNCs do not substitute for domestic effort. They can only provide access to tangible and intangible assets and catalyse domestic investment and capabilities. In a world of intensifying competition and accelerating technological change, this complementary and catalyst role can be very valuable. But the globalisation is also feared and often condemned because it sometimes brings instability and unwelcome change. It exposes workers to competition from imports, which can threaten their jobs, it undermines banks and even entire economies when flows of foreign capital overwhelm them. Since globalisation has its dangers, countries need to prepare their own capabilities to harness their potential.

TNCs are principal drivers of the globalisation process, which defines the new context for development. There is more space for firms to pursue their corporate strategies, and enjoying more rights than human resource development. The obvious question is: should these increased rights be complemented by firms' assuming greater social responsibility? The notion of social responsibility of TNCs encompasses a broad range of issues of which environmental, human and labour rights have attracted most attention in recent years. In a liberalising and globalising world economy, this question is likely to be asked with increasing frequency and insistence. Governments now focus more on imposing the broader setting in which TNCs operate—macro-economic management, infrastructure provision, human capital, competition policy, and the like. In short, they seek to entice TNCs to do what they would like to see done, as opposed unilaterally seeking to impose their objectives on them. More often than not, it a matter of the right policy mix of carrot and stick, reflecting, of course, the specific attributes and objectives of countries and companies.

Economic development remains an urgent need. Globalisation – which links countries closer than ever before with each other – reinforces this need. TNCs can affect development, by complementing domestic investment and by undertaking trade and transfer of knowledge, skills and technology. Changes in technology, demand, and economic structure will make the exchange of services an increasingly important form of trade in the 21st century. Falling communication costs and the use of common international standards for professional services contributed to the large jump in service trade.

Policy benchmarking in all areas is becoming more common which, in turn, puts more pressure on countries to innovate in the policy areas. There is widespread reduction and removal of trade barriers, deregulation of internal markets, privatisation and liberalisation of technology and investment flows at the national level. Many developing countries and economies in transition have concluded bilateral treaties to protect FDI and avoid double taxation. At the international level, regulation has intensified and is being harmonised.

The WTO Uniform Law the World Over: World trade involves a number of complex transactions across national borders. Thus the nature of transaction is such that more than one national law applies on the transaction. Uniform laws on trade transactions are a must in today's world where goods export is in the region of 5.5 million. The second point to be understood is that international trade facilitates efficiency. Each country should specialize in the production of those goods and services in which it has abundant factor endowments. For example, a country with a surplus of power should produce energy intensive commodities like aluminium. The country should not produce goods where it is deficient in the required factor endowments. Similarly, a country with abundant land and water should produce cotton and develop the textile industry. The free flow of international trade in aluminium and textile between the countries in the above example according to the factor endowments ensures that both countries are better off with trade compared to the no trade situation with each country producing its own aluminium and textiles.

WTO Rules Govern Trade Between Nations : The World Trade Organization (WTO) is the main international body dealing with the rules of trade between nations. The WTO agreements, negotiated and signed by the main trading nations (except China, Russia and the Muslim countries of the Middle East like Saudi Arabia). These documents provide the legal ground rules for international commerce. The agreements are like contracts, which bind governments to keep their trade policies within the boundaries set by the agreements. In other words, the policies have to be "WTO compatible". WTO is an inter governmental organization, nonetheless, the rules apply to business they focus on how producers of goods and services, exporters, and importers conduct their business.

There is increasing pressure on WTO to respond to the needs of civic society. It is strongly felt that the interests of the people, i.e., the workers, farmers and consumers should also be kept in mind by the WTO. Global issues like poverty, environment, labour should get full attention. This point was first highlighted in the Ministerial conference at Geneva in 1998 on the occasion of the 50th birthday of WTO. There were demands that WTO should follow the normal processes of civic society. General Council and dispute settlement panel proceedings should be open to the public and NGOs should be welcomed to participate in the deliberations.

The First and Second Birth of WTO (1948, 1996)

In the famous and historic Bretton Woods Conference after the Second World War, the three pillars to manage the world economy, namely the IMF, World Bank and ITO (International Trade Organization) were conceived. IMF was seen as the world body to facilitate international liquidity. World Bank was conceived as a sectoral lending institution. Both these bodies were based in Washington DC on opposite sides of the same street. They emerged as full-fledged organization from the Bretton Woods process. ITO, the third baby, was still born and remained in the shape of the GATT agreement till 1995. The fully formed body took shape only on 1 January 1995 when the organization was re-christened as WTO, the World Trade Organization. Though US was responsible for the delay finally it felt the need for a fully empowered world body in mid '80s to frame and enforce a law to combat rampant intellectual property piracy, the world over. Once the US put its might behind the Uruguay Round, the scope of the negotiations widened well beyond the scope conceived in the original Punta del Este declaration. Ultimately, the final agreement encompassed Goods, Services and Intellectual Property Rights. Subsequently, "new issues" like environment, investment, competition policy and labour are the additions of the Singapore Ministerial. Geneva ministerial added E-commerce and trade facilitation to the agenda. In the aborted Seattle ministerial, biotechnology was mooted as yet another field for action by WTO.

The main text is the Marrakesh Agreement establishing the World Trade Organization and its annexes, altogether about 430 pages long. Annex 1 covers the Multilateral Agreements on Trade in Goods (which in turn includes GATT and numerous other agreements such as those on agriculture, textiles, anti-dumping, subsidies, etc.), the General Agreement on Trade in Services, and the Agreement on Trade Related Intellectual Property Rights. Annex 2 is the Understanding on Rules and Procedures Governing the Settlement of Disputes. Annex 3 deals with the Trade Policy Review Mechanism. Annex 4 includes the Plurilateral Trade Agreements signed by some of the WTO members. Ministerial Decisions and Declarations.

The WTO trading system envisages the basic principles such as:

a. Non-discrimination between countries: The MFN Treatment

b. Non-discrimination within a country: National Treatment

c. Freer Trade: Gradually, through Negotiation

d. Predictability: Through Binding and

e. Promoting Competition.

These principles are the foundation of the multilateral trading system.

Non-discrimination between countries - The MFN Treatment: WTO philosophy is that trading system should be without discrimination – a country should not discriminate between its trading partners (they are all, equally, granted "most-favoured-nation" or MFN status). MFN means that every time a country lowers a trade barrier or opens up a market, it has to do so for the same goods or services from all its trading partners

– whether rich or poor, weak or strong. The trading partner should be a member of WTO. Thus a country can charge higher duty on imports from China without attracting the ire or WTO dispute settlement process.

If a country improves the benefits that it gives to one trading partner, it has to give the same "best" treatment to all the others. WTO members so that they all remain "most-favoured". No country, as long as it is a WTO member, can be "less favoured".

Exceptions for Regional Trade and Unfair Trade: Some exceptions are however allowed. For example, countries within a region can set up a free trade agreement that does not apply to goods from outside the group, or a country can raise barriers against products from specific countries that are considered to be traded unfairly. And in services, countries are allowed, in limited circumstances, to discriminate. Thus countries in customs unions like the European Common Market or NAFTA can charge lower duty on imports from other members as compared to non-markets under the exception clause of MFN. Anti dumping duties can be levied on specific countries or companies on discriminatory basis provided the rules under GATT 1994 are followed.

Non-discrimination within a Country: National Treatment: Imported and locally-produced goods should be treated equally – at least after the foreign goods have entered the market. The same should apply to foreign and domestic services and to foreign and local trademarks, copyrights and patents.

Predictability - Through Binding: Sometimes, promising not to raise a trade barrier can be as important as lowering one, because the promise gives businesses a clearer view of their future opportunities. The multilateral trading system is an attempt by governments to make the business environment stable and predictable. In the WTO, when countries agree to open their markets for goods or services, they "bind" their commitments. For goods, these bindings amount to ceilings on customs tariff rates. The countries cannot exceed the bound rates under any circumstances. Similar binding commitments are being made now for services like telecom.

Promoting Fair Competition : The WTO is a system of rules dedicated to open and fair competition. The tariff reduction and elimination exercises go hand in hand with measures to reduce or eliminate services. The net result is that domestically produced goods face much the same environment regarding taxes and subsidies as those produced in other countries. The "level playing field" between foreign and local goods encourages and fosters competition with the corresponding positive effect on efficiency and consumer welfare. The Singapore Ministerial Conference, in fact, set up a separate working group to research into the relationship between trade and competition policy.

Policy Legal Framework, Reservation & Other Issues, of Small Scale Enterprises in the Twenty First Century

The Small Scale Enterprise (SSE) sector has emerged as an engine of growth in most of the developed and newly industrialized countries. India's vision of emerging as an economic power in the 21st century can be realised through the promotion and development of the Small and Medium Enterprises (SMEs). In fact, the SME is the sector of the Millennium. The role that small scale enterprise sector has to play in the next ten years must be viewed in the dynamic context of a changing world. It must address to the requirements of the time and the changes which are taking place both within and outside the country.

Liberalization and globalisation is the order of the day. Market forces will determine the system and manner of production. The allocation or resources within the sector must be governed by the criteria of efficiency, productivity and competitiveness. The SSEs will have to move from a regime of a protective environment to a competitive environment. The role of Government is to be that of a facilitator.

India is a member of WTO. Thus the policy of the SSE Sector in India will have to be WTO compatible and must be in tune with the provisions of the WTO on all issues including the basic issues like actionable and non-actionable subsidies, patents, tariff and non-tariff barriers, sanitary and phyto-sanitary measures, etc. Subsidies, support and incentives to the SME sector do not come under the category of 'actionable' subsidies as long as they are horizontal in their application. The Government should take up adequate measures to increase awareness on WTO provisions among the SSI entrepreneurs and take appropriate measures to protect Indian SSI sector through bound rates, information/data to prove dumping and help in introduction of anti-dumping measures, create a legal cell to take care of legal problems faced by the SSI units on account of WTO conditions. The DC (SSI) should create a separate Division on WTO, supported by adequate experts in various disciplines.

The concept of market is changing very fast. The term 'domestic market' is gradually vanishing. For that matter the term 'international market' also may become irrelevant soon. There will only be one market and hence the products of the SSI sector must be competitive within the country as well as outside. The products are to be sold increasingly with 'brand names' hence the future of SSE development must focus on promoting brands for SSI products.

Rapid scientific and technological advancement is taking place in the developed world. The developing countries experience problems relating to technology, raw material and capital. Besides, these countries are under severe pressure to brace up for global competition and to upgrade their skills, competence and technology. More focussed attention needs to be placed on these three areas. Information technology should be utilised to the fullest at all levels. SSE should take advantage of e-commerce, e-marketing, etc. and internet facilities by making their presence felt through websites.

While formulating policies and programmes for the development of small scale enterprises, the following points must be remembered: (a) at a time when employment is stagnant in the agricultural sector and large industry sector is passing through near 'zero employment growth', it is only in the small enterprises, besides the service sector, where employment has been growing. In a labour surplus economy like India, the need for policies and programmes for employment generation is of prime importance; and (b) the SME Sector suffers from certain handicaps and as such it needs special support.

Reservation

The reservation of products for exclusive manufacture in the SSI sector should continue for the present because the reserved items of the SSI sector are making significant contribution to employment, output and exports. The position may be reviewed from time to time, taking into account the developments and strength of the concerned sector and the market situation and implications of GOI agreements with WTO.

De-reservation of some selected export thrust items could also be considered since the country is losing valuable foreign exchange by production of low value added items by using traditional or low-grade technology. Production of reserved items could be allowed to be taken up by non-SSI units, subject to minimum export obligation of 30 per cent to be achieved in the first three years. Thereon 30 per cent export each year is to be achieved. Presently it is 50 per cent.

The endeavour of the governments should be to make the sector WTO compliant and more competitive during the transition period by way of sensitilization to WTO provisions, keeping import duty at bound rates, maintenance of duty differential on raw materials and finished goods, providing interest support for technology upgradation and easy access of credit to them.

In order to make SSI products competitive in both the internal and international markets, it is necessary to adopt State of the Art technology. The investment ceiling of those items which are important from the angle of exports and also play an important role in employment generation, could be suitably enhanced to Rs. 5 crores, e.g. leather products, ready-made garments, hosiery, hand tools, toys, packaging material, auto components, pharmaceuticals, food processing, etc.

Facing the Challenge of WTO Agreement

The World Trade Agreements and negotiations have a direct impact on all economic activities including the development and promotion of the small-scale sector. WTO Agreements are likely to affect the SSI sector in the following ways:

(i) Removal of QRS will allow free and cheap imports and will result in stiff competition to the SSIs.

(ii) In view of the Agreement of TRIPS, it would be difficult for the SSI sector to continue with the reverse engineering and manufacture many items without paying royalty to the patent holders.

(iii) In terms of Sanitary and Phyto-sanitary measures, SSIs will have to adopt international standards with regard to quality, health and hygiene.

REFERENCES

Arun Goyal, WTO in the New Millennium (Ed) Academy of Business Studies, New Delhi, 2000.

Narasaiah, M.L., WTO and the Developing Countries, Discovery Publishing House, New Delhi, (2001)

Bhalla VK. and S. Shiva Ramu, International Business Environment and Management', Anmol Publications Pvt. Ltd., New Delhi, 2000.

8

SME's in the Era of Globalization—WTO Implications

M S Bhagwtgita[1]

The glabalization era presents SME's with both challenges and threats. Threat is the growing competition from overseas while the challenge lies in the new opportunities opened before them. The terms "export" and "import" are being replaced in the worlds business dictionary by a new term "COOPETETION" the combination of "Cooperation and Competition". Both the challenge and the threat demand more sophisticated and professional support mechanism. The involvement of SME's in the highly developed industrial economies like Japan, Germany, France contributes 85% SSI sector and employees 70% of the industrial workforce. This is true with India also.

WTO Genesis

WTO was established on 1 January 1995, governments had conducted the Uruguay Round negotiations on 15 December, 1993 and Ministers have given their political backing to the results by signing the final Act at a meeting in Marrakesh, Morocco in April 1994. The Marrakesh Declaration of 15 April 1994 affirmed that the results of Uruguay Round would strengthen the world economy and lead to more trade, investment, employment and income growth throughout the world. WTO is the embodiment of the Uruguay Round result

1 Faculty member and Convener Academic Council, National Institute of Small Industry Extension Training, Yousufguda, Hyderabad 500 045.

and the successor to the General Agreement on Tariff and Trade (GATT). WTO has got at about 140 members, and India is one of the founder members of WTO. It has privilege and immunities similar to those accorded to the specialized agencies of the UN. It has a separate council for the goods, services, trade and quasi-judicial bodies to adjudicate disputes.

WTO's main task is to make, the multilateral trading system, credible and transparent. Its main principle is to act as 'fair trade policeman' and ensure multilateral trade rules, carry out recommendations and rulings and compensate complaints by the member countries concerned.

WTO Agreements have become an integral part of the international training. It has become the driving force behind the development of free and fair trade in the world at present. Agriculture, e-commerce, labour environment, biotechnology, investment and competition policy remain as main issues.

The main functions of the WTO are:

1. Administering and implementing the multilaterial and plurilateral trade agreeement.
2. Acting as a forum for multilaterial trade negotiations
3. Seeking to resolve trade dispute
4. Over seeing national trade policies and
5. Cooperating with other international institutions involved in global economic policy making.

WTO agreement contains about 29 individual legal texts covering everything from agriculture to textiles/clothing, services to government procurement, rules or origin and intellectual property augmented by more than 25 additional ministerial declarations, decisions and understandings which spell out further obligations and commitments for WTO members.

The legal text of WTO agreements is a list of about 60 agreements, annexes, decisions and understandings. The main legal "Cover Note" is the Final Act embodying he Reults of the Uruguay Round of Multilaterial trade and its annexes. The Details of the annexes are:

1. (Annexe-1) Covers the Multilateral Agreements on Trade in Goods (which in turn includes GATT and numerous other agreements such as those on agriculture, textiles and anti-dumping, subsidies etc) the General Agreement on Trade Related Intellectual Property Rights.
2. (Annexe-2) Contains Understanding of Rules and Procedures governing the Settlement of Disputes.
3. (Annexe-3) Deals with the trade policy review mechanism.
4. (Annexe-4) This includes the Plurilateral Trade Agreements, signed by some of the WTO members.
5. (Annexe-5 & 6) These include ministerail decisions and declarations.

On 26Th March 1997, 40 countries accounting for more than 92% of the world trade in information technology products, agreed to eliminate import duties and other charges on these products by 2000 (by 2003 or 2005 in the case of some development country members). As other tariff commitments, each participating country is applying its commitment equally to export from all WTO members (i.e. on a most - favored-national basis), even any members are not being signatories to ITA (Information Technology Agreement).

BASIC PRINCIPLES OF THE WTO TRADING SYSTEM

1. Non discrimination between countries: MFN Treatment
2. Non discrimination within a country: National Treatment
3. Feer Trade: Gradually, through negotiation
4. Predictability through binding
5. Promoting competition.

With the emergence of WTO conditions, the basic principles of trade, regional groupings, barrier free movement, mergers & acquisitions, foreign direct investment, bilateral agreements, emergence of revolutionary changes in IT, popularity of service sector which forced the world economy as well as India has made customer a king. In the concept of global village, the SSI sector has to up grade, modernized, adopt and imbibe modern management practices, quality improvement etc. which calls for the WTO agreement.

Distinctions between GATT and WTO

GATT	WTO
1. Ad hoc and provisional	1. WTO Agreements are permanent, sound legal basis because members have ratified the agreements and tells about how to function.
2. Its members are Contracting Parties (officially only a legal text with no legal organization)	2. WTO has got members.
3. Deals with trading goods	3. WTO covers services and intellectual properties rights as well.
4. Dispute Settlement based on consensus of all members.	4. WTO dispute settlement is faster and automatic, rulings cannot be blocked by a majority.
5. It operates along with WTO	5. It is independent.

RELECTIONS ON WTO

India's Hon'ble Minister for Commerce Mr. Murasoli Maran pointed out that there are inherent imbalances and inequalities in certain WTO agreements, which should be corrected. He also expressed concern over the inadequate implementation of WTO Agreements particularly, textiles and agriculture, which have crucial significance for developing countries, trade interests. He also expressed concern over anti-dumping subsidies, intellectual property, TRIMs and the non-realization of expected benefits of agreements such as textile and agriculture during implementation have been a matter of grave concern. The special and differential treatment clauses remained virtually inoperative.

General Implications of WTO

1. The impact is on every economic activity either in agriculture, trading, service or manufacturing.
2. World markets are opening up due to lowering of tariffs, dismantling of protections.
3. Development countries will have greater opportunities in sectors in which they have cost based competitive advantage.
4. Export markets have become toughter because of competition between developing countries.
5. Quality concern and standardization of products will be a big challenge in developing countries.
6. In the global arena of markets, cost audit is the need of the hour.
7. Since the information technology has developed leaps and bounds and knowledge based society emergence is also one of the problems.
8. With good legal backing system and procedures awareness is also an imperative.
9. WTO's emphasis on standardizing trading services has a profound impact on the Indian industry particularly on SSIs.
10. As information on WTO and its clauses is available only with few hands, it is causing great difficulty in meeting with the norms (guidelines and procedures).

WTO Impact on SSI

Even though, SSI Sector produces over 7500 items will have to be aware of the patents, production including technological patterns, trademarks and industrial designs etc. Since 95% of the SSI units are in the nature of tiny micro enterprises and run by single man show, with lack of capital, and do not have access to the poor economies of scale, bargaining power, information backing and modern management practices etc. In these circumstances the Indian SSI enterpreneur has to be guided on WTO provisions agreements which are likely to effect in the areas of Quantitative Restriction on SSI reservation. Removal of Quantitative Restrictions means dismantling the reservation of SSI policy, which means many of SME's specially in the consumer goods sector will find it difficult to survive as more and more imported products will be in the Indian market. They have to compete with low cost products coming from neighbouring countries (LDC) such as Nepal, Bangladesh, Sri Lanka and China. Since the domestic market is open to foreign countries, the advantage of low labour cost, which our SSI enjoys, may be beyond our point. Which means the domestic consumer prefers low cost products, low end products, will face international competition from export oriented developing countries (About 624 reserved items out of 812 have been shifted to OGL).

Due to the challenges posed by the anti-dumping measures the SMEs have to be carefully understand the provisions and procedures. There are certain provisions (special and differential provisions) that are intended to benefit the developing countries but may act against the SME's, when it comes to trade among the developing countries. The Article 5.8 of the Agreement provides that, the volume of dumped imports shall normally be considered negligible if dumped import from a particular country is found to be less than 3 of the imports. While subsidies are not allowed and there are a few subsidies, which are listed as Permissible Subsidies (Actionable Subsidies like Duty Entitlement Pass Book Scheme-DEPB, Export promotion of Capital Goods Scheme-EPCG, Income-tax benefit U/Sec. 80HHC), and there are others, which are permissible (Non-Actionable Subsidies) called Green Subsidies. Permissible subsidies are those which are permissible till they do not hurt the interest of other members (a subsidy specific to an enterprise, group of enterprise, industrial sector or designed geographical location, is permissible). Permissible Non-Actionable Subsidies are those which are granted on the basis of objective criteria that are economic in nature and horizontal in application and do not favour certain enterprises over others and are not specific. Importing countries cannot levy countervailing measures on Non-Actionable Subsidies, i.e., subsidies given by the Government to SME's, identified on the basis of their size or number of employment would be Non-Actionable.

Indian industry society has to learn a lesson to be competitive without the presence of subsidies. In this regard, SME's have to face serious challenges as the Government subsidies to small enterprises are Non-Actionable. WTO presupposes that an enterprise knows the implication of all provisions in a country where 95% of SSI's are tiny units, this "knowledge" is a big question mark. The other reasons being the SSI sector is adversely affected by

1. Slow technological up-gradation (lack of capital)
2. Poor infrastructure (power failure, communication links, water, etc.)
3. Obsolete laws, rules and regulations etc.
4. Lack of awareness among SSI & WTO provisions
5. Unorganized sector data is poor
6. Lack of common test facilities
7. Tariff reduction and required protection
8. Anti-dumping practices
9. Subsidies and countervailing measures
10. Technical barriers to trade and investment based SSI definitions
11. Agreement on trade related investment measures (TRIMS)
12. Trade related intellectual property
13. SAARC commitments (South Asia Preferential Trading Agreement)

Emerging Issues Before SME's

1. Production and packing for competitive price, i.e., financial and technological capability;
2. Labour Standards-Labour intensive industries;
3. Lack of awareness on rules, rights and obligations;
4. Knowledge about new opportunities in trade;
5. Lobbying of SSI Associations, about world trade information;
6. Cluster approach; and
7. Good Marketing Strategy- Creation of brand image.

In this regard data bank creation on WTO, and industry-institution and universities tie-ups for flow of information, investment in technology infrastructure and human resources rather than subsidies is the need of the hour. In order to be more competitive and cost-effective in the global scenario of WTO, the SME's will have to gear up in tune with the changes in the market trends and consumer behavior. The SMEs should acquaint with themselves about WTO provisions and procedures. In this regard, the voluntary intervention, by NGO's associations and other agencies with the help of government support, may act as a facilitator, thorough solicitors/legal advisors and experts, and open discussions, seminars, awareness camps etc.

9

Globalisation: Challenges of Small-Scale Industries

Prof. C. Suryanarayana*

Ever since the country got Independence in 1947, the Government of India has given a special emphasis to promote small-scale industries, as they are the vehicles of creating additional employment through low capital investment. Reservation of 807 items (Industrial Policy Statement, 1977) and encouraging support from the Government brought much progress to the Small-Scale Industry (SSI) sector. The small-scale industries generated employment to be the tune of 170 lakh persons in 1998-99. Employment in SSI to the total employment in the country constitutes around 6 per cent. But the notable fact that about 60 per cent of the nation's workforce is employed in agricultural activities. Further, a substantial increase is noticed in exports contribution by this sector. Despite the fall in the rate of production from 21.4 per cent during the period 1973-74 to 1980-81 to 18.0 per cent (1990-91 to 1998-99), the rate of growth in exports increased from 22.6 per cent to 34 per cent during the same period.

The state has recognized the significance of SSI sector and the Industrial Policy Resolution of 1856 clearly stated that "small-scale industries provide immediate large-scale employment; offer a method of ensuring a more equitable distribution of national income and they facilitate an effective mobilization of resources of capital and skill, which might

* Professor, Dept. of Commerce and Management Studies, Andhra University, Visakhapatnam (A.P.)

otherwise remain dominant. Some of the problems that unplanned urbanization tend to arise will be avoided by the setting up of small centers of industrial production all over the country[1]. B.S. Minhas, a former Planning Commission Member observed that the heavy industries were essentially capital intensive, and only lip service was paid to encouraging labour-intensive production in agriculture and industry, while all the time, encouraging capital-intensive production[2]. It is also pertinent to mention here that Gandhian planning aims at attainment of maximum self-sufficiency in village communities. It focuses on rehabilitation, development and expansion of cottage industries side by side with agriculture. One should not mistake Gandhiji's emphasis on Swadeshi as a narrow nationalism. It implied as an extended link between the villages, the nation and the global system. It is the autonomy of the individual and of institutions and of the maximum self-reliance of the nation[3]. Gandhi is not against all machinery but protests against the craze for machinery and its indiscriminate multiplication. He believes that the factory system using extensive machinery made become a source of exploitation of labour by a few capitalists. Nehru - Mahalanobis growth model, undoubtedly, have their relevance and merits but assigned low points to the development of agriculture and small-scale industry sector, which are the backbones of Indian Rural Economy. The economic problems faced by the country, namely, inflationary rise in prices, unemployment, industrial sickness, growing inequalities, mounting poverty, etc., are the outcomes of greater emphasis on large-scale industry. Emphasizing on the employment potential, Karve Committee stated that the principle of self-employment is at least as important to a successful democracy as that of a self-government[4]. The Committee felt that large-scale industry may be given preference where they are necessary (i.e., capital goods industries and the

---

1. Planning Commission, *Second Five-Year Plan*, Govt.of India, New Delhi, p. 47.
2. Minhas, B.S., 'Planning and the Poor', p. 3.
3. Rudder Datt and K.P.M. Sundaram, *Indian Economy*, S. Chand & Company Ltd., New Delhi, 1999, p.153.
4. Report of the Village and Small-Scale Industries Committee, Government of India, 1955, Karve Committee.

building up of social and economic infrastructure, etc.) and in other spheres of production small-scale enterprises may be encouraged. There are certain other product lines in which small units poses a definite advantage over the large-scale units. There are certain other product lines in which small units carrying out certain operations or making certain parts of delivery to a large or patent firm. The complementary is of mutual advantage both to small-scale and large-scale units[1]. The net output to capital ratios during 1967 and 1979 are worked out to be 3 to 4 times that of the large-scale sector. Prof. P.C. Mahalanobis also considered household or cottage industries create employment opportunities by about fifteen or even twenty times greater in comparison with large-scale industries. One striking feature, worth mentioning here; along with the increasing trend of modernization of small-scale enterprises is that capital output ratio is observed to be higher by 4 times to that large-scale enterprises during 1993-94.

On the other side of the coin, argument against SSI sector from some quarters, that the average pay in small-scale enterprises is quite lower than it is in large-scale enterprises. It may be true that some small entrepreneurs exploit labour in the vital absence of trade unions. Evidences shows that in developed countries like USA, UK, Japan, etc., a worker in a small-scale is earning 80 per cent or even more of the wage earned by his counterpart in a large enterprise. At present, in India too, this ratio reached a level of about 50 per cent and it may gradually increase in a short period of time.

One of the prominent reasons for slow growth of SSI in India is the policy of administrators. It played a role of promoter and regulator with over ambitions. States should not think of promoting small industrial enterprises even in the remote villages of the country. It may not be possible on the economic grounds. The International Perspective Planning Team pointed out the policy of trying to implant large amount of industry in the backward areas as directly in villages is doomed to failure and cannot be justified economically. The focus for industrial development under a dispersal policy should be neither the

---

1. Jaya Prakash Reddy R., 'Problems and Development of Small-Scale Industries in India, Ashish Publications, New Delhi, 1991, p. 2.

metropolis nor the village, but rather the large range of potentially attractive cities and towns between the two extremes[1]. It is also true that some small-scale entrepreneurs are much interested in benefits and subsidy packages offered by the state. With deliberate intentions, they utilized the funds for their personal ends. Discouraging SSI sector in this ground means plucking out the organ, which is suffering from illness rather than curing the disease.

Economic Liberalization – State Policy on SSI

The Government of India announced its policy on SSI sector on 6th August 1991. Its primary objective is to impart more vitality and growth – impetus to SSI to enable it to contribute its might (mite) fully to the economy, particularly in terms of growth of outputs, generation of employment and exports, several measures have been taken to promote and develop SSI sector such as:

i) Widening the scope of National Equity Fund Scheme to cover projects to up to Rs.10 lakhs for equity support, i.e., up to 15 per cent.

ii) Single Window Loan Scheme been enlarged to cover projects up to Rs.20 lakhs with working capital margin up to Rs.10 lakhs.

iii) Allowing equity participation by other industrial undertakings in the SSI, not exceeding 24 per cent of the total share holding.

iv) Offering factoring service to SSI through Small Industries Development Bank of India (SIDBI).

v) Establishment of Technology Development Cell (TDC) as a wing of Small Industries Development Organization (SIDO).

vi) Assisting SSI units to market their product through National Small Industries Corporation (NSIC).

vii) Promoting of entrepreneurship through large number

---

1. Report of the International Perspective Planning Team, 1963, p. 13.

of Entrepreneurship Development Programmes (EDPs).

The recent policy aimed at preparing the Indian entrepreneur to meet the challenges that they have faced in view of opening up our economy to world markets. Moving toward a situation of 'free trade' results in internationalization of the economy. The impact of free trade and the role and impact of World Trade Organization should be observed with caution for the survival and growth of Indian industry in general and SSI in particular.

The World Trade Organization (WTO) emerged on January 1995 by the Uruguay Round of General Agreement on Tariffs and Trade (GATT) in order to remove the tariff and non-tariff barriers to import and export and restrictions on the inflow and outflow of capital among the member countries. India also joined as a member country of WTO. In the light of this, she had to change her long advocated policy of import-substitution and trade practices of multiple controls, restrictive regulations and wide range of state intervention. India has no other opinion but the situation that are prevailing in domestic and external front in the early 90's made it to accept the stipulation of IMF and IBRD and to opt for membership in WTO. The high rate of inflation (13 per cent), huge fiscal deficit, adverse BOP position and reversal of NRI currency flows compelled the country to adopt package of Structural Adjustment Programme (SAP).

Table 1 shows the value of production of goods and services and the volume of exports of SSI sector during 1973-74 to 1996-97.

The number of small-scale industries units has been increased from 4.2 lakhs in 1973-74 to 28.57 lakhs by the end of 1996-97 registering a growth rate of around 9 per cent. Similarly, it generated employment to 4 million persons in 1973-74 and it rose to 16 million in 1996-97 with a growth rate of 6 per cent. It is notable that with an increase of six per cent employment, the SSI sector could enhance the generation of output by 18 per cent. Even if the inflationary rise is considered at the prices of 1980-81, the rate of increase in production is about 11 per cent. Worth mentioning point here, is the rate of growth in output of

SSI sector is quite significant (11 per cent). Therefore, development of SSI yields positive and higher growth rate for the development of economy. If a big push is given to the small-scale sector, it can become a stabilizing factor in a capital-scarce economy like India by providing a higher output capital ratio as well as a higher employment capital ratio.[1]

Table 1: Production in and Exports of SSI Sector

Year	*Production*	*Exports*	*% (2) in (1)*
		(Rs. in Crores)	
1973-74	7,200	393	5.45
1977-78	14,300	845	5.90
1980-81	28,060	1,643	5.85
1985-86	61,228	2,769	4.52
1990-91	1,55,340	9,100	5.85
1991-92	1,78,700	13,883	7.77
1992-93	2,09,300	17,785	8.50
1993-94	2,41,648	25,307	10.47
1994-95	2,93,990	29,068	9.89
1995-96	3,56,213	36,470	10.24
1996-97	4,18,863	40,355	9.63
Compound Annual Rate of Growth			
1973-74 to 1980-81		21.4	22.6
1980-81 to 1990-91		18.6	18.6
1990-91 to 1996-97		18.0	28.2

Sources: Hand Book of Industrial Statistics (1987) and RBI, Report on Currency & Finance (1996-97)

Exports

The value of exports of SSI sector increased from Rs.393 crores in 1973-74 to Rs.40,355 crores in 1996-97. During 70s and 80s, the proportion of exports of SSI out of its total value of production is around five per cent (4.52 per cent to 5.90 per

1. Rudder Datt & K.P.M. Sundaram, *Indian Economy*, S. Chand & Co. Ltd., New Delhi, 1999, p. 617.

cent). The exports of SSI sector significantly increased from 7.77 per cent to 34 per cent during 1991-92 and 1998-99.

Export opportunities have helped several units of readymade garments, canned and processed fish, leather sandals and chappals, food products, hosiery and marine products, woolen knitwear etc., to increase the utilization of production capacity from about 50 per cent to 80 per cent. On the other side, the share of imports of SSI sector constituted about 34 per cent of the total exports of the country.

Challenges of Globalization

The globalization has a remarkable impact on the industrial development of the country. The world economy, at present, is characterized by increasing integration of world markets for goods and services, capital and technology lows, comparative advantage will be more and more man-made and determined by a country's ability to harness the forces of modern sciences and technololgy[1]. The Indian industry, more specifically, the small entrepreneurs need to absorb, adopt and assimilate new technologies into their production process and organize production process efficiency to meet the global standards of goods and services. It is necessary in view of the encouraging cross-border trade in goods and services, which is increasing at a higher rate and Indian SSI sector has the opportunities to get a sizeable share of it if concrete efforts are made to improve their operative efficiency. The global trade in the areas of electronic and computer components, automobile components, utilities, paper and office products, consumer goods, food products, construction materials, video games, recorded magnetic tapes, etc., would have a greater export potential in the next decade. Similarly, the service sector also has a potential market for small entrepreneurs in the areas of communication, information technology and Internet, e-commerce services. International Data Corporation estimated that the number of Internet users would increase to 500 million by 2005 and the Asia accounts for 170 million. This is the potential size of the customer base for global electronic buying and selling.

---

1. Jyotsna Rajuput, 'Globalization and Emerging Trends of Industrial Development', *Yojana*, Vol. 45, March 2001, pp. 34-39.

The emergence of China as one of the major trading countries of the world will pose a threat to the manufacturers of India. China's total trade reached $ 324 billion in 1998, which is 3 per cent of the world trade, it emerged as 10th largest trading country and expected to reach to the second place with 10 per cent share in the world trading by 2020. After the China's entry into the WTO, within five years it causes loss of 40 million jobs in the world. Of these, 5-10 million jobs in agricultural sector, 10 million in the state sector and 20 million in the private sector industries[1]. This should be an eye opener to the Indian entrepreneurs. No longer, the Government of India protects them by imposing qualitative and restrictions on imports, trade barriers and non-trade barriers etc. The Small Enterprises need to attain competency in their relative fields of production of goods and services to counter attack the intrusion of foreign goods and services into the domestic market. Reduction in costs, improvement in quality, innovative ideas in production and technology, product utilities, product attributes would certainly make the Indian enterprises to compete with foreign manufacturers.

Further, State's policy of de-reserving about 600 items coupled with the entry of Multi National Corporations (MNCs) put heavy pressure on the survival, growth and development of small-scale enterprises. Medium and large-scale firms have a relative advantages over small-scale enterprises in respect of procurement of funds, import of technology, research and development, recruitment and development of, technical, professional and managerial personnel, marketing network and product promotion. Some of the Indian Companies has achieved high growth in sales volume, profit, and net worth, upgrade of technology and creating brand image for their products. They are competing not only in the domestic market but also spread their tentacles to the foreign markets. Many of these organizations depend on several components, consumables and some services on SSI sector. The Indian SSI sector should substitute foreign suppliers. The tapping of potential market would be possible only by enriching the quality of their output,

---

1. Bhattacharya b., *Implications of China's Entry into WTO*, Vol.11, No.4, Focus WTO, November-December 2000, pp.1-3

competitive prices and prompt deliveries. Mass communication media sector like satellite TV components, Internet, fax and telecommunications, etc., provides a good opportunity for the Indian SSI sector to penetrate into both domestic and global markets.

The Indian planners have set eight per cent growth rate of industrial sector in 90's. Nevertheless, the realized growth rate is less than the targets expect two years.

The lower growth rate in the manufacturing sector has pulled down the growth of GDP of the country. Several SSI units find it difficult to achieve the growth owing to the economic recession and competing with MNCs. Competitiveness is the key to success. According to the Global Competitiveness Report-1999 of the World Economic Forum, India has slipped to 52nd position of the world out of 56 countries surveyed in terms of people with requisite technical skills. But high level of commitment, motivation and strict discipline were mostly found missing in our organizational culture. In the present day complex and globally competitive economic environment, small-scale industries should show increasing concern on achieving productivity through which they can assure of survival and growth. Productivity is not a mere rationalization or reducing consumption of resources but is concerned more with making available products and services that enhance the quality of life and accelerate economic development[1].

In the coming years, India should pave the way to becoming a major player in the global market. As a first step in this direction, the Indian entrepreneurs need to produce goods and services with quality, competency and at affordable prices. The small-scale enterprises should be supported by the large-scale enterprises for outsourcing credit facilities and by the Government for providing sufficient infrastructure and R & D facilities.

---

1. Khader, S.A., 'Strategic Perspectives for Building Productivity Culture', Yojana, No.5, May 2000, pp.10-18.

10

WTO and Its Implications to Small-Scale Industries

Dr. G. Tulasi Rao* & Dr. T. Kama Raju**

World trade has undergone a structural change during the last five decades since the establishment of GATT in 1948. With the emergency of WTO in 1995, as a regulatory body of the world trade, the economic boundaries of the nation for all the practical purposes have expanded enormously much beyond their frontiers and the trade mechanism no longer different in and abroad. World trade partners are required to follow uniform rules and procedures of world trade.

The Indian trade both domestic and foreign is under severe pressure due to the impact of WTO. The threat being faced by SSI is much severe than that of medium and large-scale sector. The impact of WTO is likely to create some far reaching implications in SSI thereby this sector is gradually loosing its base.

The concerns of the SSI development in India have generally been expressed in terms of its parts rather than the whole. Technology, credit, raw materials, price have often been highlighted as the problems, and several public institutions, ranging from government agencies down to FDI, have justified their own role as problem solver rather than as active agents of change. The government is under obligation to lift the Quantitative Restrictions (QRs) balance of 715 (items) on imports

* Associate Professor and Assistant Professor, respectively, Dept. of Commerce & Management Studies, AU Dr. B.R. Ambedkar P.G. Centre, Etcherla, Srikakulam.

on April 1, 2001. Large number of industries has already been facing stiff competition from imports from MNCs of developed countries. There have been instances of large-scale dumping of cheaper imports over the last three years when there has been a big slump in commodity prices world over.

Before 1990, QRs are imposed on imports of about 8000 items. The figure came down to 2700 items in 1997 during EXIM policy 1992-97. Earlier, the Indian government had reached an agreement with major trading partners (European Union, Japan, Australia and Canada) other than US to phase out QRs by 1, January 2003.

The US had approached the dispute settlement body of WTO in 1997 and complained against India that it is not phasing out its QRs on imports for 2700 products in six years as per the rules laid down in WTO. The defensive argument of India that it is not still free from BOP crisis, was rejected by dispute settlement body. Hence, India under compulsion must lift its QRs on imports within six years as laid down in the WTO agreement. India has already lifted its import restrictions on 2000 products for the SAARC countries. India is now forced to remove all import curbs ahead of its proposed March 31, 2003 dead line.

Majority of the items in the list of 715 on which QRs are lifted on imports are reserved items of SSI. They include food, textile, garments etc. These industries should brace for future shock. A little over 52 per cent of the things, which will become freely importable over year 2000 and 2001 fall into two broad sectors food and textiles. According to estimates 1999, sales for domestic manufacturers in these sectors amounted to Rs.1,04,797 crore, which comprises about 5 per cent of Indians GDP.

India has already gone beyond its commitments made to over various trading partners by freeing a total of 894 items of imports during the announcement of EXIM policy 1997-2002. Another 414 items have been partially liberalized by being put on special imports license list (SIL). Consequently, 665 items remain on the restricted list, 72 on the casualized list, and 298 on the open general license (OGL). Now India is left with last

715 items after the announcement of the EXIM policy in April 2001 and these will have to be lifted with effect from April 1, 2001. Then the fate of SSI would be changed from bad to worse.

The lifting of QRs on imports will have multidimensional effect on the survival and growth of SSI products of MNCs have the advantage of global branding, latest technology and cost advantage and are offered out highly competitive prices. The removal of the remaining QRs would lead to an anomalous situation in the case of products reserved for the SSI sector as the reserved items could be imported freely. It would not make sense therefore to continue with reservation of product lines alongside free imports. What is not understood is the government's continuous reluctance to do away the reservation of items from SSI sector even when the items in the reserved list will face open competition from imports. Once the QRs on imports are lifted , reservation of items for the SSI sector would have no meaning.

The government's decision to reduce customs duties on list of inputs of the SSI combined with the enhancement in the exemption limit on excise will improve the price competitiveness of the domestic SSI sector and help the industry to compete against import items at cheaper prices, particularly, from countries like China. SSI manufacturing products including toys, video games, electronic calculators, security systems and photographic accessories and parts will among the immediate beneficiaries of the government decision.

The concessions and other benefits recently announced by the government will empower the SSI sector to some extent, which is alive to the fact that it would have to compete in the world market particularly due to the effect of WTO. It is too pessimistic to think that the adverse effects of WTO will have immediate effect of flood of imports. It is not a cakewalk for the foreign brands to penetrate into the remote rural markets. Unless appropriate policy measures are initiated to make the SSI sector competitive in the global market, there is always a potential danger ahead.

11

Challenges of WTO Agreements for Small Industry Development

Dr. J. Revathy* & Prof. K.V. Rao**

Significance of Small Industry in India

Small Business Units (SBUs) are viewed increasingly as an important vehicle for meeting both the growth and equity objectives of developing economics. The contribution of SBUs to the industrial growth is significant. Viewed in terms of turnover, value addition and exports, the share of SBUs is relatively high. For example, in Malaysia, SBUs constitute the majority of all industrial establishments, accounting for at least one half of industrial employment and value added[1]. In Singapore SBUs in manufacturing, commerce and the service sectors constitute approximately 87 percent of business, 42 per cent of employment, 25 per cent of value added and 16 per cent of direct exports[2]. Taking India as an example, small business units in India accounted for about 40 per cent of the gross turnover in the manufacturing sector, about 45 per cent of the manufacturing exports and 35 per cent of total exports[3]. Similarly, employment generated by this sector stood at 167.2 lakhs which constitutes 59.8 per cent of the total employment in the organized sector of the country[4].

SBUS, being labour intensive, are believed to provide more

* Dr. J. Revathy, Head, Dept. of Commerce & Management Studies, VRS & YRN College, Chirala-523157, A.P.

** Prof. K.V. Rao, Dept. of Commerce & Management Studies, Nagarjuna University, Nagarjuna Nagar-522 510, Guntur, A.P.

employment and earning opportunities for unskilled workers. As unskilled workers may often underemployed or unemployed, small-scale industry therefore contributes towards reducing poverty and inequality. Research in six developing countries shows that, collectively, small establishments account for most industrial employment. That may be true of many countries, if not most[5]. In developing countries much manufacturing employment is found in rural areas. Further, SBUS tend to be more dispersed then larger enterprises and can thus contribute to the promotion of a more balanced development process.

They have the ability to accelerate rural industrialization by foregoing linkages between the more organized industrial sector in the urban areas and the rural manufacturing enterprises that often produce a variety of inputs for industries located in urban areas. In this way, SBUS also provide employment for a large section of the rural population, especially in the off-season, thus smoothing out variations in rural incomes and consumption[6]. Further, there is also evidence that SBUS can create jobs for a relatively lower level of investment and are particularly suitable for an economy with a surplus of low-skilled labour. The number of small units, value of production and employment have gone up quite substantially. The total number of SBUS have increased to 31.21 lakh in 1998-99 from just 20.9 lakh in 1991-92, and the output has increased from 1,78,699 crores to 5,27,515 crores in 1998-99. Further, the value of employment has gone up to 171.6 lakh persons from 129.8 persons during the same period[7].

In spite of phenomenal growth in the SBUS, sickness in the industry is growing year after year. Of the total number of cases referred to BIFR expansion include Board for Industrial and Financial Reconstruction cases pertaining to SBUS are substantial. As per the provisional data compiled by RBI, the total number of sick/weak units financed by scheduled commercial banks increased to 3,09,013 as at the end of March 1999 from 2,24,012 as at the end of March 1998[8]. The SSI sick units constitute 99 per cent of total number of sick/weak units, they accounted for 22.2 per cent of the total outstanding bank credit. The studies sponsored by RBI have identified factors like deficiencies in the project appraisals, shortage of raw materials, power crisis, transport and financial bottlenecks as the reasons for growing sickness in the small industry. The independent research studies undertaken by individual researchers have also identifies several factors like the above being responsible for the failure of SBUS. An international planning team invited to suggest measures for the development of SBUS found as early as in 1954 that there was a severe lack of capital as well as credit largely because of low productivity and over population[9]. S.P. Mathur on the basis of his study in Agra Region reported that finding adequate fixed and working capital was the greatest bottleneck in the growth of small industry[10].

Genesis of WTO Agreements

The process of disciplining international trade started with the signing of an Agreement in 1947 in Geneva immediately after the Second World War by 23 non-communist countries. This agreement was called General Agreement on Tariffs and Trade (GATT). Since the idea of having an International Trade Organization under UN could not fructify, GATT was the only agency for promoting non-discriminatory trade among member nations, which rose to 96 in 1998. However, GATT remained confined to two basic functions, viz., tariff reduction and removal of non-tariff barriers. GATT took major decisions by having discussions and negotiations through meetings among member nations. Between 1947 and 1986, GATT had seven rounds of meetings. The eighth round began in Uruguay in 1986 and concluded in 1994, which led to the emergence of the World Trade Organization (WTO). This is before the most talked about meeting in the area of International Trade. The profit prepared and submitted by the then Secretary General Dunkel has attracted lot of hue and carry among the most developing nations.

The World Trade Organization came into being in 1st January 1995 as an outcome of the signing of final Act on 15th April 1994 at Marrakech. WTO has emerged as the only Body dealing with the Rules of Trade between the nations. With headquarters in Geneva, Switzerland, it has 135 members including India.

As the only regulatory body for the world trade, WTO's

objective is to ensure freer more transparent and more predictable trading regime in the world. It is based on a sound legal system and its agreements are ratified by the Parliaments of the member countries.

WTO's Agreements cover all the original treaty provisions of GATT relating to trade in goods and also cover new areas like trade in services, trade related intellectual property issues and trade related investment measures. The basic objective of WTO is to ensure global free trade and reductionof tariff and non-tariff barriers. The ultimate objective of WTO is to expand production and trade and allow the optimal use of world resources. Its procedures are based on the principles of transparency, predictability and certainty. WTO has an effective dispute settlement mechanism with built-in cross retaliatory provisions and is poised to become a forum for continuous negotiations. The ministerial conference is the forum for discussion and thus an apex body for decision making. The conference meets every two years. So far, three conference have been held. The first in Singapore (1996), second in Geneva (1998) and third in Seatle (December 1999). The last conference remained inconclusive. The activities of WTO cover the three areas of interest, viz, trade in goods, trade in services and trade related investment measures.

GATT and Small Industry

The following are some of the general implications of GATT on small industry:

Main Criteria

The entire edifice of GATT is built on five basic rules i.e.,

(i) Protection to domestic industry to be provided through tariffs only.

(ii) Non - tariff barriers like import licensing, quotas, other form of restrictions will have to be eliminated.

(iii) Reduction in tariff and other barriers to trade to be done though negotiations. Tariffs are to be bound against subsequent increases on most of the products,

(iv) Most Favoured Nation Principle - No discrimination among member countries. Exceptions however, exist for regional preferential agreements like EU, NAFTA, ASEAN, SAPTA, etc., for the MFN rule.

(v) National Treatment - same treatment to imported products and domestic products.

Phasing out of Quantitative Restrictions: Since overnight elimination of Quantitative Restrictions (QRs) was not possible, flexibility was granted for eliminating QRs in a specific time frame. Developing countries including India were given more time to adjust. Delayed removal of QRs was allowed to countries having Balance of payments problems to restrict imports. The Agreement requires the developing countries to **take price based measures** (such as import surcharge) instead of quantitative restrictions (as restrictive import licensing). Quantitative restrictions were abolished by WTO Members in agriculture and ink its place tariffs were applied, making the process more transparent. Similarly for textiles, quotas levied by many developed countries on import of textile products from developing countries are to be phased out in a specific time frame by 1st January, 2005 completely.

Subsidies :- While some subsidies are not allowed (called Prohibited Subsidies), there are a few subsidies which are listed as Permissible (Actionable Subsidies) and there are others which are Permissible (Non-Actionable Subsidies) called Green Subsidies.

Unfair Practices :- GATT rules deal with two types of unfair ractices which distort conditions of competition. There are:

(i) If the goods benefit from the subsidies and

(ii) If goods are dumped in the foreign market.

The Agreement on Anti- Dumping Practices and Agreement on Subsidies and Countervailing Measures authorize countries to levy compensatory duties on import of product benefiting from "unfair trade practices." The criteria and procedures employed by both the Agreements for determining injury are similar.

Trade Related Investment Measures (TRIMS): Governments often impose conditions and restrictions on direct flow of foreign investment in accordance with certain national priorities. Conditions that can affect trade are known as Trade Related Investment Measures. The Agreement prohibits use of five types of TRIMS which are as follows:

- Local Content Requirement (LCRs) involving use of certain kinds of local inputs in production.
- Trade Balancing Requirement limiting use of import content in proportion to exports of investing companies.
- Trade Balancing Requirement placing restrictions on import to an amount ior value of the product exported.
- Exchanging Restrictions implying restrictions on access to foreign exchange to an amount of foreign exchange earnings attributable to the enterprise.
- Domestic sales requirement requiring a company to sell certain products locally.

WTO and Indian Industry

The process of economic reforms with emphasis on liberalisation and globalisation started in India in June 1991 and the domestic industry has been trying to adjust to the changes since then but within the limits of Indian conditions. The programme has been a phased one. The freedom of phasing may not be available once the WTO conditionalities become operative. The Quantitative Restrictions (QRs) on imports maintained on Balance of Payments (BOP) grounds were notified to WTO in 1997 for 2714 tariff lines (at 8 digit level). With improvement in BOP, the Committee on BOP Restriction had asked India to phase out plans for remaining these QRs. India had an Agreement with its trading partners (except USA) to phase out its QRs in next 6 years i.e. by March 2003. For this bilateral Agreements were signed with the trading partners but USA disputed the need for India to maintain QR as the latter's BOP position had considerably improved. India lost in Th is legal battle and has been asked to remove the QRs by 01-04-2001. As on date, the number of tariff lines on which QRs exist , has come down to 1429 this includes 685 items under Special Import License (SIL). The QRs on 714 tariff lines are to be removed by 31st March, 2000 and balance 715 to be removed by 31 st March, 2001. The biggest challenge before Indian Industry is to radically change its mindset. Industry can not continue to survive behind high tariff barriers or non tariff barriers like import licensing.

Impact of WTO on Small Scale Industries

The Small Scale Industries, which are defined in terms of the investment limit in plant and machinery (as on date the maximum limit not exceeding Rs. 100 lakhs for SSI/ancillary units (it has been reduced from Rs. 300 lakhs w.e.f.24.12.99) and Rs.25 lakhs for Tiny units), are a vital constituent of the Indian Economy. More than 7500 products are produced by more than 31.20 lakh small unit over the country. They provide employment more than 17 million people, i.e. next only to agriculture. The production (Current Prices) accounts for Rs. 5,27,515 crores. The Export is to the tune of Rs. 49,481 crores by the end of the 1998-99. The share of SSI sector in the total exports is more than 35%.

The WTO , which is going to affect every economic activity - both in terms of goods and services, will definitely have an enormous impact on the small scale sector, which consists of multidimensional target groups which vary from small tiny unit (one man show) to highly qualified and conversant Technocrats having access to the intranet and other sort of facilities.

Over the years, particularly upto 1991, the Government policy has been to give as much as protection to small units to enable it to come up to fulfill the major obligation lto strengthen the socio-economic base of the country and to encourage industry to reach every nook and corner of the country to overcome the regional imbalances. In 1991, first time the government came out with a special and separate package for strengthening of small, tiny and village enterprises, wherein emphasis was laid on easy access of credit instead of subsidized and concessional credit, modernisation and upgradation of technology, provision of 24% equity participation by other industrial undertakings including foreign investors for upgradation of technology modernisation of ancillarisation and sub-contracting, developing infrastructural facilities, strengthening marketing and export market to enable the sector to easy and greater access to both national and international markets, etc. The emphasis of the measures was to enable the Sector to contribute its might fully to the economy, particularly in terms of growth of output, employment and exports.

Consequently a number of measures have already been taken which ranged from enhancement of an investment limit, delicensing of the sector, simplification o f registration, withdrawal of restricted list for manufacture, implementation of self-employment oriented projects like PMRY, developing backward areas to strengthen infrastructure facilities though introduction of IID schemes, simplification and decentralization of banking provisions and earmarking of credit for the sector, opening of specialized bank branches exclusively for SSI, simplifications of the Government Purchase Programme, ensuring prompt payment to small units by enacting and amending the Delayed Payment Act of 1993, opening of Tool Rooms, etc. Introduction of ISO-9000 scheme for upgradation of technology, introduction of information through Electronic Media (Interact) to enable easy access to information, involvement of NGOs and Association in subcontracting programmes and training programmes, etc.

These measures have paid dividends and have installed a ray of hope in the entrepreneurs. The sector has been able to fact the openness of market more effectively than the overall industrial sector within the country. It is quite apparent from the fact that the over all growth rate of the small-scale sector is more than 7.4% against the overall growth of 4% of the industrial sector as a whole.

However, WTO agreements and negotiations has thrown challenges of different type and the agony is that most of the small units are unaware of these agreements and Negotiations and do not know as to how they are going to affect them and how they should deal with them. As is a known fact that majority of small units are single unit show, they do not have money, expertise and manpower tc deal with the situation. Even if they have in a few cases, they are not aware as to how to deal with situation, to whom a approach and how to approach.

Not only the small units but the government has also to think over its existing policies and programmes after having an in-depth study and to carry out necessary changes immediately. They have to take lead in making the Sector aware of the implications and equip it with all the support to make it able to safeguard itself and to avail optimum benefit.

It is new of this that an attempt has been made top find out in short the implications of the Agreements and Negotiations of WTO till date, measures taken by the Government and the need of the hour.

New Measures Initiated

The reservation policy has not been of must help to the small enterprises. For instance, in 1995, out of the 8.36 items, 233 were not ever manufactured by small units. And over 80 per cent of small units produced just 5 per cent of the reserved items. By April, 1997 the number of products reserved for small units cam down to 821, following the dereservation of 15 items. Ironically, the present system of incentives of SSIs rightly felt that neither the investment ceiling nor reservation can guarantee efficiency.

Impact of WTO on Indian Small Scale Sector

The umbrella of the WTO is likely to create some far-reaching implications for the SME sector in India, specifically with regard to their competitive ability and integration with the global markets. Most of the problems arise due to the unorganized nature of this sector, lack of data and information, use of low technology, sometimes obsolete technology and poor infrastructure in the country. WTO will affect all types of SSI units whether producing for the domestic market or for the international market. The SSI sector, which produces over 7,500 items will have to aware of the patents of products including even of the technological patents, trademarks, industrial designs, etc. 95% of the SSI units are in the nature of tiny, micro enterprises and are weak. Many of them are one man shows. Their capital base is poor and does not have access to the economies of scale. Their bargaining power is low and do not have access to the information and modern management practices. They constitute most vulnerable segment of the SSI sector. Hence, they need to be guided and supported. Balance 5% of Ssi units are in the category of modern SSIs and have already established global links. But, they are also tiny when compared to SME sector of developed countries. Thus, they have only relative advantage and not absolute advantage and they also need to be guided on WTO provisions and also on the safeguards available to them. It must also be understood that Indian small enterprises have certain inherent strengths, which helped them raise their share in total exports to 35% even in the face of tough global competition. The sector possesses the advantage of immovableness and flexibility. Their inventories are low and have weathered many adverse situations successfully and boldly. Indian SMEs have also advantages of local of raw material and word class till besides cheap labour, which could be harnessed to the advantage[14]. At the same time, it is essential to note their vulnerability in the context of emerging global environment resulting into:

i) Loss of protected environment;

ii) Greater competition from imports;

iii) Reduction in conventional subsidy as these are required to be WTO friendly. Many subsidies (viz., export subsidy) are contestable

iv) Widening knowledge and technology gap as a result of revolutionary change in technology;

v) Quality and standard gap;

vi) Inability to match the prescribed hygiene and health standards prescribed under sanitary and phyto-sanitary standards (e.g., food, animal, plant disease, other safety standards);

vii) Increased export risk;

viii) Difficult environmental regulations and costly prescriptions; and

ix) Lack of awareness and information on WTO provisions.

India is already in the process of phasing out QRs by bringing more and more items in the Open General License (OGL) category. The anomaly being the continuance of certain products in the reserved list for small industry, while being shifted to the OGL category. Due to India losing its case to USA in the Dispute Settlement Body of WTO, physical controls (mainly licensing) have to be removed by 1.4.2001. If QRs are removed, policy of reservation becomes redundant. Already about 620 reserved items of a total 812 have been placed under OGL. Most of the remaining items of the reservation list will be out of the cover of protection latest by 31st March 2001 and thus the reservation policy will have only a limited relevance that too with domestic large-scale units.

Due to the total removal of QRs many of the SMEs, especially in the consumer goods sector, would find it difficult to survive; competition will intensify as more imported products find easy access to the Indian market. Items reserved for the SSIs will not face competition from similar products being imported freely except for a low tariff barrier from all over the world and produced by large-scale global manufacturers.

When the domestic market is fully open to competition from foreign goods, the advantage of low labour cost, which our SSIs claim to enjoy, may not work beyond a point. The domestic consumers prefer better quality to low cost products. Low-end products will also face international competition from export-oriented developing countries. Even on the cost level there may be stiffer competition coming from low cost producers from the neighbouring Least Developed Countries (LDCs), such as Nepal and Bangladesh, Sri Lanka and China, which are already offering tough competition.

Marketing Problems: While the domestic market is going to be fully exposed to external competition, the SMEs may have to be cautious against possible dumping by their competitors from abroad, which may be difficult to establish in many cases. What is also significant is that the cost of anti dumping investigations may be prohibitive for the SMEs. On the other end, anti dumping charges by the importing countries may do serious damage to the export prospects as well. The SMEs would need to understand the challenges posed by the Agreement on Anti-Dumping Measures.

There are certain provisions (Special and Differential Provisions) that are intended to benefit the developing countries, but may act against the SMEs when it comes to trade among the developing countries. Article 5.8 of the Agreement provides that the volume of dumped imports shall normally be considered negligible if dumped import from a particular country is found to be less than 3% of imports of the like products, unless countries, which individually account for less than 3% of the imports of the like products collectively account for more than 7% of the import.

SSIs in India are unable to defend or take counteractive measures primarily due to their ignorance, weak NGOs, lack of necessary data and problem of accessibility to information. Organizations like NSIC will have to play a pivotal role in this regard. Government assistance for fighting legal battles will also be needed.

Managerial and Technical Effectiveness: The SMEs would have to take note of growing Technical Barriers to Trade (TBT) in view of high technical standards, set by the developed countries. These are emerging as major non-tariff barriers to access markets of the developed countries. The arrangement on TBT provides for differential and more favourable treatment to the developing country members. But this hardly respected by the developed countries. One of the basic problems of our SMEs is their technological weakness.

Investment-based on definition of SSI unit has at times been found contrary to the objective of technology upgradation and/ or setting up of units with minimum technological standards. The SMEs are likely to be deprived of market access not only in the case of technology intensive items but even for many labour intensive items. Most of the countries define their SMEs in terms of employment or turnover and thus when any dispute arises they will not treat an Indian SSI as a small enterprise. The first official definition of SSI was fixed in 1950 in terms of investment in fixed assets and the strength of workforce in the unit. The criterion underwent a number of modifications over the period.

In the later part of fifties, the change effected in defining an SSI was mainly a shift from a workforce criterion to an investment criterion. In 1966, the original value of plant & machinery was adopted the sole criterion for defining SSI. Since most of the countries use employment or turnover criterion for defining SSI, there is need to examine the SSI definition and link it to the criterion of employment as is prevalent in most of the countries.

The WTO Agreements would be a continuous process, and regular monitoring/study would be required to assess their impact on the SSI sector. SSI associations would have to be taken into confidence, and made aware of the implications of WTO agreements.

- Indian SSEs are at present incapable of visualizing the things in their right perspective because they are technologically, financially, organizationally very weak as compared to global SMEs. Hence, we may have to redefine the SSI definition so that – SSI, are able to match with them and become comparable with global SSIs. In fact the SSIs should convert themselves into small-scale enterprises which would include services. Investment based definition has often been found coming in the way of technology upgradation.
- Gradual phase out of the Reservation Policy for the SSIs, compatible with the EXIM Policy supported by a package of assistance for the affected units.
- Small industries to reposition themselves in certain strategic sectors where India has proven comparative advantages. We should pay more attention to clusters as our future strategy of development.
- Evolve a bold marketing strategy for key SSI produces and promote their brand image because even a good quality product needs to be marketed properly.
- A strong SSI desk on WTO to be created with a strong legal backup in the concerned Government Departments and Industry Associations.
- Develop India as the sourcing point and as a sub-contracting base. Support to schemes/measures, which enhance linkages between large and small units.

- Technological upgradation at par with the best, to achieve low cost of production, better quality and economies of sale.
- Focussed attention on clusters and key products.
- A change in the role of government from protection to promotion by assuming the role of facilitator.
- Diversification of SSI export item.
- Build up a strong database of products, process and cost of production in India and abroad.
- More advocacy required so that small enterprises' voice is heard on all forms in India and outside.
- Prepare inventory of technical standards.
- Expanding the role of Information Technology and making full use of Website E-mailing be adopted.

Conclusions

In the era of globalization, protection to SSI sector could be given through multilateral process. Government intends to keep tariff levels (custom duties) at not higher than 35% and with 10% surcharge, the tariff would be 38.5%. Tariff levels might even be brought down further in tho coming years. There are now four slabs of duties, 35%, 25% 15% and 5% with surcharge of 10% continued.

The Export-Import Policy 2000-2001 has placed 58 items that are reserved for SSIs on the Open General License (OGL) list and 198 more items from the reserved list will be freed on April 1, 2001. Thus at present, 624 out of 812 items that figure in the reserved SSI list can be imported freely under OGL. On April 1, 2001 more items will become freely importable. Imports will enjoy a clear edge over products produced within the country. Quantitative Restrictions (QRs) on 1429 items would be lifted by April 1, 2001 more items will become freely importable. Imports will enjoy a clear edge over products produced within the country. Quantitative Restrictions (QRs) on 1429 items would be lifted by April 1, 2001; on 714 of them, restrictions have already been removed from April 1, 2000. Earlier, during 1996-

99, on as many as 1914items. QRs have been lifted. Many of these items are consumer goods including domestic appliances and food items. Union Commerce Minister is of the opinion that withdrawal of QRs would not affect SSI sector adversely as sufficient safeguards such as tariffs and anti-dumping measures would be available. Besides, it is time to remove QRs as these exist at present only in six countries. Removal of QRs has not so far resulted in significant rise in imports. The new Policy will provide focussed fillip to export of gem and jewelry, software, pharma, agro-chemicals and bio-technology, rationalise a raft of export promotion schemes, and simplify procedures to cut down transaction cost. State Governments will be assisted based on their export performance for granting assistance for export-related infrastructure development.

Very soon, other benefits like post-export Duty Entitlement Pass ook (DEPB), and Export Promotion Capital Goods (EPCG) and other schemes are also likely to be axed or substantially modified. With that our Export-Import Policy will be WTO compatible, but our exports may become uncompetitive in the process. Dismantling of QRs, lowering of tariffs, opening of reserved categories, reduction in subsidies for exports, legislation on Trade Related Intellectual Property Rights (TRIPs) etc., need to be taken into account to analyze the challenges placed before the SSI sector. Government should act as a facilitating agency for SSI sector by providing subsidy on R & D projects, ensure protection through WTO – friendly measures, providing focussed policy treatment, and level playing ground for SSI sector. There is an urgent need to strengthen SSI sector to face challenges of WTO.

REFERENCES

1. Economic and Social Commission for Asia and the Pacific, Industrial Restructuring in Asia and the Pacific, Bangkok, 1991, p.214.
2. Small Scale Enterprises, Economic Survey, Government of India, 1997- 98, p.109.
3. Ibid., p.109.
4. Ibid., p.109.

5. I.M.D. Little, 'Small Manufacturing Enterprises in Developing Countries', World Bank Economic Review, Vol. No. 2, 187, p. 204.

6. Raising Finance for Small Enterprise Development, Industrial Development Global Report, United Nations Industrial Development Organization, 1977.

7. Small Scale Industries Economic Survey, p.109.

8. Small Scale Industries Economic Survey, p.109 & 110.

9. Revathy, J., "Financial Management Practices of Small Business Units", Thesis submitted to Nagarjuna University, Nagarjuna Nagar.

10. Mathur S.P. Economics of Small Scale Industries in Agra Region. Thesis submitted to Agra University, Sundeep Prakasam, Agra, 1979.

11. Implicational of WTO on Small Enterprises, Dr. C.S. Prasad, Laghu Udyog Samachar, January- March 2000 volume XXIV NO. 6 to 8 p-4.

12. Ibid p.7

13. World Trade Organisation Agreement its impact on Small Scale Sector, Anil Kumar, Laghu Udyog Samachar, January-March 2000 volume XXIV No. 6 to 8 p.32 & 33.

14. Impact of WTO Agreements on Small and Medium enterprises in India – T.P. Bhat, Vikrant Sayena and Anihuman Gupta, The Indian Journal of Commerce, Vol.53, No. 1& 2, January-June 2000, p6-11.

12

WTO Scenario: Strategies for Small Industry Development

Prof. C. Suryanarayana* & Dr. V. Krishna Mohan*

The economic boundaries of nations for all practical purposes have expanded enormously much beyond their geographical limits and the rules of trade are applicable uniformly in domestic as well as international zones. The economic environment is changing very fast and the changes are visible in multiple forms and from different directions. The economic reforms with emphasis on liberalization, privatization and globalizations alerted us to produce quality products at competitive prices. Organizations, whether big or small, are compelled to upgrade technology, cut costs, improve quality and adopt innovative management strategies.

The role played by Small-scale Industry (SSI) in the process of economic development is no doubt significant. It is contributing about 36% GDP, 35% to India's exports and employing 16.72 millions (1997-98). Their number also increased perceptibly from 1,35 million in 1985-86 to 2.57 millions in 1994-95.

The emergence of World Trade Organization (WTO) and its conditionalities, Small-scale Industries will have to compete on their own to find a place for themselves in the domestic as well as international markets. They will have to improve the quality

* Prof. C. Suryanarayana and Dr. V. Krishna Mohan are Coordinator and Dy. Coordinator respectively of the UGC Special Assistance Programme, Department of Commerce and Management Studies, Andhra University, Visakhapatnam.

of products and be efficient and competitive in order to survive and grow. While technology up-gradation is inevitable for SSIs, the size of investment, as per the recent definition, is considered a severe credit crunch, inadequate knowledge of marked dynamic and acumen, inadequate infrastructure, poor R & D, low productivity of manpower etc.

The WTO agreement does not discriminate on the basis of size of industries or enterprises. Hardly there is single agreement of WTO, which is directly dealing with SSIs. Under the WTO scenario, Indian SSIs might face competition both from MNC's and from Indian large-scale companies. The market access agreements encompassing TRIPS & TRIMS means that import of goods will increase in all product categories including reserved items of SSIs. Reduced tariff rates would effect the Indian SSIs depending upon the level of import intensity of exportable items and demand for importable products.

The objectives of this paper is to examine the strengths, weaknesses, opportunities and threats for the development of Small-scale Industry under WTO regime and to offer some suggestions to improve competitiveness of SSIs.

The paper observes that the small-scale units, not only played a crucial role in providing large scale employment opportunities at lower capital cost than large scale industries, but also helped in industrialization of rural and backward areas, thereby reducing regional imbalance, assuring more equitable distribution of national income and wealth. SSI units are also supplementary and complimentary to large and medium scale units as ancillary units.

The Government of India has helped the small-scale sector through supportive policy measures since adoption of planned economy model. The basic policy support for SSI sector has its roots in the Industrial Policy Resolution of 1956. Further, the Industrial Policy Statement, 1977, laid emphasis on reservation of items. The reservation of economically viable and technologically feasible products to be exclusively manufactured by SSIs began with a list of 47 items, which was gradually extended to many products. Other policy supports, which could be listed are excise exemption, credit under priority sector lending from banks and financial institutions, marketing support through reservation of items for products from SSI sector for government purchases, providing infrastructure facilities like sheds, plots in industrial estates, technological support, new management techniques, training and entrepreneurship development.

Though this sector has shown substantial progress, its major problems like inadequate credit flow from banks and financial institutions (FIs), inadequate infrastructure facilities, low quality standards of products, use of obsolete technology, plant, machinery and equipment, inefficient management techniques, etc. are still inhibiting the sector. Besides, this sector has to face challenges of competition from the opening up of economy to globalisation, need for increasing exports and meet WTO commitments.

The policy support provided so far has acted as a catalyst in promoting this sector. However, the Planning Commission felt an urgent need to review the policy measures so as to make this sector more growth oriented and enable it to withstand the pressure from global competition. The Industrial Policy measures announced in 1991 laid special thrust on promotion and strengthening of small, tiny and village industries. Besides effecting changes in investment limits, equity participation, etc., a new scheme of Integrated Infrastructure Development for SSIs with the participation of State Governments and Financial Institutions was initiated and a pro-active role for NGO sector was mooted.

In order to protect the interest and facilitate their rapid development of SSI sector, the Government in pursuance of its policies, have initiated a number of support measures from time to time which include policy of reservation, revision of investment ceilings, modernisation, technology upgradation, marketing assistance, etc. The emerging economic scenario in the changed liberalised and competitive economic environment has necessitated structural and fundamental changes in the policy framework put into place for the development of this vital sector of the economy. Accordingly, there has been a shift in focus from "protection" to "promotion". In the post-reform period, a number of steps including partial de-reservation, change in investment limits, facilitating foreign participation, establishment of growth centres, export promotion, marketing assistance and incentives for quality improvement, etc. have been taken by the government for strengthening of this sector.

The SSI sector has proved its mettle even in the changed liberalised economic environment of the country. The steps required for opening up of the economy have affected the operations of this sector, throwing open new opportunities and challenges at the same time. The need of the hour undoubtedly is to provide sustenance through suitable measures to strengthen it for converting the challenges into opportunities for scaling new heights.

Impact on Small-scale Sector

The emerging regime of liberalisation of international trade and deregulation and privatisation of internal economy, in the light of WTO, has rendered the small-scale industry (SSI) sector highly vulnerable. The umbrella of WTO is likely to create some far reaching implications for the SSI sector in India, specifically with regard to their competitive ability and integration with the global markets. Most of the problems arise due to the unorganized nature of this sector, lack of data and information, use of low technology sometimes obsolete technology and poor infrastructure in the country. WTO will affect all types of SSI units whether producing for the domestic market or for the international market.

The SSI sector, which produces over 7,500 items will have to be aware of the patents of products including even of the technologic al patents, trademarks, industrial designs, etc. 95% of the SSI units are in the nature of tiny micro enterprises and are weak. Many of them are one man shows. Their capital bases are poor and do not have access to the economies of scale. Their bargaining power is low and do not have access to information and modern management practices. They constitute most vulnerable segment of the SSI Sector. Hence, they will need to be guided and supported since they are also employment generators for the economy. Balance 5% of SSI units are in the category of modern SSIs and have already established global links. But, they are also tiny when compared to SSI sector of developed countries. Thus they have only relative advantage and not absolute advantage and they also need to be guided on WTO provisions and also on the safeguards available to them. It must also be understood that Indian small enterprises have certain inherent strengths, which helped them raise their share in total exports to 35% even in the face of tough global competition. The sector possesses the advantage of immovableness and flexibility. Their inventories are low and have weathered many adverse situations successfully and boldly. Indian SSIs have also advantage of local raw material and word class skill besides cheap labour, which could be harnessed to the advantage. At the same time, it is essential to note their vulnerability in the context of emerging global environment resulting into:

- Loss of protected environment
- Greater competition from imports
- Reductions in conventional subsidy as these are required to be WTO friendly. Many subsidies (viz., export subsidy) are contestable
- widening knowledge and technology gap as a result of revolutionary change in technology
- Quality and standard gap
- Inability to match the prescribed hygiene and health standards prescribed under Sanitary and Phyto-sanitary standards (e.g., food, animal, plant disease, other safety standards)
- Increased export risk
- Difficult environmental regulations and costly prescriptions and
- Lack of awareness and information on WTO provisions.

In the light of the fast changing global scenario, the SSIs are required to analyze the strategies being followed by their counterparts in countries like China, Japan, South Korea, etc. and accordingly improve their competitiveness through: (i) Technology Upgradation and absorption to manufacture their products most cost effectively ND also with quality consciousness, (ii) R&D efforts to introduce market oriented innovative Products; (iii) Product diversification in tune with the requirements of medium and large scale industries and at times some sister concerns; (iv) changing the mind set of the Indian entrepreneur to quickly move from the local and regional perspective to the global outlook.

Greater understanding and awareness on the part of entrepreneur about the standards and guidelines set out by WTO to make their products acceptable in global markets. Market intelligence and knowledge would make the Indian entrepreneur to suitably adopt and respond to the challenges posed by the fast changing markets. The ethical and moral values always rule the roost in global business. The Indian entrepreneur ought to nurture this to improve his competitiveness in the domestic as well as international markets.

Quality consciousness should be ingrained in the small entrepreneur and employees too in order to gain a competitive advantage in the liberalized business environment. The impact of human re-engineering and retraining on the productivity and quality should not be lost sight off if the small enterprises are to play a vibrant role in the economic development of India.

13

Quantitative Restriction: Some Insights

Dr. A.V. Shukla*, Ms. V. Prabhu** & Mr. V. Varshney@

The business environment of the country these days is abuzz with the fast approaching dead line of 1st April 2001 when the Government of India is committee to removing @Quantitative Restrictions (QR's) thereby opening the flood gates into the country. Fears are being expressed that the local industry in general and the SSI in particular is likely to be crushed under the onslaught of heavy imports and the virtual flooding of markets with cheap imports particularly from countries like China.

This paper attempts to present the entire perspective in clear terms removing ambiguities, misunderstandings, misconceptions if any so as to promote clear understanding of the likely future business scenario in the country.

What Are QR's?

QR's or Quantitative Restrictions refer to limits set by countries to curb imports (or exports). These can be in the form of quotas, licensing requirement or in the form of canalizing of imports – i.e., allowing only a few players or entities to import

* Reader, PG Dept. of Business Administration & Management, Amaravati University, Amaravati and Accredited management Teacher (AIMA).

** Participants – MBA Programme.

@ Quantitative Restrictions were removed form 1st April 2002. The paper was written before this date.

specific things. QR's are thus measures, other than tariffs or duties, taken to restrict imports (or exports).

The noted economist Dr. Anne Krueger has described QR's, licenses and restrictions as "rent-seeking activities", which carry a premium or windfall profits for the quota holder. That is why some analysts in India have defined QR's as Quota Raj", which breeds corruption and inefficiency.

QR's in India – The Background

Under the GATT (General Agreement on Tariffs and Trader), imports have to be controlled only through tariffs or custom duties and not through quantitative restrictions such as quotas, licences, etc. All member countries have to abide by its provisions. There are, however, some exceptions to this rule. One such exception is that a country can take recource to QR's on grounds of Balance Of Payments (BOP) difficulties. It is under this exception that India has been maintaining QR's. Till 1993, India's BOP situation had been unfavourable. However, since 1994-95 there has been a steady improvement in the country's foreign exchange (FE) reserves position.

Table 1: Total FE and Total Imports

Year ending on 31st March	*Total FE reserves at the end of financial year*	*Total imports During the year*
1993	09.8	21.88
1994	19.3	23.88
1995	25.2	28.65
1996	21.7	36.69
1997	26.4	39.13
1998	29.4	41.48
1999	32.5	42.39
2000	38.0	42.20

It can be seen from the above table that FE reserves have gradually improved.

Why QR;s are being Removed?

With the improvement in the Balance of Payments position, certain members of WTO (World Trade Organization) disputed, around 1995, India's need or justification to continue Quantitative Restrictions for BOP reasons. Ultimately, India had no alternative but to agree to the phase out QR's.

By 1997, India could negotiate with most of the trading partners, with the exception of USA, to arrive at a mutually agreeable solution for phasing out these QR's. Under the agreements, the QR's were to be withdrawn over a six-year period ending 31st March 2003. USA, however, felt that the period was too long and filed a dispute against India in the WTO. The Dispute Settlement Panel of WTO, which was constituted in November 1997 to adjudicate, ruled against India. India filed an appeal before the Appellate Body of WTO against the findings of the Panel but the Appellate Body also upheld the findings of the Panel challenged by India. Consequently, India is now obliged to withdraw QR's. An Agreement was signed between India and USA for determining the reasonable period of time, under which QR's on the remaining 1429 tariff were to be removed by 1st April 2001, of which QR's on 714 were to be removed before 1st April 2000. Incidentally, out of the 136 members of the WTO, QR's are being maintained only by 5 countries other than India, i.e., Tunisia, Nigeria, Pakistan, Bangladesh and Sri Lanka. They are also in the process of phasing out the QR's. No other country maintains QR's except textile quotas, which also have to be phased out by 1sr January 2005, under the Agreement on Textiles and Clothing.

The Likely Impact

Removal of QT's it is felt, has both advantages and disadvantages what remains to be seen is what will be the ultimate outcome?

The advantages of the removal of QR's can be summed up as follows:

- Firstly, consumers will benefit as they will get a wider choices of goods and services at a lower prices;

- Secondly, freer trade is likely to bring down prices and help in keeping the level of inflation low;
- Thirdly, the Government is also likely to benefit from higher customs duties on imports, e.g., things, which were being bought in the markets from abroad through various other channels can now be brought through legal channels, thus generating revenue for the country (a case in point could be that of freeing of gold imports, which has resulted in told now being imported through legal channels, with Government earning substantial revenue through customs duty);
- Fourthly, it would lead to easier access to imported raw material and capital goods for the domestic manufacturers leading to faster industrial growth; and
- Finally, competition from imports can lead to upgradation in the quality of domestic products and increased productivity leading to increased competitiveness of the Indian domestic industry, which could help in pushing our exports. This means not only value for money for the consumers, but also in the long-run development, which may help in placing and domestic industry on a stronger footing to face international competition and to become global players. In a sense, therefore, removal of QR's can be viewed as not only a challenge but also an opportunity for the Indian Industry to initiate steps for enhancing their competitiveness, given the fact that there are no alternative except to removing QR's. In a country as diverse as India, there are bound to be a wide range of winners and losers, arising from any significant reforms. Although the above scenario presents a rather bright picture, it is only one side of the spectrum. The other side has its disadvantages, demerits, flaws, the important ones of which follow:

1. Dumping :

Dumping means exporting a product at lower than its normal price, which can be assessed based on its domestic sale price or cost of production or sale price in other countries.

Although there are anti-dumping duties, which can be imposed if there is dumping and a casual link is established between dumping and injury to the domestic industry dumping can have its negative effects on the Indian market. China is a classic example, its products are pouring into the country. Their unique feature being low cost. With the average Indian consumer being price sensitive these products would satisfy the needs of the middle class and rural sector, which form the bulk of the Indian market.

2. Because of lower import barriers and deregulation in industry, foreign investment has increased tremendously. In 1991 it was about $ 150 bn. a year, by 1997 it had surged to 2 bn. and is still heading.

The reason being, with a population of over 980 m, India presents a very lucrative market, companies such as Procter and Gamble, Asea Brown Boverl and Alfa Laval have substantially increased their presence in the burgeoning Indian market.

This means Indian companies now face fiercer competition from abroad. While some of the big industrial houses such as Tata and Hindustan Lever have managed to diversify their product lines to keep up, others are being squeezed out of the market. Take for example the case of Bajaj, the second largest scooter manufacturer in the world. Since 1991, Bajaj has lost significant market shares to companies that have their own design and development units. These winners are able to offer the customer updated products developed with Indian conditions and customers in mind.... Hero, TVS, Suzuki, LML.

The arrival of Coca Cola and Pepsi in 1993 had a devastating impact on locally produced beverages. Local coals such as Thump Up and Campa Cola have driven out of the market by these giants. In fact, Coke has taken over the factories of Campa Cola. Companies, such as Parle and Tata have disappeared as soft drinks and soap manufacturers. As a result, Indian entrepreneurs have resisted the influx of other multinationals such as Kentucky Fried Chicken etc.

Every sector has been and will further be affected, and the public sector is no exception. In fact the public sector has faced a much severe blow. Previously, public enterprises operated under a system of government-administered prices, quotas and controls, which they managed to manipulate for their own profit. Once import restrictions were lifted, many public sector units ran into difficulties, as their inefficiencies were exposed. The alcohol-based chemicals are a good example. Almost all the manufacturers had to shut down because their operations had become uneconomic in relation to cheaper imports. Companies that were used to compete with state enterprises experienced a major shock when markets were liberalized in 1991. Steel is a good example; SAIL, TISCO and INDAL have gone traumatic adjustments, which still continue.

Major changes have occurred in the automobile industry. Production rose from 2.4 m. units in 1991 to 3.99 m. units in 1997. Sales have risen from 2.8 m. units to 3.5 m. units over the same period. What caused the growth? In 1993, the Indian car industry was de-licensed allowing 100% foreign ownership in some cases. This spurred Mitsubishi, Honda, Ford and General Motors to start up joint ventures with Indian partners. For instance, Suzuki Motors of Japan has increased its stake in the former state owned carmaker Maruti Udyog Ltd. to 50%.

The above effects are, although not a result of the removal of QR's but removal of QR's is only going to add to the burden. This bleak scenario is going to worsen. It is feared SSI's are going to see the end of the day. Although the government affirms the fact that there has been no surge in imports, and the imports have shown only fractional changes what is feared is that this is only the beginning and every change is gradual.

Presently, the consumers are happy, the products pouring in are satisfying their desires. They may enjoy Swiss chocolates, Venezuelan coffee, Dutch cheese, Australian juice and French caviar. But – aren't they only accelerating the alienation of Indians from their own traditional culture? Some people ask.

The latest rumours going around are those, Chinese rice is available at Rs.7 kg. in bagfuls. The quality is supposedly as good as the 'Kolum' or the 'Sona Masuri' rice eaten in many of our homes. News from the cold storages indicates the availability of American chicken legs (sold internationally as bye products, as the American looks at the chicken as breast and breast alone!) at Rs.38 a kg! On the face of it this all sounds tempting. Globalization is surely here, but all through the back-door.

No doubt, the removal of QR's will trigger off a number of effects: a new class of customers who will exercise the kind of choice that its peers across the world have long enjoyed; and an entirely new business ecosystem with a new class of entrepreneurs focused on importing and distributing imported items; a major shift in brand perception, of those already available and those coming in. but above all, there could well be a significant socio-economic fallout which, more than anything else makes the removal of QR's a far more significant event than merely a new legislation coming into force.

Conclusion: With the present scenario, one can be thankful to the progressive easing of QR's. Today, it is theoretically possible for everybody to buy items made anywhere in the world, across product categories. But still, the prices of many of these imported items are almost at par or even lesser compared with their desi counterparts.

The consumer seems to only gain, but what one must ponder about is, are they really gaining? Or is this a short-term disguised paradise?

14

The Impact of WTO on Indian Industries

Prof. M. Chandrasekhar*

In 1995, WTO emerged as a regulatory body of world trade. According to WTO, trading nations are required to adhere to uniform rules of trade and the trade procedures are based on the principles of transparency, predictability and certainty. The trade between countries has been in existence from time immemorial. A system of some regulatory mechanism was prevalent among some countries in order to protect their industries from competition created counterparts in other countries. The WTO is expected to play the role of regulator of the world trade by ensuring tho implementation of the various provisions of the new trade agreement.

The main functions of WTO include administering and impelling the multilateral trade agreements, acting as a forum for multilateral trade negotiations, resolving trade disputes, overseeing national trade policies etc. WTO is a system of rules dedicated to open, fair, and undistorted competition.

In recent times, developing countries like India, Indonesia, Malaysia, Egypt, Cuba, Pakistan are demanding the correction of a number of imbalances in WTO rules and regulations.

The objectives of the paper include identifying challenges and threats from WTO to Indian industries, and to offer suitable suggestions to overcome them.

Challenges and Threats to Indian Companies

For almost 45 years, Indian companies have lived under

the shelter of protection. They are marked by low productivity, lack of research and development, unplanned growth, and above all, lack of competency.

The biggest challenge ever faced by the Indian industry is coping with foreign competition. India has a disadvantage of being a 'RIP VAN WINCKLE' of the emerging market economies. In the light of the changed economic situations, Indian companies should have strategic alliance, joint ventures that are the best options for getting the latest technology and upgrading operations to global standards. The challenge of meeting global competition may involve, for most companies, reorganizing business, shedding non-core activities, identifying business focus, etc.

MNCs, which are facing saturated markets and limited avenues for investment, are looking toward India for new markets and challenges. A critical analysis of some of the industries reveals the actual impact of WTO on Indian industries. Industry wise analysis of the issues ins [presented in the following paragraphs.

Electronics

The global ctv brands started flowing into India. Samsung, LG, Akai, Thomson, Sansui, Aiwa, etc., have become household names in India. With the advent of global brands, the Indian companies, which are producing washing machines, refrigerators, are affected with low sales, and low margins and low brand equity. Electronic gadgets, audio, video sets etc flooded into Indian market which trend is at the cost of SSI sector development.

Automobiles

The automobile giants like Ford, GM, Hyundai, Daewoo, have entered India. They are poising a threat to the very existence of Indian car manufacturers. Maruti has lost its market share significantly. Second hand imported cars are permitted from April 1st 2001. The import of second hand cars from the countries like Japan, Germany, France, Korea, etc., will affect the Indian automobile companies.

Other Sectors

MNCs, which are having an advantageous position in telecommunications and other sectors, want India to throw the domestic, market, open for their entry. Similarly, the use of patent rights is being pushed and this has resulted in the price of medicines rising sharply in India. The opening up of the insurance sector will lead to drying up of our savings. CII, Bombay Club, ASSOCHAM have become wary of MNCs as they swallow Indian firms by various kinds of devices.

Soft Drinks

Parle was the leader in the soft drink industry. The company has been taken over by Coca Cola. Duke and Sons has been sold to Pepsi Foods. The Indian soft drink companies have been sold to MNCs.

Due to the fear of global giants, a lot of mergers and takeovers are taking place in recent times. The number of joint ventures has also increased from 285 in 1991 to 524 in 1996.

Agriculture

India is potentially the strongest agricultural nation in the world, with the largest area under cultivation, low cost labour, good climatic conditions; agriculture can be developed to generate enormous profits, employment and exports. In recent times, the imports from Taiwan, China are affecting the agriculture industry, fruit juice, milk are also being imported and are sold at cheaper rates in India.

Textiles

The developed countries have been taking steps to cut our textile exports as they are making strong inroads in the countries under the European Union and United States of America. The imposition of anti-dumping duties is the other protectionist measures initiated by the countries of European Union. Since the anti-dumping duties raise the landed costs of the fabrics, they are likely to adversely affect our exports. Since this sector accounts for about 32 per cent of the total export earnings, the act of protectionism will hit the textile industry seriously and this in turn will affect our agricultural and rural economy with which this sector has close links.

Small-scale Industries

SSIs survived in India for many years because of protection given by government through subsidies, tax holiday, infrastructure facilities, and reservation of some areas, etc. These days SSIs are finding it difficult to survive as some of the area have been de-reserved. As a result, SSIs are facing stiff competition from MNCs, medium scale and large-scale industries. Many SSIs are becoming sick due to reasons as lack of finance, lack of marketing, state of the art technology, imports; majority of SSIs is suffering from inadequate infrastructure such as power, communication, transportation, water etc. The entrepreneurs do not have global exposure to face foreign competition. Anti-dumping laws also cause serious damage to the prospects of SSI exports. Out of 812 products reserved for SSIs, 230 products are not made in India; as they are reserved for SSIs, other big companies are not allowed to make them. If people want to buy those goods they have buy foreign goods. SSIs have to manufacture on a large-scale, adopt modern technology by infusing fresh investment to face competition from foreign goods. SSIs have a fear that they may lose SSI status if they invest more than the prescribed amounts. As a result, SSIs are trying to remain as SSIs to get government subsidies and incentives by adopting outdated and archaic technology. The existing financial institutions do not cater to the needs of entrepreneurs. They are not ready to undertake risks. There is bureaucratic delay in disbursing loans, lots of paper work, which in turn, escalate the cost of project resulting either in their abandonment or in their turning non-viable.

India is flooded with toys, electronic goods from China. The government is supposed to give encouragement and protection to domestic companies so that they can face foreign competition in terms of price, quality etc. It is learnt that to import goods as many as 25 permissions are required, for exporting to other countries as many as 50 permissions are needed. This shows the attitude of government towards exports and imports. The Indian manufacturing is very high. Some of the Asian countries are having cost advantages. They are able to sell at cheaper rates in India. These days a lot of goods are coming from China. From April 1st onwards, quantitative restrictions are removed and these things are sounding a death knell to some of Indian companies. It is believed that most of Indian companies have not concentrated much on exports since independence. The companies are not quality conscious. Most of the Indian companies never faced competition because of the protection given by the government. With the advent of liberalization, privatization and globalization, the Indian industries are facing stiff competition. The share of manufacturing sector has come down to 24.7 per cent in 1998-99 from 28.03 per cent in 1991-92. The imports from China started increasing steadily. During the last six months goods worth of Rs.3,224 crores imported from China. In recent times, imports have increased from the countries like Britain, Hong Kong, France, Australia, Indonesia, Germany, Indian consumers prefer to buy goods from other countries, as they are cheap. As a result, Indian companies are forced to reduce their production. The investments in the areas like textiles, cement, chemicals where there is foreign competition started declining.

Competition from China

China has started economic reforms in 1978. The GNP has been growing at a compound annual rate of 8.8 per cent per annum. The privatization of state firms is frequently regarded as necessary for fostering production. In China, few state companies have been privatized and the largest contribution of industrial growth has come from enterprises, which are publicly owned. The Chinese experience suggests those privatization matters less than competition and autonomy for achieving efficiency.

Since India is a signatory to the WTO it is obliged to meet its commitments. Under the agreement, Indians has to reduce import tariff on industrial and agricultural products in a span of 6 to 10 years.

Suggestions

The government should create right market conditions by giving Indian companies the same flexibility and access to input as global competitors. This means Indian firms must be allowed to tap cheap global finance, buy any technology they like etc. We need institutes for improving a wide range of human skills. We need to greatly upgrade our 'knowledge infrastructure' and this means creating institutes for international law, intellectual property rights, foreign languages and other issues that must be mastered by any global player. 'Michael Porter' has stressed in 'the competitive advantage of nations' that successfully exporting countries have manufacturing clusters accompanied by skill centers and India needs to create world class skill centers in diamond cutting, jewellery design, garment design and related export-oriented fields.

Companies have to spruce up all aspects of operations, in terms of technology and design, material procurement, manufacturing processes, quality levels, finance techniques, and dynamics of marketing for export promotion, taking fair advantage of the liberalized environment provided by the government. Timely decisions and responses, firm delivery dates, assumed quality norms, pro-customer policies are needed to succeed in global pursuits. Productivity has to improve in all areas of management and the entire work force should wake up to the new realities through meaningful counseling and HRD techniques. A thorough reshaping of attitude and redesign of work methods is imperative to bring in a totally new culture of activity and achievement. International production sharing as Peter Drucker calls it has been resorted to by many developed countries whereby unskilled and semi-skilled assembly of foreign supplied components is performed in factories located in low wage countries and skilled operations are retained in developed countries possessing technology and expertise. This gives a chance for gradual upgradation of skills in the developing countries in course of time after diffusion of technology.

The pressure is mounting on India to liberalize its import regime by lowering tariff rates and dismantling quota restrictions. To gear up for global competition, there is a need to rewrite many of the laws, policies, and methods of implementation. It is imperative to restructure and remodel the functioning of institutional mechanisms. The development-oriented institutions such as banks, R & D organizations and trade promotion bodies have to meet the new challenges emerging from the global market.

Industry has to focus attention on exports and a sizeable part of its production should be exported. To compete with the global players, we have to produce goods in a massive scale. When economic barriers are being brought down under the WTO framework, it is indispensable to gear up Indian industries for global competitiveness. Acquisitions and mergers are becoming the order of the day. Several companies are actively involved in marketing tie-ups, strategic alliances and joint production ventures. The system and style of management is rapidly changing for the better. These are signs of a move into the global market. Still Indian industry has many miles to go before it becomes a major global player.

Indian companies should not perceive threats as danger signals but should try to assess their own strengths and weaknesses and try to convert the threats into opportunities.

Conclusion

Awareness in Indian industries is spreading fast to restructure and concentrate on core competence. Many enterprises are hiving off some areas and expanding the areas of competence to reap the benefits of economies of scale. Indian companies have to shake off the lethargy of years to improve performance on aspects of cost, quality, lead-time, and service to customers. Indian companies have to change their corporate culture, management styles and compensation structure in order to attract professionals who could help them develop appropriate business and marketing strategies for growth. Globalization, if it has any meaning for the developing countries, should help to improve the lot of 85 per cent of the world population living in these countries. They are able to take advantage of the unequal bargaining power at the WTO and force the developing countries to open up their potentially huge markets to foreign goods and services and capital.

REFERENCES

1. The Survey of Indian Industry, 1996, 1997, 1998, 1999.
2. Mainstream, July 12, 1997.
3. The Economic Times, April 16, 1994.
4. The Economic Times, April 30, 1994.
5. The Economic Times, March 9, 1995.
6. The Economic Times, January 8, 2000.
7. Business World, September 5, 1995.
8. Business World, September 20, 1999.

15

WTO Agreement: A Boon or a Bane to the SSI Sector

Mr. Israel Raju Vuram*

It is no accident that India today operates the largest programme for the development of small industry as in any developing country[1]. Certain special Characteristics of the small industry sector (SSI) make it unique in the Indian industrial scenario. These characteristics include the decentralized nature of the sector, its small size, greater reliance on local raw material and indigenous technology, employment intensity and its suitability in rural areas with limited use of techno-economic infrastructure. The SSI sector, as an important segment of the Indian economy, accounts for around 95% of the Industrial units, 40% of the manufacturing sector's output, 36% of exports and provides direct employment to 18 million persons in around 3.2 million registered SSI units in the country[2]. The sector enjoys the pride of being the second largest employer in the country and offers a wide spectrum of products. It serves as a Greenfield for the nurturing of entrepreneurial talent enabling the small-scale units to graduate into medium scale.

---

* *Commerce Lecturer, ACTS Degree College, and Research Scholar,* Dept. of Commerce and Management Studies, Andhra University, Visakhapatnam.

1. Ram K. Vepa, "Modern Industries in India", Saga Publications, New Delhi, 1988, p. 18
2. SIDBI Report on small-scale Industries Sector-2000, SIDBI, Lucknow, 2000, p. 1.

Emergence of WTO

The economic boundaries of nations for all practical purposes have expanded enormously much beyond the geographical limits and the rules of the trade are no longer different for domestic zone and international zones.

Trading partners are required to follow uniform rules of trade. The process of discipline in international trade started with the signing of an Agreement in 1947 in Geneva immediately after the Second World War by 23 non-communist countries, an agreement called General Agreement on Tariff and Trade (GATT). Since the idea of having an international trade organization under UN could not fructify, GATT was the only agency to promote non-discriminatory trade among member nations, which rose to 96 in 1988. GATT had held seven rounds of meetings. The eighth round began in Uruguay in 1986 and concluded in 1994, which led to the emergence of the World Trade Organization (WTO).

The World Trade Organization came into being on 1st January 1995 as outcomes of the signing of final Action on 15th April 1994 at Marrakech. WTO has emerged as the only body dealing with the Rules of Trade between the nations. With headquarters in Geneva, Switzerland it has 135 members including India. The basic objective of WTO is to ensure global free trade and reduction of tariff and no-tariff barriers. The ultimate objective of WTO is to expand production and trade and allow the optimal use of world resources. Its procedures are based on the principles of transparency, predictability and certainty.

Impact on WTO on Indian Small-scale Sector

The umbrella of the World Trade organization is likely to create some far-reaching implications for the SME sector in India, especially with regard to their competitive ability and integration with the global markets. Most of the problems arise due to the unorganized nature of this sector, lack of data and information, use of low technology sometimes obsolete technology and poor infrastructure in the country. WTO will affect all types of SSI units whether for the domestic market or for the international Market.

Reservation Policy for SSI units

Article XVIII of GATT provides for the imposition of Quantitative Restriction on imports for balance of payments reasons. India is already in the process of phasing out quantitative restrictions by bringing more and more items in the Open General Licensing Category(OGL). If QRs are removed, policy of reservation becomes redundant. Already about 620 reserved items of a total 812 have been placed under OGL. Most of the remaining items of the reservation list will be out of the cover of protection latest by 31st March, 2001 and thus the reservation policy will have only a limited relevance that too with domestic large scale units. Due to the total removal of QRs many of the SMEs, especially in the consumer goods sector, would find it difficult to survive, competition will intensify as more imported products find easy access to the India market.

As Quantitative Restrictions have to be removed, the protection level by way of tariff also has to come down. The SMEs have to note that India is committed to a ceiling tariff bindings of 40% on finished goods and 25% on intermediate goods, machinery and equipments. Reduced protection has already resulted into reduced competitive strength of SSI units. Tariff protections is bound to be scaled down significantly in the future.

Anti Dumping Practices

While the domestic market is going to be fully exposed to external competition, the SMEs may have to be cautious against possible dumping by their competitors from abroad, which may be difficult to establish in many cases. What is also significant is that the cost of anti dumping investigations may be prohibitive for the SMEs. On the other hand, anti dumping charges by the importing countries may do serious damage to the export prospects as well.

Trade Related Investment Measures (TRIMS)

In the domestic market, again there may be reasons to feel concerned when the agreement of Trade Related Investment Measures (TRIMS) comes into force which prohibits five types of investment conditions. The Government may have to do away with the criteria of local area content and dividend balancing. This may prove to be a big jolt to development of sub-contracting and result in loss of domestic market for the SMEs. Impact may be severely felt in the emerging sectors of Indian Industry and especially in automobiles, consumer electronics, white goods, electrical machinery, electrical appliances, etc.

Trade Related Intellectual Property Rights (TRIPS)

Intellectual Property Rights (IPR) are considered as a tool to create wealth through knowledge. Inventions and technical information flow very quickly all over the world and other can easily copy them. It is essential that fruits of R&D are adequately protected throughout the world under the harmonised protection system. WTO-TRIPS agreement recognized that widely varying standards in the protection and enforcement of intellectual property rights and the lack of multilateral framework of principles, rule and disciplines dealing with international trade in counterfeit goods, be streamlined in the form of rules and disciplines. Second hand imports of automobiles will be allowed with the removal of QRs by 2001 A. D. Import of second hand vehicles form abroad unless properly monitored might have adverse implications for the domestic automobile industry and also for the small-scale vendors and sale-contractors.

Trade and Investment

In the event of multilateral agreement on investment and its eventual enforcement, the SMEs may have to struggle for survival in a completely unprotected environment in the domestic market. Agreement on Trade and Investment would be primarily about 'National Treatment' and 'Most Favoured Nations' treatment, probably, in that environment SMEs of the other Member Countries would need to be given same treatment in India as is given to other SMEs and the implications may indeed be far reaching.

Government Procurement

In India, the Government is a substantially large buyer as well as a large investor. For the SMEs, the Government is a big support as far as market is concerned. There are reservation policies and also price support mechanism for purchase of products from the small-scale sector but product reservation, are non-statutory. If it challenged SMEs who face marketing problems will be adversely affected. In the event of a multilateral agreements, the market constituted by Government may have to be opened up to foreign competition and the system will have to be made more transparent.

Sustainability of Export Obligation

At present, 812 items are reserved for exclusive manufacture in the field of small-scale sector. Any non-SSI unit, which wants to manufacture, reserved item had to undertake 75% export obligation. It had been felt that this is too high a percentage, as under this condition, an undertaking has to export three times of the quantity of products it sells in the domestic market. It is difficult for many industrial undertaking to achieve this target. This change had also become necessary because even in the case of 100% export oriented units where export obligations of 100 had been prescribed, at the start of the scheme, the same were subsequently reduced to 75% and in some cases even to 50%. Since December 1997, the export obligations have been restricted to 50% in case of all the reserved items. It is expected that reduced export obligations of 50% will enable the units to get competitive advantages by selling 50% of the products in the domestic market.

What need to be done

- Indian SSEs are at present incapable of visualizing the things in their right perspective because they are technologically, organizationally very weak as compared to global SMEs. Hence we may have to redefine the SSI unit in tune with international SME definition so that SSI should convert themselves into small-scale enterprises which would include services. Investment based definition has often been found coming in the way of technology up gradation.
- Evolve a bold marketing strategy for key SSI products and promote their brand image because even a good quality product needs to be marketed property.

- A strong SSI desk is to be created in WTO with a strong legal backup in the concerned Government Departments and Industry Associations.
- Develop India as the Sourcing Point and as a Sub-contracting base supporting to schemes/measures, which enhance linkages between large and small units.
- Technological up gradation at par with the best, to achieve low cost of production, better quality and economies of scale.
- Build up a strong database of products, process and cost of production in India and abroad.
- Expanding the role of Information Technology and making full use of Website. E- mailing be adopted.

16

Challenges of Small Industry in the Post Liberalization Period

Dr. V. Krishna Mohan*

This paper reviews the strengths of small-scale sector in India and examines the policy interventions of Government of India. It focuses on the winds of change in terms of challenges thrown open to small-scale sector. This paper gives new ideas, which require greater emphasis in future years.

INTRODUCTION

Global Economic landscape has witnessed a profound transformation in the recent years. There is little doubt that The process of economic liberalization and globalization has been instrumental in promoting efficiency, new capital investment and faster economic growth in many nations. However, it has also led to a degree of competition, which was virtually non-existent in the earlier era of protectionism and planned development. It is now imperative for companies as well as global managers to understand what globalization is, the factors responsible for its rapid spread across nations and what it implies in terms of their business units to pursue global strategic goals and demanding that they act on a global mandate.

As a sequel to their transformation, the small industry sector has come into prominence. The small enterprise management

---

* *Associate Professor, Dept.* of Commerce and Management Studies, Andhra University, Visakhapatnam

has assumed greater importance in the post-liberalisation economy. The development of small-scale enterprises is generally believed to contribute substantially to employment creation and generation of income. Particularly for low-income population groups. In this context, management of over 35 lakh small enterprise units is of great significance and importance in the wake of emerging global competitive economy.

Small-scale sector with strong basics, is now caught up in winds of change, which are ushering in contemporary industrial culture, business ethics resplendent the enterprise of a new generation. Small-scale industry opened their frontiers by absorbing new technology to sharpen their artistic skills and deepening their creativity to be competitive in the global market.

SMALL ENTERPRISES IN INDIA

The present economic scenario in India has created an excellent climate of the development of small enterprises, although the Indian economy traditionally been agro-based, with a sizeable part of its GDP being contributed by agriculture, a notable contributor to the nations's GDP is from m the small-scale industrial sector, the village, cottage and small industrial units with a very low capital base dominated the SSI sector in the early years. With the increasing pressure of population, which has grown from 350 million in 1947 at the time of independence to over 985 million as on now, there has been a necessity for speedy industrialization of Indian economy so as to generate more and more leaving apart the large scale industries. The SSI sector needs to develop with greater commitment to create employment and to promote wealth maximization. In the post-liberalisation period, the focus has been on starting of new SSI and strengthening existing ones.

The paradigm shift in economy witnesses that the small-scale sector has remained a very active participation in Indian growth. To illustrate this,

- Over 95% of the total industrial units are in the small-scale sector numbering 2.7 millions
- SSIs have 15.3 million workforce, representing 80% of the total industrial workforce

- Over 40% of the turnover of the manufacturing sector comes from the SSIs, i.e. Rs.3,40,650 million out of Rs. 21,19,680 million.

POLICY INTERVENTIONS

The Government of India has always been highly supportive of the SSI sector. A large number of fiscal and other types of concessions/ incentives have been made available to this sector. Support policies have undergone several changes in tune with the liberalized national and international scenario. The major incentive include:

- Revision in ceiling on investment in plant and machinery in SSI units from 3.5 million to 6.0 million in 1991 and recently to Rs.10 million in December 1997. This is primarily intended to facilitate acquisition of better technologies on concessional terms.
- Large industries are permitted to invest in equity of SSIs up to 24%
- Indirect taxes and import levies have been significantly moderated. Import duties have been started down form 100% to as low as 5% on some inputs, as now.
- Capital goods/technology imports have been made easier.
- Indian investment in joint ventures abroad has been liberalized.
- SSI sector is exempt form payment of excise duties up to a turnover of Rs. 1 crore. Liberal policy of reservation and concession has been extended to this sector the sector can thrive and prosper.

The provisions available to large industries to take up equity up to 24% in SSI is a major step to participate in the equity of ancillaries and intermediate product manufacturing and bring to bear their technological and managerial capabilities on the running of such SSIs.

THE WINDS OF CHANGE

Currently, India has been undergoing sea changes which

will enable medium and large-scale industries and foreign concerns open to world markets which is happening in almost all developing countries. In the industrial and economic scenario, there are dynamic liberalization aimed at free market orientation and participation in the process of globalisation . The policy of integrating national and global economies has already started to show results by a spurt in foreign investment in Indian industries, the setting up of new joint ventures, etc., a new a era of growth has begun in the history of Indian industrial growth.

In the wake of deregulation, removal of some of the earlier protectionist measure and the opening up of an insulated economy to a competitive market, the small-scale industries would also face new challenges.

Globalisation has opened up opportunities which the SSI sector must seize to be globally competitive both in the terms of prince and quality. For this, they must improve upon he existing levels of technology, quality and market information. In future years, the country may open up further by allowing such imports, which are hitherto restricted to production by SSIs only. This means that competition in the domestic market and international market is going to become an inevitable challenge.

So far, the availability of protection and a large insatiable domestic market, fairly free of fierce competition have helped the growth of SSIs. There is, therefore, an apprehension, despite the government's assurance regarding the importance placed by it on the role of SSIs, whether there will be now a stunting or even cessation in the activities of the SSE sector.

I will not perhaps be factual I said that such apprehension will not come true. There will certainly be mortality in some of the units, a reduction in the speed of growth of a few more. The winds of change will, however, hurt mostly those which are inefficient, unprepared for the change and also not flexible enough to adopt their functioning to the change.

1. **Need for Strategic thinking**: as globalisation process gets incorporated into the Indian scene, industry has to reorient its production and marketing strategies. Strategies adopted

for marketing and development oaf marketing network will assume greater importance for SSI units due to impetus given to large enterprises to tap domestic and international markets. The use of foreign brand names and a wider market base, is the context of rapidly changing market conditions, will call for greater efforts on the part of small enterprises to remain competitive. Strategy is a game of the mind. It is the art of creating and designing route to desired business destinations on an uncertain, shifting and un-marked commercial map. It is strategic thinking involving a long-term vision that would enable the entrepreneur to foresee the emerging patterns and to plan a proper position for himself myopic enterprises often lapse into history, sooner or later. A mission for the enterprise has to be developed form the long-term vision. Detailed strategies would need to be evolved in pursuit of continued relevance in the changing market place.

2. **Focus on Core Competencies**: Core competency is an important factor often ignored. Companies have gone in for indiscriminate diversification into totally unrelated areas. This could have been due to the difficulties during the pre-liberalisation era for getting licenses, making the focus of management to obtain licenses in whatever areas are of interest to them. To urge for diversification is fast dying down and enterprises are now focusing on core competencies, when large industries have realized the futility of broadband operations, the SSIs would surely need to draw appropriate inferences and stick to areas of core competence. Certain concepts have undergone a quiet change. In materials, a machines or men. It is not capacity utilization but capability utilization. Production is not merely in volume but more in the assessment of value addition.

3. **Planning innovativeness:** Being innovative beings in the difference; and this difference gives a competitive edge to any unit. It is no longer possible to be competitive without being innovative. As change entails new products, new investment, new techniques, training and, above all, new risks, in most organization, there is resistance to change.

However, in the present context, change is inevitable. Therefore, plan for it with a long-term vision.

4. **Quality consciousness:** In the coming years only quality products will attract the buyers. Quality is the total concept. Industry has to ingrain this concept right from their rawmaterial sourcing to production of final goods, To be competitive is to be in a position to produce offerings of a firm at a better quality and lower price. Quality means not only conforming to specifications and standards; but it should be a habit. It reefers to productivity, competitive costs, timely delivery and total satisfaction of the consumer. Quality function in fact, is the technique to anticipate, identify and translate the expectation of the customer. Units must remember, excellence is not a goal, but a way of life.

5. **Technology Management:** Education is a vital element in the successful management of technology. For maximizing effectiveness, one needs to manage technology as an investment and not a mere cost. Appropriate mechanism to assess new and emerging technologies needs to be cultivated.

6. **Marketing Orientation:** The customer will be the king in the growth of the organization. Organizations, like those in Japan, which worked knowing this dictates, flourished. Quality, consistency, durability and service after sale at low price are the final expectation of a customer. The transition will be from the business philosophy of product-orientation to customer orientation. Manufacturing and delivery systems must be quick to meet the customer's needs, flexible enough to introduce new product range.

7. **Export Promotion:** Problems of export oriented SSI units need attention on priority basis. These include finance, technology up-gradation, raw materials, quality assurance, packaging, market intelligence, etc. the Government mechanism should be geared for this task. Industry associations should play a leading role in studying the requirements of member units and share the responsibilities with the governmental agencies. Consortiums of export units are being encouraged to assume greater

responsibilities. Participation in international exhibitions, gathering market intelligence and facilitating tie-up with importers in other countries will sped up the process. The merging thrust areas for exports are electronics, computer software, textiles, leather goods, food processing industries and a wide range of technology services. setting up of JVs ad collaborations in developing countries is a recent activity, which needs to be cased upon in view of the high potential.

8. **Role of Associations and Voluntary bodies:** Associations and voluntary bodies are being encouraged to take over responsibilities for setting up sub-contracting exchanges, entrepreneurship development institutes and other management training institutes, take initiative for developing quality consciousness among small-scale entrepreneurs and infuse the necessary enthusiasm to adopt energy saving, environmental assessment and audit, and pollution control directions for the larger interest of the industrial sector. They can also play an important role in setting up R&D centres, testing facilities and consortia marketing both domestically as well as for export. These associations or voluntary organizations can be motivated by the SSI promoting agencies in order to take up responsibility for co-ordinating and organizing training programmes for the benefit of small, tiny and micro enterprises.

9. **Mindset of the Entrepreneur:** It is the mindset of the entrepreneur, which is the most important of all. The entrepreneur must develop a mindset that would not allow his to rest unless he keeps pace with changes in the domain of the enterprises. When once mindset is cast, half the battle is won. A work of caution here is that the Generals alone do no win battles. They need support form the rank and file. If they all think in unison, the ultimate impact will be the highest.

Conclusion: The process of liberalization has given rise to several challenges to the SSI in India, but has also opened up vast opportunities. Many large-scale industries are reducing the number of vendors and laying down stringent quality standards. Many of these large industries buying supplies and components form SSI sector have talking of effective price cuts. By implication, unless the SSIs discard their conservatism and go for adopting themselves to the situation, their survival is at stake. It is only by adopting the best management practices, they can ensure survival and entry to global markets.

The need, therefore, for small industries, is to appreciate the changes as harbingers of new opportunities, and a redefinition in focus aimed specifically at industrial growth and widening of markets, hither to unexplored. Exports hold strategic potential not only for enhances sales and price but also for access to new technologies, strategic alliances even with competitors, interactions with different markets and cultures. These will help improvement in manufacturing process and also maturity in attitudes.

In the prevailing environment, small-scale sector is exposed to new challenges, risks and opportunities that have been alien to them in the past. The emerging forces for globalization, de-regulation and technology transfer as well as increasing and shifting demands of customers are changing the contours of small-scale industries, in the days to come, there will be considerable shift in the way entrepreneurs can perceive business opportunities. Opportunities that are likely to merge in the new environment can be categorized as follows:

1. Tie-ups for joint venture within and outside the sector
2. Growth in demand for differentiated products.
3. Access to new technology and process of manufacture based on flexible manufacturing system to serve the demand for differentiated products
4. Access to markets which are not homogenous and rapidly changing

Similarly the funding and resource patterns of small-scale industries will undergo a sea change with existing public sector financial institutions and banks moving towards privatisation and more private companies entering the field. With this, financial assistance schemes will become flexible, customer oriented and appraisal techniques will be modified to meet individual needs. This will have considerable impact on the traditional mode of project formation and planning for small enterprises.

To be ready to face challenges of liberalisation in SSI, the enterprise will need to strengthen in some directions. I shall discuss some of them are; they are not new ideas but certainly need greater emphasis in future years.

REFERENCES

1. Cook Paul and kirkpatrick C, Privatisation Policy and Performance: An ovcrview, Whatsheef,1988.
2. T.S. Papola, Report on Restructuring in Indian Industry, Planning Commission, Government of India, May 1996.
3. Corporate Restructuring Strategies: Strategies and Implications, All India Management Association, Excel Books, New Delhi, 1996.
4. S.S. Bhanmdare, Indian Industry in Post-Liberalisation Era: Some Critical Issues, Forum of Free Enterprise Booklet, Mumbai, August 2001.
5. P. Narayana Reddy (ed) Impact of Liberalization on Industries in India, CBIT, Hyderabad, Novemeber, 1999.
6. P. Narayana Reddy (ed), Challenges in Management, CBIT Publication, Hyderabad, November, 2000.

17

Development of SSI Sector in the Context of WTO: A Focus on Financial Implications

- S. Prabhakar Reddy*

The SSI is currently defined in terms of investment ceiling on the original value of the installed plant and machinery. Different segments of SSI are SSI undertakings. Ancillary Industrial Undertakings, Tiny Enterprises, Women Entrepreneurs enterprises, Small Scale (Industry related) Service and Business, Enterprises (SSSBEs) and Export Oriented Units (EOUs).

For determining the status of Small Scale Industrial Undertakings, the investment limit in Plant & Machinery has been reduced to Rs. 100 Lakhs from Rs. 300 lakhs with effect from 24.12.1999. However, units, which secured provisional registration as SSIs prior to 24.12.99, will enjoy the status of SSIs even though their investment in Plant & Machinery is over Rs. 100 lakhs but up to Rs. 300 lakhs. A unit is treated as Tiny Enterprise where investment in Plant and Machinery does not exceed Rs.25 lakhs irrespective of the location of the unit.

As per the survey, the SSI registered units had a predominance in food products followed by metal products, wood products, machinery parts and hosiery and garments this. Survey also indicated that 72.37% of total SSI enterprises are located in Rural areas and 27.63 % are located in Urban areas.

* *Deputy General Manager*, Andhra Bank Zonal Office, Visakhapatnam

Institutional Support Structure to SSI

Different National and State level institutions operating in the country for meeting the credit requirements of the SSI sector include Small Industrial Development Bank of India, Commercial Banks, Regional Rural Banks, Co-operative Banks, Development Financial Institutions, NABARD, NSIC, Statutory bodies like KVIC, KVIB, Coir Board etc. The range of assistance offered covers promotional measures, financing and extension support through appropriate schemes aimed at setting up of new projects and expansion, diversification and strengthening of the existing units.

Policy Initiatives

Some important policy decisions of various agencies towards the improvement of credit flow to SSI sector are detailed below:

1. Computation of working capital limits as 20% on projected turnover has been increased to Rs. 500 lakhs.
2. Delayed payment to SSI & Ancillary Industrial undertakings Act 1993 was amended in 1998 providing for the setting of "facilitation council" at the state level. Banks have been asked to ensure that form January 1998 onwards not less than 25% of the total inland credit purchases of the borrowers should be bills drawn by the seller concerned, including SSIs
3. More thrust is given for encouraging micro credit finance
4. The investment limit of SSI units has been reduced from Rs. 300 lakhs to Rs. 100 lakhs.
5. Women entrepreneurship needed to be encouraged by way of formulating special schemes and development of women enterprise clusters.
6. The reservation of items for exclusive manufacture by SSIs was formulated in order to ensure the bulk production of consumer goods in the SSI sector. As on February 1999, the total number of reserved items to SSI was 812.

WTO and its Implications on SSIs in India

World Trade organization came into existence in 1995 January. As the only regulatory body of world trade, WTO's objective is to ensure freer, more transparent and more predictable regime in the world. There is no economic activity in the world that will go unaffected by World Trade Organization. After the Uruguay Round of talks new agreements viz, General Agreement on Trade in Services (GATS) and Agreement on Trade Related Aspects of Intellectual Property Rights (TRIPS) have been added.

WTO Agreement cover

1) Goods	-	All Industrial Products, Consumer Durables.
2) Services	-	Banking, Insurance, Consultancy etc.
3) Intellectual Property	-	Patents, Copyrights, Trademarks.

General Implications of WTO

- WTO and its agreements have a great impact on every economic activity be it agriculture, trading, service or manufacturing.
- World markets are opening up due to lowering of tariff and dismantling of other restrictions in developed and developing countries. Enlightened entrepreneurs have greater opportunities to benefit form their comparative advantages.
- Domestic markets are increasingly exposed to threat because of lowering of tariff leading to freer entry of foreign goods and because of foreign companies establishing manufacturing bases locally.
- The developed countries will benefit by opening of service sector and tightening of intellectual property rights.

- Export markets will become tougher because of competition among developing countries having similar comparative advantages.
- Products from developing countries will face tougher quality standards in developed markets.
- The international trade is increasingly becoming knowledge based. The entrepreneurial ability will come to fore in the new environment.

Impact of WTO agreement on Indian Small Business

- Impact will be on entire gamut of trade in goods. Competition will intensify as more imported products find easy access. Around 75% of the products reserved for Small Industries are already in OGL rest to be allowed in due course. Removals of Quantitative Restrictions (QRs) set to further increase import of products form China, Korea, Thailand etc. countries.
- Only those industries whether producing for domestic or foreign markets, which have international vision will survive and grow.
- Indian exporters of electrical machinery, consumer articles, pharmaceuticals, detergents, automobiles, household electric/electronic gadgets, insecticides, chemicals, fertilizers, toys etc., will benefit as imports of these products are subject to mandatory product standards. However as agreement also covers PPM (Process and Production Methods), it could be used for discriminating against Indian exports for agri/food/phama products.
- Companies exporting fresh/processed fruit/vegetables, juices, meat, dairy products etc., should understand the mandatory standards as they have serious implications for their business in agri/processed foods and dairy products.
- Regarding subsidies, the agreement prohibits export subsidies but allows permissible subsidies. Developing

countries have to phase them out by 2003 and should freeze their level and coverage during transitional period.

- By 1st Jan 2000, developed countries cut tariffs by 40% developing countries by 30% in five equal installments which ahs resulted in massive increase in competition for domestic manufacturers.

In the context of changed business environment and the challenges offered by WTO and globalization there is a great role to the three key players in the economy viz. The Government and Policy Makers, Business Associations and the Business.

Indian businesses are under the impression that WTO and its agreements affect only those who are in international trade, importing or exporting something and do not affect those who are producing and selling domestically. This however is not true and the fact is that no business, none whatsoever operating in any field will remain unaffected by the WTO agreements.

The ability of business to benefit from the improved institutional frame work that has resulted form Uruguay Round will depend greatly on their knowledge of the trade rules and privileges, their awareness of the new opportunities for trade that have been created by different countries and the initiative thy show in bringing to the notice of their governments their problems *in selling so that Government can raise the issues at appropriate levels under WTO.*

With the advent of WTO the Scenario for SSI may change in the following respects

- More Industrial /Technology parks with all facilities for small industries will be established.
- Quality will be uppermost concern in customer-oriented economy and ISO 9000 and other standards need to be followed.
- Rapid Technological obsolensce exerts tremendous pressure on SSI to upgrade modify process technologies.

- Small units will be environments friendly and necessary certifications will have to be obtained.
- Access to global markets, tie-up with foreign partners for import of technology and buy-backs.
- Preferential treatment in allotment of infrastructure facilities, setting up of mini-insductrial units and cluster industries.
- Thrust on agro-industries , food processing industries, export promotion industries and high technology industries
- Greater weightage to tiny units will continue
- Co-operative arrangements between units manufacturing the same products will consolidate.
- Making available integrated (composite) term loan for higher amounts on preferential terms.
- Collateral guarantee form institutions will boost the establishment of tiny units.
- Credit rating institutions will play a prominent role in acting as intermediaries and arranging loans etc.

The Outlook

- For SSIs the globalization of economic activities has two interfaces. For some, the process opens new opportunities to expand and grow, for others a much larger group. The process poses a threat from abroad.
- In view of emerging WTO regime and a high level reservation redundancy, there may be a need to reconsider orienting of the existing Government Policies so as to achieve a phased dereservation of 812 reserved items.
- To curtail the bureaucratic intervention and number of inspections, various measures have been taken in the recent past. It was, however, suggested by the industry associations to simplify the procedures further,

- Stamp duty and registration charges leviable on instruments of mortgage need to be rationalized, so as to make innovative financial instruments viable and catalytic in the flow of credit to the SSI sector.
- At present, the SSI units are required to pay tax at regular intervals, at times in advance, which strains their cash flow. In this direction, rationalization of tax structure on the lines of a three tier bases 1) Federal Tax, 2) State Tax and 3) Local Tax as prevalent in some overseas economics be considered.
- In view of the increasing need for funds by the SSI sector, it has been suggested that RBI may consider advising banks to deploy at least 25 per cent of their Net Bank Credit to the SSI sector.
- The capacity building for SSI sector in terms of infrastrucural facilities, availability of raw material, R&D. Development of human skills, dissemination of information and formation of industry clusters need to be developed to take advantage of new opportunities.
- The Government might encourage the setting up of private industrial estates so that there is an element of competition in providing industrial infrastructure services.
- During the phase of transition the development process, different sectors of the economy need a steadily increasing level of technology (in products and processes), a high degree of research and development, coordination between research laboratories and the user groups, quality standardization.
- To encourage Research and Development in the SSI sector, provision of suitable fiscal incentives could be considered. It has been suggested that a "Renewal/ Upgradation of Technology Fund for SSI Units" be created and the contribution made by the units out of their profits be exempted from income tax.
- There are number of entrepreneurship development institutes set up both by the Government and the Non-

Government sector for the development of human skills. While the existing set of institutes has been helpful in creating a pool of technically qualified persons and in upgrading the skills of human resources, there is, however need to establish additional facilities in the light of changes emerging in the technology and managerial arena.

- To enable the SSI entrepreneurs in facing the emerging challenges, there is a need for creating awareness about the implications of WTO and educating entrepreneurs suitably.
- It may be desirable to conduct product-wise market research on the implications of WTO and other related aspects. The out come of such studies could be made available to Industry Associations/Entrepreneurs for wider market understanding and use by the members and SSIs at large.

State-wise Estimates of SSI Units, Employment and Fixed Investment

States/UTs	*No. of Units ('000)*	*Employ-ment ('000)*	*Fixed Investment (Rs.million)*	*Employ-ment Per unit*	*Investmt. per unit* (Rs.'000)
Andhra Pradesh	132.79	837.21	16,935	6.3	127
Arunachal Pradesh	4.60	20.66	7,406	5.0	161
Assam	29.83	146.22	14,821	4.9	497
Bihar	291.17	473.63	8,105	1.6	61
Delhi	130.22	1,171.96	26,040	9.0	200
Goa	5.76	39.43	2,191	6.8	380
Gujarat	156.73	862.93	55,119	5.5	352
Haryana	89.50	504.14	15,182	5.6	170
Himachal Pradesh	27.25	114.49	5,643	4.2	207
Jammu & Kashmir	26.10	113.22	NA	4.3	NA
Karnataka	208.58	1,017.20	38,512	4.9	185
Kerala	177.38	819.28	26,303	4.6	148

(Contd...)

Madhya Pradesh	286.43	675.87	13,509	2.4	47
Maharashtra	234.94	1,562.60	2,26,016	6.7	962
Manipur	6.09	30.28	375	5.0	62
Meghalaya	3.27	18.59	247	5.7	75
Mizoram	3.90	23.46	580	6.0	149
Nagaland	0.78	3.90	NA	5.0	NA
Orissa	32.44	214.07	8,702	6.6	268
Punjab	197.34	854.00	34,050	4.3	173
Pondicherry	4.28	34.74	2,257	8.1	527
Rajasthan	94.26	402.87	24,390	4.3	259
Sikkim	0.30	2.90	161	9.7	542
Tamil Nadu	324.63	2,921.64	77,910	9.0	240
Tripura	2.01	9.11	145	4.5	72
Uttar Pradesh	357.96	1,469.18	34,880	4.1	97
West Bengal	167.13	614.64	NA	3.7	NA
A and N Island	1.05	4.51	79	4.0	75
Chandigarh	2.96	28.30	8,247	9.6	2,786
Dadra &Nagar Haveli	0.87	11.65	1,530	13.4	1,758
Daman & Diu	1.46	24.38	NA	16.7	NA
Lakshwadeep	0.12	0.52	9	4.2	75

SECTION - III

DIC and Small Industry Development

The Genesis, Scope and Functions

Healthy expansion of SSI sector was deterred by factors such as improper supply of raw materials, absence of technical advise, lack of organised marketing of the products and inability to make best use of export opportunities. Funding agencies were reluctant to provide the required credit facility at the right time to small units in rural areas. Lack of technical sophistication to manufacture high quality products, inadequate research and development effort, underutilisation of capacity due to proliferation of units in the same industry and heavy burden of local taxes also retarded the progress and affected the efficiency of small units. The institutional framework for rendering technical and managerial counseling for SSIs did not come forth at the right time and right quality and quantity due to operational problem of these institutions. This had made the Govt. to consider the need for establishing a new agency with limited operational area, which can render a variety of services, needed by the SSI sector under one roof. This idea has materialised in 1978 when the Govt. of India has decided to establish District Industry Centres (DIC) to provide all the services and support required by small and village entrepreneurs.

With the establishment of DICs, the long cherished idea of making district a focal point of industrial planning and development was crystallised. The DICs are considered as an institutional innovation to assist small industrial units at three important stages viz. Pre-investment, investment and post-investment stages. They are also considered as a single-window of clearance for industrial units. They will perform a variety of functions such as economic investigation of the districts' raw materials and other resources, supply of machinery and equipment, provision of raw material, arrangement of credit facilities, taking effective step for marketing and a cell for quality control, research and extension.

Objectives: The DICs are established to fulfill the following specific objectives.

1. To create more employment opportunities to the rural unemployed youth.
2. To reduce the regional imbalances and to increase industrialisation.
3. To bring down the concentration of economic power and economic inequalities and
4. To step up the people's standard of living.

The objective of DIC have been setout conforming to the plan objectives of establishing socialistic pattern of society. Ensuring social and economic equality to all sections of society and providing employment to all able bodied men and women formed the basic philosophy of economic planning. Industrial policy has its roots in the overall economic policy envisaged.

Functions: For achieving growth and development in the industrial economy of a district through the specific objectives as mentioned above, the functions of the DIC are classified into developmental and regulatory which are given here.

1. To survey existing, traditional and new industries, and raw materials and human resources; to identify schemes and make market forecasts for different items; to prepare sample techno-economic feasibility reports and offer investment advice to entrepreneurs;
2. To assess the machinery and equipment requirements of small-scale, tiny and village industries; indicate the locations where machinery and equipment for different plants may be available for entrepreneurs, to liaison

with research institutions and arrange for the supply of machinery on hire purchase basis;

3. To arrange for training of entrepreneurs of small and tiny units and liaison with small industries service institute, small industrial extension training institute and other institutions, to keep abreast of research and development in selected product lines and quality control methods;
4. To ascertain the raw material requirements of various units, their sources and prices and to arrange for their bulk purchases and distribution to entrepreneurs;
5. To liaison with lead banks and other financial institutions, appraise applications, monitor the flow of industrial credit in the district, and arrange for financial assistance to entrepreneurs;
6. To organise marketing outlets, to liaison with government procurement agencies, convey market intelligence to entrepreneurs, organise market surveys and market development programmes;
7. To give particular attention to the development of Khadi and Village and other cottage industries, to liaison with State Khadi and Village Industries Board and organise training programmes for rural artisans;
8. To provide immediate aid required by entrepreneurs in respect of power supply, licences required under municipal and health departments and Factories Act for establishment of industries;
9. To assist entrepreneurs in allotment of worksheds or sites required for establishment of industries in industrial estates;
10. To help in arranging loans to educated unemployed belonging to scheduled castes, scheduled tribes and socially or economically backward communities for starting industries under special employment schemes;
11. To help in extending suitable technical training to rural youth to pursue self-employment schemes;

12. To assist in arranging grant of central and state government concessions and interest free sales tax loans, to provide capital for purchase of plant and machinery, construction of buildings and allotment of sites to new industrialists;

Originally the DICs had discharged these functions. As the DICs found it very difficult to carryout various activities in view of their large and pervasive nature, the Government redesigned the functions of DICs

Announcing the Industrial Policy Statement of 1977 Mr. George Fernandes, the then Union Minister of Industries made the following statement in the Parliament.

"That in each district there will be one agency to deal with all the requirements of small and village industries. This will be called **District Industries Centre (DIC).** Under the single roof of DIC, all the services and support required by small and village entrepreneurs will be provided. These will include economic investigation of the district's raw materials and other resources, supply of machinery and equipment, provision of raw materials, arrangement for credit facilities, an effective step for marketing and a cell for quality control, research and extension".

The DIC, therefore, is expected to provide all the services and facilities to entrepreneurs under a single roof for setting up small and village industries. Looking at the objectives of DICs there are three important functions which the DICs could discharge profitably.

DICs should act as a data bank, an information bank and a dissemination centre, for giving prompt up-to-date and reliable information to anybody trying to set up a small-scale unit and the information would not only be with regard to licensing procedures but also about what is in the realm of feasibility and what is not.

Another area is regulatory work of registration, deregistration, monitoring and utilisation of credit, raw materials, processing of cases regarding supply of machinery on hire purchase, marketing assistance, etc.

The third aspect in which the DICs can play an effective

role is with regard to interlinkages with different institutions such as electricity department, department of water works, municipality/ panchayat, town planning, commercial banks, etc. The DICs should function in close coordination with all agencies related to industrial development at the district level. To ensure this there should be a single line of command operating from the DIC for the entire field staff connected with industrial promotion activities and diffusion of direction and responsibility should be avoided to enable DICs adopt a result-oriented approach.

The DIC programme made rapid progress soon after its introduction by the Central Government. The state governments were quick in responding to the centre's initiative and established DICs in a number of districts quite fast.

The trust of the small-scale and cottage industries was shifted from the big cities and State capitals to the district head-quarters. In each district, it was proposed to have a single agency to deal with all the requirements of small and village industries. This agency was called 'District Industrioo Contre' (DIC). Undor the single roof of the DIC, all the services, facilities and support required by the small and village entrepreneurs were provided. The DIC is now regarded as a 'mini-secretariat' at the district level with the authority to provide all the inputs to rural entrepreneurs. In other words, it seeks to take the administration to the district level, and not force the entrepreneurs to run to the State capital.

Organisational Structure of DIC

Each DIC is headed by one General Manager (G.M); who is responsible for the overall coordination and development of small-scale industries including village industries in the district, and ensure the implementation of action plans drawn up for promoting and developing small-scale, cottage and village industries in the district. The GM is the kingpin of the DIC programme. He has to provide leadership to the team operating under him. He should be an effective instrument in initiating the massive programme of rural industrialisation; identification of growth centres in the district.

The GM is assisted by four Functional Managers. They look after four disciplines viz. 1) Economic Investigation-Information & Infrastructure (EI & II), 2) Credit, 3) Raw Materials & Marketing, 4) Village Industries & Training (VI&T). They are to be assisted by three project managers and a number of extension officers.

The functional managers should be of proven ability and experience, having qualities of leadership, organisational ability and executive capability. They should have sufficient experience in executing industrial development programmes. They should be able to find solutions to all the administrative, financial and other possible bottlenecks.

Inferface with other Agencies (Chart Enclosed)

The chart briefly explains the various types of assistance required by small industrial units at the pre-investment, investment and post-investment stages, the role of the various central, state and district level agencies associated with the development of small industry and the linkage between DIC with the above agencies.

The DICs have not been able to fully fulfil the objectives with which they has been established. Their functioning has been a subject of criticism reasons is manifold. The DIC have been beset with with a number of problems and issues that have impeded their effective functioning. Any research, workshop, or seminar on DICs needs to address various issues that are listed below:

- The DIC's are supposed to interact and coordinate a large number of other industry promoting agencies such as KVIB, Handicrafts Development Corporation, DRDA, SETVIS, CMEY, SERSIB, etc. It has been observed that the DIC's have not been able to render the needed expertise. As a result, the village and tiny sector progress to the level and degree as anticipated.
- It is feared that the functionaries of DIC's and other industry promoting agencies as mentioned above have not been fully realized mission of speedy

industrialization of rural India and large-scale promotion of village and cottage industries has remained as an unfinished agenda.

- The single window system introduced with a view to reduce the burden of entrepreneurs and expedite the process of sanctioning the projects and DIC to act as an effective nexus and institutions at District level and failed miserably. The entrepreneur's woes have remained perennial. The multiple window system has been in practice despite the governmental efforts to replace it with single window system, its feasibility and practicability be reviewed.
- Co-ordination is lacking between DIC's and the funding agencies like commercial banks, APSFC, SIDBI, etc. Projects recommended by the DIC for financial assistance have been abnormally delayed and rejected due to some reason or other and consequently the entrepreneurs are frustrated and demotivated.
- The promoting agencies, especially DIC's are required to identify the project keeping in view the resource potential of the region, the market potential of the product and the competitive environment. Sometimes all the three factors are not paid required attention. The entrepreneurs are also not able to get the timely counseling and guidance.
- There is haphazard growth of industries without regard to the backwardness of the region or mandal. Dispersal of industries, and backward area development, which is one of the principal objectives of DIC's, has not been achieved.
- The R&D facilities required by the SSI units are neither created nor provided. The necessary technical and managerial assistance provided by the DIC's is observed to be very limited. The DIC functionaries are engrossed totally in several unrelated tasks and assignments. Much of the valuable time and energies of the personnel is consumed in discharging other duties for which they are not primarily meant for.

- The major functionaries of DIC's are not given an opportunity to updatetheir knowledge and skills with regard to changing business environment, modern technology and its adaptability and knowledge about success stories of small enterprises in various countries etc. Needless to say, the DIC functionaries need to acquire professional capabilities and managerial skills, and strategies to increase effectiveness and efficiency of DIC's.
- The functionaries of DIC's are not given necessary training inputs in the technical, managerial and entrepreneurial lines on a continuous basis. They are supposed to be mentors, trainers of the entrepreneurs. The style of functioning of DIC's, its work culture and ethos has got to be reoriented towards entrepreneur-centered and enterprise-centered.
- DIC's are often criticized on the grounds of red-tapism, favoritism and bureaucratic approach.
- The DIC's are supposed to impart training of potential and existing entrepreneurs in different aspects of entrepreneurship and enterprise development. DIC's have not been able to perform this function effectively, which might be attributable to reasons such as:
  (i) The personnel in DIC's are saddled with multiple responsibilities;
  (ii) Non-availability of competent trainers;
  (iii) Lack of suitable modern infrastructure;
  (iv) Lack of adequate resources;
- Effective and efficient functioning of DIC's is a function of the information resource base created by these centers. Data and information regarding the resource potential of the District as a whole and its mandals, availability of manpower and their skills, market information and intelligence, general business environment, etc are vital and the DIC's have not been able to create database and act as a potential information source to entrepreneurs.

- Use and benefits of modern information technology at various levels and by various functionaries is yet to be explored to improve productivity.
- Not infrequently the potential entrepreneurs raise their hue and cry against DIC's for not being able to get their project cleared at the earliest which is not due to DIC's ineffectiveness but due to the impediments created by other agencies who are also a party to clear the project. The matter of the fact is that apart from DIC's, other agencies connected with the project clearance are observed to have been bound by their own norms and guidelines that often become impediments in the speedy clearance of the projects ultimately by the DIC's. As a result, most of the time DIC's are becoming scapegoats.
- Though the objective of all the promoting agencies is one, which being promotion of industries, with a collective effort, every agency is guided by its own norms and procodures which are tantamounting to conflicting views and interpretations and dampening the spirit of the entrepreneurs as well as the DIC functionaries. How to overcome this paradox is a serious concern.
- Restructuring of the organization and redesigning of roles of various functionaries is imperative in the light of issues identified and to make these centers suitably respond to the challenges posed to the changing industry and business scenario. Functional and professional autonomy of DIC's coupled with the necessary powers and accountability also constitutes crucial matters that deserve the attention of the Policy makers, association of SSI's, Entrepreneurs and academicians.
- The study conducted by IIM-Ahmedabad observed that none of the DICs even had all the seven functional managers and none even had any project manager recommended by the review committee. It further observed that no attention was paid to the qualifications and experience of managers.

- Although the DICs have been promoting industrial units, they are not monitoring the progress and performance of the units nurtured by them. Periodic review of the performance of the units by the DIC would have rescued the units from becoming sick. This dimension deserves the attention of all those concerned with the SSI sector.
- Less focus is given for human resource development. Adequate investment in human resource development is not made in order to prepare and sharpen the DICs' manpower to confidently accept challenge in the changing techno-economic and business environment.
- It is no exaggeration to mention that the Documentation Centres of the majority of the DIC's are not worth mentioning from the standpoint of acquisition of latest literature, updating the project profiles, developing and updating database and networking.
- Though the DICs have clear objectives, they don't have vision strategy for entrepreneurship development and industrialization. There is no perspective plan with regard to new industries to be promoted based on the district resource potential surveys from time to time, market demand surveys and environmental and locational aspects of backward areas in the district. As such the DIC's could not establish themselves as potential centers for entrepreneurship development and effective institutions to accelerate the pace of the industrialization of the district.
- In view of the challenges posed by the liberalization and privatization, the SSI sector needs to be made more competitive both in the domestic and international markets. The DIC's, being focal centers, are required to reorient themselves with appropriate strategies and structure to make the SSI sector more vibrant in the contemporary global economic scenario.

REFERENCES

Rao, T.V., *Development of Small Scale Industries: Role of DICs*, Anmol Publications Pvt. Ltd., New Delhi, 1995.

Elizabeth Martin, *Management for the Smaller Company*, D.B.Taraporevala Sons & Co. Pvt. Ltd, Bombay, 1979

Uma Kapila (Ed), *Indian Economy Since Independence*, Academic Foundation Publishing, Ghaziabad, 2000.

18

Impact of District Industries Centres on Rural Industrialization

* Prof. L. Venugopala Reddy, ** Prof. P.B. Appa Rao &
*** Dr. T. Suresh Kumar

In a developing country like India with its large population in villages it is in all reality, a herculean task to provide full employment to its citizens without undertaking industrial decentralization on a wide scale on the country side. This is possible as Gandhiji said, only through the establishment of small-scale, cottage and village industries. It is regrettable that Indian planning based on materialistic socialism rather than on Gandhiji's ideas of economic development, failed to solve the problem of poverty and unemployment. In this paper the 'Impact of the District Industries Centres on Rural Industrialization' has been discussed on the basis of the secondary data. For this purpose ten-year period commencing from 1986-87 has been selected.

1. Rural Industries Projects Programme (RIIP)

Though emphasis on promotion of rural industries was a part of the framework of the planning in India from the very

* Professor Sri Krishnadevaraya Institute of Management, Sri Krishnadevaraya University, Anantapur.

** Professor, Department of Commerce, Sri Krishnadevaraya University, Anantapur.

*** Lecturer in Commerce, Govt. Degree College, Dharmavaram, Anantapur.

beginning, the real effective step was taken in 1962 when the Rural Industries Projects Programme (RIIP) was launched to foster the rural crafts and to hasten the small-scale industries in rural areas. The project was envisaged as a package programme with the objectives of:

(i) providing necessary inputs to the small-scale units and to the artisans,

(ii) guiding them in getting scarce raw materials and in marketing their products,

(iii) counseling them and giving information relating to different schemes, and

(iv) assisting them in securing necessary financial assistance from the State Government and financial institutions. By the year 1977-78, 112 districts in 22 States and 6 Union Territories were covered by RIIP, out of which 92 Districts were industrially backward. During the period (1962-1978) 2,15,100 industrial units were established under RIP Programme with a fixed capital of Rs.24,471 crores and working capital of Rs.187.27 crores. In view of the policy of further expanding the rural industrialization it is proposed to extend the RIP Programme so as to cover the entire country and RIPs were converted into District Industries Centres in 1978.

District Industries Centres (DICs)

District Industries Centres were set up in December 1978 in pursuance of the New Industrial Policy statement issued by the Government of India in 1977. The main thrust of the District Industries Centres was on the development of industrial units, which create employment opportunities in rural and semi-urban areas with an objective of single window delivery of the various inputs required for industrial promotion, growth and development. Prior to this, the entrepreneur had to approach several agencies in order to get these facilities. The chief objectives of District Industries Centres are:

(i) To provide the required technical, managerial, financial and other types of guidance and counsel and help them in obtaining the necessary raw materials, marketing facilities and other inputs required for setting up and developing industrial units.

(ii) To help them in procuring the required licenses, permits, incentives, subsidies, etc., that are offered by departments of Central and State Governments.

2. Industrial Development of the District through the District Industries Centre is Measured Through

(i) the number of units established or set up,

(ii) employment generated,

(iii) financial assistance provided,

(iv) the number of rural artisans assisted, and

(v) the number of rural artisans trained.

When all the above are achieved through the District Industries Centre, it comes under achievement of industrialization/rural industrialization through the District Industries Centre.

The first three aspects, i.e., (I) the number of units established or set up, (ii) employment generated and (iii) financial assistance provided are concerned with both urban and rural industrialization. The last two factors, i.e., (i) the number of rural artisans assisted, and (ii) the number of rural artisans trained are concerned with only rural industrialization. The effort of the District Industries Centres is not confined exclusively to rural industrialization.

The last three aspects, i.e., (I) financial assistance provided, (ii) the number of rural artisans assisted, and (iii) the number of rural artisans trained in District Industries Centres indicate the 'effort' of the District Industries Centre. The first two aspects, i.e., (I) the number of units established or set up, (ii) employment generated in DICs indicate the 'result' of the effort put in by the District Industries Centre.

3.1. Promotion of the New Units

The District Industries Centre has actively engaged in providing various types of assistance, particularly to the cottage, small-scale and village industries. During the period 1988-89 to 1997-98, 5,948 small-scale and tiny units have been set up in Anantapur district with the help of District Industries Centre, as against a target of 5,598, thus establishing a record of 106 per cent achievement. The target was not achieved in 1993-94 and 1994-95 as the percentage of achievement being 99.6 per cent and 99 per cent respectively. The data further reveals that the percentage of achievement was 111 per cent in 1988-89 and 135 per cent in 1997-98. It may be due to concerted efforts put in by the District Industries Centre in promoting rural industries (Table 1).

3.2. Employment Generated

The employment generated through the setting up of industrial units in the District during 1988-89 to 1997-98 (presumably due to the efforts of the District Industries Centre) was for 54,316 persons. Table 1 shows year-wise break up of targeted employment generation and actual employment generation. In eight out of 11 years the achievement was either 100 or more than cent per cent. In the other three years the achievement was less than 100 per cent. In 1994-95 the achievement was substantially low. The percentage of achievement in that year was only 30 per cent. The next lowest level of achievement, as far as employment was concerned, was 53 per cent in 1995-96. The reasons are not known.

3.3. Credit Assistance

One of the functions of the District Industries Centre is to arrange for credit to the entrepreneurs from commercial banks and other financial institutions. Performance of the District Industries Centre in this regard during the period under study was remarkable, as it was three times more than of the target. Except in 1994-95 achievement exceeded the target. The total financial assistance sanctioned was Rs.932.206 thousands as against a target of Rs.582.892 thousands, thereby resulting in 160 per cent achievement (Table 1).

3.4. Artisans Assisted

The District Industries Centre officials identify village artisans like carpenters, blacksmiths, potters, basket –makers etc., and recommend them to different commercial banks for sanctioning loans required for the purchase of tools, implements and raw materials, so that the earning capacity of artisans increases. During the period under study 38,245 artisans were assisted as against a target of 30,313. Similar to the case of number of units set up, credit sanctioned, and employment generated, achievement in respect of the number of artisans assisted too exceeded the target (Table 1).

3.5. Rural Artisans Trained

During the period (i.e., 1988-89 to 1997-98), the District Industries Centre, Anantapur thought of giving training to 11,467 rural artisans but actually trained 13,163 artisans. The achievement exceeded the target by 15 per cent (Table 1).

3.6. Small and Tiny Unit Set up in the District and Caste Category of the entrepreneurs (Year-wise)

During the ten years period (1988-1998) small and tiny units have been set up. Of them, 6.55 per cent of the units have been set up by SC entrepreneurs and 0.48 per cent of the units have been set up by ST entrepreneurs. BC entrepreneurs have been set up 28.5 per cent of the units. As many as 64.4 per cent of the units have been set up by OC entrepreneurs. From this it can concluded that in spite of variety of incentives provided, very less number of SCs and STs are starting the small and tiny units. Efforts to develop entrepreneurship among SCs and STs have been continued and further intensified. The possibility of developing entrepreneurship among SCs and STs depends upon social, economic and educational factors.

Out of 5,618 small tiny units set up during the ten years period 368 (6.55 per cent) units have been set up by SC entrepreneurs. On an average they have set up average number of units set up by the SC entrepreneurs per annum is 36.8 units. In terms of percentage, small and tiny units set up by SC entrepreneurs varied between 1.3 and 24.45. In 1990-91 and 1991-92 unusually more than 20 per cent units have been set up by SC entrepreneurs. The reasons are not known.

The number of units set up by ST entrepreneurs in different years never exceeded 1 per cent except in 1993-94. From this it can be understood that entrepreneurial activity among STs very poor.

In three out of ten years, the percentage of small and tiny units set up in the district by BC entrepreneurs is less than 25 per cent. In other seven years under consideration BC entrepreneurs have been set up the units. On the whole, during the ten years period under the consideration 28.53 per cent of the units have been set up by the BC entrepreneurs in the district. Hence, it can be assumed that participation of the backward community people in the entrepreneurial activity has been satisfactory.

On the whole, during the ten years period 64.44 per cent of the units have been set up by the OC entrepreneurs. The percentage of the units set up by the OC entrepreneurs varied between 58.32 in 1990-91 and 73.31 in 1993-94.

Number of units set up in different years during the ten years period showed an increasing trend (Table 2).

4. Number of Small and Tiny Units Set up in the District

Number of small and tiny units set up in the district during 1988-98 has been given in Table 3. Average number of the units set up per annum, in the district, during the ten years period was 562.3. Of the 5,623 units 3,412 (60.68 per cent) units were set up in rural areas thus working out an average of 3,412 units per annum. This is more than the average number of units (2211 units) set up in the urban areas of the District during the same period.

Coefficient of correlation between the number of units set up in rural and urban areas is 0.8059. That means that there is a positive significant correlation between the number of units set up in rural and urban areas in the district.

Under growth rate of the units set up in the rural areas is 18.34. It is less when compared to linear growth rate of the units set up in the urban areas (22.56). That means though the average number of units set up in rural areas per annum is more than the average number of units set up per annum in urban areas of the district, the number of the units set up in the rural areas during the period increased at a lesser rate than the number of units set up in the urban areas.

4.1. Number of Agro-based Small and Tiny Units Set up in the District

Number of agro-based small and tiny units set up in the district during 1988-98 has been given in Table 4. Average number of agro-based units set up in the district during the ten years period was 116.5 per annum. Of the 1,165 agro-based units set up in the district during the period 951 (81.63 per cent) units were set up in the rural areas thus working out an average of 95.1 units per annum. This is more than the average number of units (21.4 units) set up in the urban areas of the district during the same period.

Coefficient of correlation between the number of agro-based units set up in the rural and urban areas is 0.1475. that means there is a positive insignificant correlation between the number of units set up in rural and urban areas in the district.

Linear growth rate of the agro-based units set up in rural areas is 2.21. It is more when compared to linear growth rate of the agro-based units set up in urban areas (-0.38). Linear growth rate of the agro-based units set up in urban areas (-0.38) is negative thus recording a negative growth. Average number of units set up in rural areas per annum is more than the average number of units set up in urban areas per annum in the district. The growth rates are very less when compared to the growth rates of all the small and tiny units set up in the district during the period. It can be taken as an indication of very low importance accorded by the District Industries Centre to the growth of agro-based units in the district. Because of affinity, which agro-based industry has with the rural areas the number of agro-based units set up in the rural areas during the period might have been more than the number of units set up in the urban areas.

4.2. Number of Chemical-based Small and tiny Units Set up in the District

Number of chemical-based small and tiny units set up in the district during 1988-98 has been given in Table 5. Average number of chemical-based small and tiny units set up in the district during the ten years period under consideration was 13.8 per annum. Of the total 138 chemical-based small and tiny units set up in the district during the period, 68 (49.28 per cent) units were set up in the rural areas itself. It works out to be 6.8 units per annum. This is less than the average number of units (7.0 units) set up in the rural areas of the district during the same period.

Coefficient of correlation between the number of chemical-based small and tiny units set up in rural and urban areas in the district during the ten years period is 0.3717. That means there is a positive insignificant correlation between the number of units set up in rural and urban areas in the district during the period under consideration.

Linear growth rate of the chemical-based small and tiny units set up in rural areas is 052. It is less than the linear growth rate of the chemical-based small and tiny units set up in urban areas (0.75). That means average number of the units set up in rural areas per annum is less than the average number of units set up in urban areas per annum in the district during the ten years period under consideration. The growth rates are very less when compared to the growth rates of all the small and tiny units that have been set up in the district during the period. From this it can be said that chemical units have got urban affinity.

4.3. Number of Small and tiny Engineering Units Setup in the District

Table 6 shows the number of small and tiny engineering units set up in the district during the ten years period commencing from 1988-89 to 1997-98. Average number of engineering small and tiny units set up in the district during the ten years period under consideration was 138.3 per annum. Of the total 1,383 engineering small and tiny units set up in the district during the period, 673 (48.66 per cent) untis were set up in the rural areas itself. It works out to be 67.3 units per annum. This is less than the average number of units (71.0 units) set up in the urban areas of the district during the same period.

Coefficient of correlation between the number of engineering small and tiny units set up in rural and urban areas in the district during the ten years period is 0.8728. That means there is a positive significant correlation between the number of units set up in rural and urban areas in the district during the period under consideration. Though the engineering units in both rural and urban areas increased, in the urban areas they have increased slightly at a higher rate. This may be due to widespread market in the urban areas.

Linear growth rate of the engineering small and tiny units set up in rural areas is 7.74. It is slightly less than the linear growth rate of the engineering small and tiny units set up in urban areas (8.95). That means average number of the units set up in rural areas per annum is less than the average number of units set up in urban areas per annum in the district during the period under consideration. The growth rates are higher when compared to the growth rates of all the small and tiny chemical units set up in the district during the period. Many of the engineering units are service industrial units.

Linear growth rate of the engineering small and tiny units set up in urban areas (8.95). That means average number of the units set up in rural areas per annum is less than the average number of units set up in urban areas per annum in the district during the period under consideration. The growth rates are higher when compared to the growth rates of all the small and tiny chemical units set up in the district during the period. Many of the engineering units are service industrial units.

4.4. Number of Forest-based Small and Tiny Units Set up in the District

Table – 7 shows the number of forest-based units set up in the district during the ten years period commencing from 1997-98. Average number of forest-based small and tiny units set up in the district during the ten years period under consideration was 22.8 per annum. Of the total 228 forest-based small and tiny units set up in the district during the period. 117 (51.32 per cent) units were set up in the rural areas itself. It works out to be 117 units per annum. This is more than the average number of units (11.1 units) set up in the urban areas of the district during the same period.

Coefficient of correlation between the number of forest-based small and tiny units set up in rural and urban areas in the district during the ten years period is 0.3687. that means there is a positive correlation between the number of units set up in rural and urban areas in the district during the period under consideration. But the correlation is not to be considered as significant. Though the forest-based units in both rural and urban areas increased. In the rural areas they have increased slightly at a higher rate. This may be because of traditional nature of the industry and localized weight losing raw material.

Linear growth rate of the forest-based small and tiny units set up in rural areas is 0.88. It is slightly more than linear growth rate of the forest-based small and tiny units set up in urban areas (0.52). That means average number of the units set up in urban areas per annum in the district during the period under consideration. The growth rates are lower when compared to the growth rates of all the small and tiny chemical units set up in the district during the period. Many of the forest-based units are timber depots.

4.6. Number of Livestock-based Small and Tiny Units Set up in the District

Table – 8 shows the number of livestock-based small and tiny units set up in the district during the ten years period commencing from 1988-89 to 1997-98. Total number of livestock-based small and tiny units set up in the district during the period was only 46. Average number of livestock-based small and tiny units set up in the district during the ten year period under consideration was 4.6 per annum. Of them 27 (58.70) units were set up in the rural areas. It works out to be 2.7 units per annum. This is more than the average number of units (1.9 units) set up in the urban areas of the district during the same period.

Coefficient of correlation between the number of livestock-based small and tiny industrial units set up in rural and urban areas in the district during the ten years period is –0.0625. That means correlation between the two is negative and weak. Of all the types of the units about which so far discussed, it is the first type of industry in which there is negative correlation between the units set up in rural and urban areas of the district. Though the livestock-based units in rural areas increased from two in 1988-89 to live in 1997-98 the livestock-based units set up in the urban areas decreased from four in 1988-89 to three in 1997-98. This may be because of traditional nature of the industry.

Linear growth rate of the livestock-based small and tiny livestock-based small and tiny units set up 0.02. It is slightly more than the linear growth rate of the livestock-based small and tiny units set up in urban areas (-0.04). That means average number of the units set up in rural areas per annum is more than the average number of units set up in urban areas per annum in the district during the period under consideration. The growth rates are lower when compared to the growth rates of all other types of small and tiny units set up in the district during the period. Many of the livestock-based units are kambal (woolen blanket) weaving units, which are traditional in nature.

4.7. Number of Small and Tiny Mineral-based Units Set up in the District

Table – 9 shows the number of small and tiny mineral-based units set up in the district during the ten years period commencing from 1988-89 to 1997-98. Average number of mineral-based small and tiny units in the ten years period under consideration was 71.6 per annum. Of the total 716 mineral-based small and tiny units set up in the district during the period 640 (89.39 per cent) units were wet up in the rural areas itself. It works out to be 64 units per annum. This is more than the average number of units (7.6 per cent) set up in the urban areas of the district during the same period.

Co-efficient of correlation between the number of mineral-based small and tiny units setup in the rural and urban areas in the District during the ten years period is –0.4562. That means there is a negative correlationbetween the number of the units setup in the rural and urban areas in the District during the period under consideration. Though the mineral-based units in the rural areas increased from 77 in 1988-89 to 85 in 1997-98 the mineral-based units setup in the urban areas increased from 6 in 1988-89 to 10 in 1997-98 thus recording a growth of 67 per cent. This is because of plenty of raw material available in the District.

Linear growth rate of the mineral-based small and tiny units setup in the rural areas is 3.77. It was less than the linear growth rate of the mineral-based small and tiny units setup in the urban areas(1.10). That means average number of the units setup in the rural areas per annum is more that the average number of the units setup in the rural areas per annum is more that the average number of units ssetup in the urban areas per annum in the District during the period under consideration. The growth rates are more when compared to the growth rates of all the small and tiny units setup in the District during the period.

4.8. Number of Textile Small and Tiny Units Setup in the District

Table 10 shows the number of textile small and tiny units setup in the District during the ten years period commencing from 1988-89 to 1997-98. Total number of textile small and tiny units setup in the District during the period was 788. Average number of textile small and tiny units setup in the District during the ten years period under consideration was 78.8. Of them 481 (61.04) units were setup in the rural areas. It works out to be 48.1 units per annum. This is far more than the average number of units (30.96 units) setup in the urban areas of the District during the same period.

Coefficient of correlation between the number of textile small and tiny industrial units set up in the rural and urban areas in the district during the ten years period is 0.3230. That means correlation between the two is positive but not but not cognizable. Textile units in rural areas increased from 15 in 1988-89 to 100 1997-98 thus recording linear growth rate of 5.15. The textile units set up in the urban areas have increased from 21 in 1988-89 to 37 in 1997-98 thus recording a linear growth rate of –0.85. In the rural areas of the district, population belonging to weaver community is large in number. Many of them are inclined to start textile units. This is the reason for setting up a large number of textile units are handlooms and power looms.

LGR of rural areas is more than LGR of urban areas. That means average number of the units set up in the rural areas per annum is more than the average number of units set up in the district during the period under consideration.

4.9. Number of Miscellaneous Small and Tiny Units Set up in the District

Table 11 speaks of the number of miscellaneous small and tiny units set up in the district during the ten years period commencing from 1988-89 to 1997-98. Total number of miscellaneous small and tiny units set up in the district during the period was 1159. Average number of miscellaneous small and tiny units set up in thedistrict during the ten years period under consideration was 115.9. Of them 455 (39.26) units were set up in the rural areas. It works out to be 45.5 units per annum. This is far less than the average number of units (70.4 units) set up in the urban areas of the district during the same period.

Coefficient of correlation between the number of miscellaneous small and tiny industrial units set up in the urban areas in the district during the ten years period is 0.8386. That means correlation between the two is positive and cognizable. Miscellaneous units in the rural areas increased from 44 in 1988-89 to 103 in 1997-98 thus recording a linear growth rate of 5.63. The miscellaneous units, set up in the urban areas of the district, have been increased from 41 in 1988-89 to 183 in 1997-98 thus recording a linear growth rate of 12.52. From this it can be concluded that relatively a large number of miscellaneous units have been set up in the urban areas than in the rural areas.

Coefficient of correlation between the units set up in the rural and urban areas is positive and significant in case of engineering units, miscellaneous units and all units; is positive but not significant in case of agro-based units, chemical-based, forest-based units and textile units; and is negative but not significant in case of livestock-based units and mineral-based units.

Linear Growth Rate for all units set up in the rural areas during the ten year period under consideration is the highest (18.34). It is followed by engineering units (7.74), miscellaneous units (5.63), textile units (5.15), agro-based units (2.21) and chemical-based units (0.52).

Linear Growth Rates of mineral-based units and livestock-based units set up in the rural areas of the district during the ten years period and consideration are negative. Linear Growth Rate of all units set up, in the urban areas of the district, during the ten year period under consideration, is the highest (22.556). It is followed by miscellaneous units (12.52), engineering units (8.95), mineral-based units (1.10), chemical-based units (0.75) and forest-based units (0.52). Linear Growth Rates of textile units, agro-based units and textile-based units are negative.

5. Investment in Small and Tiny Units Set up in the District

Investment in the small and tiny units set up in the district during the ten years period under consideration has been shown in Table 4.14. Industrialization in the district, contributed by the District Industries Centre, is not only in the number of units set up but also by the amount invested in those units.

Total amount invested in the units set up during the ten years period was Rs.97,12,241. Of which 69.23 per cent of the amount was invested in the units located in the rural areas. This is a good sign. The amount invested in the rural units in 1988-89 was Rs.85,350. That became Rs.12,34,020 in 1997-98. It may be due to the efforts put in by the government and other development agencies.

The amount invested in the units located in the urban areas increased from Rs.1,28,785 in 1988-89 to Rs.6,45,850 in 1997-98 thus recording an increase of 501.49 per cent. In all the ten years investment in rural units was more than 50 per cent of the investment in all the units. In terms of per cent, investment in urban units increased from 14.65 in 1988-89 to 34.36 per cent of the total investment in 1997-98. On the other hand, investment in rural units decreased from 85.35 per cent to 65.64 per cent in 1997-98.

5.1. Investment in Agro-based Small and Tiny Units Set up in the District

Investment in the agro-based small and tiny units set up in the district during the ten years period under consideration has been shown in Table 15. Total amount invested in the agro-based units set up during the ten year period commencing from 1988-89 to 1997-98 was Rs.21,45,432. Of which as much as 73.82 per cent of the amount was invested in the units located in the rural areas. This is a good indication of contribution of the District Industries Centre for rural industrialization. The amount invested in rural units in 1988-89 was Rs.99,552 and the amount invested in 1997-98 was Rs.3,27,000. It may be partly due to the efforts put in by the government and other development agencies and partly due to affinity between the areas and agro-based units.

The amount invested in the units located in the urban areas increased from Rs.40,070 in 1988-89 to 1,32,250 in 1997-98 thus recording 330.05 per cent increase in the decade concerned. In no year, investment in rural units was less than 50 per cent of the investment in all the units. In terms of per cent investment in urban units increased from 28.70 in 1988-89 to 28.80 per cent of the investment in 1997-98. Investment in rural units decreased marginally by 0.1 per cent.

5.2. Investment in Chemical-based Small and Tiny Units Set up in the District

Investment in the chemical-based small and tiny units set up in the district during the ten year period under consideration has been shown in Table 16 Total amount invested in the chemical units set up during the ten years period commencing from 1988-89 to 1997-98 was Rs.10,68,131. Of which 91.58 per cent of the amount was invested in the units located in the rural areas. This is a considerable proportion of the total investment. The amount invested in rural units in 1988-89 was Rs.98,820. That decreased to Rs.35,480 in 1997-98. Investment in rural based chemical small and tiny units was nil in 1995-96. As much as 99.53 per cent of the year's investment flowed into rural-based units in 1993-94. In 1990-91 also the proportion of the investment in rural-based units was 97.70 per cent. There is no definite trend in the investment.

Coefficient of correlation between investment in rural and urban units is negative and insignificant (-0.4116). Linear Growth Rate of the units located in the rural areas is also negative (-3.85) thus indicating negative growth of rural chemical industrial units.

The amount invested in the chemical units located in the urban areas increased from Rs.1,450 in 1988-89 to 9.050 in 1989-90. It then felt to 3,295 in 1990-91. Any how, the trend is quite erratic. In percentage terms also no trend is dissemble. In terms of per cent, investment in urban units increased from 1.18 in 1988-89 to 34.17 in 1997-98. On the whole, investment in urban-based chemical units increased.

5.3. *Investment in Engineering Small and Tiny Units Set up in the District*

Investment in the small and tiny engineering units set up in the district during the ten years period from 1988-89 to 1997-98 has been given in Table 17. Total amount invested in the engineering units set up during the ten years period under consideration was Rs.11,01,546. Of which 59.93 per cent of the amount was invested in the engineering units located in the rural areas. The amount invested in rural units increased marginally from Rs.1,18,120 in 1988-89 to Rs.1,32,670 in 1997-98. The amount invested in the units located in the urban areas increased from Rs.20,875 in 1988-89 to 47,660 in 1997-98 thus recording an increase of 128.31 per cent. In the first ten years investment in engineering units located in the rural areas was more than 80 per cent of the investment in all the units. In terms of per cent of the investment in urban units increased from 15.02 in 1988-89 to 26.43 per cent in 1997-98. On the other hand, investment in rural units decreased from 84.98 per cent in 1988-89 to 73.57 per cent in 1997-98.

5.4. *Investment in Forest-based Small and Tiny Units Set up District*

Investment in the small and tiny forest-based units set up

in the district during the ten years period under consideration has been shown in Table – 18.

The amount invested in both rural and urban forest-based units set up during the ten years period commencing from 1988-89 was Rs.1,90,484. Of which 56.14 per cent of the amount was invested in the units located in the rural areas. The amount invested in the rural units in 1988-89 was Rs.4,920. That increased to Rs.25,420 in 1997-98. The increase was more than 400 per cent.

The amount invested in the forest-based units located in the urban areas decreased from Rs.5,690 in 1988-89 to Rs.5,230 in 1997-98. Investment in rural forest-based units in 1989-90, 1991-92, 1992-93, 1995-96 and 1997-98 was more than 50 per cent of the total investment. It was as low as 16.25 per cent of the total investment. It was as low as 16.25 per cent in 1994-95.

Investment in urban forest-based units also decreased from Rs.5,690 in 1988-89 to Rs.25,420 in 1997-98. In relative terms also investment in urban forest-based units decreased from 53.63 per cent to 17.06 per cent in 1997-98. Coefficient of correlation between the investment in rural and urban forest-based units is 0.1711, which though positive very insignificant. Linear growth rates are also positive but less than one, thus recording an insignificant annual growth of forest-based units in the district.

5.5. Investment in Livestock-based Small and Tiny Units Set up in the District

Year-wise investment particulars in the small and tiny livestock-based units in the district are given in Table 19. An amount of Rs.31,233 was invested in the livestock-based units set up during the ten years period commencing from 1988-89. Of which, 61.78 per cent of the amount was invested in the units located in the rural areas. That means a major share of investment was in the rural units during that period. The amount invested in rural livestock-based units increased from Rs.1,100 in 1988-89 to Rs.2,890 in 1997-98.

The amount invested in the units located in the urban areas increased marginally from Rs.1,290 in 1988-89 to Rs.1,700 in 1997-98 thus recording an increase of mere 31.78 per cent. In four out of ten years there was no investment at all in the units located in the rural areas. In the same way in three out of the ten years investment in urban livestock-based units was nil.

Coefficient of correlation between the investment in the rural and urban livestock-based units during the ten years period under consideration was positive and significant. Linear growth rate of the units located in the rural areas during the ten years period was very less and negative (-0.32). Whereas linear growth rate of the units located in the urban areas was positive though very less (0.11).

5.6. Investment in Mineral-based Small and Tiny Units Set up in the District

Investment in the small and tiny units set up in the district during the ten years period under consideration has been shown in Table 20.

Total amount invested in the units set up during the ten years period commencing from 1988-89 was Rs.28,39,987. Of which as much as 87.61 per cent of the amount was invested in the mineral-based units located in the rural areas. This is considerable. The amount invested in rural units in 1988-89 was Rs.3,66,850. That became Rs. 5,47,050 in 1997-98. It may be because of availability of minerals in certain rural areas of the district.

The amount invested in the units located in the urban areas increased from Rs.1,14,650 in 1988-89 to Rs.1,37,500 in 1997-98 thus recording an increase of 19.93 per cent. Proportion of investment in rural mineral-based units varied from 69.46 per cent in 1994-95 to 98.15 per cent in 1991-92. In five out of ten years the proportion was more than 90 per cent of the investment in all the units. In terms of per cent investment in urban mineral-based units decreased from 3.03 in 1988-89 to 2.45 in 1997-98. On the other hand, investment in rural units increased slightly from 96.97 per cent to 97.55 per cent in 1997-98.

Linear growth rate of the units located in the rural areas (22.99) is much higher than the linear growth rate of the mineral-based units located in the urban areas (8.26). That means investment in the rural mineral-based units is increasing at a higher rate than the growth of investment in the units located in the urban areas.

5.7. Investment in Textile Small and Tiny Units Set up in the District

Investment in the small and tiny units set up district during the ten years period under consideration, has been shown in Table – 21. Investment in the textile units set up in the district during the ten years period commencing from 1988-89 was Rs.9,78,540. Of which slightly more than 50 per cent of the amount was invested in the textile units located in the rural areas in the district. The amount invested in textile units located in the urban areas increased from Rs.15,870 in 1988-89 to Rs.1,02,220 in 1997-98.

The amount invested in the units located in the urban areas from Rs.15,870 in 1988-89 to Rs.1,02,300 in 1997-98 thus recording an increase of 544.61 per cent. It is a phenomenal increase of the investment in urban textile units. Coefficient of correlation is 0.8458 thus indicating a positive significant relationship between the investment in the established units in rural and urban areas. Linear growth rates are moderate though positive.

5.8. Investment in Miscellaneous Small and Tiny Units Set up in the District

I· vestment in the small and tiny units set up in the district during the ten years period under consideration has been shown in Table –22. Total amount invested in the units set up during the ten years period commencing from 1988-89 was Rs.13,46,038. Of which only 27.69 per cent of the amount was invested in the units located in the rural areas. This is very low. The amount invested in the rural units in 1988-89 was Rs.17,490. That became Rs.70,290 in 1997-98.

The amount invested in the units located in the urban areas increased from Rs.32,075 in 1988-89 to Rs.3,24,540 in 1997-98 thus recording an increase of 911.82 per cent. No specific trend in the investment dissembles. In terms of per cent, investment in urban units increased from 64.71 in 1988-89 to 82.20 per cent of the total investment in 1997-98. On the other hand, investment in rural units decreased from 35.29 per cent to 17.80 per cent in 1997-98.

Correlation between the investment in rural and urban based miscellaneous units is 0.6157 thus indicating a positive significant relationship. Linear growth rate of investment in rural units is much less than growth rate of investment in urban units.

6. Employment in Small and Tiny Units Set up in the District

Employment in the small and tiny units set up in the district during the ten years period commencing from 1988-89 has been shown in Table – 24. Altogether 28,090 persons were employed in 5,623 small and tiny units set up in the district during the period under consideration. Employment generated was five persons per unit approximately. Average investment per person was Rs.345.75

Number of persons employed in the units located in the rural areas was 17,935. This works out to be 63.65 per cent in the total employment generated. Percentage of the small and tiny units set up in the rural areas was 60.68, percentage of the investment in the units located in the rural areas was 69.23 and the employment generated was 63.85. These percentages are very close to one another. Employment per unit in the rural areas was 5.26 and is more than employment per unit in the urban areas (4.59 persons per unit). Linear growth rate of employment in rural areas was 94.78 but it was less than the linear growth rate of employment in rural areas was 94.78 but it was less than the linear growth rate of employment in the units located in the urban areas (116.94). There is positive correlation between the employment in the units located in the rural areas and the employment in the units located in the urban areas (0.7423). That means employment in both rural and urban units increased during the period but employment in the units located in the urban areas increased at a faster rate.

6.1. Employment in Agro-based Small and Tiny Units Set up in the District

Employment in the agro-based small and tiny units set up

in the district during the ten years period commencing from 1988-89 has been given in Table – 25. Number of persons employed in 1,165 agro-based small and tiny units set up in the district during the period under consideration was 5,008. Employment generated per one unit established during the decade was 4.3 persons. Average investment per person was Rs.428.40. It was more than average investment per person of all the units (Rs.345.75).

Number of persons employed in the agro-based units located in the rural areas was 3,909. This works out to be 78.06 per cent in the total employment generated in the agro-based units established in the district during the period. Percentage of the agro-based small and tiny units set up in the rural areas was 78.06, percentage of the investment in the agro-based units located in the rural areas was 73.82 and the employment generated was 78.06. These percentages are comparable with each other. Employment generated per unit in the agro-based ur˙ts established in the rural areas in the rural areas in the district during the period concerned was 4.11 and is more than the employment generated per unit in the agro-based units established in the urban areas (5.14 persons per unit) during the period.

Linear growth rate of employment in the units that were established in the rural areas during the ten years period was 26.33. It was more than the linear growth rate of employment in the agro-based units located in the urban areas (-1.72). That is employment in the agro-based units set up in the rural areas increased during the period at a considerable rate between employment in the agro-based units located in the urban areas decreased over the period though marginally.

There is negative correlation between the employment in the agro-based units located in the rural areas and the employment in the agro-based units located in the urban areas (-0.0453).

6.2. Employment in Chemical Small and Tiny Units Set up in the District

Employment in the chemical small and tiny units set up in the district during the ten years period commencing from 1988-

89 has been depicted in Table – 26. Number of persons employed in 138 chemical small and tiny units established in the district during the period under consideration was 1,057. Employment generated per chemical unit established was 7.67 persons which is greater than the number of persons employed, per agro-based unit established. Average investment per person was Rs.1029.45. It was more than the average investment per unit of both agro-based units and 'all the units' (Rs.345.75).

Number of persons employed in the chemical units located in the rural areas was 619. This works out to be 58.56 per cent in the total employment generated by the chemical units set up in the district during the period. Percentage of the chemical small and tiny units set up in the rural areas was 49.28, percentage of the investment in the chemical units located in the rural areas was 91.58 and the employment generated was 58.56. Investment appears to be relatively high in these units. Employment per unit in the chemical rural units was 9.10 and is more than employment per unit in the urban areas (6.26 persons per unit). Linear growth rate of employment in rural areas was –3.02. It is more than the linear growth rate of employment in the chemical units located in the urban areas (5.12). There is negative correlation between in the chemical units located in the rural areas and the employment in the chemical units located in the urban areas (0.1982). That means employment in rural chemical units decreased during the period but employment in the chemical units located in the urban areas increased.

6.3 Employment in Engineering Small and Tiny Units Set up in the District

Employment in engineering small and tiny units setup in the District during the ten years period commencing from 1988-89 has been shown in table 27. Number of persons employed in 1,383 engineering small and tiny units setup in the District during the period under consideration was 4,817. Employment generated per one engineering unit established during the period was 3.48 persons. Average investment per person was Rs.228.68. It was less than the average investment per unit of all the units (Rs.345.75).

Number of persons employed in the engineering units located in the rural areas was 2,377. This works out to be 49.35 per cent in the total employment generated in the engineering units setup in the District during the period. Percentage of the engineering small and tiny units located in the rural areas was 48.66, percentage of the investment in the engineering units located in the rural areas was 59.93 and the employment generated was 49.35. That means proportion of investment in engineering units was more than the proportion of engineering units located in the rural areas was 3.53 and is more than the employment generated per unit established in the urban areas(3.44 persons per unit). Linear growth rate of employment in rural areas was 22.89. It was less than the linear growth rate of employment in the engineering units located ion the urban areas (34.27). There is positive and significant correlation between the employment in the engineering units located in the rural areas and the employment in the engineering units located in the urban areas(0.8070). That means employment in both rural and urban units increased during the period.

6.4 Employment in Forest-based Small and Tiny Units Set up in the District

Employment in the forest- based small and tiny units setup in the District during the ten years period commencing from 1988-89 has been given in table 28. Number of persons employed in 228 forest –based small and tiny units setup in the District during the period under consideration was 1004. Employment generated per one forest-based unit established during the period was4.4 persons. Average investment per person employed during the period was Rs.189.73. It was lesser than average investment per unit of all the units(Rs.345.75).

Number of persons employed in the forest-based units located in the rural areas was 487. This works out to be 48.51 per cent in the total employment generated in the forest-based units in the District during the period. Percentage of the forest-based small and tiny units setup in the rural areas was 51.32, percentage of investment in the forest-based units located in the rural areas was 56.14 and the employment generated was

48.51. Proportion of the employment generated was less than proportion of the number of units and investment made.

Employment per unit in the forest-based rural units was 4.16 and is lessor than employment per unit in the urban areas (4.66 persons per unit). Linear growth rate of employment in rural areas was only 5.63. It was more than the linear growth rate of employment in the forest-based units located in the urban (4.04). There is a positive correlation between the employment in the forest-based units located in the rural areas and the employment in the forest-based units located in the urban areas(0.6763). That means employment in both rural and urban units increased during the period but employment in the forest-based units located in the urban areas increased at a lesser rate.

6.5 Employment in Livestock-based Small and Tiny Units Set up in the District

Employment in livestock-based small and tiny units setup in the District during the ten years period commencing from 1988-89 has been given in table 29. Number of persons employed in 46 livestock-based small and tiny units setup in the District during the period under the period under consideration was 3.59 persons. Average investment per person was Rs.189.29. It was lesser than average investment per unit of all the units (Rs.345.75).

Number of persons employed in the livestock-based units located in the rural areas was 96. This works out to be 58.18 per cent in the total employment generated in the livestock-based units in the District during the period. Percentage of the livestock-based small and tiny units setup in the rural areas was setup 58.70, percentage of the investment in the livestock-based units located in the rural areas was 61.78 and the employment generated was 58.18. That means proportion of the amount invested livestock-based units was more than the proportion of the actual number of the units established and the number of persons employed in those units.

Employment per unit in the livestock-based rural units was 3.56 and is less than the employment per unit in the urban areas

(3.63 per unit). Linear growth rate of employment in rural areas was -0.19. It was less than the linear growth rate of employment in the livestock-based units located in the urban areas (o.42). There is negative correlation between the employment in the livestock-based units located in the rural areas and the employment in the livestock-based units located in the urban areas (-o.0659). That means employment in livestock-based rural units decreased marginally whereas employment in the urban units increased marginally during the period.

6.6 Employment in Mineral-based Small and Tiny Units Set up in the District

Employment in the mineral-based small and tiny units setup in the District during the ten years period commencing from 1988-89 has been given in table 30. Number of persons employed ion 716 mineral-based small and tiny units set6up in the District during the period under consideration was 6,860. Employment generated per unit was 9.58 persons. Average investment per person was Rs.413.99. It was more than the average investment per unit of all the units (Rs.345.75).

Number of persons employed in the mineral-based units located in the rural areas was 6,001. This works out to be 87.48 per cent in the total employment generated in the mineral-based units in the District during the period. Percentage of the mineral-based small and tiny units setup in the rural areas was 89.39, percentage of the investment in the mineral-based units located in the rural areas was 87.61 and the employment generated was 87.48. These percentages are comparable.

Employment per units in the mineral-based units was 9.38 and is less than the employment per unit in the urban areas (11.30 persons per unit). Linear growth rate of employment in the rural areas was 17.05. It was less than the linear growth rate of employment in the mineral-based units located in the urban areas (17.91). There is positive correlation between the employment in the mineral-based units located in the rural areas and the employment in the mineral-based units located in the urban areas (0.5502). That means employment in the both rural and urban units increased during the period.

6.7 Employment in Textile Small and Tiny Units Set up in the District

Employment in the Textile small and tiny units setup in the District during the ten years period commencing from 1988-89 has been shown in table 31. Number of persons employed in 788-textile small and tiny units setup in the District during the period under consideration was 4,888. Employment generated per unit was 6.15 persons. Average investment per person was Rs.201.84. It was less than average investment per person of all the units (Rs.345.75).

Number of persons employed in the textile units located in the rural areas was 2,882. This works out to be 49.45 per cent in the total employment generated in the textile units in the District during the period. Percentage of the textile small and tiny units setup in the rural areas was 61.04, percentage of the investment in the textile units located in the rural areas was 50.58 and the employment generated was 59.45. That means 61.04 per cent of the textile units located in the rural areas claim 50.58 per cent of the investment and 59.45 per cent of employment.

Employment per unit in the textile rural units was 5.99 and is less than the employment per unit in the urban areas (6.40 persons per unit). Linear growth rate of employment in rural areas was 12.12. It was more than the linear growth rate of employment in the textile units located in the urban areas (- 1.68). There is positive correlation between the employment in the textile units located in the rural areas and the employment in the textile units located in the urban areas (0.6784). That means employment in both rural and urban units increased during the period but employment in the textile units located in the urban areas decreased.

6.8 Employment in miscellaneous Small and Tiny Units Set up in the District

Employment in the miscellaneous small and tiny units' setup in the District during the ten years period commencing from 1988-89 has been given in table 32. Number of persons employed in 1,159 miscellaneous small and tiny units setup in the District during the period under consideration was 4,331.

Employment generated per unit was 3.74 persons. Average investment per person was Rs.310.79. It was less than average investment per person of all the units (Rs.345.75).

Number of persons employed in the miscellaneous units located in the rural areas was 1,564. This works out to be 36.11 per cent in the total employment generated in the miscellaneous units in the District during the period. Percentage of the miscellaneous small and tiny units setup in the rural areas was 39.26, percentage of the investment in the miscellaneous units located in the rural areas was 27.69 and the employment generated was 36.11. That means 39.26 per cent of miscellaneous units located in the rural areas claim 27.69 per cent of the total investment in the miscellaneous units and 36.11 percentage of the employment generated by all the miscellaneous units set up in the District. Employment per unit in the miscellaneous rural units was 3.44 and is less than the employment per unit in the urban areas (3.93 persons per unit). Linear growth rate of employment in rural areas was 13.98. It was less than the linear growth rate of employment in the miscellaneous units located in the urban area (58.59). There is positive correlation between the employment in the miscellaneous units located in the rural areas and the employment in the miscellaneous units located in the urban areas (0.8047). That means employment in both rural and urban units increased during the period.

Conclusion

Performance of the DIC on the whole is satisfactory. As far as the number units setup employment generated, number of rural artisans assisted are concerned in eight out of ten years the achievement exceeded the target. In all the ten years, under consideration assistance in the form of credit provided through the DIC exceeded the targets. During all the ten years the number of the rural artisans trained was more than 100 per cent of the artisans estimated to be trained.

Category-wise distribution of the entrepreneurs assisted is not even. There is lot of scope for developing and assisting ST and SC entrepreneurs. In rural areas relatively more number of SC,ST and BC entrepreneurs have been assisted when compared to SC, ST and BC entrepreneurs assisted in urban areas. Efforts may be taken to assist more number of SC, ST and BC entrepreneurs in the District.

Table 3: Number of Small and Tiny Units Set up in the District (Year-wise)

Year	*Rural*	*Urban*	*Total*	*Trend Values*	
				Rural	*Urban*
1988-89	288 (66.36)	146 (33.64)	434 (100)	258.67	119.56
1989-90	271 (64.99)	146 (35.01)	417 (100)	277.01	142.13
1990-91	319 (63.93)	180 (36.07)	499 (100)	295.35	164.69
1991-92	359 (68.94)	164 (31.36)	523 (100)	313.69	187.25
1992-93	270 (59.34)	185 (40.66)	455 (100)	332.03	209.82
1993-94	332 (62.41)	200 (37.59)	532 (100)	350.37	232.38
1994-95	294 (54.55)	245 (45.45)	539 (100)	368.71	254.95
1995-96	358 (54.57)	298 (45.43)	656 (100)	387.05	277.51
1996-97	418 (57.73)	306 (42.27)	724 (100)	405.39	300.07
1997-98	503 (59.60)	341 (40.40)	844 (100)	423.73	322.64
Total	3412 (60.68)	2211 (39.32)	5623 (100)	--	--

Coefficient of Correlation = 0.8059
t Value = 3.85
LGR of Y (Rural) = 18.34
Coefficient of Y (Rural) = 20.37
LGR of Z (Urban) = 22.56
Coefficient of Z (Urban) = 30.69

Calculated value of t (3.85) is more than the table value (2.306). Hence, the given Correlation Coefficient is significant.

Source: Records of the District Industries Centre, Anantapur.

Note: Figures in parentheses are percentages on row totals.

Table 4: Number of Agro-based Units Setup in the District (Year-wise)

!	*Rural*	*Urban*	*Total*	*Trend Values*	
				Rural	*Urban*
1988-89	106 (82.81)	22 (17.19)	128 (100)	85.15	23.09
1989-90	81 (78.64)	22 (21.36)	103 (100)	87.36	22.72
1990-91	83 (82.18)	18 (17.82)	101 (100)	89.57	22.34
1991-92	70 (77.78)	20 (22.22)	90 (100)	91.78	21.96
1992-93	82 (70.09)	35 (29.91)	117 (100)	93.99	21.59
1993-94	120 (84.51)	22 (15.49)	142 (100)	96.21	21.21
1994-95	85 (85.86)	14 (14.14)	99 (100)	98.42	20.84
1995-96	127 (82.47)	27 (17.53)	154 (100)	100.63	20.46
1996-97	95 (86.36)	15 (13.64)	110 (100)	102.84	20.08
1997-98	102 (84.30)	19 (15.70)	121 (100)	105.05	19.71
Total	951 (81.63)	214 (18.37)	1165 (100)	--	--

Coefficient of Correlation = 0.1475
t Value = 0.42
LGR of Y (Rural) = 2.21
Coefficient of Y (Rural) = 18.37
LGR of Z (Urban) = -0.38
Coefficient of Z (Urban) = 26.94

Calculated value of t (0.42) is more than the table value (2.306). Hence, the given Correlation Coefficient is significant.

Source: Records of the District Industries Centre, Anantapur.

Note: Figures in parentheses are percentages on row totals.

Table 5: Number of Chemical-based Units Setup in the District (Year-wise)

Year	*Rural*	*Urban*	*Total*	*Trend Values*	
				Rural	*Urban*
1988-89	5 (62.56)	3 (37.50)	8 (100)	4.45	3.62
1989-90	3 (42.86)	4 (57.14)	7 (100)	4.98	4.37
1990-91	4 (44.44)	5 (55.56)	9 (100)	5.50	5.12
1991-92	6 (37.50)	10 (62.50)	16 (100)	6.02	5.87
1992-93	2 (28.57)	5 (71.43)	7 (100)	6.54	6.62
1993-94	10 (62.50)	6 (37.50)	16 (100)	7.06	7.38
1994-95	26 (74.29)	9 (25.71)	35 (100)	7.58	8.13
1995-96	0	7 (100)	7 (100)	8.10	8.88
1996-97	2 (18.18)	9 (81.82)	11 (100)	8.62	9.63
1997-98	10 (45.45)	12 (54.55)	22 (100)	9.15	10.38
Total	68 (49.28)	70 (50.72)	138 (100)	--	--

Coefficient of Correlation = 0.3717
t Value = 1.13
LGR of Y (Rural) = 0.52
Coefficient of Y (Rural) = 104.77
LGR of Z (Urban) = -0.75
Coefficient of Z (Urban) = 39.38

Calculated value of t (1.13) is more than the table value (2.306). Hence, the given Correlation Coefficient is significant.

Source: Records of the District Industries Centre, Anantapur.

Note: Figures in parentheses are percentages on row totals.

Table 6: Number of Engineering Units Set up in the District (Year-wise)

Year	*Rural*	*Urban*	*Total*	*Trend Values*	
				Rural	*Urban*
1988-89	33 (45.21)	40 (54.79)	73 (100)	32.47	30.75
1989-90	66 (58.93)	46 (41.07)	112 (100)	40.21	39.69
1990-91	34 (43.59)	44 (56.41)	78 (100)	47.95	48.64
1991-92	50 (60.24)	33 (39.76)	83 (100)	55.69	57.58
1992-93	42 (47.19)	47 (52.81)	89 (100)	63.43	66.53
1993-94	64 (46.38)	74 (53.62)	138 (100)	71.17	75.47
1994-95	87 (44.85)	107 (55.15)	194 (100)	78.91	84.42
1995-96	84 (40.98)	121 (59.02)	205 (100)	86.65	93.36
1996-97	132 (50.57)	129 (44.43)	261 (100)	94.39	102.31
1997-98	81 (54.00)	69 (46.00)	150 (100)	102.13	111.25
Total	673 (48.66)	710 (51.34)	1383 (100)	--	--

Coefficient of Correlation = 0.8728
t Value = 5.06
LGR of Y (Rural) = 7.74
Coefficient of Y (Rural) = 42.75
LGR of Z (Urban) = 8.95
Coefficient of Z (Urban) = 47.78

Calculated value of t (5.06) is more than the table value (2.306). Hence, the given Correlation Coefficient is significant.

Source: Records of the District Industries Centre, Anantapur.

Note: Figures in parentheses are percentages on row totals.

Table 7: Number of Forest-based Units Set up in the District (Year-wise)

Year	*Rural*	*Urban*	*Total*	*Trend Values*	
				Rural	*Urban*
1988-89	6 (40.00)	9 (60.00)	15 (100)	7.75	8.78
1989-90	13 (54.17)	11 (45.83)	24 (100)	8.62	9.30
1990-91	10 (47.62)	11 (52.38)	21 (100)	9.50	9.81
1991-92	10 (62.50)	6 (37.50)	16 (100)	10.38	10.33
1992-93	12 (60.00)	8 (40.00)	20 (100)	11.26	10.84
1993-94	12 (48.00)	13 (52.00)	25 (100)	12.14	11.36
1994-95	5 (23.81)	245 (45.45)	21 (100)	13.02	11.87
1995-96	11 (61.11)	16	18 (76.19)	13.90 (100)	12.39
1996-97	21 (50.00)	7 (38.89)	42 (100)	14.78	12.90
1997-98	17 (63.38)	21 (50.00)	26 (100)	15.65	13.42
Total	117 (51.32)	9 (34.62)	228 (100)	--	--

Coefficient of Correlation = 0.3687
t Value = 1.12
LGR of Y (Rural) = 0.88
Coefficient of Y (Rural) = 38.23
LGR of Z (Urban) = 0.52
Coefficient of Z (Urban) = 38.95

Calculated value of t (1.12) is more than the table value (2.306). Hence, the given Correlation Coefficient is significant.

Source: Records of the District Industries Centre, Anantapur.

Note: Figures in parentheses are percentages on row totals.

Table 8: Number of Livestock-based Units Set up in the District (Year-wise)

Year	*Rural*	*Urban*	*Total*	*Trend Values*	
				Rural	*Urban*
1988-89	2 (33.33)	4 (66.67)	6 (100)	2.78	2.09
1989-90	5 (62.50)	3 (37.50)	8 (100)	2.76	2.05
1990-91	1 (50.00)	1 (50.00)	2 (100)	2.75	2.01
1991-92	0	0	0	2.73	1.96
1992-93	11 (100)	0	11 (100)	2.71	1.92
1993-94	0	4 (100)	4 (100)	2.69	1.88
1994-95	0	1 (100)	1 (100)	2.67	1.84
1995-96	0	0	0	2.65	1.79
1996-97	3 (50.00)	3 (50.00)	6 (100)	2.64	1.75
1997-98	5 (62.50)	3 (37.50)	8 (100)	2.62	1.71
Total	27 (58.70)	19 (41.30)	46 (100)	--	--

Coefficient of Correlation = -0.0625
t Value = 0.18
LGR of Y (Rural) = -0.02
Coefficient of Y (Rural) = 124.00
LGR of Z (Urban) = -0.04
Coefficient of Z (Urban) = 83.05
Calculated value of t (0.18) is more than the table value (2.306). Hence, the given Correlation Coefficient is significant.

Source: Records of the District Industries Centre, Anantapur.

Note: Figures in parentheses are percentages on row totals.

Table 9: Number of Mineral-based Units Set up in the District (Year-wise)

Year	*Rural*	*Urban*	*Total*	*Trend Values*	
				Rural	*Urban*
1988-89	77	6	83	80.96	2.64
	(92.77)	(7.23)	(100)		
1989-90	65	5	70	77.19	3.74
	(92.86)	(7.14)		(100)	
1990-91	109	3	112	73.42	4.84
	(97.32)	(2.68)	(100)		
1991-92	125	1	126	69.65	5.95
	(99.21)	(0.79)	(100)		
1992-93	32	7	39	65.88	7.05
	(82.05)	(17.95)	(100)		
1993-94	28	7	35	62.12	8.15
	(80.00)	(20.00)	(100)		
1994-95	20	11	31	58.35	9.25
	(64.52)	(35.48)	(100)		
1995-96	34	8	42	54.58	10.36
	(80.95)	(19.05)	(100)		
1996-97	65	18	83	50.81	11.46
	(78.31)	(21.69)	(100)		
1997-98	85	10	95	47.04	12.56
	(89.47)	(10.53)	(100)		
Total	640	76	716	--	--
	(89.39)	(10.61)	(100)		

Coefficient of Correlation = -0.4562
t Value = 1.45
LGR of Y (Rural) = -3.77
Coefficient of Y (Rural) = 53.02
LGR of Z (Urban) = 1.10
Coefficient of Z (Urban) = 58.90

Calculated value of t (1.45) is more than the table value (2.306). Hence, the given Correlation Coefficient is significant.

Source: Records of the District Industries Centre, Anantapur.

Note: Figures in parentheses are percentages on row totals.

Table 10: Number of Textile Units Set up in the District (Year-wise)

Year	*Rural*	*Urban*	*Total*	*Trend Values*	
				Rural	*Urban*
1988-89	15 (41.67)	21 (58.33)	36 (100)	24.95	34.55
1989-90	14 (38.89)	22 (61.11)	36 (100)	30.09	33.69
1990-91	47 (52.22)	43 (47.78)	90 (100)	35.24	32.84
1991-92	76 (56.30)	59 (43.70)	135 (100)	40.38	31.98
1992-93	31 (39.24)	48 (60.76)	79 (100)	45.53	31.13
1993-94	73 (82.95)	15 (17.05)	88 (100)	45.53	30.27
1994-95	49 (70.00)	21 (30.00)	70 (100)	50.67	29.42
1995-96	38 (57.58)	28 (42.42)	66 (100)	55.82	28.56
1996-97	38 (74.51)	13 (25.49)	51 (100)	60.96	27.71
1997-98	100 (72.99)	37 (27.01)	137 (100)	71.25	26.85
Total	481 (61.04)	307 (38.96)	788 (100)	--	--

Coefficient of Correlation = 0.3230
t Value = 0.97
LGR of Y (Rural) = 5.15
Coefficient of Y (Rural) = 54.41
LGR of Z (Urban) = -0.85
Coefficient of Z (Urban) = 47.45

Calculated value of t (0.97) is more than the table value (2.306). Hence, the given Correlation Coefficient is significant.

Source: Records of the District Industries Centre, Anantapur.

Note: Figures in parentheses are percentages on row totals.

Table 11: Number of Miscellaneous Units Set up in the District (Year-wise)

Year	*Rural*	*Urban*	*Total*	*Trend Values*	
				Rural	*Urban*
1988-89	44 (51.76)	41 (48.24)	85 (100)	20.16	14.05
1989-90	24 (42.11)	33 (57.89)	.57 (100)	25.79	26.58
1990-91	31 (36.05)	55 (63.95)	86 (100)	31.42	39.10
1991-92	22 (38.60)	35 (63.95)	57 (100)	37.05	51.62
1992-93	58 (62.37)	35 (61.40)	93 (100)	42.68	64.14
1993-94	25 (29.76)	59 (70.24)	84 (100)	48.32	76.66
1994-95	22 (25.00)	66 (75.00)	88 (100)	53.95	89.18
1995-96	64 (39.02)	100 (60.98)	164 (100)	59.58	101.70
1996-97	62 (38.75)	98 (61.25)	160 (100)	65.21	114.22
1997-98	103 (36.14)	182 (63.86)	285 (100)	70.84	126.75
Total	455 (39.26)	704 (60.74)	1159 (100)	--	--

Coefficient of Correlation	=	0.8386
t Value	=	4.36
LGR of Y (Rural)	=	5.63
Coefficient of Y (Rural)	=	55.06
LGR of Z (Urban)	=	12.52
Coefficient of Z (Urban)	=	62.32

Calculated value of t (4.36) is more than the table value (2.306). Hence, the given Correlation Coefficient is significant.

Source: Records of the District Industries Centre, Anantapur.

Note: Figures in parentheses are percentages on row totals.

Table 14: Investment (Rs.'000) in Tiny and Small Scale Units Set up in the District (Year-wise)

Year	*Rural*	*Urban*	*Total*	*Trend Values*	
				Rural	*Urban*
1988-89	756.412 (85.35)	128.785 (14.65)	879.197 (100)	467.63	67.79
1989-90	448.09 (77.88)	127.296 (22.11)	575.386	513.13 (100)	112.48
1990-91	609.142 (64.64)	333.251 (35.36)	942.393 (100)	558.62	157.16
1991-92	382.179 (53.22)	335.948 (46.78)	718.127 (100)	604.11	201.85
1992-93	472.265 (65.74)	246.11 (34.26)	718.375 (100)	649.61	246.53
1993-94	997.272 (77.59)	287.987 (22.41)	1285.259 (100)	659.10	291.21
1994-95	443.295 (67.08)	217.522 (32.92)	660.817 (100)	740.59	335.90
1995-96	540.064 (65.39)	285.883 (34.61)	825.947 (100)	786.09	380.58
1996-97	846.79 (69.02)	380.08 (30.98)	1226.87 (100)	831.58	425.26
1997-98	1234.02 (65.64)	645.85 (34.36)	1879.87 (100)	877.07	469.95
Total	6723.529 (69.23)	2988.712 (30.77)	9712.241 (100)	--	--

Coefficient of Correlation	=	0.6271
t Value	=	2.28
LGR of Y (Rural)	=	45.49
Coefficient of Y (Rural)	=	39.52
LGR of Z (Urban)	=	44.68
Coefficient of Z (Urban)	=	59.74

Calculated value of t (2.28) is more than the table value (2.306). Hence, the given Correlation Coefficient is significant.

Source: Records of the District Industries Centre, Anantapur.

Note: Figures in parentheses are percentages on row totals.

Table 15: Investment (Rs.'000) in Agro-based Industrial Units Set up in the District (Year-wise)

Year	*Rural*	*Urban*	*Total*	*Trend Values*	
				Rural	*Urban*
1988-89	99.552 (71.30)	40.07 (28.70)	139.622 (100)	84.78	38.36
1989-90	132.105 (87.49)	18.883 (12.51)	150.988 (100)	101.13	42.31
1990-91	115.712 (63.93)	38.24 (24.84)	153.952 (100)	117.49	46.27
1991-92	134.109 (61.24)	84.863 (38.76)	218.972 (100)	133.85	50.23
1992-93	151.59 (65.80)	78.79 (34.20)	230.38 (100)	150.20	54.18
1993-94	126.134 (58.85)	88.18 (41.15)	214.314 (100)	166.56	58.14
1994-95	175.64 (89.93)	19.66 (10.07)	195.30 (100)	182.91	62.10
1995-96	98.924 (68.27)	45.97 (31.73)	144.894 (100)	199.27	66.06
1996-97	223.04 (93.81)	14.72 (6.19)	237.76 (100)	215.63	70.01
1997-98	327.00 (71.20)	132.25 (28.80)	459.25 (100)	231.98	73.97
Total	1583.806 (73.82)	561.626 (26.18)	2145.432 (100)	--	--

Coefficient of Correlation = 0.4520
t Value = 1.43
LGR of Y (Rural) = 16.36
Coefficient of Y (Rural) = 41.93
LGR of Z (Urban) = 3.96
Coefficient of Z (Urban) = 64.87

Calculated value of t (1.43) is more than the table value (2.306). Hence, the given Correlation Coefficient is significant.

Source: Records of the District Industries Centre, Anantapur.

Note: Figures in parentheses are percentages on row totals.

Table 16: Investment (Rs.'000) in Chemical-based Units Set up in the District (Year-wise)

Year	*Rural*	*Urban*	*Total*	*Trend Values*	
				Rural	*Urban*
1988-89	120.96 (98.82)	1.45 (1.18)	122.41 (100)	117.00	5.09
1989-90	5.178 (36.39)	9.05 (63.61)	14.228 (100)	113.14	5.99
1990-91	123.289 (97.70)	3.295 (2.60)	126.584 (100)	109.29	6.90
1991-92	26.76 (56.25)	20.81 (43.75)	47.57 (100)	105.44	7.80
1992-93	3.93 (41.28)	5.59 (58.72)	9.52 (100)	101.58	8.71
1993-94	622.439 (99.53)	2.94 (0.47)	625.379 (100)	97.73	9.61
1994-95	40.41 (24.02)	14.18 (25.98)	54.59 (100)	93.87	10.52
1995-96	0	6.00 (100)	6.00 (100)	90.02	11.42
1996-97	18.10 (64.76)	9.85 (35.24)	27.95 (100)	86.17	12.33
1997-98	35.48 (65.83)	18.42 (34.17)	53.90 (100)	82.31	13.23
Total	996.546 (91.58)	91.585 (8.42)	1088.131 (100)	--	--

Coefficient of Correlation = 0.4116
t Value = 1.28
LGR of Y (Rural) = -3.85
Coefficient of Y (Rural) = 180.05
LGR of Z (Urban) = 0.90
Coefficient of Z (Urban) = 69.27
Calculated value of t (1.28) is more than the table value (2.306). Hence, the given Correlation Coefficient is significant.

Source: Records of the District Industries Centre, Anantapur.

Note: Figures in parentheses are percentages on row totals.

Table 17: Investment (Rs.'000) in Engineering Units Set up in the District (Year-wise)

Year	*Rural*	*Urban*	*Total*	*Trend Values*	
				Rural	*Urban*
1988-89	118.12 (84.98)	20.875 (15.02)	138.995 (100)	62.88	26.27
1989-90	82.804 (82.05)	18.114 (17.95)	100.118 (100)	63.57	30.24
1990-91	48.095 (60.09)	31.949 (39.91)	80.044 (100)	64.27	34.21
1991-92	13.226 (14.41)	78.80 (85.59)	92.066 (100)	64.97	38.18
1992-93	84.253 (67.76)	40.09 (32.24)	124.343 (100)	65.67	42.15
1993-94	18.585 (39.50)	28.47 (60.50)	47.055 (100)	66.36	46.13
1994-95	35.845 (43.65)	46.272 (58.35)	82.117 (100)	67.06	50.10
1995-96	41.69 (46.93)	47.148 (53.07)	88.838 (100)	67.76	54.07
1996-97	84.82 (50.84)	82.02 (49.16)	166.84 (100)	68.46	58.04
1997-98	132.67 (73.57)	47.66 (26.43)	180.33 (100)	69.15	58.04
Total	660.148 (59.93)	441.398 (40.07)	1101.546 (100)	--	--

Coefficient of Correlation = -0.2220
t Value = 0.64
LGR of Y (Rural) = 0.70
Coefficient of Y (Rural) = 58.63
LGR of Z (Urban) = 3.97
Coefficient of Z (Urban) = 46.93

Calculated value of t (0.64) is more than the table value (2.306). Hence, the given Correlation Coefficient is significant.

Source: Records of the District Industries Centre, Anantapur.

Note: Figures in parentheses are percentages on row totals.

Table 18: Investment (Rs.'000) in Forest-based Units Set up in the District (Year-wise)

Year	*Rural*	*Urban*	*Total*	*Trend Values*	
				Rural	*Urban*
1988-89	4.92 (46.37)	5.69 (53.63)	10.61 (100)	6.45	5.82
1989-90	7.59 (61.26)	4.80 (38.74)	12.39 (100)	7.39	6.39
1990-91	319 (63.93)	180 (36.07)	14.084 (100)	8.34	6.95
1991-92	359 (68.94)	164 (31.36)	10.04 (100)	9.28	7.51
1992-93	270 (59.34)	185 (40.66)	43.2055 (100)	10.22	8.07
1993-94	332 (62.41)	200 (37.59)	18.99 (100)	11.16	8.64
1994-95	294 (54.55)	245 (45.45)	13.045 (100)	12.10	9.20
1995-96	358 (54.57)	298 (45.43)	10.90 (100)	13.04	9.78
1996-97	418 (57.73)	306 (42.27)	26.57 (100)	13.98	10.32
1997-98	503 (59.60)	341 (40.40)	30.65 (100)	14.92	10.88
Total	106.94 (56.14)	83.544 (43.86)	190.484 (100)	--	--

Coefficient of Correlation	=	0.1711
t Value	=	0.49
LGR of Y (Rural)	=	0.94
Coefficient of Y (Rural)	=	81.94
LGR of Z (Urban)	=	0.56
Coefficient of Z (Urban)	=	53.20

Calculated value of t (0.49) is more than the table value (2.306). Hence, the given Correlation Coefficient is significant.

Source: Records of the District Industries Centre, Anantapur.

Note: Figures in parentheses are percentages on row totals.

Table 19: Investment (Rs.'000) in Livestock-based Units Set up in the District (Year-wise)

Year	*Rural*	*Urban*	*Total*	*Trend Values*	
				Rural	*Urban*
1988-89	1.10 (46.03)	1.29 (53.97)	2.39 (100)	3.35	1.69
1989-90	7.10 (59.30)	4.873 (40.70)	11.973 (100)	3.03	1.58
1990-91	5.55 (97.80)	0.125 (2.20)	5.675 (100)	2.72	1.47
1991-92	--	--	--	2.40	1.36
1992-93	1.155 (100)	--	1.155 (100)	2.09	1.25
1993-94	--	2.35 (100)	2.35 (100)	1.77	1.14
1994-95	--	0.20 (100)	0.20 (100)	1.46	1.03
1995-96	--	--	--	1.14	0.92
1996-97	1.50 (51.72)	1.40 (48.28)	2.90 (100)	0.83	0.81
1997-98	2.89 (62.96)	1.70 (37.44)	4.59 (100)	0.51	0.69
Total	19.295 (61.78)	11.938 (38.22)	31.233 (100)	--	--

Coefficient of Correlation	=	0.5892
t Value	=	2.06
LGR of Y (Rural)	=	-0.32
Coefficient of Y (Rural)	=	123.87
LGR of Z (Urban)	=	0.11
Coefficient of Z (Urban)	=	123.07

Calculated value of t (2.06) is more than the table value (2.306). Hence, the given Correlation Coefficient is significant.

Source: Records of the District Industries Centre, Anantapur.

Note: Figures in parentheses are percentages on row totals.

Table 20: Investment (Rs. '000) in Mineral-based Units Set up in the District (Year-wise)

Year	*Rural*	*Urban*	*Total*	*Trend Values*	
				Rural	*Urban*
1988-89	366.85	11.465	378.315	145.36	-1.98
	(96.97)	(3.03)	(100)		
1989-90	174.145	9.24	183.385	168.35	6.28
	(94.96)	(5.04)	(100)		
1990-91	190.087	12.015	202.102	191.35	14.53
	(94.05)	(5.95)	(100)		
1991-92	132.32	2.50	134.82	214.34	22.79
	(98.15)	(1.85)	(100)		
1992-93	120.88	20.218	141.098	237.33	31.05
	(85.67)	(14.33)	(100)		
1993-94	118.867	28.68	147.547	260.32	39.30
	(80.56)	(19.44)	(100)		
1994-95	130.51	57.37	187.88	283.31	47.56
	(69.46)	(30.54)	(100)		
1995-96	302.01	41.08	343.09	306.30	55.82
	(88.03)	(11.97)	(100)		
1996-97	405.51	155.44	560.95	329.29	64.07
	(72.29)	(27.71)	(100)		
1997-98	547.05	13.75	560.80	352.28	72.33
	(97.55)	(2.45)	(100)		
Total	2488.229	351.758	2839.987	--	--
	(87.61)	(12.39)	(100)		

Coefficient of Correlation = 0.2824
t Value = 0.83
LGR of Y (Rural) = 22.99
Coefficient of Y (Rural) = 56.85
LGR of Z (Urban) = 8.06
Coefficient of Z (Urban) = 122.46
Calculated value of t (0.83) is more than the table value (2.306). Hence, the given Correlation Coefficient is significant.

Source: Records of the District Industries Centre, Anantapur.

Note: Figures in parentheses are percentages on row totals.

Table 21: Investment (Rs. '000) in Textile Units Set up in the District (Year-wise)

Year	*Rural*	*Urban*	*Total*	*Trend Values*	
				Rural	*Urban*
1988-89	21.42 (57.44)	15.87 (42.56)	37.29 (100)	33.97	37.26
1989-90	15.86 (34.69)	29.854 (65.31)	45.714 (100)	37.42	39.72
1990-91	76.362 (53.89)	65.325 (46.11)	141.687 (100)	40.87	42.19
1991-92	57.134 (47.37)	63.47 (52.63)	120.604 (100)	44.32	44.66
1992-93	60.162 (49.97)	60.231 (50.03)	120.393 (100)	47.77	47.12
1993-94	49.972 (38.90)	78.485 (61.10)	128.457 (100)	51.22	49.59
1994-95	38.83 (72.86)	14.465 (27.14)	53.295 (100)	54.68	52.05
1995-96	46.49 (53.32)	40.70 (46.68)	87.19 (100)	358.13	54.52
1996-97	35.54 (73.44)	12.85 (26.56)	48.39 (100)	61.58	56.99
1997-98	93.22 (47.68)	102.30 (53.32)	195.52 (100)	65.03	59.45
Total	494.99 (50.58)	483.55 (49.42)	978.54 (100)	--	--

Coefficient of Correlation = 0.8458
t Value = 4.48
LGR of Y (Rural) = 3.45
Coefficient of Y (Rural) = 45.37
LGR of Z (Urban) = 2.47
Coefficient of Z (Urban) = 59.73

Calculated value of t (4.48) is more than the table value (2.306). Hence, the given Correlation Coefficient is significant.

Source: Records of the District Industries Centre, Anantapur.

Note: Figures in parentheses are percentages on row totals.

Table 22: Investment (Rs. '000) in Miscellaneous Units Set up in the District (Year-wise)

Year	*Rural*	*Urban*	*Total*	*Trend Values*	
				Rural	*Urban*
1988-89	17.49 (35.29)	32.075 (6.714)	49.565 (100)	13.63	28.01
1989-90	22.508 (40.93)	32.482 (59.07)	54.99 (100)	18.88	43.41
1990-91	43.537 (19.95)	174 (80.05)	218.265 (100)	24.14	58.81
1991-92	11.28 (10.85)	92.725 (89.15)	104.005 (100)	29.39	74.22
1992-93	20.285 (42.01)	27.996 (57.99)	48.281 (100)	34.65	89.62
1993-94	53.535 (52.92)	47.632 (47.08)	101.167 (100)	39.91	105.03
1994-95	19.94 (26.80)	54.45 (73.20)	74.39 (100)	45.16	120.43
1995-96	44.70 (30.82)	100.335 (69.18)	145.035 (100)	50.42	135.84
1996-97	69.21 (44.51)	86.30 (55.49)	155.51 (100)	55.67	151.24
1997-98	70.29 (17.80)	324.54 (82.20)	394.83 (100)	60.93	166.65
Total	372.776 (27.69)	973.263 (72.31)	1346.038 (100)	--	--

Coefficient of Correlation = 0.6157
t Value = 2.21
LGR of Y (Rural) = 5.26
Coefficient of Y (Rural) = 55.90
LGR of Z (Urban) = 15.40
Coefficient of Z (Urban) = 89.19

Calculated value of t (2.21) is more than the table value (2.306). Hence, the given Correlation Coefficient is significant.

Source: Records of the District Industries Centre, Anantapur.

Note: Figures in parentheses are percentages on row totals.

Table 24: Employment in the Tiny and Small Scale Units Set up in the District (Year-wise)

Year	*Rural*	*Urban*	*Total*	*Trend Values*	
				Rural	*Urban*
1988-89	2014 (77.05)	600 (22.95)	2614 (100)	1366.98	489.27
1989-90	1426 (72.24)	548 (27.76)	1974 (100)	1461.76	606.21
1990-91	1567 (66.88)	776 (33.12)	2343 (100)	1556.55	723.15
1991-92	1850 (64.59)	1014 (35.41)	2864 (100)	1651.33	840.09
1992-93	1311 (58.03)	948 (41.97)	2259 (100)	1746.11	957.03
1993-94	1480 (62.79)	877 (37.21)	2357 (100)	1840.89	1073.97
1994-95	1015 (53.79)	872 (46.21)	1887 (100)	1935.67	1090.91
1995-96	1378 (54.21)	1164 (45.79)	2542 (100)	2030.45	1307.85
1996-97	3009 (65.89)	1558 (34.11)	4567 (100)	2125.24	1424.70
1997-98	2885 (61.61)	1798 (38.39)	4683 (100)	2220.02	1541.73
Total	17935 (63.85)	10155 (36.15)	28090 (100)	--	--

Coefficient of Correlation	=	0.7423
t Value	=	3.13
LGR of Y (Rural)	=	94.78
Coefficient of Y (Rural)	=	35.34
LGR of Z (Urban)	=	116.94
Coefficient of Z (Urban)	=	37.13

Calculated value of t (3.13) is more than the table value (2.306). Hence, the given Correlation Coefficient is significant.

Source: Records of the District Industries Centre, Anantapur.

Note: Figures in parentheses are percentages on row totals.

Table 25: Employment in Agro-based Units Setup in the District (Year-wise)

Year	*Rural*	*Urban*	*Total*	*Trend Values*	
				Rural	*Urban*
1988-89	411 (79.96)	103 (20.04)	514 (100)	272.40	117.62
1989-90	249 (80.32)	61 (19.68)	310 (100)	298.73	115.90
1990-91	267 (77.17)	79 (22.83)	346 (100)	325.07	114.19
1991-92	385 (66.84)	191 (33.16)	576 (100)	351.40	112.47
1992-93	340 (58.22)	244 (41.78)	584 (100)	351.40	110.76
1993-94	354 (79.55)	91 (30.45)	445 (100)	377.73	109.04
1994-95	280 (85.63)	47 (14.37)	327 (100)	404.07	107.33
1995-96	467 (82.51)	99 (19.49)	566 (100)	430.40	105.61
1996-97	658 (92.94)	50 (7.06)	708 (100)	456.73	103.90
1997-98	498 (78.80)	134 (21.20)	632 (100)	483.07	102.18
Total	3909 (78.06)	1099 (21.94)	5008 (100)	--	--

Coefficient of Correlation	=	0.0453
t Value	=	0.13
LGR of Y (Rural)	=	26.33
Coefficient of Y (Rural)	=	30.35
LGR of Z (Urban)	=	-1.72
Coefficient of Z (Urban)	=	55.01

Calculated value of t (0.13) is more than the table value (2.306). Hence, the given Correlation Coefficient is significant.

Source: Records of the District Industries Centre, Anantapur.

Note: Figures in parentheses are percentages on row totals.

Table 26: Employment in Chemical-based Units Set up in the District (Year-wise)

Year	*Rural*	*Urban*	*Total*	*Trend Values*	
				Rural	*Urban*
1988-89	129 (87.16)	19 (12.84)	148 (100)	75.51	20.78
1989-90	10 (27.03)	27 (72.97)	37 (100)	72.48	25.90
1990-91	65 (80.25)	16 (19.75)	81 (100)	69.46	31.01
1991-92	44 (36.67)	76 (63.33)	120 (100)	66.44	36.13
1992-93	14 (27.45)	37 (72.55)	51 (100)	63.41	41.24
1993-94	184 (81.78)	41 (18.22)	225 (100)	60.39	46.36
1994-95	86 (74.14)	30 (25.86)	116 (100)	57.36	51.47
1995-96	0	44 (100)	44 (100)	54.34	56.59
1996-97	11 (14.10)	67 (85.90)	78 (100)	51.32	61.70
1997-98	76 (48.41)	81 (51.59)	157 (100)	48.29	66.82
Total	619 (58.56)	438 (41.44)	1057 (100)	--	--

Coefficient of Correlation = -0.1962
t Value = 0.57
LGR of Y (Rural) = -3.02
Coefficient of Y (Rural) = 91.29
LGR of Z (Urban) = 5.12
Coefficient of Z (Urban) = 50.40

Calculated value of t (0.57) is more than the table value (2.306). Hence, the given Correlation Coefficient is significant.

Source: Records of the District Industries Centre, Anantapur.

Note: Figures in parentheses are percentages on row totals.

Table 27: Employment in Engineering Units Set up in the District (Year-wise)

Year	*Rural*	*Urban*	*Total*	*Trend Values*	
				Rural	*Urban*
1988-89	207 (61.42)	130 (38.58)	337 (100)	134.69	89.80
1989-90	243 (60.90)	156 (39.10)	399 (100)	157.58	124.07
1990-91	115 (45.63)	137 (54.37)	252 (100)	180.47	158.33
1991-92	160 (54.98)	131 (45.02)	291 (100)	203.36	192.60
1992-93	189 (51.78)	176 (48.22)	365 (100)	226.25	226.87
1993-94	164 (43.73)	211 (56.27)	375 (100)	249.15	261.13
1994-95	192 (35.42)	350 (64.58)	542 (100)	272.04	295.40
1995-96	264 (42.44)	358 (57.56)	622 (100)	294.93	329.67
1996-97	531 (51.50)	500 (49.50)	1032 (100)	317.82	363.93
1997-98	312 (51.74)	291 (48.26)	603 (100)	340.71	398.20
Total	2377 (49.35)	2440 (50.65)	4817 (100)	--	--

Coefficient of Correlation = 0.8070
t Value = 3.87
LGR of Y (Rural) = 22.89
Coefficient of Y (Rural) = 46.88
LGR of Z (Urban) = 34.27
Coefficient of Z (Urban) = 48.95

Calculated value of t (3.87) is more than the table value (2.306). Hence, the given Correlation Coefficient is significant.

Source: Records of the District Industries Centre, Anantapur.

Note: Figures in parentheses are percentages on row totals.

Table 28: Employment in Forest-based Units Set up in the District (Year-wise)

Year	*Rural*	*Urban*	*Total*	*Trend Values*	
				Rural	*Urban*
1988-89	24 (36.36)	42 (63.64)	66 (100)	23.36	33.51
1989-90	43 (50.00)	43 (50.00)	86 (100)	28.99	37.57
1990-91	34 (40.00)	51 (60.00)	85 (100)	34.62	41.59
1991-92	47 (67.14)	23 (32.86)	70 (100)	40.25	45.64
1992-93	51 (53.68)	44 (46.32)	95 (100)	45.88	49.68
1993-94	43 (45.74)	51 (54.26)	94 (100)	51.52	53.72
1994-95	13 (19.12)	55 (80.88)	68 (100)	57.15	57.76
1995-96	35 (60.34)	23 (39.66)	58 (100)	62.78	61.81
1996-97	111 (44.05)	141 (55.95)	252 (100)	68.41	65.85
1997-98	86 (66.15)	44 (33.85)	130 (100)	74.04	69.89
Total	487 (48.51)	517 (51.49)	1004 (100)	--	--

Coefficient of Correlation	=	0.6763
t Value	=	2.60
LGR of Y (Rural)	=	5.63
Coefficient of Y (Rural)	=	56.73
LGR of Z (Urban)	=	4.04
Coefficient of Z (Urban)	=	60.93

Calculated value of t (2.60) is more than the table value (2.306). Hence, the given Correlation Coefficient is significant.

Source: Records of the District Industries Centre, Anantapur.

Note: Figures in parentheses are percentages on row totals.

Table 29: Employment in Livestock-based Units Set up in the District (Year-wise)

Year	*Rural*	*Urban*	*Total*	*Trend Values*	
				Rural	*Urban*
1988-89	8 (47.06)	9 (52.94)	17 (100)	10.47	5.02
1989-90	14 (53.85)	12 (46.15)	26 (100)	10.28	5.44
1990-91	5 (62.50)	3 (37.50)	8 (100)	10.08	5.85
1991-92	0	0	0	9.89	6.27
1992-93	44 (100)	0	44 (100)	9.70	6.69
1993-94	0	14 (100)	14 (100)	9.50	7.11
1994-95	0	3 (100)	3 (100)	9.31	7.53
1995-96	0	0	0	9.12	7.95
1996-97	9 (40.91)	13 (59.09)	22 (100)	8.92	8.36
1997-98	16 (51.61)	15 (48.39)	31 (100)	8.73	8.78
Total	96 (58.18)	69 (41.82)	165 (100)	--	--

Coefficient of Correlation = -0.0659
t Value = 0.19
LGR of Y (Rural) = 0.19
Coefficient of Y (Rural) = 133.25
LGR of Z (Urban) = 0.42
Coefficient of Z (Urban) = 86.58

Calculated value of t (0.19) is more than the table value (2.306). Hence, the given Correlation Coefficient is significant.

Source: Records of the District Industries Centre, Anantapur.

Note: Figures in parentheses are percentages on row totals.

Table 30: Employment in Mineral-based Units Set up in the District (Year-wise)

Year	*Rural*	*Urban*	*Total*	*Trend Values*	
				Rural	*Urban*
1988-89	968 (95.56)	45 (4.44)	1013 (100)	523.38	5.31
1989-90	691 (92.50)	56 (7.50)	747 (100)	540.43	23.22
1990-91	339 (93.13)	25 (6.87)	364 (100)	557.48	41.13
1991-92	705 (98.60)	10 (1.40)	715 (100)	574.53	59.04
1992-93	291 (83.88)	58 (16.62)	349 (100)	591.58	76.95
1993-94	206 (75.18)	68 (24.82)	274 (100)	608.62	94.84
1994-95	219 (74.49)	79 (26.51)	298 (100)	625.67	112.76
1995-96	290 (75.13)	96 (24.87)	386 (100)	642.72	130.67
1996-97	1239 (80.04)	309 (19.96)	1548 (100)	659.77	148.58
1997-98	1053 (90.31)	113 (9.69)	1166 (100)	676.82	166.49
Total	6001 (87.48)	859 (12.52)	6860 (100)	--	--

Coefficient of Correlation	=	0.5502
t Value	=	1.86
LGR of Y (Rural)	=	17.05
Coefficient of Y (Rural)	=	60.73
LGR of Z (Urban)	=	17.91
Coefficient of Z (Urban)	=	92.98

Calculated value of t (1.86) is more than the table value (2.306). Hence, the given Correlation Coefficient is significant.

Source: Records of the District Industries Centre, Anantapur.

Note: Figures in parentheses are percentages on row totals.

Table 31: Employment in Textile Units Set up in the District (Year-wise)

Year	*Rural*	*Urban*	*Total*	*Trend Values*	
				Rural	*Urban*
1988-89	117 (46.99)	132 (53.01)	249 (100)	233.65	204.18
1989-90	106 (53.27)	93 (46.73)	199 (100)	245.78	202.50
1990-91	563 (65.77)	293 (34.23)	856 (100)	257.90	200.81
1991-92	405 (51.99)	374 (48.01)	779 (100)	270.02	199.13
1992-93	180 (46.65)	242 (57.35)	422 (100)	282.14	197.44
1993-94	432 (68.79)	196 (31.21)	628 (100)	294.26	195.76
1994-95	167 (64.23)	93 (35.77)	260 (100)	306.38	194.07
1995-96	158 (44.01)	201 (55.92)	359 (100)	318.50	192.39
1996-97	252 (75.00)	84 (25.00)	336 (100)	330.62	190.70
1997-98	502 (66.05)	258 (33.95)	844 (100)	342.75	189.02
Total	2882 (59.45)	1966 (40.55)	4848 (100)	--	--

Coefficient of Correlation	=	0.6784
t Value	=	2.61
LGR of Y (Rural)	=	12.12
Coefficient of Y (Rural)	=	56.24
LGR of Z (Urban)	=	-1.68
Coefficient of Z (Urban)	=	46.88

Calculated value of t (2.61 is more than the table value (2.306). Hence, the given Correlation Coefficient is significant.

Source: Records of the District Industries Centre, Anantapur.

Note: Figures in parentheses are percentages on row totals.

Table 32: Employment in Miscellaneous Units Set up in the District (Year-wise)

Year	*Rural*	*Urban*	*Total*	*Trend Values*	
				Rural	*Urban*
1988-89	150 (55.56)	120 (44.44)	270 (100)	93.51	13.05
1989-90	70 (41.18)	100 (58.82)	170 (100)	107.48	71.64
1990-91	179 (51.00)	172 (49.00)	351 (100)	121.46	130.23
1991-92	104 (33.23)	209 (66.77)	313 (100)	135.44	188.82
1992-93	202 (57.88)	147 (42.12)	349 (100)	149.41	247.41
1993-94	97 (32.12)	205 (67.88)	302 (100)	163.39	305.99
1994-95	58 (21.25)	215 (78.75)	273 (100)	177.36	364.58
1995-96	164 (32.35)	343 (67.65)	507 (100)	191.34	423.17
1996 97	198 (33.45)	394 (66.55)	592 (100)	205.32	481.76
1997-98	342 (28.41)	862 (71.59)	1204 (100)	219.29	540.35
Total	1564 (36.11)	2767 (63.89)	4331 (100)	--	--

Coefficient of Correlation = 0.8047
t Value = 3.83
LGR of Y (Rural) = 13.98
Coefficient of Y (Rural) = 50.46
LGR of Z (Urban) = 58.59
Coefficient of Z (Urban) = 77.33

Calculated value of t (3.83) is more than the table value (2.306). Hence, the given Correlation Coefficient is significant.

Source: Records of the District Industries Centre, Anantapur.

Note: Figures in parentheses are percentages on row totals.

19

Changing Role of District Industries Centres

D. Nagayya*

Overview

In 1978, a major structural innovation was undertaken in building up Institutional support for small enterprises, by establishing district industries centres (DICs) in each of the districts all over the country in a phased manner during 1978 to 1981. The DIC functions under the Commissioner of Industries at the state level, and is headed by a General Manager, who is assisted by expert managers (up to seven). Three functional managers common to all DICs are in the fields of **Economic Investigation, Village Industries and Credit.** The other four expert managers vary according to the local needs of the districts. The areas in which these managers function are: **Machinery and Equipment; Research, Extension and Training; Raw Materials, and Marketing.** In some states, one of them is designated as project manager with technical background, and a few years experience of having worked in an industry or associated with counseling of entrepreneurs. The DIC structure also envisaged functionaries at sub-divisional level in a district. They are known as Assistant Managers and Industrial Promotion Officers operating are sub-divisional level. In some states, industrial promotion officers with technical background have

1 Consultant on Small Enterprises at Guntur and former Director (Industrial Dev.) National Institute of Small Industry Extension Training(NISIET), Hyderabad.

been posted at block/taluk level, with nearly five to nine IPOs in different parts of the district. DICs focus on developing small, tiny and cottage or micro enterprises, and generate more employment opportunities among rural and backward areas, and in smaller towns between 20,000 to 50,000 population.

The DIC is expected to provide the ' critical mass' of capabilities at the district level, which may provide under a single roof various facilities and information, and obtain necessary clearances from the concerned authorities through the DIC. The intention is that an entrepreneur does not have to run from pillar to post for these time consuming tasks, and may obtain necessary and requisite information and counseling at one point. The 430 DICs operating in the country now cover almost the entire country, with the exception of the metropolitan cities.

The DIC programme for the first time attempted to carry the 'message' of industrialization to rural areas in a systematic and organised manner. The focus of the programme was on s mall towns (population between 20,000 to 50,000). An Important merit of the programme was that it brought industrial development administration virtually nearer to the door steps of entrepreneurs.

DICs as a centrally sponsored programme implemented by the state governments is coordinated by the Office of the Development Commissioner (Small Scale Industries) at the Center. Central Government provided 50 per cent assistance for the DICs in terms of staffing at Functional Managers and General Managers level, apart from meeting the capital expenditure in full. Beginning from 1993-94, the scheme has been transferred to the states and since then, the states have been meeting the entire expenditure on DICs. The Center continues to provide the DICs support, such as development of information centres and computerization, evaluation studies, and preparation of project profiles, technical literature , etc., apart from promotional schemes such as common facility centres, Research and Development centres, etc. One of the important activities of DICs in the context of self employment is the implementation of Prime Minister's Rozgar Yojana from 1993-94.

Broad grouping of functions performed by DICs is as follows:

1. **Regulatory functions:** Registration of SSI units, activities connected with policy implementation, administrative work including settlement of disputes, implementation and monitoring of programmes of both central and state governments.
2. **Recommendatory assistance from government agencies for:** Machinery, finance, procurement of materials, registration and licenses.
3. **Promotional:** Preparation of project reports, district action plans, entrepreneurship development, surveys, consultancy and escort services.

DICs are mostly burdened at present with the work relating to registration of SSI units and PMRY. Infrastructure through industrial estates, industrial areas and industrial clusters is another area where DIC functions as an effective line with the concerned specialised corporation looking after infrastructure development in the state.

Assessment of the Performance of DICs by Various Studies and Committees

The paper attempts a review of the performance of DICs as brought out by recent studies and all India committees, and reflects over the changing role of DICs in the fast changing international and national business environment, and brings out a few directions for the future to strengthen the field agency for accelerating industrial promotion with focus on rural areas, smaller towns, and micro and tiny sector enterprises, i.e., smaller among small enterprises which have great potential for widespread dispersal and dynamism, which need to be strengthened to face the competitive environment.

Recent studies referred to in this context are : (i) evaluation of 55 DICs carried out in 1988 covering a number of states by five management and research institutions in different parts of the country; (ii) NCAER - FNST study of 1993 dealing with *Structure and Promotion of Small Scale Industries in India*, a comprehensive empirical study on small enterprises based on responses from the field across the country, which has formed the basis for liberalisation in the SSI sector; (iii) *Report of the Expert Committee on Small Enterprises* of the Union Ministry of Industry chaired by Abid Hussain (1997) (Expert Committee Report); and (iv) *Report of the Study Group on Development of Small Scale Enterprises*(2001) of the Planning Commission chaired by S.P. Gupta (Study Group Report).

Single Window Service

DICs were expected to provide extension services to the fast growing SSIs under one roof and act as a 'single window' for all the clearances and formalities required in setting up and running small enterprises. For the fulfillment of these objectives, they were expected to liason with extension agencies like Small Industries Service Institutes (SISIs)and other concerned departments and organizations. However, the programme seems to have failed to achieve these avowed objectives. The technical expertise and information required by entrepreneurs available at the level of DICs is very weak. Technical and economic information at DICs has not been updated, and wherever it has been updated, the same has been done on the basis of information received from the state government, SISIs and state corporations. An evaluation study of DICs undertaken by a few premier institutes in 1988 indicated that the 'single' window' concept has hardly worked, and DICs by virtue of lack of technical expertise have not been of any significant help to entrepreneurs in providing guidance in the selection of products and project formulation.

Information Services

The two major agencies in the field, namely, the SISIs and DICs, are not well equipped to render economic, technical and managerial guidance to a vast number of small scale enterprises. They are themselves handicapped by lack of access to adequate and updated information. The information linkages of DICs / SISIs with other agencies are weak. No where, a systems approach has been evolved. The main source for upgradation of information seems to be the circulars received from the government and other sources, which shows inadequacy of the system. The information system is not geared to meet the growing, changing and diverse needs of small enterprises. The institutions, entrusted with the job, are bogged down on account of lack of resources and organizational problems, as a result of which aspects relating to information have been neglected. Besides, there is lack of coordination between various agencies at district and state level in particular. SEs should strive to keep themselves abreast of the latest information on technology, marketing, management, or for that matter all aspects affecting their competitiveness and growth.

Out of various services rendered by DICs, their major activity is confined to registration of SSE units (provisional and permanent), and activities relating to implementation of Prime Minister's Rozgar Yojana (PMRY) scheme; and other activities received considerably less attention. For updating or preparation of new product profiles, DICs have been devoting some attention.

DIC is the Weakest Link of Extension Services

DIC that forms the largest support network is constrained by regulatory work, paucity of human resources of the required skills. DICs continue to the weakest link in the chain of extension agencies at Central and State levels, though Dic is the most spread out organisation to provide such services. Despite their shortcomings, the DICs need to be strengthened as there is no alternative to them at the district level. DICs should be helped to utilize the services of specialilsed agencies operating at the state and central level. Greater degree of systematization is needed to ensure their effectiveness.

Over the years, DICs have failed in their avowed objective of acting as a 'single window' for clearances, and have not been able to effectively liaison with the concerned departments. During the field survey, it has been revealed that banks have withdrawn their officials from DICs who were earlier posted as credit managers. In matters like credit, power water, raw materials, factory accommodation, etc., the concerned departments and organisations do not seem to be readily willing to shed their power and authority. In fact, it has been found that even within the state, for Department of Industries, in some states, proper coordination is found wanting which ultimately affects the functioning of DICs.

In pursuance of the overall policy of liberalisation, Government of India set up a committee in 1991 to go into the question of simplification of rules and procedures in respect of small entrepreneurs. The committee is reported to have made recommendations in regard to change in labour laws, factories act, environment laws, excise laws, and on reorientation of the roles of DICs and inspectors of various central and state departments. The matter is being pursued by another committee appointed by the Government of India in 2001 with the Cabinet Secretary as the Chairman to look into a number of aspects relating to simplification of matters procedures and laws. This needs constant monitoring and updating with reference to the changing needs of small enterprises.

A number of state governments have initiated steps to liberalise the rules and procedures for small industries. It is learnt that in Punjab, visits of inspectors to small units has been done away with, and in a few states inspectors would visit units only with the approval and under the direction of senior officers. In Karnataka and a few other states, provisional and permanent registration by DICs is to be issued across the counter as soon as the application is submitted and efforts are being made to reduce paper work in other departments like labour, urban development, finance, etc.

The application of a large number of acts, regulations and pro9cedural formalities at various stages of establishment and running the enterprises continue to be a major irritant to small entrepreneurs, and adversely affects their operations. For the emerging new class of young, educated and technically qualified persons, it is a frustrating experience.

With regard to procedural problems with banks/financial institutions, the report observed that a format of about 20 pages is to be filled in by small entrepreneurs which is too time consuming and cumbersome for smaller among small units seeking relatively lower amounts of assistance. Further, small entrepreneurs do not have the requisite education and skill in financial matters to understand their implications and fulfill these requirements. Some of them are, therefore, reluctant to approach banks and financial institutions, more particularly the latter.

Observations by Evaluation Studies

The DIC programme has not up to the expectations. An evaluation of 55 DICs in the country by five institutions in 1988 reveals the following shortfalls in the programme:

- DICs have become bureaucratic. This may be attributed to the fact that bulk of their staff has been drawn from those who were working in the Directorate of Industries Offices.
- Single Window' concept has not materialized in practice. The delegation of powers to DICs is not adequate.
- Credit managers, though drawn from lead banks have not been quite effective in getting adequate financial assistance, and in changing the conservative attitude of banks. In any case, credit managers deputed from lead banks have since been withdrawn.
- Technical and Professional expertise of specialized staff in the DICs is not adequate is meet the growing requirements.
- Excessive inspections by multiple agencies and consequently corruption, continue.
- State level coordination committee do not meet frequently, and guidance provided by them to DICs is inadequate.
- Inspection with voluntary agencies is limited.
- Data provided by DICs about their performance is not found to be always reliable. The tendency is to pad performance statistics, and thereby provide an unduly rosy picture.

Suggestions for Revitalizing DICs

A few suggestions for revitalizing DICs are presented in this section.

1. Expert Group's recommendation to restructure DICs and DEPAs

The Expert Group (1997) recommends that a completely new look be taken on the functioning of the DICs in order to make them more promotional rather than regulatory. DICs would acquire additional significance if they can weave a web of linkages with other institutions. They should function as key conduits for information flowing from availability of channels for discrimination to local business firms. The DICs can function with greater efficiency if they can draw on other resources from business. They can work in association with local councils constituted of members from industry, banks, training institutions, etc. The function of the councils should be to solve the day-to-day problems encountered by entrepreneurs.

The Expert Group suggested that DIC structure should be changed as District Enterprise Promotion Agency (DEPA). It should be constituted as a broad based district level society wit representation formt he departments of industry, revenue, labour, environment and sales tax, banks, financial institutions, state industry corporations, small industry associations, and the local governments. The representatives of specialized promotional agencies of the central and state governments could be standing invitees to this body. Conceptually, this body can be developed as an autonomous agency functioning as a single stop service for information, grievance redressal, clearances coordination and project planning. At the central level, the Ministry of Small Scale Industries, and Agro and Rural Industries could be renamed as Ministry of Small Scale Industries and Business Enterprises, coordination at the policy level and conceptual level can be brought about through the renamed ministry.

The new agency suggested at the district level, DEPA, could be made more autonomous and service oriented. Effective support of SSIs now requires greater technical expertise than is presently available in the DICs. An autonomous structure would help in making it possible to recruit people with appropriate expertise, which would otherwise not be feasible within the current government structure. The effort must be to form public-private partnerships so that government could continue to provide substantial funding support-say, sliding form 90 per cent in the first year to 50 per cent in period of 10 years. The rest should be raised form industry association partners, and from fees collected for the service rendered. The funding pattern will have to vary between districts. Those districts, which have industry clusters, would be able to contribute larger proportion of funds whereas in less developed districts, the government would have to shoulder greater responsibility. Such restructured DEPAs should function as centers for bringing together different local institutions on an organized basis to solve local day-to-day problems. Local councils could be formed to provide the basis for initiating promotional activities which are necessary for the support of SSEs in the district in order to encourage specific support activities. The government should set up a fund at the state level by pooling resources form various organisations including entrepreneurs, from which funds could be made available for various activities.

The state government, in essence, act as a facilitator and oversees the entire programme to ensure that the programme implementation is more result oriented or performance oriented, and not merely target oriented.

The Expert Group also suggests that the DEPAs should have a special focus for the assistance of tiny units. Each DEPA must have experts to primarily work for specific requirements of respective entrepreneurs in the tiny sector. Developing barefoot consultants to guide entrepreneurs at the field level with the active involvement of DEPA becomes necessary. Panel of consultants at the district level drawn from technical and other educational and training institutions, industry and other specialized organisation can be entrusted with this special responsibility of counseling entrepreneurs, and conducting specialized studies.

Other suggestions

- The General Manager(GM), DIC is generally drawn among the official of State Directorates of Industries. The extension services to be rendered by DICs require a number of attributes in GM, particularly a high level of motivation and commitment combined with professional expertise and management capabilities. The appointment of GM and Managers should not be a routine affair. They should be drawn from diverse sources including the Government.

- It is important for DICs to have a panel of consultants to supplement the expertise available in the DICs to handle various roles.

- Among the specialized areas in which work can be initiated by DICs in relation to the scope available in the district, mention made of (i) information updating with reference to the SSI sector, of the state and district, and few prominent industry groups in the micro, tiny and SSI sector including village industries, partly based on secondary sources, and partly first hand collection of data from the field, (ii) active liaison with state and national level organizations on existing and prospective industries relevant for the district, and to extend a helping hand to these organizations for mobilizing data needed by them form industrial units in the district, (iii) to act as an aggressive technical and managerial consultancy organisation to support local industries with the help of a panel of consultants wherever necessary, (iv) to envisage the pattern of growth for different industries based on a realistic field situation, and (v) to focus on entrepreneurship development, vocational training, and skill development by keeping in touch with the relevant organizations. In short, what is being suggested is (a) an aggressive forward looking approach to improve the industrial base, and also the competitive strength of existing units, and (b) to have an effective dialogue with various quarters within the district and within

> the rest of the state in particular, to support the entire range of industrial sector of the district. Though in a small way, these tasks are being performed at the resent, lot more desires to be accomplished through a concerted action of the revitalized DIC, with the support of all relevant central and state level agencies.

Technological, economic and managerial information, and market intelligence for domestic and export markets needs to be far more systematized and collected b the concerned specialized agencies, and made available to DICs. DICs form part of the total system of decentralized industrial development. Systems approach is envisaged to make the best use of the district level set up.

REFERENCES

1. Government of India, *Ministry of Industry* (1997), Report of the Expert Committee on Small Enterprises (Chairman: Abid Hussain), New Delhi.
2. Nagayya, D. (1998), *Impact of Economic Liberalization on Small Industry*, Hyderabad, National Institute of Small Industry Extension Training (NISIET) (Study sponsored by National Small Industries Corporation, New Delhi).
3. National Council of Applied Economic Research and Friedrich-Naumann-Stiftung (NCAER)-FNSt) (1993), *Structure and Promotion of Small Scale Industries in India—Lessons for Future Development*, New Delhi, NCAER.
4. Small Industries Development Bank of India (SIDBI)(2000), *SIDBI Report on Small Scale Industries Sector*, 2000, Lucknow.

20

Performance of DIC: A Case Study of Nellore District

* K. Lavanya Latha & ** Prof. BEVVN Murthy

History

Developing countries, particularly India, mostly rely on the performance of agricultural and industrial sectors for their economic development. The agricultural sector has a vast employment potential but is unable to absorb the fast multiplying population. This situation calls for developing alternatives to meet the needs of needs of ever-growing population. So planners and economists focused attention on accelerating the economic growth through rapid industrialization in the post-independent and planning era. In fact industrialization has been assigned high priority in the development of economy and accorded top priority in the successive five-year plans for achieving the socio-economic objectives. In an attempt to encourage the humbler industrialists and to instill the spirit of industrialization among them, DIC and industrial estate plays an important role. The famous Tafford Park Estates Limited called "The Mother of Industrial Estates" was established in the year 1896 in Manchester, England[1], is the first industrial estate. The concept of industrial estate found its way right across the Atlantic through the United States in 1899, i.e., the year in which the Cleaning Industrial District, Chicago started its operation[2].

* Research Scholar, School of Business Management, S.V. University, Tirupathi.

** Professor, School of Business Management, S.V. University, Tirupathi.

In 1950s the planners of the developing countries like India realized the importance and usefulness of the industrialization. The example of the developed countries was the trendsetter. The invaluable experience gained by such countries tempted the developing nations to make use of the industrial estates as a tool for industrialization in general. As a result of such tendencies, countries like Canada, Puerto Rico, Jamaica, Mexico, Brazil, Irish Republic, Denmark, Finland, Switzerland, Nigeria, India and Pakistan found their place in the world map of industrial estates in 1950s. Thus it was during 1950s that the industrial estates were brought into limelight worldwide. The trend of 1950s continued through 1990s and there after.

In India, though a tiny estate seemed to be set up at Hadapsar[3] by the Poona Municipal Corporation 1952, the real beginning is said to be made in 1955 when an estate was started near the Baktinagar railway station at Rajkot by the erstwhile Sourashtra state[4]. The Rajkot estate may be described as the fore founder of the industrial estates programme in India. Due to the advantages associated with the estate programme the Government of India[5] launched the largest ever programme of industrial estate development through DIC during the five-year plans.

A new concept, known as Functional Industrial estates, was added for units engaged in similar business, making it easy to provide common facilities peculiar to a particular industry. Electronic estate in Pune and Hyderabad, automobile parts in Vijayawada etc., are few examples (Pannalal 1994).

The following are the main objectives of DIC :

- To encourage the growth and registration of SSI units,
- To encourage the self-employment schemes like Prime Minister Rozgar Yojana to educated unemployed youth,
- Recommending for assistance from government agencies for machinery, finance, procurement of materials, registration and licenses,
- Marketing assistance to the SSI units,
- Preparation of project reports and district action plans,

- Providing financial assistance to artisans through banks and also giving subsidy through DRDA,
- Implementations of industrial cooperative societies,
- Encourage entrepreneurship development and training,
- Administrative work including settlement of disputes,
- Activities connected with policy implementation.

Resilient SSIs

Small enterprises, i.e., small scale units, not only played a crucial role in providing large scale employment opportunities at lower capital cost than large scale industries, but also helped in industrialization of rural and backward areas, thereby reducing regional imbalance, assuring more equitable distribution of national income and wealth. SSI units are supplementing and complimentary to large and medium scale units as ancillary units. Considering the large employment level and backlog of creation of new jobs to provide employment to all able people today hopes are pinned on the small scale sector. The Government is making all efforts to provide conducive atmosphere, level playing ground and policy support to enable the SSI sector to achieve higher levels of production, exports and employment.

The Government of India has helped the small scale sector through supportive policy measures since adoption of planned economy model. The basic policy support for SSI sector has its roots in the Industrial Policy Resolution of 1956. Further, the Industrial Policy Statement 1977, laid emphasis on reservation of items. The reservation of economically viable and technologically feasible products to be exclusively manufactured by SSIs began with a list of 47 items, which was gradually extended to many products. Presently, 811 items are on the reserved list. Other policy supports which could be listed are excise exemption, credit under priority sector lending from banks and financial institutions, marketing support through reservation of items for products from SSI sector for government purchases, providing infrastructure facilities like sheds, plots in industrial estates, technological support, new management techniques, training and entrepreneurship development.

The Small-Scale Industry (SSI) sector has emerged over five decades as a highly vibrant and dynamic sector of the Indian economy. Today, this sector accounts for about 95 per cent of the industrial units and is contributing about 40 per cent of value addition in the manufacturing sector, nearly 80 per cent of manufacturing employment and about 35 per cent of exports (both direct and indirect). More than 32 lakh units are spread all over the country producing over 7,500 items and providing employment to more than 178 lakh persons.

Current Status

The real objective of a DIC goes beyond mere development of SSI units through industrial estates, self-employment schemes like PMRY etc. The SSI unit should become in the long run a large scale sector. PMRY program provides a platform to young and talented individuals to dream of becoming large players in future. Due to their economic significance, DIC has to be managed efficiently to deliver the goods. It should take care of sites and sheds requirements adequately and must provide amenities and facilities of standard variety of available prices. The facilities should be total and not in parts.

The present study is undertakes to ascertain the performance of DIC. Nellore, the one of the important business center in Andhra Pradesh. The following are the objectives of the Study:

- To analyze the physical performance of the estate in terms of number of plots and sheds developed and allotted,
- To analyze the performance of self-employment scheme like PMRY in terms of sanctions and grounded.

Methodology of the Study

For the purpose of achieving the above objectives, secondary data was collected from the official records of APIIC, Nellore regarding the performance of SSI units during last five years and to study the progress of PMRY, self-employment schemes among people. The available data was properly analyzed and modified to suit the study requirements. The major findings of the study in the form of physical performance of estate and SSI units, its target and achievements are presented below.

Analysis

Table – 1 gives the data regarding the number of plots and sheds developed and allotted in Nellore district on 31.3.2001. Basically plots and sheds are with centralized provision of all inputs and infrastructure facilities. Main regions of Nellore town like APIE, Wood Complex and Autonagar PH1 all the developed plots are allotted with no vacant plots. Here 100% of achievement took place. Autonagar PH2 of Nellore town which is having highest plots 387, only 360 are allotted with 27 vacant plots. Here achievement is 93%. Industrial Estate of Gudur, Kavali and Pannmgedu have 22,40,48 plots. Out of which 20, 35, 37 are allotted and 2, 5, 1 are remain vacant IIDC. Tada have 151 plots with 60 allotted plots and remaining 91 are vacant. Here achievement is the lowest i.e., 39.7%. In IDA, Ventachalam number of plots developed remain vacant.

Table 1: Statement showing the vacancy position in the existing Industrial Estates/Industrial Development Areas of the Nellore District as on 31.3.2001

Name of IE/IDA	*Plots*				*Sheds*			
	Deve-loped	*Allo-tted*	*Vacant*	*%*	*Const-ructed*	*Allo-tted*	*Vacant*	*%*
1. APIE, Nellore	97	97	--	100	--	--	--	--
2. Wood Complex	103	103	--	100	--	--	--	--
3. Autonagar PH1	250	250	--	100	--	--	--	--
4. Autonagar PH2	387	360	27	93.0	42	18	24	42.8
5. Indl.Estate Gudur	22	20	2	90.9	6	6	--	100
6. Indl.Estate Kavali	40	35	5	87.5	--	--	-- --	
7. IDA Pannamgedu	38	37	1	97.3	--	--	--	--
8. IIDC Tada	151	60	91	39.7	--	--	--	--
9. IDA, Venkatchalam	146	--	146	--	--	--	--	--

Source : Records of APIIC, Nellore.

Coming to sheds, only 42 sheds are constructed in Autonagar PH2 of Nellore town of which 18 are allotted and remaining 24 are vacant. Here 43.8% of achievement takes place. Industrial Estate, Gudur shows all the constructed 6 sheds are allotted with 100% of achievement.

The demand for plots in urban area is more where as these are no takers in rural Venkatachalam and few in Tada. Entrepreneurs prefer to have the enterprise in urban against rural because of priority to the urban towns despite the Venkatachalam and Tada are on the national highway.

This indicates that in Nellore district industrialists are interested to take plots other than sheds. Here is because of sites located in villages are not having proper transport and water facilities.

Table – 2 indicates acres of land acquired and developed. Here mostly all regions in Nellore district the land acquired and developed, only IE, Gudur 18.99 acres of land developed out of 26.47 acres of land acquired. APIIC has proposed to acquire an extent of 25.17 acres in Karur village of Tada mandal for the expansion of IIDC, Tada Wood Complex in Nellore town have highest working units, i.e., 98% and IIDC Tada have lowest 5 units.

Table 2: Details regarding geographical area covered & working units of IDA/IE in Nellore District

Name of the Estate	*Extent of Land (in acres)*		*No. of Units Working*	%
	Acquired	*Developed*		
1. APIE, Nellore	33.28	33.28	60	62
2. Wood Complex	51.95	51.95	101	98
3. Autonagar, PH1	36.68	36.68	213	85
4. Autonagar, PH2	60.74	60.74	215	60
5. Indl. Estate, Gudur	26.47	18.99	19	95
6. Indl. Estate, Kavali	29.50	29.50	24	68
7. IDA, Pannamgeda	24.24	24.24	22	60
8. IIDC, Tada	108.00	108.00	5	8
9. IDA, Venkatachalam	67.03	67.03	-	-

Source : Records of APIIC, Nellore.

It could be observed that the percentage of sick units is less in Nellore where as it is highest in Tada, Pannamgedu. This indicates that 65% of entrepreneurs are satisfied with IE/IDA and only 45% of entrepreneurs are dissatisfied.

Table – 3 indicates that there is a gradual increase in number of SSI units in Nellore district for five years. In 1995-96, 1131 SSI units are installed with investment 1064.64 lakhs, which is increased to 1772 during 1999-2000. This clearly indicates that entrepreneurs of Nellore district are4 more interested in SSI units.

Table 3: Progress of SSI in Nellore District

Year	*No. of Units*	*Investment (Rs. in lakhs)*	*Employment*
1995-96	1131	1064.52	6066
1996-97	1275	1373.52	7058
1997-98	1301	1489.90	6438
1998-99	1446	1728.322	6376
1999-2000	1772	2886.17	8893

Source : Records of DIC, Nellore.

A scrutiny of Table – 4 yields that there is gradual increase in installing SSI units from 1995 to 2000 from basic target but in 1997-98, 5% decrease in expected target. This is due to many of entrepreneurs have switched to aqua farms which gives profits in a short run. Coming to employment, it fluctuating from 1995 to 2000. This is due to scarcity of skill workers in their respective regions. Credit assistance gradually increased from basic target from 1995 to 2000.

From 1995 to 1999, DIC failed in providing assistance to artisans from expected target. But from March 1999 to 2000, the DIC encouraged the unemployed youth through self-employment schemes. So in this year there is 58% increase in expected target, which is a good achievement of DIC. In these years training provided to artisans is less from expected target due to many unemployed youth are with basic technical background came forward how are already skilled ones.

This table indicates that entrepreneurs and artisans of Nellore district are increased in installing SSI units.

Table – 5 indicates that % sanctions against target was gradually decreased from 110% to 22% 1999 and got increased to 60% during 1999-2000. % groundings over target also got decreased from 60% to 31% from 1996 to 2000. This is due to not advertising regularly in daily newspapers by Commissioner of Industries.

Table 5: Progress of PMRY in Nellore District

(Rs. in Lakhs)

Programme	*Target*	*Sanctions*			*Grounded*		
Year	*No.*	*No.*	*Amount*	*%*	*No.*	*Amount*	*%*
1995-96	--	--	--	--	--	--	--
1996-97	1160	1278	988	110	692	504	60
1997-98	1230	951	680	75	523	366.60	43
1998-99	1230	265	188	22	--	--	--
1999-2000	1210	730	522	60	540.10	372	31

Source : Records of DIC, Nellore.

Conclusions

The study presents as contrasting picture of DIC and IE of Nellore district. In terms of plots and sheds allotted, there exists a huge demand for plots from urban entrepreneurs. Many of plots are occupied but no sheds have been constructed in many areas. This indicates the poor vision towards sheds by the entrepreneurs of Nellore district. As far as infrastructure is concerned, many rural estates are ill equipped and have failed to meet the burgeoning requirement of SSI units.

In a nutshell, it can be said that instead of simply increasing either the number of estates of sheds, it is better to equip them with all the necessary infrastructure facilities, which really contribute to the success of industrial estate programme.

It is observed that the majority of artisans were inclined to set up their units. The artisans are not aware of modern marketing techniques and their utility in business. The DIC has to bring new schemes like providing financial assistance through banks by giving subsidy, providing marketing assistance etc.

The Commissioner of Industries has to communicate well to meet the exact target in implementation of PMRY through advertisement in daily newspapers inviting applications from the candidates. Interviews for selection of candidates has to be held for every three months.

DIC is the innovative nodal agency for providing centralized inputs and infrastructure to small and medium enterprises located in IE/IDAs. The DIC should act like incubators used to provide life-supporting facilities to immature born children protect them by providing proper infrastructure facilities. The performance of DIC greatly remains the performance of Estates/ SSI units. This article made an attempt to analysis the performance of DIC in terms of industrial estates developed. This article ends with suggestions for overall improvements of DIC and to take the mantle of entrepreneurship to every corner of the district to meet the twin challenges of unemployment and under utilization of resources.

Summary and Suggestions

In the light of the above, the Government has to look into number of recommendations made by study group for development of small enterprises under Chairmanship of S.P. Gupta.

- The study group has also made a number of recommendations on fiscal and financial measures covering;
- Setting up of targets for tiny and SSI units for credit from banks and Fis under priority sector lending;
- Measures for strengthening resource support to SIDBI and to make available cheaper resources for on-lending at low interest rates to SSI sector;
- Setting up of a special venture capital type fund of

Rs.500 crores to be named as Laghu Udyog Nirman Nidhi for equity support;

- Standardization of procedure and simplification of forms by banks;
- Exemption from excise registration and visits of excise registration and visits of excise inspectors until the turnover reaches a limit of Rs. 50 lakh with a system of self-declaration;
- More effective monitoring f credit flow to SSI sector by the Monitoring Committee of local institutions;
- Raising the limit of composite loans from Rs.10 lakhs to Rs.25 lakhs to encourage tiny units to get term loan and working capital from same bank/FI.

The study group has recommended following measures for technology upgradation and modernization of SSI un its.

- Setting up of a Technology Bank for collection and dissemination of information about technology sources.

To provide increased marketing support to the SSI sector, the study group has recommended that:

- Up to 33 per cent of government purchases may be done from SSI sector on the lines of USA.
- Industry status to all types of consortium industries so that they can avail finance from banks and FIs.
- Subsidization of participation of SSI units up to 50 per cent in air fare for export related buyer-seller meets.

REFERENCES

1. William, Bredo, *Industrial Estates : Tool for Industrialization*, Asia Publishing House, Bombay, 1962, p. 10.
2. *Ibid.*
3. Study of Industrial Estates, Central Small Industries Organization, Ministry of Industry, Government of India, New Delhi, 1966 (mimco), p. 5.
4. P.C. Alexander, *Industrial Estates in India*, Asia Publishing House, Bombay, 1963, p. 17.

5. N. Gangadhara Rao and M. Gangadhara Rao, Industrial Estates and India's Experience, *Indian Journal of Social Sciences*, September-December, 1973, p. 246.

6. S.P. Gupta, *Report of Study Group on Development of Small Enterprises*, Planning Commission, Government of India, 2001.

21

District Industries Centres (DICs): Future Perspectives

* Dr. T.V. Rao

The DICs as the focal point of industrial development at the district level came into existence in the year 1978. The DICs are supposed to provide pre-investment, investment and post-investment assistance to the industrial sector (particularly the Small-Scale Industries (SSI) and Village industries).

Two and half decades have already passed by and it is pertinent to review the performance of the DICs, their achievements and areas of failure.

The objective of this paper is to throw light on what is expected of the DICs, what they have done and what will be the future direction.

What is Expected?

The DICs are established on the recommendations of the NISIET study group. The objective is to make the district as the center for planning and promoting industrial development. It should provide pre-investment, investment and post-investment assistance mainly to the small industry, act as a single window of clearance, provide vital information to the entrepreneurs about the availability of resources at the district level, and assist the small industry in matters relating to the supply/availability of

---

* The author published the doctoral thesis on the working of DICs in the book titled 'Development of Small-Scale Industries – Role of DICs', published by Anmol Publications Pvt. Ltd., New Delhi, 1995.

machinery/marketing/credit/infrastructure and a host of other services.

The DICs are to be manned by highly trained, well-motivated, professional and functional managers ably assisted by three project officers.

The DICs are supposed to establish liaison with other departments of Central and State governments operating at the district level and act as a single window of clearance at the district level[1].

They were vested with the additional responsibility of administering the SEEUY program and also imparting the requisite skills to the rural youth in order to enable them to secure self-employment.

What happened?

The author had the opportunity to look into working of DICs and their organizational structure. In the course of the study, number of DIC officials and beneficiaries were contacted and their views and opinions were gasthered.

A macro level survey was done on the working of DICs in the state of Andhra Pradesh by collecting secondary data. It was supplemented by an intensive analysis of the functioning of DICs in four districts, Rangareddy, Krishna, Anantapur and Mahaboobnagar.

The main findings of the study are:

- After the establishment of DICs there is substantial growth in units, investment and employment generated;
- Structural shifts have taken place in the composition of SSI as the importance of rubber, petroleum, chemical and non-metallic mineral industry increased;
- The share of SC and ST beneficiaries in the number of SSI and artisan units established, employment generated and increased;

1. See enclosed charts "DIC AS NODAL AGENCY" and "DIC – INTERFACE WITH OTHER AGENCIES"

- DICs in Telangana region performed better than their counterparts in Andhra and Rayalaseema regions;
- The DICs are supposed to be manned by fresh recruits with requisite professional skills placed as functional managers. Contrary to the declared policy these posts were filled up by promoting the officials of the industries department. As a result the zeal and initiative of young professionals was lost;
- There is lack of uniformity and absence of any scientific methodology in conducting techno-economic survey of the districts;
- The non-appointment of the three project officers also impaired the effective functioning of DICs;
- The bank official at the district level lamented that the DIC assistance was not forthcoming in loan recoveries;
- Project and product profiles prepared by the DICs are not based on any objective criterion and lack of relevance;
- There are multiple agencies working at the district level catering to the needs of small, tiny and village industries such as DRDA, KVIB, and Handicrafts Board, etc. Unfortunately, there is lack of proper cooperation and coordination amongst them;
- As a single window the DICs failed miserably in coordinating with the central and state government departments operating at the district level. This problem is arising, as the other departments are not willing to share their powers with the DICs;
- As a nodal agency the DIC performance is very poor and all the evils of government departments entered them. The DICs virtually rendered no assistance to the needy entrepreneurs;
- Under the SEEUY program the DICs rendered valuable assistance as most of the rural youth have derived substantial benefits under the ISB component

but the unfortunate story is that they preferred to establish service units in place of industrial units and their choice was influenced by family background, friends and relatives. Most of them selected traditional ventures rather than diversified new areas;

- The number of woman beneficiaries under the SEEUY program was very low;
- The author has taken up the case study of the artisan complexes established at Lingojiguda and Nutankal in Ranga Reddy district, Atkur, Kondapally in Krishna district, Lepakshi and Kothakota in Anantapur districts. It is observed that the working conditions of these artisans are poor and that proper facilities such as power, water, etc., were not provided to them;
- The artisans were not getting enough assistance from any agency at the district level in matters relating to supply of raw materials, credit, modernization of machinery, and marketing. The artisan complexes have become residential houses rather than production centers; and
- Much of the governmental funds were wasted in the construction of rural industrial estates and artisan complexes due to selection of wrong locations. Most of the industrial sheds remained unoccupied and un-utilized.

Future Perspectives

The presence of DICs as the prime industrial planning and promotional agency at the district level is essential and not at all disputed. There is lot of apathy and despair in their working. The single window and nodal agency concepts still remained in their premature stage, which is the root cause of beneficiary discontent.

The post-liberalization scenario has completely changed the complexion and content of the economic environment. it unleashed the competitive force. Produce or perish is the rule of the day. There is no scope for survival of the weak and inefficient.

Quality and competitiveness alone can make the industrial units to stay in the market.

It is under this backdrop, that a thorough review of the functioning of DICs is essential. The small industry is not excluded from facing the challenges of competitive forces. It is the unbound responsibility of the DICs to safeguard and to protect them. In a way the future survival small industry depends on how best the DICs can assist the beneficiaries and how they discharge their onerous responsibilities. The DICs can no longer remain as district information centers. They should rather become the District Development Centres. They should rather become the District Development Centres. The government should arm the DICs with greater powers and responsibilities. Professional functional managers are to be appointed to man the DICs. They should be given more powers to act and also functional autonomy vis-à-vis accountability. They, in turn should prepare an action plan for modernizing the plant and machinery of the SSI wherever possible and necessary provide marketing assistance, encourage and motivate the beneficiaries in producing new, quality and competitive products. They should also provide technical consultanct service.

The DICs should work with vision and mission and make the single window concept a virtual reality. Falling to live up to the expectations of the new challenging economic environment by this vital district level agency may cause a disaster not only to the DICs but also to a large number of beneficiaries dependent on it.

Table 2
Industrial Profile of the District

S.No.	Sector	Number of Units in 1990			Number of Units in 1995			Number of Units in 2000		
		SSI	L&M	Total	SSI	L&M	Total	SSI	L&M	Total
1.	Agro based	89	0	89	133	0	133	244	0	244
2.	Forest based	211	0	211	468	0	468	244	0	244
3.	Mineral based	6	0	6	48	0	48	33	1	34
4.	Marine based	0	0	0	0	2	2	0	0	0
5.	Textile based	1	0	1	31	0	31	131	0	131
6.	Engineering	450	0	450	44	1	45	384	0	384
7.	Chemical	36	0	36	29	0	29	25	1	26
8.	Livestock	23	0	23	16	1	17	36	0	36
9.	Building material	75	0	75	27	0	27	72	1	73
10.	Miscellaneous	87	0	87	424	0	424	1217	3	1220
	Total	978	0	978	1220	4	1224	2308	6	2314

Table 2.2
Performance Under PMRY

S.No.	*Year*	*Target*	*Sponsored*	*Sanctioned*	*Grounded*	*Trained*
1.	1993-94	243	368	180	134	180
2.	1994-95	1500	2152	1214	878	1130
3.	1995-96	1650	3469	1705	1301	1622
4.	1996-97	1650	3038	1668	1271	1365
5.	1997-98	1770	3103	1832	1336	1597
6.	1998-99	1786	3759	1862	1311	1490
7.	1999-00	1743	4045	1876	1292	1080
8.	2000-01	1758	3889	1954	1080	1122
9.	2001-02	1700	3373	1734	928	1057
	Total	13800	27196	14025	9311	10446

22

SSI Sector in East Godavari District–Role of District Industries Centre

Dr. J. Chandra Prasad & K. Nageswara Rao

India today operates the largest number of programs for promotion and development of small-scale sector as compared to any other developing country. Small-scale industries, power looms, and other traditional villages industries has, through tho last four decades, displayed a phenomenal growth in terms of output, employment and exports. The sector's contribution towards widening of the entrepreneurial base, promotion of rural industrics and ancillary support to large and medium industries has also been tremendous. This sector presently produces nearly 7,500 items ranging from simple products to highly sophisticated/ technology-based products.

SSI Sector—The Positive Focus

Various empirical studies that the characteristics of capital per worker, output per worker, value added per worker, ratio of capital and value added, are below:

	Small	*Medium*	*Large*
Capital per worker (Rs.)	57012	61249	287679
Output per worker (Rs.)	327569	308923	465384
Value added per worker (Rs.)	38509	42865	98791
Gross output/Capital ratio	0.17	0.20	0.61
Value added/value of output ratio	0.12	0.14	0.21

The status of SSI sector is evident from that in 1998-99 it accounts for 55% of total industrial product in India (1998-99), 35% of total export.

The Initiatives in India

A policy of positive discrimination towards small enterprises, is the offspring of the freedom movement, and more specifically the Quit India movement, where Khadi (hand-woven textiles) evolved as the symbol of this policy thrust. The national governments policy was concretized in the Industrial Policy (IPR) of 1948, Following the approached outlined by the IPR, an institutional network involving, the All India Cottage Industries Board and six other specific Boards, was set up during the First Five-Year plan period.

The second Five-Year Plan and the Mahalonobis model, which provided its theoretical under spinning, came out with a clear statement on the respective roles of small and large industry in the policy and strategy of development in the country.

The Third major phase of small enterprise development in the country was inaugurated by the mid-1980s. This era has been marked by a further focus on project-based approaches, and mounting arguments for intermittent widening of the limits of the small-scale sector (through definitional hikes in investment limits). The liberalization regime, formally inaugurated in 1991, brought forward a new policy of small scale and tiny industries with significant focus on loosening the protective applicable to this sector. With a view to make the district as a focal point for industrial development, the government of India DICs, at the district levels, constitutes a single agency providing all the services, facilities and support required to set up the industrial units and for their successful functioning. These centers are with the objective orientation of promotion and widespread dispersal of small and cottage industrial units in rural and urban areas.

The objective of the paper is to study the widening horizons of small-scale industry under the aegis of District Industries Centre and to suggest ways for further activism.

East Godavari District – A Profile

East Godavari located in the geographical and cultural background of the river Godavari is predominantly agro-based. The headquarters is located at Kakinada. It lies on the north east coast of Andhra Pradesh and is bounded on the north by Visakhapatnam district and state of Orissa. On the east south by the Bay of Bengal and on the West by Khammam and West Godavsri district.

The district is located between the northern latitude of 16 degree and 18 degree and between eastern longitudes of 81 degrees and 82 degree 30'. It occupies an area of 10,807 sq. kms. And has a population of 45,40,937 as per 1991 census. The district consists of 57 revenue mandals with 9 towns grouped under 5 revenue divisions. The district can be broadly divided into three zones, viz., the agency or hill tracts, the delta and the uplands. Delta area constitutes the whole of Konaseema, parts of Kakinada and Rajahmundry revenue divisions. The district presents a vast expense of rice fields founded by plantains, betal and coconut gardens and innumerable plantains groves.

About 68% of the population are engaged in agriculture and its allied activities. Paddy is the main crop, other important crops being groundnut, pulses, coconuts, sugarcane, bajra, mango, tobacco, cashew, banana, etc. Paddy is grown on 2.8 lakh hectares producing 4.27 lakh tones, sugarcane grown on 17,000 hectares producing 13.00 lakh tones. The coconut grown on 27,000 hectares with an annual yield of around 40.70 crores nuts. Sericulture, cashew plantations and oil palm are encouraged in a big way.

The agriculture products and its by-products and the vital inputs for agro-based industries like : rice, flour, oil mills, sago and starch products, coconut products, solvent extraction plants, tobacco producing and redrying plants. Coir and allied products, coconut products, fruit products like mango jelly, cashew kernels, cashew shell oil and palm fibre. To bring additional area under mulberry cultivation for increase in the production of coconuts and silk yarn production national sericulture project (1989-90 to 1993-94) with the World Bank assistance has been in operation.

The area under forest is 2.85 lakh hectares and stands third in coastal Andhra in production of bamboo, timber, beedi leaves and firewood. The total forest production is 5.878 hectares. Teak is grown in 82.8 hectares, bamboo in 378 hectares and eucalyptus in 1605 hectares. And milk projects at Rajahmundry and Kakinada taken up Dairy Development Corporation.

Important minerals in the district are graphite, fire clay, china clay, laterite and bauxite. Basing on these minerals there is a good number of Mangalore tile units, bricks kilns, graphite crucible units, ceramic and refractory units. Granite deposits are also available. This gives scope for granite polishing units for the first time to be set up in the district. Kakinada stands first in Andhra Pradesh with 43% total state fish production. The inland fish is 28,341 M.T. catch while marine fish is about 5,66,00 MT per annum.

Good number of fish products and prawn processing units with filling being given for brackish water fish development, more units are possible, nylon fish net manufacturing units are already encouraged.

Salt cultivation in and around Kakinada. It mostly concentrated in Gurajanapalli, Penugudur, Chollangi and Chollangipet villages.

Besides 5 licenced salt factories comprising an area of Asc 222.00, there are unlicenced salt cultivators cultivating in an area of Acs. 750,000. In all the production is 33,660 Mts. The average yield is about 15 tonnes per acre, which is low. This necessitated modernization of salt farms.

Industrial Estates/Industrial Development Areas

There are five industrial estates and three industrial development areas in the district. All infrastructural facilities like power, water and internal roads are providing in these areas to enable quick implementation of projects proposed to be taken by the entrepreneurs. The details of industrial estates are as follows:

Registered Units

It can be analysed from the table that the food and agro-based small-scale units are dominating with 32.68 per cent. Out of 9,546 units 3,120 units belonged to food and agro-based category followed by engineering based units 1,796 (18.81 per cent), forest-based units 1,254 units (13.13 per cent) and mineral-based units 767 (8.03 per cent).

Investment

The operation efficiency depends not only on management but also on the level, availability and effect utilization of investment. Generally, in any small industries the investment position is weak which need to be taken care of. It is observed from the table that total 9,546 units account for 18.8 per cent of units assume 51.31 per cent of the total investment share is only 26.81 per cent. Food and agro-based units are not investment-oriented compared to engineering based units.

Employment

Small-scale units provide a plenty of employment opportunities in the district economy. The 9,456 small units sheltered 83,117 employees. The highest employment is observed in food and agro-based category with 35.55 per cent as evident from the table. Both mineral and engineering-based units are having the same employment potential with 12.82 and 12.78 respectively. It also reveals that a minimum of only 0.68 per cent of total employment is provided from the animal-based units.

District Industries Centre

The District Industries Centre, Kakinada came into being from 1.3.1981. The major structural innovations in the industrial policy for creation of single agency to meet the requirements of small and village industries and to achieve the objective of efficient and effective promotion of cottage and small scale industries.

The main aim of the DIC is to develop coordination with entrepreneurs from rural areas and with various institutions such as banks, consultancy organizations, district development agencies.

The DIC targeted to tackle in an effective manner, the various structural changes in the field of development of village and small-scale industries and correct the imbalance.

The DICs, in general, are aimed at providing the following facilities:

- Documentation Cell facilitating the entrepreneurs to choose their industry;
- Financial assistance through nexus with various agencies such as banks, financial institutions, Andhra Pradesh Small-Scale Industries Corporation, National Small Industries Corporation Limited, etc., for provision of machinery and working capital.
- Export promotion;
- Marketing facilities, etc.

The District Industries Centre also quickens the rural industrialization with Nodal Agency and District Advisory Committee for expeditious clearance and up, not save the time but also develop the industries in the right direction.

Industrial Horizon of East Godavari – A Focus on SSI

38 large and medium scale industries with investment of 267.84 crores employing 17.119 persons are functioning in the district and 11 projects involving capital investment of Rs.1820.17 crores with an employment potential up to 2,990 are under implementation. Another 28 major and medium projects having scope of employment are awaiting implementation.

The main lines of manufacture among the existing industries are agro-based industries such as paper mills, straw board making, sugar factories, textiles, liquid glucose, industrial alcohol, automobile component manufacturing industries such as break drums tie-rod ends brushes, etc. The district offers immense potential for setting up a number of medium and small-scale industries.

There are 9,546 small-scale units registered in the district functioning with a capital investment of Rs.199.49 crores with an employment potential of 83,177 persons. The details of the small scale units existing in the district as on 31.3.1999 category-wise is shown hereunder:

Conclusions

The data-based analysis so far and the personal observation and interaction with the entrepreneurs of the select units help to make some noteworthy reflections. The financial disability of small-scale industries in the district is deplorable. Their internal resources are so small that they have no surplus to live on during the period of business strain. There should be support by the banks and financial institutions. The credit worthiness should not be judged in terms of value of assets but in terms of the ability of an enterprise to do the job and earn profit.

Due to lack of proper marketing channels the products of SSI are sold at un-remunerative prices. The small entrepreneurs are not aware of the market information with regard to price, place, quality, quantity fashions, so an efficiently market information system is desirable at the district level to make the small entrepreneurs aware.

Reasonable segregation of market should be carried out, so that the consumer goods, and other products of large scale consumption are allotted to small industries. Promotional agencies should be developed in the East Godavari district which could assist the small units in general and specially carrying out the initial spade work, idle land reservation, clearance of plans from local authority producing the services of architect or engineering construction of factory premises and registration with directorate of industries, etc.

It is necessary to provide more infrastructure facilities, especially in rural areas to attract rural entrepreneurs to start small industries. All the industrial estates and industrial development areas come up are in and around, cities, and big towns. There should be a programme to set up mini-industrial estates near mandal headquarters and major panchayats. There should be a package approach, by way of providing land, sheds, credit, machinery, raw material, licence, power etc., thereby inconvenience caused will be reduced.

Though the DICs are supposed to function as single agency for providing all services under one roof, entrepreneurs are to run around multiple agencies for support and services. To facilitate the entrepreneurs, the DICs need to establilsh a workable nexus with other SSI promoting and service institutions.

The DIC should improve its professional character and develop machinery for the evaluation and follow up of SSI to prescribe timely directions and corrections.

INDUSTRIAL DEVELOPMENT AREAS

Name of the Estate/ Development Area	*Extent Acres*	*Available*	*Allotted*	*Vacant*	*Available*	*Allotted*
Existing :						
1. Self-Employment Estate, Kakinada	6.80	10	10	--	15	15
2. Indl. Development Area, Kakinada	46.72	48	48	--	20	20
3. Indl. Development Samalkot	25.75	22	22	--	28	28
4. Assisted Private Indl. Estate, Dowleswaram	34.31	58	58	--	17	17
5. Indl. Development Area, Dowleswaram	168.31	17	--	--	--	--
6. Indl. Development Area, Kadiyam	73.48	Undeveloped land has been acquired and allotted				
7. Mini Industrial Gopalapuram	2.64	2	2	--	5	5
8. Mini Industrial Area, Ramachandrapuram	15.68	30	16	14	4	4

INDUSTRIAL DEVELOPMENT AREA AS FOLLOWS

S. No.	*Name of the Estate/ Development Area*	*Extent (Acres)*	*Remarks*
Under Implementation :			
1.	Industrial Development Area, Kakinada	61.63	Taken proposals of land and development of land is in progress
2.	Industrial Development Area Sarpavaram	142.07	Already taken possession
Proposed During VII Plan :			
1.	Autonagar, Kakinada	202.87	
2.	Industrial Development Area (beach road), Kakinada	500.00	Initially
3.	Industrial Development Area, Kotapadu	1097.00	
4.	Industrial Development Area, Rajakagraharam	500.00	
5.	Autonagar, Rajahmundry	57.63	
6.	Industrial Estate, Tuni	48.47	
7.	Mini Industrial Estate, Ramachandrapuram	38.00	

Category	*Units*	*% to Total*	*Invest-ment*	*% to Total*	*Employ-ment*	*% to Total*
Food and Agro-based	3,120	32.68	5,34,877	26.81	29,521	35.51

23

District Industries Centres—The Outlook

Er. H. Shivaji Rao
Chartered Engineer
Secretary,COSI (A.P)

It is imperative that no organization can be static all the time with age old philosophies and policies especially in the light of the general euphoria created by the liberalization policies set up by Government of India and enacted in 1991 and the globalization of all economy in the recent past. The organizations both Government and non-Government need to consider this in setting up their goals and targets.

The liberalization of policies have scared the Small Scale sector of the Industries that they would be really effected due to the decontrol of industry, increased competition and market oriented reforms. The development of Industries and in particular the small scale Industries, being the responsibility of State Governments, the District Industries Centres, which were setup with a purpose to develop industrial base in the respective revenue districts at all the headquarters of Districts, have prime responsibilities in the development of Industries.

Government of Andhra Pradesh have promulgamated certain orders in 1995 to make procedures eased for the new industrial entrepreneurs in S.S.I Sector having given a considerable thought over the past G.O.M.S. No. 611 dated 01-12-1986 and G.O.M.S.No.41, dated 29-03-1995 and the recommendations by the Commissioner of Industries in 1994 & 1995.

To establish an Industry, a prospective entrepreneur is required to obtain clearances/approvals from the following agencies prior to start off of the unit in addition to other regulations.

(i) Approval of village Panchayat, if the industry is proposed to be set up in a Panchayat area and that of Municipality if the unit is to be set up in a Municipal Area and from an Urban Development Authorities of the location if the unit is to be set up in the Urban Areas.

(ii) Approval of the Town Planning

(iii) Approval of Factories Inspector

After careful consideration and to encourage entrepreneurs with less of Governments' Bureaucracy hurdles, based on the proposals sent by the Commissioner of Industries, and after holding discussions with related Non-Governmental Organizations, representing various industrial associations, Government issued orders that all Small Scale and Tiny Industries operating with power up to 30 HP, and employing up to 30 persons be exempted form obtaining clearances / approvals stated above, subject to the following conditions.

1. The S.S.I. units should not be set up in residential area in case of villages.
2. The industrial units shall not violate zonal regulations in Municipal Area where zonal regulations are in force.
3. The S.S.I. shall not utilize boilers in the manufacturing process.
4. The SSI units have taken necessary steps and measures to ensure health and safety of workmen.
5. The SSI units shall be registered as SSI with D.I.C in order to take the above privilege, the units shall at the time of registration certify before the D.I.C that the above conditions have not been violated in a pro forma

specified for this purpose by the Department. The SSI Registration Certificate is issued by the Department only after enquiring that the above declaration is made on a Rs.20/- stamp paper.

The liberalized procedure is not applicable for those units which do not register themselves with D.I.C.'s and in such case they will be required to obtain approvals/clearances form the above said authorities individually.

The Government further clarified that not withstanding this exemption from obtaining approvals/clearances, by the SSI units, the relevant laws will be applicable for operation of these units and Government has taken concurrence of the various Authorities prior to issuing this order.

The Single Window System, that DIC's have ventured to adopt few years back to curtail the delays in obtaining these approvals by the Industrial Entrepreneurs was not very effective. The reason being that DIC's have not taken the necessary initiatives to obtain the approvals properly excepting they were acting as Postal Medium. The monthly SSI review meetings held in presence of the District Administration, has succeeded in pushing the matter to certain extent but not completely.

Therefore these revised orders, have to a large extent helped the promoters to save time in grounding the unit.

Presently DIC's are engaged in the following activities in relation to setting up new Industries.

1. They receive application from the units for registration as on SSI.
2. They scrutinize, forward the applications for obtaining clearances from the different departments. They participate in SSI Review Meetings and ascertain that the approvals are give by the concerned departments.
3. Once the unit is grounded, the applications for subsidies are processed and recommendations made for release of subsidies.

In other words the DIC's are more engaged in processing the registration and subsidy allotment, rather than promotion of Industries, despite the fact that each DIC has more than 3 to 4 Industry Proportion Officers employed located not only at the district head quarters but also at the division head quarters within the district.

It is time that each DIC maintain a library of typical industrial projects and list of selective Industries suggested for Srikakulam district to assist new entrepreneurs. There is no proper coordination to conduct periodical seminars / training programme for prospective entrepreneurs. Some times, they organize such training programmes with the assistance of SISI or certain Non-Governmental Organizations. But there is no follow up programme after the training is conducted. So the percentage of grounded units after the EDP courses is very low.

With the present global communication net work D.I.C's can attend to more developmental activities than what they are handling at present. Programmes such as CMEY, PMRY can also be handled but need not engross completely in only these activities. Despite the above, there is a substantial growth in the industries set up during the last decade, as shown by Department of Industries, with number of industries established increasing year by year as seen from the following table.

	1992-1993	1993-1994	1994-1995	1995-1996	1996-1997	1997-1998
No. of Units Established	14,645	16,211	17,190	19,869	23,307	30,164
Investment In Rupees (Crores)	152	146	157	211	238	243

Some of the items that should be concentrated are:

1. Reservation of certain Industries to be manufactured only in SSI Sector.
2. Fiscal Concessions, supply of scarce raw material and concessional credit.
3. Support for marketing
4. Infrastructure support
5. Technical Support for modernization and expansion

6. Training in Human Resources Development
7. Problems faced by existing Industrial Units

The D.I.C's based on their studies, surveys and experiences should be identifying and updating the selective list of industries more suitable for the Districts than to continue publishing the same old lists year by year.

The DIC's should be able to prepare case histories on the sick industries, if necessary with the assistance of local Industrial Associations, enlighten the reasons for such sickness for the benefit of new entrepreneurs so that they would not be repeated.

The DIC's shall be able to ascertain the exact need of total project cost and form a cell to guide the new entrepreneurs in how best the project can be financed, by giving their know how on various financial undertakings who come forward for such assistance. DIC's shall also concentrate on the follow up of newly grounded units and where necessary advise them on the tendencies to sickness and preventing measures. It cannot but be emphasized that several industrial units tend to sickness for various reasons and may of them could be controlled at the preliminary stages. Such guidance is very much essential for the new under takings. Sustaining the existing units help more in the development of industrial sector, than promoting only new industries.

Similar to the EDPs, which are conducted for the purpose of promoting new industrial units, seminars and workshops are to be held for the existing units periodically in a general forum and discuss their operational problems, either financial, marketing or processing techniques.

It is necessary that the modern techniques shall be implemented to avoid obsolences of the age old processing methods for better profit margins. DIC's have to take active role, being nearer to the industry, in this regard, as the Government has come forward to subsidize such investments.

DIC's shall have their own technical cell to review the technical and economical aspects of new projects and if necessary coordinate with APITCO., etc., and ensure that a new project has to no burgs which can lead to sickness, prior to grounding itself.

In present days, the tendency of most entrepreneurs is not to run the industry, but to set up an industry only to get the subsidy en-cashed. Once the subsidy is in hand, the industry becomes sick and the bankers are facing a bad recovery situation. The author does not opine that all entrepreneurs are like this but this tendency exists amongst many of the new entrepreneurs. Recently the State Government has conducted seminars and meetings at various levels on VISION – 2005 and identified that this problem can be averted by developing infrastructure facilities and provide the entrepreneurs at subsidized cost instead of extending subsidy in cash. DIC's being the representatives of the State Government, should come forward in identifying those infrastructures requirements and provide them to the needy.

Several years back, the then Industries and Commerce Department, have established their own Industrial Estates and also in certain places Assisted Private Industrial Estates, taking the contribution from the interested industrial Entrepreneurs. These Industrial Estates were established at the outskirts of the towns, with adequate roads, power and water resources. The buildings also were constructed with the assistance of A.P Industrial Infrastructure Corporation.

The Industries Department even has established their own raw material service centers and Tool Room Production Units in these industrial estates with their own employment.

Though initially there was interest shown by the new Industrialists, subsequently due to improper maintenance of these infrastructure facilities, and huge rents or out right sale prices for the buildings fixed pay APIDC, there is a deterioration of occupancy in such units. At present, there are large number of vacant buildings causing heavy losses to the Government.

The most important requirement for sustenance of any industry is the marketing facilities. The DIC's can establish their own marketing cells, which can guide the new undertakings with data, and provisions for marketing their products with ease.

To sum up, DIC's shall concentrate more on development of industries by

1. Updating the Statistical information regarding of

sources of raw material, marketing outlets and suggestive list of prospective industries and making them available for the new entrepreneurs.

2. Providing infrastructure such as power, water, roads required for new industries.
3. Conducting meetings/seminars with the existing Industries and identifying any further scope of sickness and take preventive steps.
4. Conducting meetings with already sick industries and guide them to identify the reasons for sickness and assist them in averting the same.
5. Assisting the new entrepreneurs in grounding the units at the earliest to prevent any escalated costs in setting up the unit, because of this delay.
6. Conducting periodic training programmes both EDP as will as product oriented workshops and seminars.

24

DICs – Role in Changing Scenario

B. Suresh Babu,
General Manager,
DIC, Visakhapatnam

The District Industries Centres have been facing numerous problems which are of varied nature while some are in turned to it others are relating to coordination with other promoting agencies, policy mattors and the entrepreneurs themselves. In this paper some such issues are dealt with which have emanated from experiences and ground realities

Coordination: At present, any Entrepreneur, who wishes to set up an industry, has to roam around at least 5 to 6 departments viz. A.P. Industrial Infranstructure Corporation for Land, A.P. State Financial Corporation or Financial Institutions for Finance, A.P.TRANSCO for Power, A.P.Pollution Control Board for Pollution Clearance, Factories Department for Factories approval. In Small Scale Industrial sector, mostly one or two persons will only look after the affairs and it is very very difficult to move from pillar to post of various things. It is also expressed by various industrialists and entrepreneurs that considerable time is being wasted in getting varous clearances and at times it is also lacking transparency and bogged down to harassment. It is also expressed by various Industry Associations that since D.I.C. is focal point for industrial development, a system of Industry Facilitation Cell may be created at DIC where all connected departments will meet once in a week and provide all the approvals / services and necessary counseling, guidance for speedy clearances and for speedy implementation of the projects.

Further, DIC is also playing vital role on developing Ancillary Industries affiliated to Public Sector Undertakings through a mechanism of District Task Force Committees headed by District Collectors. Off late, certain issues are being brought to the notice of DICs that the parent unit is not taking care of the Ancillary Industries and it is also alleged that the orders/ works meant for Ancillary and Local Industry are been diverted and especially in the context of Visakhapatnam Steel Plant, this sort of feed back is on very high side. It is also expressed by the various Industry Associations that General Manager, District Industries Centre should be made the member of Purchase Committee of Public Sector Undertakings as representative of local S.S.I and Ancillaries as to have a transparency in the purchases from them. I opine that this sort of arrangement is the need of the hour and DICs will play key role in arbitrating the differences between the parent unit and Ancillaries.

Marketing: As a part of Marketing Assistance, DICs are also representing in various Purchase Committees of various Government Departments at State Levdel, but, when it comes to purchases of Central Government Departments, Public Sector Undertakings of State Govt. and Central Government, DICs, have no role to represent local S.S.Is. Though there is concept of NSIC Registration, the procedure to obtain such Registration is very Cumbersome and involving the inspections of S.I.S.I. Here, the Industry Associations expressed a view that S.I.S.Is. are having very few Centres and it is taking considerable time for S.I.S.I. inspections and why can't DICs are to be delegated such inspections so as things will be made easy. In my personal experience, even the attempts of Single Point Registration of NSIC are not so fruitful and I suggest DIC should be empowered as Inspecting Agency for NSIC Registration rather than SISI as to ease the things.

After Liberalization, to set up a Larger & Medium Scale unit, it requires an Industrial Entrepreneurs Memorandum from Secretariat for industrial approvals except in the case of Licensable items. IEM is nothing but an Acknowledgement of a proposal. Government of India has liberalized the procedure in so easy way that one has to send his application with required fee through post to SIA, and we will get such Acknowledgement just within a month. But in the case of SSIs, DICs used to give Provisional Registrations with Stamp & Seal of G.M./A.Ds/Field Officers as the case may be. Here, it is suggested that simply on a model of IEM and an 'Inwad' Cell in charge may be empowered to issue such Acknowledgement on Provisional Registrations. The DICs should remove the word of SSI Registration for Provisional SSI and substitute it with a wording of SSI Acknowledgement on similar lines of IEM of Government of India as in the case of Large & Medium Scale Units.

Single Window: While attuning to the process of Liberalization and Simplification, Government of Andhra Pradesh has announced in the New Industrial Policy vide G.O.Ms.No.9, Industries & Commerce Dept., Dt. That all statutory approvals will be dealt through Single Window System. District Level Committees headed by District Collectors will clear all statutory approvals up to Rs. 1.00 crore investment and State Level Committees will clear the approvals above Rs. 1.00 crore as per the guidelines. In some States Approvals/Clearances of all S.S.I. sector are being dealt at District Level and the rest at State Level. The State Government may follow the similar pattern duly rationalizing the simplification as majority of units with Rs. 1.00 crore investment are falling in the category of S.S.I. sector and the entrepreneurs are made to follow up things at State Level and itself is contrary to friendly policy towards S.S.I. sector. Further, Government of Andhra Pradesh is also extending certain incentives to S.S.I. sector through GOMs. No.9. But, when it came to processing, Government has allowed the District Level Committees to process up to Rs.15.00 lakhs investment on project cost and the rest has to go to State Level. Here, units with project cost of Rs. 25.00 lakhs are categorized 'Tiny Sector' and they are forced to follow up at State Level. It may be suggested that all incentive cases of Tiny/SSI sector (Govt. of India definition) may be processed at District Level for quick disposal and to create friendly climate.

Further, "Marketing Intelligence" is one of the Key parameter either to identify new opportunities or to sustain the healthy running of the existing units. At present, we are having number of project consultants both in Government Sector and Private Sector and the cost of Market Intelligence is very high and not available to small entrepreneurs. Here, DICs may be reformed as source of latest Marketing Intelligence and that is possible only when the DICs are provided with High Tech facilities like Internet, Fax and exposure to various exhibitions, Seminars etc. In addition, the Senior Officers of DICs are made busy with routine target oriented works rather than focus on updating and up-keeping the latest information on Market Intelligence, new technologies etc. An investment decision by an entrepreneur can't be taken simply, but it should be only with solid logic of Market Intelligence and it is the need of the hour to empower in this dimension. In this endeavor, District Industries Promotion Committee meetings will be made more fruitful by discussing on the new proposals and Brain storming on Market Intelligence.

After Liberalization, Industry Associations are playing key role in influencing Government in framing Industry friendly policies. But, of late, some Letter pad Associations are coming into picture and disturbing the healthy environment and DICs are unnecessarily burdened with the work of resolving conflicts among Associations. To increase the effectiveness, DICs are to be empowered to register/recognize the Industry Associations and further empower to conduct Elections, Seminars etc. so as to stream line the mushrooming of fake interest groups.

Further in the Liberalized Economic Scenario. 'Quality' is key factor for survival and every industry is expected to have ISO Certification. Hence, DICs may be empowered as Nodal Department to process necessary documentation for ISO Certification and Quality Certification agencies may be requested to work in coordination with DIC.

25

Working of District Industries Centres: A Case Study of Visakhapatnam District

Prof. C. Suryanarayana* & Mrs. M. Meher Karuna**

Introduction: Small opportunities are often the beginning of great enterprise. "Size" as George Meredith pointed out is a matter of opinion. Perhaps in few areas is that so true as in business and industry, where it is the character of the company, as much as any physical or financial yardstick, that determines a business is small. Executives of giant corporations have repeatedly asserted that it is not the big competitor whom they fear, it is the small one.

In India, the role of Small-Scale industries in the development of the national economy stressed by the Industrial Policy 1956. The small-scale sector provides immediate large-scale employment and offers the method of ensuring more equitable distribution of national income, promoting entrepreneurship and earning foreign exchange to the country. Small firms seem to have an edge in industries that call for personalized service, attention to detail and the flexibility to adapt quickly to changes in the business or technological environment. The small industries lead to effective mobilization

* *Co-ordinator*, UGC-SAP, Department of Commerce and Management Studies, Andhra University

** *Faculty Member,* Visakha Institute for Professional Studies, Visakhapatnam

of resources of capital skills and utilization of local resource endowment. The small-industry sector which accounts for around 95 per cent of the industrial units, and 40 per cent of the output of the manufacturing sector.

GROWTH OF SMALL SCALE SECTOR IN INDIA

The Indian small-scale sector has been fortunate to be built upon a local heritage of enterprise, dynamism and renewal. The performance of the Indian Small-Scale sector in terms of critical economic parameters such as number of units, production, employment and export during the last decade (1991-2000) is given in Table- 1.

The growth of the sector during this period is very impressive. The number of units in the small-scale industry increased by 65.97 per cent. Production-wise also the small-scale industries showed a phenomenal increase of 272 per cent from 1990-91 to 1999-2000. It is also witnessed that the sector generated employment which increased by 5.20 millions i.e. 41.5 percent. The contribution of the sector to Indian exports also increased from 96.64 billions in 1991 to Rs. 489.79 billions in 98-99 which account for an increase of 406.8 percent. Therefore it is evident that the small-scale sector in India during the last decade has grown remarkably. It is interesting to note that the SSI sector made tremendous progress in the post LPG period i.e., after 1991, without being affected by the threats of WTO and liberalization of import policy.

As can be seen from the Table-1 by the end of 1999-2002 there are 3.22 million SSI units contributing a total production of Rs.5,784.70 billions(current prices) with a total employment of 17.73 millions. This sector contributed to Indian exports to the tune of Rs. 489.79 billions (current prices) by the end of 1998-99. The small-scale sector has contributed about 40 per cent of industrial production and 36 per cent of total direct exports. This sector has been maintaining a higher growth rate than industrial sector as a whole. While the industrial sector registered a growth rate of 6.5 per cent the SSI sector registered a growth rate of 8.16 per cent in 1999-2000. It is evident from the Table-2 that the growth of the SSI sector has been higher than the growth of industrial sector throughout the period of 1991-92 to 1999-2000.

This paper analyses the working of DICs, Visakhaptanm during the last 6 years. The data relating to the SSI units promoted by the DIC, the employment generated, investment, production, the progress under PMRY, the Industry spread in the district are collected from the secondary source.

DISTRICT INDUSTRIES CENTRES

In India, the DICs came into existence in 1978 as focal points of industrial development at the district level. Before the establishment of DICs there was no agency exclusively for the development of industry at the district level. Hence the Government of India introduce in 1962 the Rural Industries Program and Rural Artisan Program in order to bring about industrial development in rural and backward areas in phased manner. These programs could not achieve the desired effect and produced only partial results. The small entrepreneurs had faced a number of hardships and delay in conceiving and executing their industrial projects, and also in getting various clearances and licenses etc. to overcome many such problems of entrepreneurs and also to accelerate the pace of Industrial development particularly in the rural areas. The Govt. of India envisages Industrial policy Statement in 1977 that " in each district there will be one agency to deal with all the requirements of small and village industries. This will be called District Industries Center (DIC) under the single roof of DIC, all the services and support required by small and village entrepreneurs will be provided, these will include economic investigation of the district's raw materials, arrangement for credit facilities, and effective step for marketing and a cell for quality control, research and extension".

DICs should act as a data and information bank and dissemination centre for setting up of small scale units which, acts as regulatory body by taking up registration, deregistration, monitoring and utilization of credit, raw materials, processing of cases regarding supply of machinery on hire purchase, marketing assistance, etc. The third aspect on which the DICs can play an effective role is with regard to inter linkages with different institutions such as electricity department, department of water works, municipality/panchayat, town planing, commercial banks, etc the DICs should function in close coordination with all agencies related to industrial development at the district level. The ensure this there should be a single line of command operating from the DIC for the entire field staff connected with industrial promotion activities and diffusion of direction and responsibility should be avoided to enable DICs adopt a result-oriented approach.

DIC-VISAKHAPATNAM

Industrial Development: The DIC, Visakhapatnam came into existence in Oct 1978. Ever since its inception the DIC with other agencies, promoted a large number of medium scale, small-scale, tiny and village industries both in urban and rural areas of the district. By the end of March 2002 there are 24,786 SSI units in the District with the total investment of Rs.21,330 lakhs, providing an employment to 2,43,000 persons. Out of the total of 24,786 units only 48.66 per cent are registered with the DIC. It is to be noted that the unregistered units of the District should be brought under the purview of DIC by insisting registration. One way of doing this is by motivating the unregistered units through counseling and by providing incentives.

The SSI sector of the District is predominantly consists of engineering and forest based SSI units. Out of the total 24,786 units , a very large number of 29.89 per cent are engineering based, followed by 21.12 per cent forest based units. Agro and food based units constituted 8.48 per cent. The investment in these units is also observed to be very low , in engineering units the average investment per units is Rs. 0.81 lakhs, while it was 0.34 lakhs per unit in the case of forest based units. It is interesting to note that in respect of agro-based units, mineral based units the average investment works out to Rs.1.73 and 2.55 lakhs respectively. In electronics and electrical based units also the average investment is a little above Rs. 1 lakh. It is evident that although the engineering and forest based units are about 46 per cent, all of them are tiny enterprises with investment of less than Rs. 1 lakh. Due to cost of technology and machinery and other processing equipment the overall investment is more in agro based, mineral based, electronic and electrical based units.

Out of the total registered units 12063 with DIC a large percentage of 62.68 are tiny units. It is revealed that the DIC promoted very small number of SSI units with more than 20 laks of investment. (37.31 per cent) .

Geographical Spread of Industries: The DIC has promoted various types of small scale industries both in urban and rural areas of the district. Mandal wise distribution of this industries is given n Table –2.

There are 43 revenue mandals in the district where SSI units were started with a formal registration with DIC. However, there is lot of variation in the industrialization of these mandals. A cursory look at the data given in the Table reveals that 42.25 percent of industries of SSI units are in the urban areas of Visakhapatnam and Gajuwaka. The industrialization is very low in rural mandals for example Bheemunipatnam, Anakapalli, Narsipatnam, Chodavaram have started industries which constituted 3.79 per cent 3.42 per cent 5.37 per cent and 4.64 per cent respectively. Even though these mandals are semi-urban in character industrial development is very insignificant. In other mandals industrial promotional activity can be considered to be very negligible. Also it is observed that the progress of industrialization in both in urban and rural mandals during 1991-92 to 2001-02 is on the declining trend. In Visakhapatnam urban mandal 312 units were started in 1991 as against 39 units started in 1999-2000 and 26 in 2000-2001 and 12 in 2001-2002. In most of the rural mandals no units were started continuously for 3 to 4 years particularly since 1998-99. It manifests that that one of the objective of DIC namely Industrialization of rural areas could not be achieved. The process of small industry development even in the urban areas is tardy and declined particularly since 1997-98 .

Performance Under PMRY: The Prime Minister Rojgar Yojana steam was launched on October 2 1993 to assist educated unemployed youth to set up self-employment ventures. Year wise performance under the scheme during 1993-94 to 2001-2002 is demonstrated in Table - 3. During 1993-94 to 2001-02, 14,025 self-employment ventures were sanctioned out of which 9,531 were actually grounded which accounts for actual achievement of 68 per cent of the ventures started. In every year the units grounded were less than the sanctioned units, this may be attributed to reasons such as non-compliance of the procedures by the individuals and delay in processing of applications and delay in sanctioning subsidies and indifferent attitude of the prospective beneficiaries.

It is appreciable that throughout the period, 1993-94 to 2001-02 the number of units sanctioned exceeded the targets. The number of educated unemployed youth trained for self-employment ventures was 10,643 during the above period. It is to be observed that the number of units grounded didn't increase in the proportion in which the sanctions were made. On the other hand a steep fall is observed in the number of units actually grounded from 1998-99 to 2001- 02. Also there was an inconsistent growth in the number of people trained. During the last five years the performance under PMRY is not very impressive, eventhough the targets and sanctioned number of units increased, the actually grounding of units didn't take place to the extent of 100 per cent. The DIC need to find out the reasons and the problems of the beneficiaries and help them to start the units. The purpose of PMRY scheme will be served only when the beneficiaries actually started the units and generated the income. The DIC should intensify its efforts in this respect by fixing up the deadline for starting the units. The procedure should be simplified and delay should be avoided to extent possible in order to motivate the beneficiaries.

Conclusion

The District Industries Centre concentrates more on promotion of industries in urban areas rather than rural areas. In many rural mandals were neglected, the objectives of the industrialization for backward areas was not achieved. The investment level of a large majority of the units is less than Rs. 1 lakh, which indicates low level of operational activity and profitability. About 70 percent of the units registered are tiny units. In the early years of starting of the programme PMRY there was an impressive growth and progress but it decelerated in the later years, in respect of grounding of units and the number of unemployed youth trained. It is suggested that the DIC should have a perspective plan of promotion of industries so that the small entrepreneurs in rural areas can be motivated. Industrial activity should be toned up by providing special incentives to those entrepreneurs would like to start small industries in rural mandals. The data bank of DICs need to be d updated to enable the prospective entrepreneurs to get educated about the availability of various opportunities to promote new ventures.

The Functioning of Nodal Agency

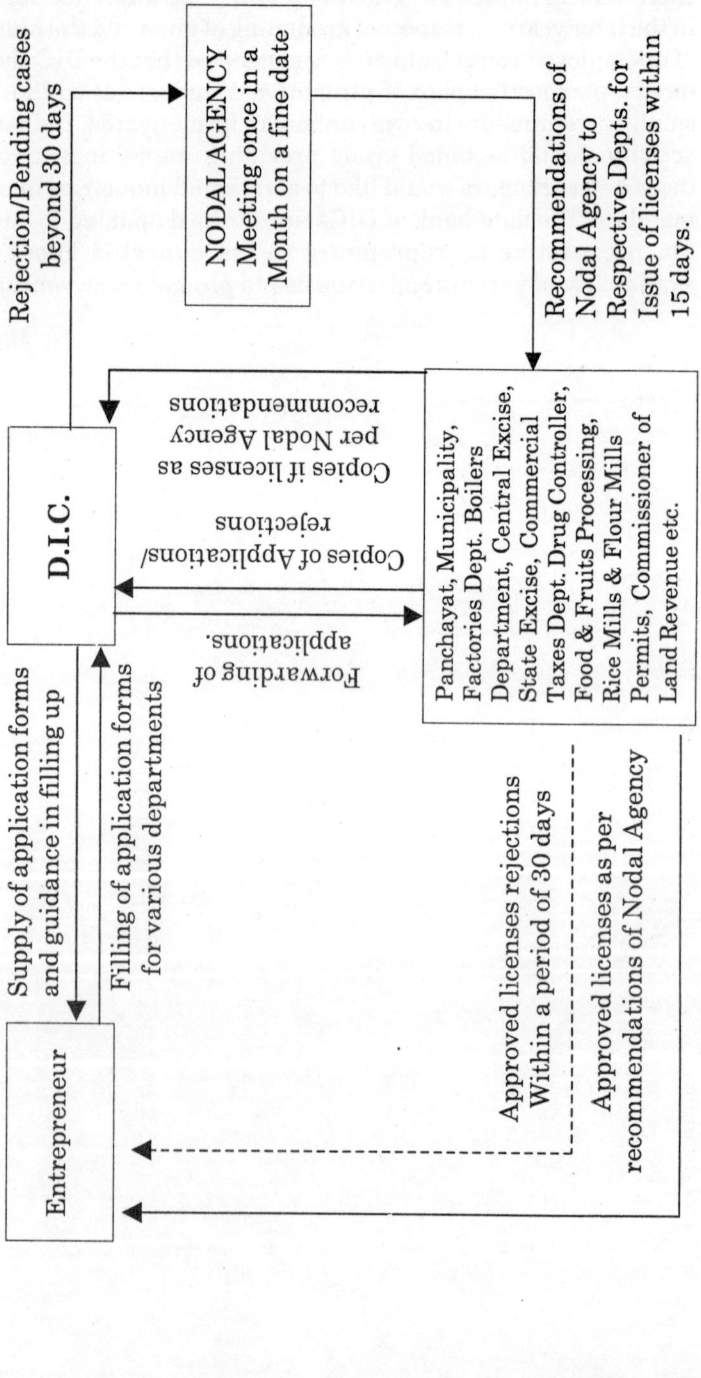

DIC - interface with other Agencies
Commissionerate of Industries

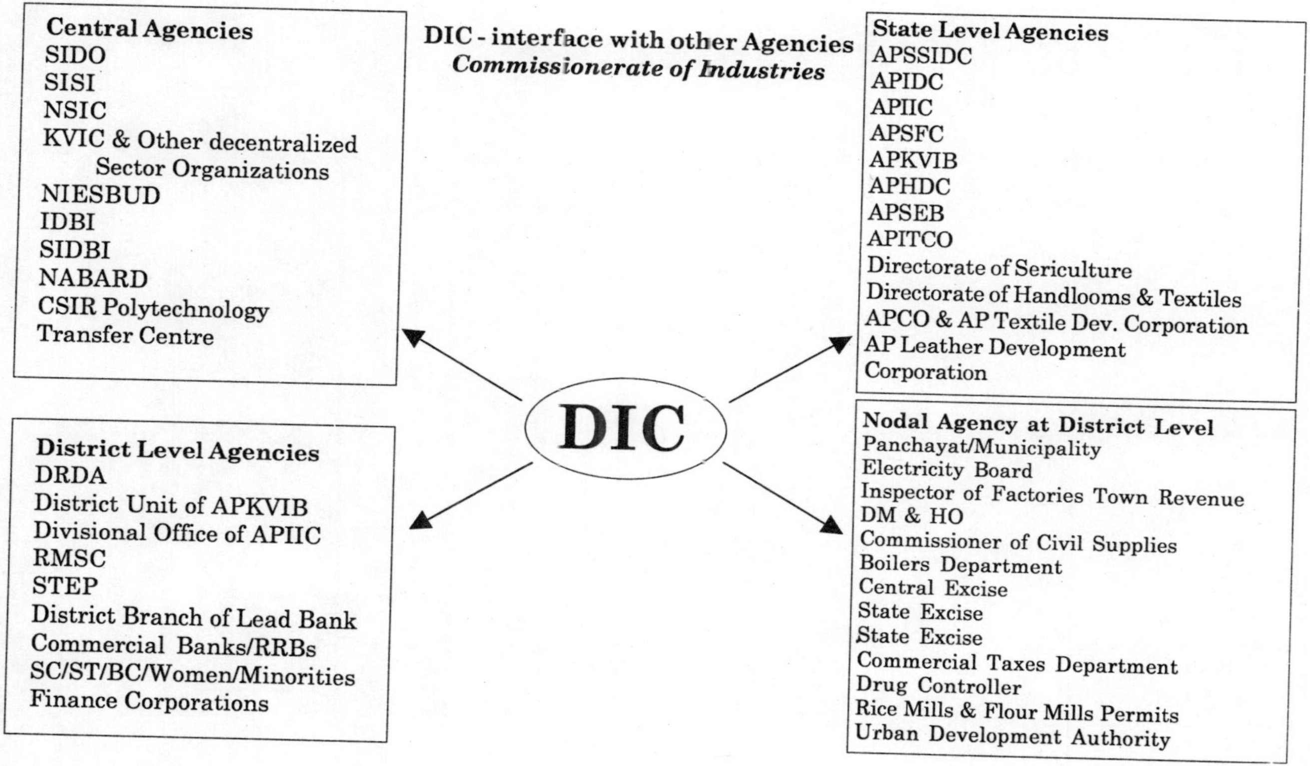

SECTION – IV

Infrastructure Development

26

Infrastructure for Small Industry Development in A.P.: A Study of APIIC

Ch. Venkateswara Rao *

Introduction : This paper has been developed from a doctoral dissertation of the researcher entitled "Development and Management of Industrial Infrastructure in Andhra Pradesh: A Study of the Role of Andhra Pradesh Industrial Infrastructure Corporation (APIIC) Limited." The paper deals with industrial development of Andhra Pradesh with regional and district analysis, study of industrial estates, and role played by APIIC. One important aspect of the paper is the feedback received from entrepreneurs' associations and individual entrepreneurs in different estates/areas promoted by APIIC in the state. All along, an effort has been made to examine the progress and performance of industrialisation and the industrial estates programme in relation to the overall goals and objectives of accelerating industrialisation. Inter-state comparison of the performance of APIIC with similar corporations of a few leading developed states has been attempted. Analysis and feedback of entrepreneurs reveal that APIIC has shown the lead in a few directions in the infrastructure programme. There are many areas where its performance can be rated as modest in relation to the performance in other states with whom comparison has been made.

* Deputy Registrar, Academic & Examinations, University of Hyderabad

1. Industrial Development of Andhra Pradesh

Industrial development of Andhra Pradesh has been studied with the help of computerised data provided by the Commissionerate of Industries of the State. Data available are for large and medium scale industries in terms of number of units, capital investment and employment; and for registered small scale units in terms of number of units, capital investment and employment. The data have been grouped district-wise in respect of units which started up to 1956, during 1956-1974,and from 1974 to 1995. Year 1956 refers to the formation of Andhra Pradesh, and the year 1974 refers to the establishment and functioning of Andhra Pradesh Industrial Infrastructure Corporation (APIIC). Data in respect of SSI units district-wise are up to end-December 1995. In respect of registered SSI units with investment in plant and machinery below Rs. 5 lakh, cumulative picture at the end of December 1995 is available district-wise. For large and medium scale units, data are given up to the end of December 1996 district-wise. Hence, this data have also been grouped for three periods: up to 1956, 1956-1974 and 1974-1996. For the purpose of aggregation, SSI data up to Dec. 1995 are added to large and medium industry data up to end-December 1996, in the absence of a better alternative.

There were 1,523 large and medium scale industries in the State with capital investment of Rs. 26,479.43 crore, providing employment for 6,41,597 persons as on 31-12-1996. Registered SSI units with investment in plant and machinery of Rs. 5 lakh and above each numbered 5,543 units, with capital investment of Rs. 783.64 crore, providing employment for 1,29,660 persons as on 31-12-1995. In addition, there were 1,12,654 registered SSI units with investment in plant and machinery below Rs. 5 lakh each, with capital investment of Rs. 1,093.38 crore, providing employment for 8,91,758 persons as on 31-12-1995. For these three categories of industries, capital investment, employment, and contribution of the three categories to the state's industrial sector in percentage terms are summed up and presented in the following table.

Present Position of the Industrial Sector in the State and the Share of Different Segments

Sl.No.	Category of Industry	No. of units	Capital investment (Rs. Crore)	Employment	Share in the total(%)	
					Capital investment	Employment
1	2	3	4	5	6	7
1.	Large and medium scale industries (as on 31-12-1996)	1,523	26,479.43	6,41,597	93.38	38.58
2.	SSI Units of Rs.5 lakh and above investment in plant and machinery each (as on 31-12-1995)	5,543	783.64	1,29,660	2.76	7.80
3.	SSI units below Rs.5 lakh investment in plant and machinery each (as on 31-12-1995)	1,12,654	1,093.38	8,91,758	3.86	53.62
Total		1,19,720	28,356.45	16,63,015	100.00	100.00

Source : Records of the Commissionerate of Industries, Government of Andhra Pradesh, Hyderabad

From the above table, it could be seen that large and medium scale industries are contributing the maximum of capital investment (93.4%), but provide employment to only 38.6 per cent of industrial work force in the state. Registered SSI units with investment in plant and machinery below Rs. 5 lakh each, account for 1,12,654 units, 3.9 per cent of capital investment and 53.6 per cent of industrial employment; registered SSI units with Rs. 5 lakh and above investment in plant and machinery each, account for 5,543 units, 2.8 per cent of capital investment, and 7.8 per cent of industrial employment. Micro SSI sector has the highest labour intensity, whereas large and medium scale sector has the highest capital intensity.

1.1 Growth of Large and Medium Scale Industries

Out of 1,523 large and medium industries operating in the

State at the end of December 1996, 1,295 (85.03%) were set up during 1974-96, 144 (9.45%) during 1956-1974, and 84 (5.52%) up to 1956. In terms of capital investment, out of total picture of Rs.26,479.43 crore at the end of December 1996, Rs.21,490.95 crore (81.16%) was added during 1974-96, Rs. 4,361.85 crore (16.47%) during 1956-74, and Rs. 626.63 crore (2.37%) up to 1956. Out of the total employment of 6,41,597 persons, employment generation during 1974-96 was 4,08,793 persons (63.71%), during 1956-74, 1,47,860 persons (23.05%), and up to 1956, 84,944 (13.24%). Growth of large and medium industries after 1974 was thus quite significant.

Reasonable amount of dispersal of a large number of large and medium industries in various districts has taken place, particularly during 1974-96 period. Apart from location of a number of central public sector undertakings, central incentives and state schemes for industrial promotion have played a key role. The role played by APIIC in developing industrial infrastructure had also been quite significant in attracting large and medium industries to a number of backward districts.

1.2 Growth of Small Scale Industries

Growth of registered small scale units analysed from the district-wise/ region-wise data is as follows:

Growth of bigger SSI units is attempted over the three periods of up to 1956, 1956-74 and 1974-Dec. 1995. Out of 5,543 bigger SSI units at the end of December 1995, 95.7% (5,305 units) were established during 1974-96. In terms of capital investment, the share of this period in the cumulative position is 96.5%. In terms of employment generation, the share of this period is 87.4%. The corresponding shares of units, capital investment and employment generation during 1956-74 period were 3.6%, 2.8% and 9.8%. The shares of the period up to 1956 were very low. Compound annual growth rates for the three parameters for the state as a whole during 1974-96 were 16.0% for number of units, 17.4% for capital investment and 10.4% for employment. The corresponding growth rates in Telangana were higher during this period. This conveys the speedy growth of bigger sized modern SSI units in a few backward districts in which special efforts were made through provision of incentives, better industrial infrastructure, nearness to the state capital, and other normal features which exert greater pull for promoting clusters of industrial units; and also a few advanced districts where momentum of growth of SSI units was already there. Districts prominent for faster growth during 1974-96 in the descending order of capital investment region-wise are: Ranga Reddy, Medak, Hyderabad, Nalgonda, Krishna, West Godavari, Visakhapatnam, East Godavari, and Chittoor. Central and state incentives, concessional finance, and organised infrastructure development contributed to acceleration of growth of SSI units. The analysis also shows that a few districts have contributed to the growth process to a greater degree, compared to many others where growth was relatively slow.

All registered SSI units put together at the end of December 1995, at the state level accounted for 1,18,197 units, capital investment of Rs. 1,877.02 crore, and employment of 10,21,418 persons. In number of units, the shares of coastal Andhra, Rayalaseema and Telangana regions were 44.3%, 12.3% and 43.4% respectively. In capital investment, the shares of the three regions were 37.0%, 10.6% and 52.4% respectively. In employment, the shares were 44.5%, 12.3% and 43.2% respectively. Districts prominent in the descending order of investment region-wise are: Ranga Reddy (Rs. 407 cr.), Hyderabad (Rs. 133 cr.) and Nalgonda (Rs. 104 cr.) in Telangana region, Krishna (Rs. 121 cr.), Guntur (Rs.109 cr.), West Godavari (Rs. 101 cr.), Visakhapatnam (Rs. 97 cr.), and East Godavari (Rs. 94 cr.) in Coastal Andhra region, Chittoor (Rs. 59 cr.), Kurnool (Rs. 53 cr.) and Anantapur (Rs. 49 cr.) in Rayalaseema region. In terms of capital investment, Telangana is more prominent because of the dominance of Ranga Reddy, Hyderabad and Nalgonda districts, followed by Medak district. With the exception of Ranga Reddy and Hyderabad districts, other prominent districts of Telangana referred to above, are at about the same level as prominent districts of Coastal Andhra region. Prominent districts of Rayalaseema region are at a much lower level. However, in terms of employment generation, Coastal Andhra scores over Telangana (44.5% and 43.3% respectively.) Ranga Reddy (91,500) and Hyderabad (88,600) districts are at the top. Prominent coastal Andhra districts stand next. These are Visakhapatnam (67,600), Krishna (65,100), East Godavari (60,200), Nellore (56,100), Guntur (55,200), West Godavari (51,500). All the four Rayalaseema districts are in the range of 29,000 in Chittoor to 35,000 in Anantapur.

1.3 Share of Backward/Non-Backward Districts

The share of backward and non-backward districts in all the large and medium scale and SS industries is shown in the following table.

Share of Backward and Non-backward Districts in Large and Medium, and SS Industries

Sl. No.	*Districts*	*Large & medium inds (%)*			*Small scale Inds (%)*			*Total Inds. Sector (%)*		
		Units	*Invest ment*	*Employm ent*	*Units*	*Invest ement*	*Employm ent*	*Units*	*Invest ement*	*Employm ent*
1	2	3	4	5	6	7	8	9	10	11
1.	Backward districts	53.2	41.0	57.5	49.0	40.5	49.4	49.0	41.0	52.5
2.	Non-backward districts	46.8	59.0	42.5	51.0	59.5	50.6	51.0	59.0	47.5

Non-backward districts have high proportion of capital investment (59.0 to 59.5 per cent) in all categories of industrial units - large and medium, as well as small, and total. Backward districts have a higher share of industrial employment, particularly in large and medium industries, as well as in total. In SSI, the proportion is slightly less by 1.2 per cent. In respect of number of units, backward districts have greater proportion of large and medium industries. In SSI as well as in total units, backward districts account for 49% as compared to 51% for non-backward districts. It also indicates that backward area industries are providing more employment than the non-backward area industries. There has, thus, been sizeable amount of dispersal of industrial activity to backward areas from 1974 in particular, largely through large and medium industries, and the resultant growth of SSI sector. Scope for further dispersal of large and medium as well as small scale units is substantial. This needs to be pursued through development of growth centres and by attracting clusters of industrial units, large and medium, small as well as tiny and artisan units.

In the development of large and medium industries, Medak district, which is in the backward districts category occupied the second place in the state, next to Visakhapatnam in terms of capital investment, and first place in terms of number of units. Khammam is another backward district, which occupies the first place in terms of employment. Overall, Chittoor, Medak, Karimnagar, Khammam and Nalgonda from backward districts category have performed well and have potential when compared to non-backward districts of the state. Even though Vizianagaram, West Godavari and Adilabad are non-backward districts, large scale industrial development has not been encouraging. In the development of SSI units, among backward districts, Nellore, Karimnagar and Nalgonda have fared better when compared to non-backward districts such as Vizianagaram and Adilabad.

2. Industrial Estates Programme in India

United Nations in its study of *Industrial Estastes - Policies, Plans and Progress: A Comparative Analysis of International Experience (1966)* defined an industrial estate as "a planned clustering of industrial enterprises offering developed sites, pre-built factory accommodation, and a variety of services and facilities to the occupants". An industrial area was defined as "a piece of land offering developed sites as an inducement for the establishment of industrial enterprises". In the Indian context, industrial estate is a facility developed exclusively for small scale units where the package of facilities provided is in greater measure. An industrial area is developed for providing developed plots to all sizes of industrial units, small, medium and large. There are industrial areas where only small scale units are accommodated. There are many aspects in common between an industrial estate and an industrial area, as both provide infrastructure for industrial units. In Gujarat, Gujarat Industrial

Development Corporation refers to both of them as industrial estates. In many parts of the country, these are referred to as industrial estates and industrial areas. In Andhra Pradesh, industrial area is referred to as industrial development area.

2.1 Objectives of the Programme

Main objectives of the industrial estates programme in India, which has been evolved over years, from 1955, are as follows:

(i) promotion of small scale industries, and stimulation of entrepreneurship on an extensive scale by providing a package of infrastructure facilities;

(ii) dispersal of industries to less developed or backward regions, small towns and rural areas;

(iii) promotion of specific category of industries, such as ancillaries and functional complexes, or specific category of entrepreneurs like technocrats, skilled persons and artisans;

(iv) relieving congestion of cities by relocating industries;

(v) promotion of export-oriented industries (free trade zones), development of nucleus complexes or any other special developmental effort for attracting a cluster of industries in a region in a planned manner;

(vi) attracting foreign investment through promotion of joint ventures or foreign concerns in industry; and

(vii) integrating industry with urban and regional planning.

2.2 Funding Pattern

In the beginning the entire cost of the industrial estates programme was met by way of loans from the Union Government to the states, the cost of land and buildings being covered by 20-year loans and of development of estates by 30-year loans, loans bearing interest @ 4.5 per annum. The scheme of assistance also included provision for subsidising the rents in appropriate instances. Loss consequent on the levy of subsidised rents, was to be borne equally by the Central and state governments up to a period of 5 years. Thereafter, losses, if any, on subsidised rents were to be borne entirely by the state governments. From the Fourth Plan (1969-74) onwards, industrial estates programme has been made a state programme. Institutional financing occupied an important place in later years. Internal generation of resources and institutional financing play a major role in recent years.

3. Industrial Estates Programme in Andhra Pradesh and Role of APIIC

Prior to the setting up of the Andhra Pradesh Industrial Infrastructure Corporation (APIIC), the Department of Industries, Government of Andhra Pradesh was performing the function of development of Industrial Estates (IEs) and Industrial Development Areas (IDAs) in the State. However, some practical difficulties were experienced in the establishment of Industrial Estates and Industrial Development Areas.

In order to avoid those difficulties, Government of Andhra Pradesh felt that it was necessary to have a separate corporation. Further, the working group appointed by the Reserve Bank of India on Financing of Industrial Estates observed that "The Government Departments with rigid rules and procedures do not seem to operate with the necessary flexibility, nor do they appear to possess the expertise to implement the schemes sucessfully". Therefore, it was recommended that the management of Industrial Estates should be entrusted to a separate corporation.

As a result, the Andhra Pradesh Industrial Infrastructure Corporation (APIIC) Ltd. was formed in 1973. This Corporation became operational after being registered as a limited company of Government of Andhra Pradesh with registration number 1630 of 1973-74 on 26th September 1973, under the Companies Act, 1956.

3.1 Objectives

Though the APIIC Ltd. was established with multisphered objectives keeping in mind the long range perspective, the following objectives were given priority for its immediate action to develop Industrial Infrastructure for speedy promotion and development of Industrial growth in the state of Andhra Pradesh.

(a) to identify potential growth centres for location of Industrial Estates (IEs) and Industrial Development Areas (IDAs) keeping in view the availability of raw materials, transport communication, banking facilities, water and power resources, and the demand for industrial goods, and to have dispersed and balanced industrial growth in the State;

(b) to provide basic infrastructure like developed land, built-up sheds, water supply, power supply, street lighting and avenue plantations;

(c) to allot developed plots and built-up sheds in Industrial Estates/Industrial Development Areas;

(d) to liaise with postal, telegraph, telephone, railway and road transport authorities, with police and fire service departments for providing common facilities in Industrial Estates/Industrial Development Areas;

(e) to provide houses to industrial workers in the Industrial Estates and Industrial Development Areas as social infrastructure;

(f) to promote common effluent treatment plants in the Industrial Estates/Industrial Development Areas.

3.2 Functions

In order to fulfil the above objectives, the Corporation has to perform several functions which can be broadly divided as follows:

a) Identification of suitable sites and land acquisition

b) Development of acquired land

c) Construction of factory sheds

d) Power and water supply

e) Industrial housing

f) Allotment of developed land (plots and sheds)

g) Fixation of price for land, developed plots, built-up sheds, etc.

h) Promoting effluent treatment schemes.

3.3 Physical Achievements of APIIC

On the establishment of Andhra Pradesh Industrial Infrastructure Corporation Ltd. (APIIC) as a company of Government of Andhra Pradesh on 26th September 1973, the Department of Industries, Government of Andhra Pradesh which used to promote Industrial Estates and Industrial Development areas, handed over 45 Industrial Estates and 15 Industrial Development Areas with 498 factory sheds on 1-1-1974, pending valuation of these assets, which have been later on valued at Rs.580.00 lakh.

As up to 31.8.1996, APIIC has promoted 226 Industrial Estates of different kinds, 20 commercial complexes and 17 industrial housing complexes in the state, total of 263 locations. As on 31.8.1996, the Corporation acquired a total land of 25,357.52 acres (10,262 hectares), and developed 13,271.82 acres (5,371 hectares). Development of land acquired works out to 52.3 per cent. In the 226 Industrial Estates/Industrial Development Areas, 17,911 plots were developed and 14,001 plots were allotted, and 3514 sheds were constructed for industrial purpose and 3,258 sheds were allotted, thereby the allotment of developed plots and constructed sheds was 78.2 per cent and 92.7 per cent respectively. In 20 commercial complexes developed in eleven districts on an area of 8.3 acres of land, 305 sheds were constructed, out of which 241 were allotted, thereby allotment of sheds in commercial complexes was 79.0 per cent. In the 17 housing complexes developed in ten districts on an area of 329.9 acres of land, 4,678 houses were constructed and 4,496 houses were allotted, thereby allotment of houses was 96.1 per cent. In the state as a whole, out of the un-developed land of 12,085.71 acres (4,891 hectares), an area of 3,890.62 acres (1,574.5 hectares) was also allotted to entrepreneurs.

In the evaluation of the industrial estates programme, difference between an industrial estate and an industrial development area has vanished and nowadays, both are serving similar purposes. Similarly, several kinds of industrial estates/areas such as mini industrial estates, rural industrial estates, satellite industrial estates, commercial complexes, electronic complexes, wood complexes, etc., are also located along with major industrial estates/areas wherever possible. As on 31-8-1996, APIIC has 15 kinds of industrial estates/areas to its credit which have been grouped into six categories based on broad nature of the estate and the physical particulars. The categories are: 1) Industrial Estates, 2) Industrial Development Areas, 3) Commercial Complexes, 4) Autonagars, 5) Mini Industrial Estates, and 6) Industrial Housing Complexes. While categories three to six are treated as independent based on the nature of the estate, the first category includes industrial estates, assisted private industrial estates, ancillary industrial estates, rural industrial estates, satellite industrial estates, and self employment industrial estates; and the second category includes industrial development areas, integrated infrastructure development centres, growth centres, wood complexes, and electronic complexes. Therefore, it could be observed that 263 locations of industrial estates of APIIC consist of 98 industrial estates, 88 industrial development areas, 20 commercial complexes, 17 autonagars, 23 mini industrial estates, and 17 industrial housing complexes.

3.4 District/Region-wise Analysis of Overall Achievements

Out of 25,357.52 acres (10,262 hectares) of land acquired in the state, Telangana region accounts for 45.4% (11,518.55 acres/4,661.5 hectares), the highest; Coastal Andhra region 42.1% (10,660.04 acres/4,314.1 hectares), the next highest; and Rayalaseema region 12.5% (3,178.94 acres/1,286.5 hectares), the least.

Out of 13,271.82 acres (5,371 hectares) of land developed in the state, Telangana region accounts for 56.4% (7,482.79 acres/3,028.2 hectares), the highest; Coastal Andhra region 28.8% (3,819.45 acres/1,545.7 hectares), the next highest; and Rayalaseema region 14.8% (1,969.58 acres/797.1 hectares), the least.

In land acquisition, eight districts, *viz.*, Ranga Reddy (4,879.67 acres), Medak (3,422.14 acres) and Khammam (1,191.37 acres) of Telangana region; Visakhapatnam (3,169.53 acres), East Godavari (2,686.11 acres), Krishna (1,136.65 acres) and Vizianagaram (1,085.56 acres) of Coastal Andhra Region, and Chittoor (1,426.95 acres) of Rayalaseema region, together account for 74.9% (18,997.98 acres/7,688.4 hectares) of land acquired.

In four districts *viz.*, Adilabad, Karimnagar and Nizamabad of Telangana region, and West Godavari of Coastal Andhra region, land acquisition and development was negligible which was between 104.56 acres to 130.11 acres in individual districts.

In terms of land development, four districts, *viz.*, Ranga Reddy (4,063.52 acres), Medak (2,141.94 acres), Visakhapatnam (1,290.79 acres) and Krishna (862.45 acres) account for 63% (8,358.70 acres/3,382.7 hectares).

3.5 Acquisition of Land in Proportion to the Area of the District/Region

Acquisition of land is at a higher proportion in Telangana region followed by Coastal Andhra Region and Rayalaseema region. When the area of Telangana region was 41.8% of the state, land acquired in the region was 45.4%. When the area of Coastal Andhra region was 33.8% of the state, land acquired was 42.1%. When the area of Rayalaseema region was 24.5% of the state, area acquired was 12.5%. It reveals that more efforts were made to acquire land in Telangana region when compared to the other two regions, or demand for industrial infrastructure in Telangana region is more. Development of industries in the districts of Ranga Reddy and Medak confirms this presumption.

Intra-regionally, a big gap could be observed between backward and non-backward districts in the acquisition of land which was almost three times in the non-backward districts of Coastal Andhra and Telangana regions. When the analysis was made between the total backward (14) and non-backward (9) districts, the share of total backward districts in land acquisition was 44.8% while it was 55.2% in non-backward districts. Similarly, development of land acquired was 44.3% in backward districts and it was 55.7% in the non-backward districts. Land acquired per 1000 sq.kms. was 58.4 acres in backward districts and 174.4 acres in non-backward districts.

The above analysis indicates that balanced regional development in the state has not yet reached even a modest success rate.

In addition to the above programmes, the Corporation has also taken up the civil works of state as well as central governments on deposit work basis for utilising its man power to the fullest extent. Further, works pertaining to the four centrally sponsored growth centres, integrated infrastructure development centres, export promotion industrial park, apparel export park, were also entrusted to APIIC as a nodal agency. Two major common effluent treatment plants, one at IDA Jeedimetla and another at IDA-Patancheru were promoted by APIIC. These are working well serving the industrial community.

4. Inter-state Comparison of Industrial Infrastructure Programme

To facilitate greater insight into the operation of the APIIC, an attempt is made to compare the role and performance as well as certain organisational aspects of the APIIC with those of its counterparts in a few states such as Maharashtra, Gujarat, Karnataka and Tamil Nadu. All the four states selected are industrially advanced states. They have had the rich tradition of investor-friendly governmental machinery at the state level, in particular. The annual reports and other information provided by the Corporations concerned and the discussions the researcher had with some of the officials of MIDC, GIDC and GGCDC and the representatives of Entrepreneurs' Associations and individual entrepreneurs of MIDC, & GIDC estates are the main sources of information for the study.

MIDC was formed in 1962 by an enactment of the state legislature under the Maharashtra Industrial Development Act 1961. GIDC was also formed in 1962 by an enactment of the state legislature under the Gujarat Industrial Development Act 1962. Minister for Industries of the state concerned is the Chairman of the Corporation in both the cases. Therefore, these corporations are enjoying greater support from the Government. APIIC was established in 1973 as a company of the Government of Andhra Pradesh and it was registered under Companies Act 1956. Both KSSIDC and KIADB have also been registered under Companies Act.

MIDC developed 195 industrial areas; GIDC has developed 274 industrial estates/areas; APIIC has developed 226 industrial estates/areas; KSSIDC and KIADB of Karnataka have developed 129 industrial estates and 71 areas respectively.

MIDC of Maharashtra has acquired about 41,000 hectares of land; GIDC of Gujarat has acquired 21,600 hectares of land; and APIIC acquired only 10,262 hectares of land. MIDC has developed 35,546 plots; 17,911 plots were developed by APIIC; 4,534 sheds/galas were constructed by MIDC; 12,291 sheds were constructed by GIDC; 3,819 sheds were constructed by APIIC; and 5,451 sheds were constructed by KSSIDC. 2,806 residential plots were demarcated by MIDC; 12,822 housing quarters were constructed by GIDC, 4,678 houses were constructed by APIIC. The number of industrial units established in the estates of MIDC was 23,095 (including projects under implementation); in the estates of GIDC functioning units were 16,304; and in the estates of APIIC the number of units established (including the projects under implementation) was 11,300. GIDC has promoted eight common effluent treatment plants, and APIIC has promoted only three common effluent treatment plants.

From all angles, industrial infrastructure development in Andhra Pradesh through the pivotal role played by APIIC, could be considered a modest attempt; and needs strengthening in certain directions for the future. APIIC has a few creditable accomplishments where it has shown the lead for other states. Implementation of Local Authority Status in the maintenance of the industrial estates of the APIIC is one in this direction.

5. Infrastructure in the Liberalised Context

World class or five-star infrastructure facilities are planned to be developed in certain locations in a large number of states for attracting NRIs and multi-nationals to start enterprises of highly sophisticated nature with export commitment. A number of specialised industrial area schemes are being implemented in various states. These include export promotion industrial parks, software technology parks, science and technology entrepreneurs parks, product-specific export promotion parks such as for apparel, leather, etc. Dry port and air cargo facilities are also being created in a number of locations for facilitating exports. States are also implementing infrastructure schemes slightly different from the earlier patterns in certain locations, including industrial estates with private sector initiative.

All along, emphasis is on private sector investment in infrastructure projects, and in developing comprehensive infrastructure facilities in various locations by joining hands with a large industrial house or by attracting capital from abroad. High level and high quality of infrastructure is being emphasised on area basis. The facilities are planned to be developed for a group of industries coming up in a region, and not for cases of individual units separately.

Social infrastructure needs to be given due weightage, whether the work is planned to be executed by the Infrastructure Development Corporation or by any other Corporation of the State Government or with private sector involvement.

The Expert Committee on Small Enterprises (1997) (Chairman: Abid Hussain) recommends that both Central and state governments redirect their existing growth centre and other infrastructure development schemes to upgrade the infrastructure available in the existing Small Scale Enterprise (SSE) clusters.

High Level Committee on Credit to Small Scale Industries (Kapur Committee, 1998) recommended that RBI might consider, in consultation with Government of India, the need to set up a Small Industries Infrastructure Development Fund (SIIDF) for developing industrial areas in and around metropolitan cities, urban and semi-urban areas which are not covered by Rural Infrastructure Development Fund of NABARD. To start with, a corpus of such a fund of about Rs.1,000 crore be kept with SIDBI for lending to state level organisations. The committee has also recommended that Rural Infrastructure Development Fund set up in NABARD (National Bank for

Agriculture and Rural Development) be used for supporting infrastructure for rural industries as well. RBI has been requested to examine the matter and permit this fund to be used for such purposes as also for provision of alternative power sources.

6 Suggestions & Recommendations for strengthening Infrastructure

Feedback received from entrepreneurs' associations and individual entrepreneurs has been consolidated in this section, with reference to the suggestions and recommendations for strengthening industrial infrastructure in Andhra Pradesh.

1) Entrepreneurs felt that infrastructure facilities like levelled plots, formation of roads, avenue plantation, drainage system, water and power supply, effluent treatment facility, industrial housing and other services like post offices, banks, schools, hospitals, etc. which were provided by APIIC were not even near the satisfactory stage. These facilities were stated to be substandard. The Maintenance of the estates was also said to be very poor. Therefore, these need to be improved to a great extent.

2) The report reveals that administration of APIIC is far below satisfactory level. However, entrepreneurs ranked administration of other governmental agencies like Inspector of Boilers, Directorate of Industries, A.P. Pollution Control Board, and A.P. State Electricity Board as nearer to the satisfactory level. Therefore, entrepreneurs have a better image of the other state level organisations and also financial institutions when compared to APIIC. The services of local bodies, *viz.*, panchayats, municipalities and corporations in the maintenance of the IEs/IDAs and other related services have been said to be below satisfactory level. Therefore, some attitudinal changes are required for improving the services provided by the APIIC and Local Bodies.

3) It was expressed by entrepreneurs that APIIC should have a liberal attitude towards entrepreneurs; it should not do real estate business; simplified procedures should be followed; it should have very cordial relations with other governmental

agencies like APSEB, APPCB, Directorate of Industries, etc.; it should provide additional borewells for supply of sufficient water; it should provide sound and high quality of infrastructure facilities; political interference should be reduced; all support services like transportation, post office, banks, schools, housing facility, canteen, health centre and police station should be provided at the estates; and full support should be extended by APIIC to Entrepreneurs' Associations regarding maintenance of estates and areas.

4) The representatives of entrepreneurs' associations are of the opinion that if the entrepreneurs' representations are attended to from time to time, it will boost the morale of entrepreneurs. The report also reveals that sound and high quality industrial infrastructure is required for accelerating industrialization of Andhra Pradesh. If infrastructure provided is inadequate as felt by entrepreneurs, prospective investors will continue to prefer to start their industries in industrially advanced states like Gujarat, Maharashtra, TamilNadu or Karnataka where better infrastructure facilities are available.

5) According to the new industrial policy of Andhra Pradesh, i.e., according to Target-2000, incentives are now made available to the whole of the state, excepting three major municipal coporation areas, irrespective of their backwardness or non-backwardness. This will certainly help in the further development of non-backward areas rather than backward areas. One important step required in this regard is to make available high quality infrastructure in more locations, particularly in backward areas, to attract medium and large industries to those locations. State-sponsored growth centres in potential centres of backward districts is the direction to be pursued.

6) The study revealed that owners of the Auto Trade & Servicing units are not willing to shift their units to the outskirts of the city/town concerned where Autonagars are developed. This trend is mostly due to the non-availability of sufficient facilities at Autonagars. This requires immediate attention of the APIIC and APPCB.

7) The Corporation could not provide the latest information about the estate-wise particulars of enterprises on total number

of industrial units, units under implementation, functioning and sick (category-wise: large, medium and small scale), investment, production, and employment. Therefore, the information of 1995 was taken. The Corporation should strive to get the information regularly from the sub-zonal/zonal offices and consolidate the same. Importance is to be given to data collection for facilitating policy decisions and for periodic reviews. After conducting an economic survey of industrial units in IEs and IDAs, a Directory of Industrial units covered by APIIC's estates and areas may be brought out. Updating it every five years is important.

8) A common services building, to be named UDYOG SADAN, is to be built in every major industrial estate to cater to the needs of APIIC, Industries Association, and any other agency for which accommodation facility is needed in that industrial belt. This may cover the office premises of the association, a large auditorium for organising meetings, one or two conference halls for smaller gatherings including training programmes, a good library, a facility for technical consultancy, and display space for organising a permanent exhibition of products manufactured in the area. The complex may include a few shopping complexes covering services as well. By adopting commercial approach, some of the activities in the complex may yield revenue annually. Display can include make and design of the machinery used, and sample products of industrial units of that area, apart from setting apart sufficient space for exhibiting products of various units by rotation. A small guest house for the use of visitors can also form part of it. The scale on which these facilities are planned can vary with the size and importance of the estate/area. In Maharashtra, Thane Small Scale Industries Association is modelled on these lines. In a number of other locations in Maharashtra and Gujarat, this type of facility is a common occurrence. It is a joint effort of the entrepreneurs and the government.

9) With the involvement of the Entrepreneurs' Associations, a number of orientation programmes may be organised in the industrial estates in the Association hall itself. These can be on entrepreneurship development, orientation to the current day policies and programmes through an interface with the functionaries of the respective organisations, awareness

programmes on priority items of relevance to entrepreneurs, such as quality certification and total quality management, environment management, environment certification, pollution control, energy audit, energy conservation, adoption of clean technologies, etc. In estates, such as mini-industrial estates, or relatively new estates situated in backward areas, where entrepreneurial response has not been encouraging, counselling and awareness camps may be organised for prospective entrepreneurs. In programmes meant for existing and prospective entrepreneurs, interface with functionaries of various departments and organisations, should be fairly frequent to clarify points of interest to entrepreneurs.

10) Small Industries Infrastructure Development Fund is to be created by SIDBI for developing industrial estates and industrial areas, as recommended by the High Level Committee on Credit to Small Scale Industries (1998). Simultaneously, Rural Infrastructure Development Fund of NABARD could be permitted to be used for industrial estates in rural and semi-urban areas.

Summing up

The paper reviewed the progress of industrialisation with focus on regional development with reference to growth of small, and medium and large industries. The second part of the paper has critically examined the performance of APIIC in promoting industrial infrastructure programme in the state from 1974. Growth of industrialisatiton has been rapid during the period 1974 - 1995. A few backward districts have become industrially advanced. Lot more remains to be done to ensure higher level of industrialisation and infrastructure programme in more backward districts. Strengthening infrastructure in backward districts which have potential for growth and have distinct locational advantages should be given a helping hand by strengthening infrastructure and by focussing the attention of various state agencies in a well-orchestrated manner.

Small industry development and infrastructure growth offer scope for greater dispersal and growth centre strategies. Cluster approach has many advantages which remain to be tapped in the State. New patterns in which high quality infrastructure growth is being promoted need to be pursued vigorously. In relation to industrially advanced states, achievements till date in Andhra Pradesh are modest. Greater decentralised effort, and greater focus on more growth centres and product oriented estates can result in balanced regional development to a greater degree. Infrastructure has a key role in this endeavour, particularly in the liberalised context. Additional programmes to be taken up by the state, in addition to those initiated by the centre need to be pursued vigorously. These can be mini growth centres through industrial estates and areas which are relatively small in size to be promoted by the state government. Some of them can be developed with the initiative of the private sector. These need to be pursued in more locations in different parts of the state. Industrial policy and small scale sector policy of the state government can provide stimulus in this direction.

REFERENCES

APIIC, *Computerised Data on Industrial Estates/Areas.* Hyderabad.

Commissioner of Industries, Government of Andhra Pradesh, *Computerised Data on Large and Medium Scale, and Small Scale Industries,* Hyderabad.

Venkateswara Rao, Ch. (1999), *Development and Management of Industrial Infrastructure in Andhra Pradesh: A Study of the Role of Andhra Pradesh Industrial Infrastructure Corporation (APIIC) Limited*, unpublished Doctoral Dissertation, Hyderabad, Jawaharlal Nehru Technological University (JNTU).

27

Strategies of Academic Institutions to Promote Entrepreneurship

Prof. BEVVN Murthy

The development of entrepreneurs and entrepreneurship is necessary in developing countries to meet the challenges posed by popula6ion growth and unemployment. The industrialized nations, technological innovations and opportunities created for human and material resources, etc. Management schools, institutions, institutions of technology, universities, etc., can play a very significant role in developing entrepreneurship in any country as has been amply demonstrated by research work done by a few specialized institutions in India. This paper presents a framework for such work in entrepreneurship development by academic institutions.

The concept of entrepreneurship gained momentum in the late fifties. The government has embarked on the development of entrepreneurship through the small-scale industry, in order to achieve rapid economic development in most parts of the country. However, the knottiest problem of dispersing industrialization through development of entrepreneurship in small towns and backward areas was that of identifying and encouraging entrepreneurs in such areas, in various offices, such a wide range of variability and inconsistency, obviously affects the quality of training and its impact. The success rate in terms of setting up enterprises and running them quite successfully by those who attended such entrepreneurial development training programmes has been quite varied ranging from anything between 5 to 60 per cent. Although success is not entirely dependent on training alone, since the support and services play an equally important role, yet the content and quality of entrepreneurship development training programmes cannot be made valued since it serves and the force to drive prospective entrepreneurs to entrepreneurial career.

Research

The following are some areas of entrepreneurship for research:

1. Development of entrepreneurs in different communities, cultures, professions and regions: The development process can be different for different categories of entrepreneurs, e.g., manufacturing entrepreneurs, professional entrepreneurs like doctors and lawyers, and rural entrepreneurs. Academic institutions need to develop different models of entrepreneurship development so that people of diverse talents and aptitudes will get opportunities in this line.
2. Selection of entrepreneurs for financial assistance, training, and development: Different selection techniques have to be identified. For example, recent work as IIMA suggested that several techniques, like attracting candidates through advertisements, screening them through carefully designed application, and selecting them through psychological tests, interviews, simulation games, and unorthodox techniques can be used. Interviews were commonly used in India (Rao and Moulik, 1976) by several agencies for selecting entrepreneurs. A few organizations that have used behavioural science tests like risk-taking and need achievement have been found to select more entrepreneurs than non-entrepreneurs for assistance and training (Rao and Moulik, 1976; and Rao, et. al., 1976). The initiation of rural entrepreneurship requires different strategies, like

reducing the technical, economic, market, and social risks (Matthai, 1976). As an outcome of these researches. IIMA and EDII organized workshops for academicians, researchers, trainers, bankers, and other developing agents working on entrepreneurship to develop and exchange experience on the selection of entrepreneurs. Different groups and institutions will further work on different techniques for identifying and selecting entrepreneurs.

3. Transfer of technology to different areas including that from urban to rural areas offer tremendous scope for developing backward areas.
4. Strategies for developing entrepreneurs in backward areas and low-income communities.
5. Development of entrepreneurial talents from early childhood through socialization in the family and in the early years of schooling: Researches have suggested that early socialization through stories narrated to children at home and in school, language taught to them, etc., influence their entrepreneurial orientation. McClelland's (1961) work has demonstrated that countries showing economic development had cultures where children were socialized to high-achievement motivation. Hence, entrepreneurs can be developed through socialization at an early age. Research on literature, materials, and other aids should be developed to acquaint children with this process.
6. Assessing the experience of agencies already developing entrepreneurs is likely to help not only the concerned agencies but also other agencies in planning their strategies. For example, a multi-disciplinary team of experts from IIMA and EDII evaluated the efforts of a local agency developing entrepreneurs, and this provided a rich experience for the concerned agency to plan their future strategies. The experience was extended on some dimensions to other agencies who were benefited by it.

7. Problems of small-scale entrepreneurs: Pathak's (1975) study on small entrepreneurs are excellent examples.

Research on entrepreneur and entrepreneurship can also be conceived in the following way:

1. Growth of industry and entrepreneurship in centers where outstanding growth has been noticed during a short period: Analysis of forces and factors sustaining such growth should throw light on the entrepreneurial process. Two studies by Pathak (1968 and 1970 and Murthy, 1982) provide examples of this.
2. Ancillary development resulting from conscious managerial decisions: In India, the experience of the Tata Engineering and Locomotive Company, Escorts, BHEL, etc. can be cited. Such ancillary developments contain within them entrepreneurship development of a type.
3. Some centers provide remarkable examples of localized industrial development. A study in progress by Pathak in three centers in Gujarat - Rajkot, Surat, and Savar Kundla – reveals that these centers demonstrated the typical transition of the artisans into industrial entrepreneurs.

Thus, entrepreneurship offers great scope for research. An international group of researchers has worked out detailed designs for conducting research in different aspects of entrepreneurship. Starting with a three-week research planning workshop at the Technology Development Institute, Hawali, in which 34 representatives from 22 institutions of six countries (India, Indonesia, Malaysia, New Zealand, Philippines, and USA) participated in 1975, a series of workshops were organized at Manila, Bandung, Penang, Hyderabad, and Ahmedabad in 1976. These workshops finalized at the workshop at IIMA, several research designs for work in five areas of entrepreneurship : (1) Identification, selection, and development of entrepreneurs, (2) general education for entrepreneurs, (3) development and testing of training programmes in business management for small-scale industry, (4) fostering local innovations and technological change, and (5) cross national evaluation of entrepreneurial development programmes. These topics were arrived at after discussions and testing out of ideas with experts in different countries. Sixteen institutions from the six participating countries are collaborating in these areas. Each country has a national design on topics of interest and there is one cross-national research design for each topic. Sharing the outcomes of such experiences will go a long way in helping each other in developing entrepreneurs.

Consultancy and Experimentation

Ample scope exists for formulating nation-wide strategies for developing entrepreneurship. Certain organizational structures can facilitate the development of entrepreneurs more than others. For example, when institutions training entrepreneurs collaborate with institutions assisting them for finance, raw material, machinery, housing, power supply, etc., in offering training and in helping them complete the formalities, enterprise building India Small Industry Extension Training Institute was founded for the purpose. In the early sixties, the first ever experiment in developing entrepreneurship was conducted. Since then there has been keen interest in developing entrepreneurs as the way approach to entrepreneurship development.

Developing entrepreneurship is becoming crucial for industrial development and alleviating the problem of unemployment. Our efforts should make entrepreneurship development a mass movement. In recent years, numerous institutions have formulated various strategies to develop entrepreneurship in different target groups. Training has been the most important component of all such strategies.

In recent years, many government as well as non-governmental agencies have committed themselves to entrepreneurship development. A number of schemes have been formulated for promoting entrepreneurship and self-employment in different parts of the country for different categories of entrepreneurs. The training conducted by these organizations vary in terms of their learning methods, other include case studies, discussions and field trips. Many choose to conduct the whole program only through simple lectures mostly by guest speakers drawn from becomes smooth. In India, an experiment is being carried out where all institutions with whom an entrepreneur should deal with are housed in the same building in each geographical region. Such organizational structures can be suggested and structured for policy makers.

Research and evaluation designs can be suggested and worked out for self-assessment by those already involved in organizing entrepreneurial development programmes. Academic institutions can also play a significant role in bringing together the experiences of entrepreneurs; trainers of entrepreneurs, bankers, and other institutions developing entrepreneurs and helping them share such experiences. The recent workshops on identification and selection of entrepreneurs conducted at IIMA exemplify such an effort. It proved useful to both practitioners and academicians.

Centers for dissemination of the information on entrepreneurship can also be established and the institutions can serve as a clearinghouse. The SIET has set an example by setting up a documentation center for small industries.

Conclusion

There are many management schools in this country producing sizeable number of management graduates; most of who seek managerial position is both private and public entrepreneurs. There is a need for these management schools for re-orientation and introduction of one or two courses into their present curriculum. The present curriculum of our school of the following courses.

Thus, academic institutions – be they management institutions, technology institutions, universities, or other institutions – interested in entrepreneurship can contribute significantly to the development of entrepreneurs and thus to the economic development of the country.

REFERENCES

Cochran, T.C., "The Entrepreneur in Economic Exchange", Entrepreneurship and Economic Development, Peter Kilby (ed.), New York, Free Press, 1971.

Gaikwad, V.R.; Shah, B.G.; Rao, T.V.; and Pareek, U., 'Entrepreneurship Concept and Approaches', Hegan, E.C., How Economic Growth Begins: A Theory of Social Change, Entrepreneurship and Economic Development, Peter Kilby (ed.), New York, Free Press, 1971.

Kilby, Peter (ed.), *Entrepreneurship and Economic Development*, New York, Free Press, 1971.

Mathai, R.J., 'Perceived Risk and Rural Entrepreneurship', paper presented at the Workshop on *Identification and Selection of Entrepreneurs*, Indian Institute of Management, Ahmedabad, October 1976.

McClelland, D.C. Power, *The Inner Experience*, New York, Irvington Publishers, 1975.

----------------, *The Achieving Society*, Princeton, D. Van Nostrand Company Inc., 1961.

----------------, and Winter, David G., *Motivating Economic Achievement*, New York, Free Press, 1969.

Nafziger, E.W., "Indian Entrepreneurship: A survey", *Entrepreneurship and Economic Development*, Peter Kilby (ed.), New York, Free Press, 1971.

Pathak, H.N., *Problems of Small Scale Entrepreneurs*, Bombay, Industrial Development Bank of India, 1975.

------------, *Growth of Diversified Industries in Baroda*, Ahmedabad, Indian Institute of Management, 1968, 50 pp. (mimeographed).

Niesbud, *Model Syllabi for Entrepreneurship Development Training Programmes*, New Delhi, 1985.

Atkinson John, 'Introduction to Motivation', Princeton, D.Van Nostrand, e. 1964.

David, C., Maclelland, *Motivating Economic Achievement*, New York, The Free Press, 1971.

Maclelland D.C., *The Achieving Society*, D.Van Nostrand, New Yo4k.

Murthy, B.E.V.V.N., *Entrepreneurship in Small Towns*, Mittal Publications, New Delhi, 1985.

Murthy, B.E.V.V.N., 'Problems of Small Scale Entrepreneurs', SEMDE, NISIET, Hyderabad.

28

Maintenance of Industrial Estates in Andhra Pradesh: Role of Industries Associations

Ch. Venkateswara Rao

Sources of Data and Methodology

This paper has been developed from a doctoral dissertation of the researcher entitled "Development and Management of Industrial Infrastructure in Andhra Pradesh: A Study of the Role of Andhra Pradesh Industrial Infrastructure Corporation (APIIC) Limited".

The records provided by the Local Authority Cell of APIIC, relevant Government Orders of the Government of Andhra Pradesh, and the views of entrepreneurs of APIIC Industrial Estates, and officials of APIIC are the sources of primary data for this purpose. Views of 114 entrepreneurs from four districts, *viz.*, Visakhapatnam, Chittoor, Ranga Reddy and Medak; 30 officials of APIIC up to the rank of Deputy Managers; and 5 representatives of the Association of APIIC Officials have been obtained through a questionnaire, and also by personal discussions. The sample of 114 entrepreneurs includes 24 representatives of industries' associations, and the representatives of 13 entrepreneurs' service societies which have been formed for the implementation of the local authority status conferred on APIIC as a nodal agency.

Introduction

Maintenance of facilities created in industrial estates and

areas has been the responsibility of municipal bodies and panchayat samities wherever APIIC transferred the estates and areas to them, as these bodies collect property tax and other taxes from entrepreneurs. As maintenance has not been virtually attended to by them for many years, APIIC and entrepreneurs have been exploring other alternatives for management of infrastructure facilities on the lines pursued in states such as Gujarat and Maharashtra. Notified Area Committee is the pattern in Gujarat, and New-Township Municipal Council is the pattern in Maharashtra for large industrial belts promoted by Gujarat and Maharashtra Industrial Development Corporations, respectively. This basically refers to greater role to be played by associations of entrepreneurs. The specially constituted committee/council is vested with powers of the municipality to collect taxes and also use them for the maintenance of facilities in the respective industrial belts. They give a part of the revenue to the local municipality or panchayat under whose jurisdiction the industrial area falls. In these two states, these patterns have been promoted in very few locations.

In Andhra Pradesh, the local authorities concerned, *i.e.*, either the Panchayat, Municipality or Municipal Corporation used to collect the property tax from Entrepreneurs located in the Industrial Estates/Industrial Development Areas of APIIC also. They were according sanctions for building plans and for installation of plant & Machinery. However, it was experienced by entrepreneurs that maintenance of their Industrial Estates/ Development Areas was neglected, and the blame has been thrown upon APIIC for the poor/non-maintenance of Industrial Estates/Industrial Development Areas. APIIC used to collect @ Rs.400/- per acre per annum towards common facilities like roads, street lights, etc. which was said to be not collected effectively, and therefore, the purpose was not served. Local authorities when approached by entrepreneurs, used to say that, as APIIC had not, yet officially handed over the Estates to them, they were unable to take up the maintenance of the Estates of APIIC. Further, local authorities were also avoiding the maintenance stating that since the APIIC was also collecting the fee @ Rs.400/- per acre per annum, it should shoulder the responsibility. On the other hand, the APIIC was claiming that when the local authority was collecting the property tax, it was incumbent on the local authority to maintain the Estates/ Development Areas.

APIIC as a Local Authority

A perspective plan prepared by the APIIC in 1985, was got approved by the standing committee constituted by the Government of Andhra Pradesh in 1986 which was meant basically for selection of sites for new locations for IEs and IDAs. Bhanuprasad Committee while going through the perspective plan as approved by the standing committee referred to above, addressed itself to the problem of maintenance of the IEs/IDAs of APIIC, and accepted the suggestion of the then Vice-Chairman and Managing Director of APIIC that the Corporation's Estates/ Industrial Development Areas may be declared by the Government as "Notified Areas".

This issue however, was actively pursued by Dr. Jayaprakash Narayan when he assumed charge as Vice-Chairman and Managing Director of APIIC in 1993. Government of Andhra Pradesh after careful consideration of the proposal of the APIIC, declared APIIC as "Local Authority" for the specified Industrial Estates /Industrial Development Areas/Autonagars, etc. of APIIC vide GO Ms. No. 519, Municipal Admn, & U.D. (J2) Dept. dt. 21.9.1994 duly amending the A.P. Municipalities Act 1965 and the Hyderabad Municipal Corporation Act 1955. Similarly, the APIIC, has been declared as "Local Authority" for some more Industrial Estates and Industrial Development Areas coming under the purview of some Panchayats, vide GO Ms. No. 113 PR Rural Development & Relief (PTS.IV) Dept. dt. 4.3.1995 duly amending the Andhra Pradesh Panchayat Raj Act 1994 (Act No. 13 of 1994). The foregoing two declarations are subject to the condition that 30 per cent of the property tax collected in these areas shall be remitted to the Municipality/ Corporation/Panchayat of that area every half year. It may be noted here that APIIC is the Local Authority in a limited sphere in the Industrial Areas/Housing Complexes set-up by it within the territorial limits of the concerned Local Body-Gram Panchayat, Municipality or Municipal Corporation as the case may be. The local body will continue to exercise all powers and functions outside the limits of Industrial Areas and Housing Complexes of the APIIC.

Powers and Function of APIIC as a Local Authority

The powers and functions of APIIC after the conferment of Local Authority status are: collection of property tax which includes education tax, library cess, etc., tax on advertisement, approval of building plans, granting of permissions for construction, establishment or installation of factory, workshop or work place in which steam or any other fuel is employed, removal of encroachments and maintenance of civic amenities like maintenance of roads, drainage, street lighting, etc., in the notified areas.

In order to create a sense of involvement and responsibility among the entrepreneurs' community, the Corporation constituted an Advisory Committee in all notified areas under the Chairmanship of the concerned Zonal Manager of the Corporation who is also designated as Commissioner of that Industrial Area, wherein membership was provided for two nominees of the Industrial Areas Manufacturers' Association/ Two-member-occupants of Industrial Areas, one representative/ nominee from Housing Allottees' Welfare Association, Sarpanch/ Councillor of the local Industrial Area, nominee of the Municipality/Gram Panchayat/Municipal Corporation (Non-official), Director of APIIC of Local Industrial Area, and Deputy Zonal Manager (Engineering)/Assistant Zonal Manager (Engineering) and Deputy Zonal Manager (Development)/ Assistant Zonal Manager (Development) as the Member-Secretary. The Advisory Committee was expected to meet periodically to suggest ways and means for collection of taxes, and decide on priority of works to be taken up in the Industrial Area, execution of schemes/works, etc. under the Chairmanship of the zonal Manager. Vice-Chairman and Managing Director of the Corporation will have absolute power/discretion to re-constitute/supersede the committee and to regulate its functions from time to time as deemed fit. The duties of the officers of different wings, *viz.*, development, engineering and accounts of the Office of the Zonal Manager, APIIC concerned were also spelt out for the smooth implementation of the programme.

Organising Training Programmes for the Officials of APIIC

A clear understanding of the statutory provisions of the Acts and Rules by all those concerned, especially by the authorities vested with such powers, is of utmost importance in providing the maintenance of civic amenities and other services. With this objective, a training programme was arranged for the Corporation field officers, initially at the National Institute of Small Industry Extension Training (NISIET), Hyderabad, and later at the Regional Centre for Urban and Environmental Studies, Osmania University, Hyderabad in collaboration with the Commissioner and Director of Municipal Administration, Andhra Pradesh, Hyderabad in 1994.

The APIIC which started functioning as local Authority in the notified areas is collecting property tax and taking up civic maintenance works and also granting building permits, etc. Though the Corporation has been utilising its total share of 70 per cent of the property tax without charging any amount towards administrative charges, it was found highly difficult to meet the expenditure on civic amenities especially due to the huge amounts required for taking up road maintenance as these were hardly taken up by the local authorities for the past 10 to 15 years. The issues of inadequacy of funds and the need to involve industrialists in civic maintenance works in the notified Industrial Areas have come up for discussion with Industrialists' Associations and at Government level also.

Formation of Industrial Service Societies

To mobilise adequate funds through donations, and to ensure speedier and total collection of property tax in the notified industrial areas for taking up prompt and satisfactory maintenance of civic services, the allottee-industrialists have come forward to offer their services and cooperation by forming exclusive non-profit making societies with all the rate payers as the members. Such societies would function as a Nodal Agency for collection of property tax in the name of the Corporation and to sanction/take up maintenance works as per the relevant rules which would promote the objective of self governance of the notified Industrial Areas by the occupant - industrialists themselves. The APIIC will continue to attend to the statutory functions of assessment, levy and demand of property tax, and other regulatory functions. However, the societies will have advisory powers on assessments and building permits. The recommendations of the society on all such matters shall ordinarily be binding on the APIIC Industrial Area Local Authority (IALA) subject to their being within the broad framework of law and relevant guidelines. These societies are named in short as "Industrial Service Societies". Other nomenclatures used are: notified municipal/gram panchayat industrial area service societies, industrial municipalities, industrial area local authorities, and entrepreneurs' service societies. As and when such societies start functioning, the concerned Advisory Committees constituted by the APIIC earlier for this purpose would be superseded.

There shall be a Managing Committee of the society elected by its General Body for a period of one year which includes Chairman, Vice-Chairman, Secretary, Joint Secretary and Treasurer. The Zonal Manager and Commissioner (Executive Officer/Special Officer as the case may be) of the APIIC IALA shall be the Ex-Officio Vice-Chairman of the Society. The members specially elected to the Managing Committee by the General Body shall not be less than 5 and more than 12. In addition, the nominees of Govt. Departments/Public Institutions like the DIC, APSEB, APPCB, concerned Local body, APIIC, UDA, etc. shall be the ex-officio members of the Managing Committee, and they shall also be invited to the General Body Meetings.

Sharing of Property Tax by APIIC & Local Bodies

The property tax will be collected by the service societies and deposited in a joint account in the name of the Industrial Service Society and the Zonal Manager, APIIC concerned. 30 per cent of the tax collected will be remitted to the Local Authority concerned as their share, every half yearly. Education tax collected should be sent to the District Educational Officer, and the library cess collected to the District Grandhalaya Samstha concerned by the Zonal Managers of APIIC periodically.

Since the Service Societies have to have manpower for

collecting taxes, the expenditure towards wages of the tax collectors and expenditure on other infrastructure for its office etc., 90 per cent of the building approval charges, and the charges collected for approving the installation of plant and machinery is given to the Service Societies by the APIIC Zonal Office as a matter of agreement between the service society and the APIIC, vide proceedings No.1125/APIIC/LAC/95 dt. 26.7.1996 of the VC & MD, APIIC. Since this amount is expected to be not sufficient, the remaining expenses will be met out of the funds raised by the members on their membership fee, donations, etc. Industrial Service Societies are now popularly known as "Industrial Municipalities".

Delegation of the Powers of UDAs/Director of Town Planning to APIIC

Further, Government of Andhra Pradesh has delegated the powers of sanction of building plans of industrial buildings hitherto exercised by UDAs/Director of Town Planning to APIIC, vide GO MS No.665 MA & UD (R) dt. 19-12-1996 in respect of the areas already specified in the Annexure - II of GO Ms No. 519 MA dt. 21.9.94 vide GO Ms. No. 665 MA & UD (R) Dept. dt. 19.12.1996, i.e., notified areas of APIIC subject to the condition that the overall supervision regarding implementation of rules/ regulations regarding building permissions will be done by the UDA/Town Planning Department, and the total fees collected in this regard should be remitted to the UDAs/Director of Town Planning. This has been done to eliminate delay and hardship to entrepreneurs in setting up their projects. However, Urban Development Authority and Department of Town Planning have yet to issue the authorisation in favour of APIIC. The matter is still under persuasion by APIIC.

Local Authority Status of APIIC – Coverage to its Estates

Even though the local Authority status conferred on APIIC is operatable at all the industrial estates of APIIC, notified industrial area service societies have been formed at 27 places covering 13 districts up to end-December 1997. The districts and places covered are given here.

Statement Showing the Particulars of Notified Area Service Societies

(End-December 1997)

Sl. No.	*District*	*Name of the Service Society*	*Year of Formation*	*Industrial Estates/Areas covered*
1	*2*	*3*	*4*	*5*
1.	Visakhapatnam	Gajuwaka Notified Municipal Industrial Area Service Society (NMIASS)	1997	AN,Visakhapatnam (IDA Vizag all Blocks - Block A to E)
2.	East Godavari	Samalkot NMIASS	1997	IE, Samalkot
3.	West Godavari	Bhimavaram NMIASS	1997	IE, Bhimavaram
4.	Krishna	a) Gudivada NMIASS	1997	IE, Gudivada
		b) Machilipatnam	1997	IE, Machilipatnam
5.	Guntur	a) Narsaraopet NMIASS	1997	IE, Narsaraopet
		b) Tenali NMIASS	1997	IE, Tenali
6.	Prakasam	Markapur Industrial Estate Development & Service Society	1997	IE, Markapur
7.	Nellore	a) Pannamgadu IDA Development & Service Society	1997	IE,Pannamagadu
		b) Gudur,Notified Gram-Panchayat Industrial Areas Service Society (NGPIASS)	1997	IE, Gudur
		c) Madduripadu NGPIASS	1997	IE, Kavali
		d) Nellore NMIASS	1997	IE, Nellore
8.	Chittoor	a) Madanapalli NMIASS	1996	IE, Madanapalli
		b) Chittoor NMIASS	1997	IE/AN, Chittoor
9.	Ananthapur	a) Kummaravandalapalli	1997	IE,Kadiri NGPIASS
		b) A Narayanapuram NMIASS	1997	IE, Ananthapur
		c) Tadipatri NMIASS	1997	IE, Tadipatri
10.	Kurnool	a) Kallur NGPIASS	1996	IE/SEIE, Kurnool
		b) Nandyal NMIASS	1997	IE, Nandyal
11.	Mahaboobnagar	Mahaboobnagar NMIASS	1996	IE, M'boobnagar
12.	Ranga Reddy	a) Qutubullapur NMIASS	1996	IDA, Jeedimetla

(Contd...)

			Phase I to V & IDA,Gandhinagar
	b) Uppal NMIASS	1996	IDA, Uppal
	c) Kapra NMIASS	1996	IDA,Nacharam, IDA, Mallapur Phase I & II IDA, Cherlapally EC Kushaiguda & Extn IHC Kushaiguda - Phase I to III & Self-Financing Housing Scheme
	d) Kattedan NMIASS	1996	SEIE, Kattedan
	e) LB Nagar, NMIASS	1996	AN, Hyderabad
	f) Kukatpally, NMIASS	1997	IE, Kukatpally APIE/IDA/SEIE Balanagar.
13. Warangal	Jangoan NMIASS	1997	APIE, Jangaon

Source: Records of APIIC.

From the above particulars, it could be seen that even though the formation of Industrial Service Societies was started in 1996 with a beginning of 8 societies, 19 societies were formed in 1997, and it is expected that by the end of the year 2000, all the viable Industrial Estates of APIIC will have the same facility. During 1998 and 1999, more locations from districts covered earlier and new locations from other districts have been covered under the scheme. It could also be noted that the scheme of self-governance by involving entrepreneurs for the maintenance of Industrial Estates has been attracted more in Coastal Andhra region (7 districts out of 9), and Rayalaseema region (3 districts out of 4) compared to Telangana region (only 3 districts out of 10). Entrepreneurs of Telangana region have to pursue the matter with the district authorities concerned and the authorities of APIIC for the implementation of the scheme wherever possible. Ranga Reddy district of Telangana region has implemented the scheme in almost all the industrial estates of APIIC.

Ambiguity in the Allocation of Duties among different wings of APIIC

It has been observed that even though the duties have been assigned to different wings of the APIIC at the Zonal Office level in operating the Local Authority Status, clear-cut guidelines have not yet been formulated defining and bifurcating the duties between the service societies and the APIIC. This has been causing procedural problems which have come in the way of maintenance works being taken up by service societies. In the absence of clear-cut guidelines and cooperation between service societies and the APIIC, the whole process becomes clumsy and the scheme cannot be implemented successfully. However, in an official meeting of the representatives of Service Societies along with officials of APIIC and others held on March 27, 1997, it has been agreed to empower the service societies for taking up of maintenance works either by themselves or through other agencies following the prescribed norms for awarding works by inviting tenders or by nomination basis and the maintenance of accounts of all the receipts and payments/expenditure. It has also been agreed that even the preparation of estimate, etc. can be taken up by the service societies either with the help of the engineering personnel of APIIC or by outside agencies as per the convenience of the service societies. This is a healthy direction for taking timely action in undertaking the maintenance works of the estates.

Tax Collection – Impact of Notified Industrial Area Service Societies of Entrepreneurs

It has been observed that in the areas where local authority status is being operated by APIIC through service societies of entrepreneurs, the societies are showing very good interest, and they are trying their best in collecting property tax from entrepreneurs. For example, when powers were vested with the APIIC at Jeedimetla Industrial Estate of Ranga Reddy District, the Corporation could collect only about Rs.8.00 lakh during the period from 1-10-1994 to 31-7-1996 (1 year and 10 months), and after this assignment was given to service societies, within a period of 6 months, i.e., from 1st August 1996 to the end of Jan. 1997, collection increased to about Rs. 27.00 lakh. The demand of annual property tax in this area was about Rs.40.00 lakh. Maintenance works in this area have been started and works costing about Rs.50,000/- only could be undertaken. Kapra Industrial Area Service Society of Ranga Reddy District could collect Rs. 35.00 lakh from 19.6.1996 till the end of February 1997. The annual demand of property tax in this area was about Rs.50.00 lakh. Maintenance works of Rs.20.00 lakh worth have been taken up. The service society of Kapra has even gone for the auction of the assets of entrepreneurs who were avoiding payment of property tax. With this kind of action, it is clear that the Local Authority status conferred on APIIC which is being operated through the entrepreneurs' service societies is welcomed by entrepreneurs in different parts of the state. The demand of property tax at Kattedan SEIE of Ranga Reddy district was about Rs.10.00 lakh per year. Kattedan Industrial Service Society was formed in 1996 and it could collect about Rs.2.00 lakh within 6 months and spend an amount of Rs.1.50 lakh by the end of March 1997 for clearing and levelling of roads of the estate. The demand of the property tax at Autonagar, Lal Bahadur Nagar of Ranga Reddy district was about Rs.14-15 lakh per year against which they could collect an amount of Rs.3.50 lakh, and spend Rs.66,000 up to 30-4-1996.

Suggestions for Effective Implementation of the Scheme

In order to make this programme more effective in the upkeep of the estates in all respects through self governance, the following suggestions are offered for the benefit of entrepreneurs. In fact, some of the neighbouring states have been observing the implementation of this scheme in all earnestness, and they are waiting for a feedback on the results which may attract them to adopt this model if it is proved to be a viable scheme in Andhra Pradesh. Maiden experience of three to four years in different locations has certainly given encouraging results. Given the support and keenness of APIIC to make the programme a success, with the full involvement of entrepreneurs, and cooperation from other governmental offices and contractors in the private sector, chances of high degree of success of the Local Authority status programme are bright.

1. All the entrepreneurs should realise that property tax is collected from them for upkeeping the maintenance of their industrial estates, and they should not try to avoid the payment of such tax. Hitherto, it was

collected by the local bodies, they never spent this amount at the respective estates, and they used to spend it elsewhere from where they get votes in the election. But it is not the case now. Therefore, all entrepreneurs should voluntarily become members of the service society concerned, and pay the property tax.

2. The APIIC should not feel that the burden of collection of property tax is on the Entrepreneurs Service Societies alone, and the Corporation is relieved of this problem. This concept is not correct, since the Government of Andhra Pradesh has conferred the Local Authority Status on APIIC but not yet on the service societies of Entrepreneurs.

3. The APIIC should cooperate in all respects with the management of the service societies in extending help in preparing work estimates, finalising tenders, issuing the work orders, work supervision and measurement, and payment of bills on time etc., This will enthuse entrepreneurs to shoulder new responsibilities over a period, when they realise that the task is in their own interest.

4. If necessary, APIIC should provide some technical staff (engineering personnel) exclusively for helping the service societies in the operation of the activities mentioned at suggestion 3 above.

5. In the long run, if the programme is proved to be successful, the Corporation may try with the help of entrepreneurs' associations in getting the conferment of Local Authority status directly on the service societies instead of keeping it with the APIIC and exercising the powers through service societies as nodal agencies.

6. As also agreed to by entrepreneurs, additional/new structures added to the existing buildings in the estates of APIIC are to be assessed following the norms in vogue at the earliest in order to increase their revenue.

7. As agreed to by entrepreneurs, the programme of levy demand and collecting the advertisement tax in the notified industrial areas following the guidelines issued by the APIIC, vide their circular No. 13827/APIIC/LAC/94-18, dated 23-5-1995 is to be initiated at the earliest which will increase the revenue of the service societies.
8. In order to mobilize the donations from the notified industrial estates of APIIC which may facilitate for tax exemption under Sec. 80 G (2) (v) of the I.T. Act, 1969, the matter is to be pursued with the Income Tax authorities both by the officials of the APIIC and entrepreneurs. This will help in strengthening the financial position of the service societies to a large extent.

Summing up

Maintenance of infrastructure facilities created in Industrial Estates and Areas of Andhra Pradesh through **Local Self Governance** by entrepreneurs' associations in the form of Notified Industrial Area Service Societies has been well established in the state. Towards the end of 1994, the programme was formally launched in the state by APIIC. By the end of December 1997, 27 locations were covered. During 1994 and 1995, APIIC was instrumental in making a beginning as nodal agency with the implementation of Local Authority Status. Later, it was resolved to form a Notified Industrial Area Service Society for each location to make the programme more effective. Eight societies were thus formed in 1996, and 19 in 1997 covering 13 districts. The programme has since been extended to many more locations in different districts. The experience has been rewarding and quite encouraging. The sound footing on which the programme has been based, and the rich experience of the state will be very helpful for many other states which are keenly observing the results of Andhra Pradesh. Full involvement of entrepreneurs and their associations in the maintenance of the facilities as well as in many other directions where there is potential for working together for the benefit of the industrial community, will go a long way in ensuring the success of the programme.

The experience of Andhra Pradesh shows that the programme has been extended to many parts of the state within a short period, and the results are quite encouraging. As a contrast, in Gujarat and Maharashtra, the notified area concept and new township municipal council pattern respectively are limited to very few prominent industrial concentrations in the state. The experience of these three states will be an eye opener for other states in the country to evolve their own patterns for the management of infrastructure facilities in Industrial Estates and Industrial Areas.

REFERENCES

Andhra Pradesh Industrial Infrastructure Corporation (APIIC), *Literature on Conferment of Local Authority Status to APIIC*, Hyderabad.

Venkateswara Rao, Ch. (1999), *Development and Management of Industrial Infrastructure in Andhra Pradesh: A Study of the Role of Andhra Pradesh Industrial Infrastructure Corporation (APIIC) Limited*, Unpublished Doctoral Dissertation, Hyderabad, Jawaharlal Nehru Technological University (JNTU).

29

Study of Managerial Aspects of Small-Scale Industries in Rayalaseema and Nellore Districts of Andhra Pradesh

M.Chandrasekar and P.Balaji Prasad*

Introduction

The significant of SSIs in Indian Economy from 1948 Industrial Policy Resolution which has recognized that SSIs where particularly suited for better utilization of local resources for achievement of local self-sufficiency. The present study primarily aims at understanding nature and structure of SSIs in 5 districts of Rayalaseema and Nellore by a sample survey of available database. To begin with the study undertakes the reviews the problems of SSI in general and survey of literature in brief.

AP Sharma classifies the marketing problems of SSI into those associated with the product and those with the market for the product. The former arose from lack of standardization; differences in the quality of materials used and lack of precision.

The latter stemmed from inadequate resources at the disposal of SSIs for identifying market outlets and trapping them profitably.

Difficulties in supply of raw materials, inferior quality of

* Professor and Associate Professor of the Faculty of School of Business Management, SV University, Tirupati.

materials, fluctuating prices, government controlled materials in some cases.

Majority of small entrepreneurs had insufficient technical and managerial background and the private agencies were not able to meet there was a case for government assistance.

Problems of labour in SSI were not discussed in general.

Sanctioning of power connection, power cuts and power fluctuations.

REVIEW OF LITERATURE

Dhar & Lydall emphasis on justification for SSIs in Indian Economy. Lakshman Studies the various issues and problems of cottage and SSIs. Nihal Singh studies the shortcomings in the management of SSIs and suggest ways for development. Reddy & Reddy: Identify the causes & curves for the morbidity in SSIs. Gangadhara Rao's study aims in evaluating the impact of programme of industrial estates on the emergence of entreprenuership and growth of small units in coastal Andhra. Murthy study presented the story of the entrepreneurs in two small towns in coastal Andhra who had their traditional culture and recently acquired skills to respond to new structures of economic opportunity in the process of improving their social and initiating a process of economic change. Sadasiva Reddy studies the pattern of development of small-scale industries in Chittore District of Andhra Pradesh. Role of districts in the department of SSI in Chittore of Andhra Pradesh is being studied by Reddappa. Srinivasulu Naidu studies the development pattern and structure of SSIs in Kurnool district. Satyanarayana discuss the finance pattern of SSI. Chandrasekara Reddy studies the role of APSFC in the industrial department of Rayalaseema. Korta: SSS & Marketing management covers Engineering Industries in Andhra pradesh state. Marketing of Groundnut, Marketing of Jaggery, Marketing of Horticultural crops, Marketing of some agricultural products, and Marketing of Tobacco.

Present Study

A database of 629 units was considered for the study. The

source of the data is from industries informatics center INDTC of commissioner of industries Govt. of Andhra Pradesh about the existing Small-scale Industries in 2001 year.

Methodology

Of the 629 a sample of 140 were selected on a simple random basis in the first part of analysis. At this stage the entire sample was subdivided based on the district and product type criteria. Thus the entire sample was arranged in the five districts and three major classes of SSI units. Such as Agro based SSIs, Industry based SSIs and Service based SSIs.

With in the Industries SSIs they were sub divided into another three categories. They are I) Chemicals II) Plastics III) Industries.

The SSIs selected as sample was studied as per their location. In Nellore there are 8 locations. In Anandapur there are 9 locations, In Kurnool there are 7 places and in Chittoor and Cuddapah there are 5 locations each.

The investment dt. Wise in general the highest no of units 67 out of 140 were in the range of Rs. 5-10 lakhs. About 44/140 in the range Rs.10-25 Lakhs. Only about 12 units were in the range of Rs. < 5 Lakhs category, (units Rs. 25-50 and 8 units >50 Category.

Employment

About 50 units were employing in the range of 5-10 work force while another 48 units in the range of 10-25 work force. 19 units between 25-50, 13 units employing more than 50 labour force.

The life span of SSIs: Out of 140 units considered for the study only 20 were started prior to 1985. About 37 units during 1985-90 or preliberalisation period. While 83 units were started after 1990. However from the data provided it is observed none of them are started after 1995.

Nellore district as benchmark sample in the study: This district sample has been retained for the study to allow the comparison to prevail in inter district comparison. Out of the three subcategories of sample Agro based SSIs Nellore and Anantapur sample data were considered for inter district comparison. Service based industry Nellore and Cuddapah are considered. While Kurnool and Chittoor were selected for industry based SSIs.

Table 1 : Classification of SSIs as Major subcategories

District	*Agro SSIs*	*Industries SSIs*	*Service based SSIs*	*Total*
Nellore	9	19	6	34
Kurnool	6	19	4	29
Cuddapah	4	11	6	21
Chittoor	7	16	4	27
Anantapur	11	14	4	29
	37	79	24	100

Table 2: Sub-Classification of Industries SSIs

District	*Other industry SSISs*	*Plastic*	*Chemicals*	*Industries SSIs*
Nellore	5	5	9	19
Kurnool	6	6	7	19
Cuddapah	4	3	4	11
Chittoor	11	3	2	16
Anantapur	12	1	1	14
	38	18	23	79

Table 3: District Wise Employment

District	*Upto 5*	*Between 5-10*	*Between 10-25*	*Between 25-50*	*More than 50*
Nellore	4	12	7	6	4
Kurnool	1	11	11	4	2
Cuddapah	0	7	8	3	3
Chittoor	2	8	11	4	2
Anantapur	3	12	11	2	2
	10	50	48	19	13

Table 4: District Wise Grounding of SSIs

District	*Before 1985*	*1985-90*	*1990-95*
Nellore	3	13	17
Kurnool	6	2	21
Cuddapah	4	6	11
Chittoor	4	6	17
Anantapur	3	10	17
	20	37	83

Table 5: Locations in the District SSIs Located

S. No.	*Nellore District*	*Kurnool District*	*Chittoor District*	*Cuddapah District*	*Anantapur District*
1.	Nellore	Kurnool	Chittoor	Cuddapah	Anantapur
2.	Tada	Nandyala	Tirupati	Rajampet	Penukonda
3.	Kotapoluru	Dharmavaram	Chandragiri	Proddutur	Tadipatri
4.	Gudur	Owk	Gajulmandyam	Pulvendula	Rayadurgam
5.	Kovvur	Kallur	Puttur	Kodur	Veligonda
6.	Duttalur	Adoni			Guntakal
7.	Thummur	Yerraguntla			Kadiri
8.	Sullurpet				Gooty
9.					Hindupur

Table 6: District wise investment in SSIs

District	*Rs. 5 Lakhs & Less*	*Between Rs. 5-10*	*Between Rs.10-25*	*Between Rs.25-50*	*More than Rs. 50*	*Total*
Nellore	0	13	14	4	2	33
Kurnool	6	12	8	1	2	29
Cuddapah	0	11	8	1	1	21
Chittoor	2	13	9	1	2	27
Anantapur	4	18	5	2	1	30
C: Totals	12	67	44	9	8	140

Agro based SSIs from Nellore and Anantapur District

First category of SSIs considered for study are agrobased units among Nellore and Anantapur districts. 9 units from Nellore district while 11 from Anantapur. Out of 9 four were paddy mills two were dal mills and one unit each from GN decorticating. Mango pulp amnd prawn feed. The geographical spread of sample from the district in this category Nellore 6 units, Gudur, Duttalur and Thummur one each.

While from Anantapur out of 11 five Gn oil & cake units three GN Decortivating units. Three Rice Mills spread over Anantapur four units, Dharmavaram, Kalyan Durg two each. Gooty, Penukonda and Kadiri one each. From Nellore out of nine units five started in 1985-90 and four units were started during 90s. Similarly from anantapur our of 11 units one GN Decorticating unit was started in pre 1985. Two rice mills and another GN Decorticating unit were started in 1985-90. Rest 7 of them started in 90s.

Industry based SSIs From Chittoor and Kurnool Districts

Out of 16 and 19 units respectively from each district three plastic based units two chemical SSI units 11 other industry units from Chittoor were studied. Six plastic based industries, seven chemical and six others in Kurnool District.

Out of 11 units six are granite based SSIs from Chittoor while five out of six plastic units from Kurnool are PVC pipe units. Three out of six other industry from Kurnool are granite/ stone based units. Out of seven chemical units from Kurnool 2 cement units 2 stone powder units and 2 gas units and one pesticide units. While 2 chemical units in Chittoor include one chemical unit and one battery charging unit.

Leather tanning, Bricks, electrical, cylinders hot min plants among five other SSIs from Chittoor. Two electrical and one anca board units also one color film unit in plastics from Kurnool district under this sub category.

The category spread of the sample units unders tudy

consisting Chittoor six, Tirupati four, Gajulamandyam three, Madanap[alli, Puttur and Chandragri one each. In Kurnool district nine from Kurnool, six from Nandyala two from Kallur, one each at Yerraguntla and Adoni.

Chandragiri battery unit is the oldest. Two PVC pipes units at Chittoor, Cylinder unit at Chittoor and brick unit at Tirupati started during 1985-90. All the other 11 units were commissioned during early 90s.

Productivity of investment: In terms of investment Granite or ceramic stoe units started at Madanapalli and Tirupati are financed more than Rs. 50 lakhs investment. They are capital intensive SSIs are available in granite PVC pipe and two ther industry plants as a source of good employment. In Kurnool district gas plant pesticide unit, electonoc unt are pre 1985 SSIs. PVC pipe unit from Nandhyala and stone powder unit started during 1985-90. Rest 14 units were started in early 90's only. It is significant to note that in Kurnool seven units and four units in Nandyala are from among this.

Service Based SSIs from Nellore and Cuddapah District

From Nellore district 6 units were observed in the sample while an equal number of units were noticed in the sample from Cuddapah district.

Two automobile repair units were financed one at Nellore and another at Gudur. One unit was financed in tyre retreading at Cuddapah. Two Ice Factories were financed both at Nellore. While three bore well digging units were financed 2 at Cuddapah another at Pulivendula. Food preservation unit at Sullurpet was oldest during 85-90 while one Graphic unit sophistcated costing more than Rs.50 lakhs work force of 5-10 in early 90s in Nellore town. Similarly laminating works unit at Proddutur and one PVC foams from Rajam Pet started before 1985. The PVC Foam unit invested more than Rs.50 lakhs earlier to 1985 itself. The food preservation unit at Sullurpet is very labor intensive Rs.10-25 lakhs employing more than 50 workforce as per the records.

Table 7: Stage Two Analysis: Agro based SSIs (dt: Nellore)

S.No	*Type of Product*	*Location*	*Invest-ment (Rs.Lakhs)*	*Employ-ment*	*Year of Production*
1.	Paddy Mills	Thummur	10-25	10-25	85-90
2.	Paddy Mills	Nellore	10-25	5-10	90s
3.	Paddy Mills	Nellore	5-10	10-25	90s
4.	Paddy Mills	Duttalur	5-10	<5	90s
5.	Dall Mills	Nellore	5-10	5-10	85-90
6.	Dal Mills	Nellore	5-10	10-25	85-90
7.	Mango Pulp	Nellore	10-25	>50	85-90
8.	Prawn Feed	Nellore	5-10	5-10	90s
9.	GN Decortication	Gudur	5-10	5-10	85-90

Table 8: Stage Two Analysis: Agro based SSIs (dt: Anantapur)

S.No	*Type of Product*	*Location*	*Invest-ment (Rs.Lakhs)*	*Employ-ment*	*Year of Production*
1.	GN Decortication	Kadiri	10-25	10-25	Pre 1985
2.	GN Decortication	Kalyandurg	5-10	5-10	90s
3.	GN Decortication	Kalyandurg	<5	<5	90s
4.	Paddy Mills	Anantapur	5-10	5-10	85-90
5.	Paddy Mills	Anantapur	5-10	10-25	85-90
6.	Paddy Mills	Dharmavaram	5-10	5-10	90s
7.	GN Oil & Cake	Dharmavaram	5-10	5-10	85-90
8.	GN Oil & Cake	Penukonda	5-10	10-25	90s
9.	GN Oil & Cake	Anantapur	5-10	<5	90s
10.	GN Oil & Cake	Anantapur	5-10	10-25	90s
11.	GN Oil & Cake	Gooty	5-10	10-25	90s

Table 9: Stage Two Analysis: Industry based SSIs (dt: Chittoor)

S.No	*Type of Product*	*Location*	*Invest-ment (Rs.Lakhs)*	*Employ-ment*	*Year of Production*
1.	Battery Charging	Chandragiri	5-10	5-10	Pre 1985
2.	Bricks	Tirupati	10-25	10-25	85-90
3.	Cylinders	Chittoor	5-10	10-25	90s
4.	Chemicals	Gajulamandyam	10-25	10-25	90s
5.	Leather tanning	Tirupati	<5	<5	85-90
6.	Electrical	Tirupati	5-10	10-25	90s
7.	Hot min plant	Puttur	10-25	25-50	90s
8.	PVC Pipes	Chittoor	<5	<5	85-90
9.	PVC Pipes	Chittoor	5-10	5-10	90s
10.	PVC Pipes	Chittoor	5-10	10-25	85-90
11.	Granite	Chittoor	10-25	10-25	90s
12.	Granite	Chittoor	5-10	10-25	90s
13.	Granite	Tirupati	>50	5-10	90s
14.	Granite	Gajulamandyam	5-10	10-25	90s
15.	Granite	Gajulamandyam	25-50	25-50	90s
16.	Granite	Madanapalli	>50	10-25	90s

Table 10: Stage Two Analysis: Industry based SSIs (dt: Kurnool)

S.No	*Type of Product*	*Location*	*Invest-ment (Rs.Lakhs)*	*Employ-ment*	*Year of Production*
1.	Gas Plant	Kurnool	5-10	10-25	Pre 1985
2.	Gas Plant	Kurnool	25-50	10-25	90s
3.	Pesticide	Adoni	<5	25-50	Pre 1985
4.	Electronic	Kallur	<5	10-25	90s
5.	Electronic	Nandyala	<5	10-25	90s
6.	Anca board	Kurnool	5-10	10-25	90s
7.	Color film	Kurnool	5-10	5-10	90s
8.	Stone Powder	Kurnool	5-10	5-10	85-90
9.	Stone Powder	Kurnool	<5	10-25	90s

(Contd...)

10. PVC Pipes	Nandyala	10-25	5-10	85-90
11. PVC Pipes	Nandyala	10-25	5-10	90s
12. PVC Pipes	Kallur	10-25	<5	90s
13. PVC Pipes	Nandyala	10-25	10-25	90s
14. PVC Pipes	Nandyala	10-25	10-25	90s
15. Granite	Nandyala	5-10	10-25	90s
16. Granite	Yerraguntla	5-10	10-25	90s
17 Granite	Kurnool	5-10	5-10	90s
18. Cement	Kurnool	>50	25-50	90s
19. Cement	Kurnool	>50	25-50	90s

Table 11: Stage Two Analysis: Service based SSIs (dt: Nellore)

S.No	*Type of Product*	*Location*	*Investment (Rs.Lakhs)*	*Employment*	*Year of Production*
1.	Food Preservation	Sullurpet	10-25	>50	85-90
2.	Graphics	Nellore	>50	5-10	90s
3.	Automobile Repair	Nellore	5-10	10-25	90s
4.	Automobile Repair	Gudur	10-25	5-10	90s
5.	Ice Factory	Nellore	10-25	5-10	85-90
6.	Ice Factory	Nellore	10-25	<5-10	90s

Table 12: Stage Two Analysis: Service based SSIs (dt: Cuddapah)

S.No	*Type of Product*	*Location*	*Investment (Rs.Lakhs)*	*Employment*	*Year of Production*
1.	Laminating Works	Proddutur	5-10	10-25	Pre 1985
2.	PVC Foams	Rajampet	>50	10-25	Pre 1985
3.	Tyre Retreading	Cuddapah	5-10	10-25	85-90
4.	Bore Well Dig Units	Cuddapah	5-10	5-10	85-90
5.	Bore Well Dig Units	Cuddapah	10-25	5-10	85-90
6.	Bore Well Dig Units	Pulivendula	10-25	5-10	90s

REFERENCES

1. Data from Industries Infromatics Centre, Commissioner of Industries, Govt. of Andhra Pradesh.
2. Shashi Bala, *Management of Small-scale Industries*, Deep & Deep Publications, 1988.
3. Nagesivanand, B., *Marketing Problems of Small-scale Industries* – A Study with reference to Chittoor District of Andhra Pradesh, 1993.

30

Role of Government in Revitalizing Sick SSI Units

Prof. K. Seshaiah & Dr. B. Ramachandra Reddy

Introduction

One of the most significant features of planned economic development in India has been the phenomenal growth of small scale industries. This sector has become an effective instrument of progress and development in terms of industrialization of backward areas and a measure of tackling the problems of unemployment plaguing the masses and the country. Development of Small-Scale sector has been one of the focus of because of its planning in India during the past half a century. Recently, small industry has become broad based by giving special recognition to the service sector in its developmental programme and it is currently referred to as the small enterprise sector, particularly in the context of generation of self employment opportunities[1].

Industrial sickness is not a new phenomenon, either in India or elsewhere. In the complex and diverse world of uncertainty, ignorance, inexperience, inefficiency, vast and rapid technological changes, changes in consumer preferences, monopolysrtic competition, growing labour power, and wise and unwise Government regulation of industry, sickness in SSI sector is not a matter of surprise. So long as sickness is sporadical, it need not cause much anxiety. However, if it assumes large proportions like an epidemic, it should be dealt with expeditiously and firmly.

1. Definition of Small Enterprises

A Study Group on development of small enterprise was constituted by the Deputy Chairman of the Planning commission in May, 1999. While constituting the study Group, representation was given to SSI associations, economists, Indian Institute of Management, Ahmedabad, SSI entrepreneurs and secretaries of various departments like Ministry of small scale Industries and Agro and Rural Industries, (SSI & ARI), Reserve Bank of India, SIDBI, FICCI etc. The study Group submitted its Interim Report on 6th July 2000. The term small-scale industry should be replaced by "Small Enterprises" which will consists of i) Tiny industrial units, ii) Small scale industrial units, and iii) Service and business enterprises. As per the Report, the three tire definition of tiny, small and medium sector are:

- Tiny units below Rs. 25 lakh investment in plant and machinery
- SSI Units Rs. 25 lakhs to Rs. 1 crore investment in plant and machinery
- Medium Unit Rs. 1 Crore to Rs. 10 crores investment in plant and machinery.

2. Definition of Sick Unit

The sick unit has been defined as one where the accumulated losses at the end of any financial year result in erosion of 50 per cent or more of its peak not worth during the immediately preceding five financial years. The net worth is the sum total of the paid-up capital and free-reserves. The free reserve means all reserves credited out of the profits and share premium account but does not include reserves credited out of revaluation of an asset, write back of depreciation provisions and amalgamation[2].

3. Symptoms of Sickness

Sickness does not develop all of a sudden. It gives out warning signals. It is a gradual process with distinct stages. There is a need for identification of various symptoms of sickness in small enterprises so that the concerned parties can check and maintained the health of units. The following are some of the Symptoms of Sickness.

- Continuous irregularity in cash credit Accounts
- Low capacity utilization
- Profit fluctuations, downward trend in sales and stagnation or fall in profits followed by contraction in the share of the market
- Higher rate of rejection of goods manufactured
- Reduction in credit summations-Whenever the companies are in financial difficulty, they open a separate account with another bank and deposit all collections therein
- Failure to pay statutory liabilities
- Larger and larger outstandings in the bill accounts.
- Larger period of credit allowed on sale documents negotiated through the bank and frequent returns by customers of the same.
- Non-submission of periodical financial data, stock statement etc., in item
- Decrease in working capital on account of increase in creditors and increase in inventories which may include large number of slow or non-moving items
- Existence of a large number of law suits against the company
- Rapid expansion and too much diversification within a short time
- Diversion of funds for purposes other than running the units
- Sudden or frequent changes in Management whether professional or otherwise dominated by one man or few individuals
- Any major change in the share holding[3].

4. Position of Industrial Sickness

The sick Industrial Companys (Special provisions) Act of 1985, classified sick units into large, medium and small units, but later the classification was made on more scientific lines. Accordingly they were grouped under non-SSI and SSI units. The following Table gives an idea of state-wise analysis of sick units in India till the end of March,2001.

Table 1: State-wise Analysis of Industrial Sickness in India

S.No	*State*	*31.03.1997*		*31.03.2001*	
		Non-SSI Sick/Weak Units	*SSI Sick/ Weak Units*	*Non-SSI Sick/Weak Units*	*SSI Sick/ Weak Units*
1	Maharashtra	399	19,360	611	8,056
2.	West Bengal	243	53,451	252	1,13,846
3	Uttar Pradesh	202	23,286	233	23,117
4	Andhra Pradesh	264	15,460	385	11,841
5	Gujarat	213	6,510	328	5,408
6	Tamil Nadu	175	9,809	317	9,959
7	Karnaataka	159	6,937	204	4,400
8	Kerala	81	8,908	76	11,144
9	Haryana	78	2,574	104	1,285,
10	Bihar	64	22,702	69	16,423
11	Madhya Pradesh	111	12,070	161	6,614
12	Orissa	62	3,408	59	6,668
13	Rajasthan	84	14,561	102	6,395
14	Punjab	62	2,466	91	1,836
15	Assam	41	10,133	56	8,632
16	Others	130	23,397	259	13,887
	Total	2,368	2,35,032	3,307	2,49,511

1. Ruddar Datt and K.P.M. Sundharam, *Indian Economy*, S.Chand & Co. Ltd, New Delhi, 2001, P.668.
2. *Business line*, 22nd Nov, 2001, p.8.

It is evident from the Table 1 that there had been an increase in the number of SSI sick units from 2,35,032 in March 1997 to 2,49,511 in March 2001. The pre centage increase in sick units over a period of 4 years in only 6. The number of SSI sick units was highest in West Bengal followed by Uttar Pradesh, Bihar, Maharashtra and so on at the end of March 1997. Similar trend is observed in the year 2001 also. The number of SSI sick units tremendously increased in West Bengal state over a period of 4 years from 53,451 to 1,13,846 (112.99%). The number of SSI sick units are gradually decreased in all the states from 31st March, 1997 to 31st March, 2001, except West Bengal, Tamil Nadu, Kerala and Orissa. Out of 2,49,511 total SSI sick units, West Bengal alone having the share of 45.6 per cent i.e., 1,13,846 units.

The total Bank Credit blocked in the sick units has increased from Rs. 13,787 crore (as on 31st March, 1997) to Rs. 19,646 crore (ason 31st March, 1999). The small scale sector has Rs.4,314 crore i.e. 22.2 percent blocked in its units while the Non-SSI sector has Rs. 15,150 crore (77.8 per cent).

5. Factors Responsible for Sickness of Small Enterprises

A review of the various studies* regarding small-scale units reveals the following:

1. Lock of management expertise is a very important factor. Young entrepreneurs start enterprises with romantic ideas. They keep high overhead costs, borrow at high rates of interest and do not care for making economies in costs, more especially during the period of infancy. Thus, inexperienced management of small units is one of the important causes of sickness.

2. Non-observance of the basic principles of business management is another major contributing factor to sickness. To start enterprises with a low equity base, to make no effort to build internal financial resources during good years, to maintain high inventories to total production, to invest short-term borrowings in medium

terms investments, etc., result in developing poor internal resilience to fight difficult times.

3. Under-utilisation of capacity caused by lack of working capital, lack of demand and non-availability of raw materials results in industrial sickness, leading to the death of small enterprises.
4. Easy approval of small-scale units by the state without proper screening of project proposals also resulted in sickness. This only under-scores the fact that assessment of viability of the projects is not made with adequate care, more especially with regard to financial viability.
5. The dead units depended mostly on their own funds i.e, on their individual savings rather than on borrowed funds. Among the dead small units, own funds accounted for 89 per cent of gross investments. For working capital requirements, these units depended on nationalized banks or co-operative banks.
6. Non-payment by the principal's to the ancillaries has been noted as an important caused of industrial sickness[4].

6. Measures to Prevent Sickness in Small Enterprises

The problem of industrial sickness in small units has to be treated differently from the problem of sickness of the large units. It is basically the problem of increasing the competitive strength and viability of the small units. For this purpose, the following measures deserve consideration:

The Reserve Bank should issue guidelines for the operation of small units and thus make professional management expertise available for the guidance of small entrepreneurs. The management expertise should acquaint the small entrepreneur with the need for a better equity base, prescribe norms for allocation of their surplus to depreciation, retained profits and expansion programmes so as to build their internal financial strength.

Since a majority of sick units die in the second or third year of their existence, a programme of monitoring and nursing them during infancy is very essential. In this way, the misuse of funds for purposes other than specified, and the factors leading to low capacity utilization can be examined and quick remedial action taken.

The Government can accord priority in allocation of scarce raw materials, extending marketing assistance and granting certain rebates and concessions to small units and more so to such units which show better record of performance.

Sickness of small units should be treated at par with scarcity/famine in agriculture and thus concessional rates of interest be charged at par with those loans, that are granted in scarcity/famine conditions in agriculture. The maximum rate of interest should be 7 per cent for small sick units to enable them to secure soft credit.

The Government should take penal action against the principals for non-payment for the delivery of goods by small units[5].

7. Other Measures Taken to Promote the SSI Sector

Two new schemes aimed at addressing the problem of collaterals faced by the SSI units and to encourage technology upgradation are:

(a) *Credit Guarantee Fund (Scheme) for SSI* – The Credit Guarantee Scheme has been launched to provide guarantee for loans upto Rs. 25 lakh extended by commercial banks, selected well performing Regional Rural Banks and other Financial institutions with out any collateral including their party guarantee.

(b) *Credit Linked Capital Subsidy Scheme for Technology Upgradation* – Government has approved this scheme on 20th September 2000, wherein 12 per cent back ended capital subsidy would be admissible on loans advanced to SSI by the Scheduled Commercial banks designated SFCs for technology upgradation in certain sub-sector.

3. *Enhancing the excise exemption limit for SSIs* – The limit has been enhanced from Rs.50 lakh to Rs. 1 crore with effect from 1st September, 2000.

4. *Improving Credit to SSIs* – steps taken to improve credit flow to SSIs are

   (i) Composite Loan Scheme Limit enhanced to Rs. 25 lakh.

   (ii) For loans upto Rs. 5 lakh, the collateral security requirement has been dispensed with.

   (iii) RBI has constituted a committee to monitor the flow of credit to SSI under the Chairmanship of its Deputy Governor.

5. *Dereservation of Readymade Garments* – The dereservation is expected to help the sector by technology upgradation, enhancement of productivity, quality consciousness, product diversification, increase in exports and innovative marketing strategies and maximizing employment opportunities.

6. *Enhancement of investment ceiling for Small Scale Service and Business (industry related) Entreprises* – The limit has been enhanced from Rs. 5 lakh to Rs. 10 lakh.

8. Details of Comprehensive Policy Package on SSI & Tiny Sector Announced by the Prime Minister on 30th August 2000

Some salient features of the package include:

Raising the exemption for excise duty limit from Rs. 50 lakh to Rs. 1 crore to improve the competitiveness of small scale sector.

Providing Credit Linked capital subsidy of 12 per cent against loans for technology upgradation in specified industries.

Conducting of the third census of small scale industries by the Ministry of SSI & ARI after a gap 12 years. This census would also cover sickness and its causes.

Raising the limit of investment in industry related service and business enterprise from the present level of Rs. 5 lakh to Rs.10 lakh.

Continuation of the ongoing scheme of granting Rs. 75,000 to each small scale enterprise for obtaining ISO 9000 certification till the end of the X plan.

SSI associations encouraged to develop and operate testing laboratories. Once time capital grant of 50 per cent will be given on reimbursement basis to such associations after detailed examination of each case.

Raising of the limit for composite loans from Rs. 10 lakh to Rs. 25 lakh.

Constitution of group under the Cabinet Secretary to suggest/recommend streamlining of inspection and repeal to redundant laws and regulations applicable to the sector.

Increasing the coverage of ongoing integrated infrastructure Development (IID) scheme to progressively cover all areas in the country with 50 per cent reservation for rural areas and 50 per cent of plots will be earmarked for tiny sector.

Raising the family income eligibility limit of Rs. 24,000 to Rs. 40,000 per annum. Under the Prime Minister's Rozgar Yojana (PMRY) with finances setting up of micro enterprises and generates employment for the educated unemployed[6].

9. Conclusion

To help the marketing of SSI Products, price performance policy of 10 per cent was made a permanent measure to project the interests SSI units. States have withdrawn this permanent preference measure. This has adversely affected the marketing of SSI products. This was uncalled for and the need of the hour is to receive this measure.

To help the growth and establishment of more and more SSI units, it is suggested that weighted deduction of 125 per cent of the salaries and wages paid by SSI units be allowed as deduction under the Income Tax Act.

A change of policies from protectionism to liberalisation has helped large Indian Industry and multinationals to enter in areas reserved for SSIs. This extreme path should be avoided since this has done more harm than good. The country should more to a middle path and permit selective liberalisation with necessary safeguards.

The development of small scale industries will rebuild the rural India and accelerated the pace of economic growth and well being of the people. The government seeking quick ways to create more employment would do well to develop projects like small scale industries which are labour intensive, quick yielding, well dispersed and capable of bringing more jobs and more consumer goods to backward areas of the country. Finally, it is the prime responsibility of all the Financial Institutions, RBI and the Government to take corrective measures for the proper development of SSI units and ways and means should be devised in such a way that there should be proper co-ordination between all concerned to avoid delays and take correct decisions and implement them properly.

REFERENCES

7. Govt. of India, VIII Five – year plan, 1992-97 vol. II, P.132.
8. Ruddar Datt and K.P.M. Sundharam, *Indian Economy*, S.Chand & Co. Ltd, New Delhi, 2001, P.676
9. Vasanth Desai, *Development of Small Scale Industrial Units*, Himalaya Publishing House, Mumbai, 2000
10. Srivastava etc., *Management and Monitoring of Industrial Sickness.*
11. Sudarshan Lal, *How to prevent Industrial sickness*, 2000, P.191
12. Govt. of India, *Economic Survey*, 2000-01, P.145.

31

Technological Development in Small Manufacturing Enterprises: Some Insights

Dr.M.Usha*

The background

Development of Small Scale Sector continues to be the central plank of t industrial development policy of the Government of India. This priority sector has be making rapid strides to carve a place for itself in terms of its contribution manufacturing output, employment and exports.

As manufacturers of final products, sub-assemblies, specialized equipment an even as suppliers to original equipment manufacturers, the small-scale units assum importance in the industrial economy of our country. While this being so, it is widel believed that small industrial units in developing countries have a poor technologic base and low research intensity measured by their research and developme expenditure. Further, it is held that the capacities of workforce employed by these unit in terms of their knowledge, skills, expertise and training are also limited. Hence th belief that small industries are ill-equipped and lack the capacity to absorb risks an bring out any technological developments. Being single-person shows by and large, it is said that they are pre-occupied with short-run problems and lack long term growth orientation. Inspite or

* *Associate Professor,* Department of Commerce, Osmania University, Hyderabad

these impressionistic views, it is recognized world over that smal industries succeed by exploiting their special strengths of flexibility, adaptability an personal touch in their relationship with both customers and employees. Indian small industries are no exception in all these respects. With the advent of New Economic Policy in 1991, Indian industry witnessed a dramatic shift from regulated and protected policy environment to a more open and competitive environment. Indian Government has been voicing time and again specially with reference to small-scale sector that protection should not breed inefficiency. Now that the protection walls collapsed and winds of competition (both from within the country and abroad) started blowing in with all gale and fury, we can say that the small industries are-in-for a major shake up.

The Indian small industrialists have realized the implication of global competition and are now gearing up to meet the changing technological requirements and world -class standards. They are aware of fact that if they have to survive and grow, they have to design or else resign and that they can no more afford to demand but have to be in demand.

Against this background and based on the premise that technological development is a source of competitive advantage to the small industries, the present paper focuses on the following issues relating to technological development in small manufacturing enterprises.

One: The various sources of technological development in the selected SSI units.

Two: The small entrepreneurs' perceptions and practices relating to technological development.

Three: The nature of technological development taking place in the sample SSI units.

The plan of the paper is as follows, while the first part is introductory in nature, Part II highlights the sample background. The various sources of technological development are examined in part III. The small entrepreneurs' perceptions and their practices relating to the technological development are presented in part IV. The nature of technological development in the sample units, which in one way are their technological achievements are analysed in Part V. Concluding observations and suggestions are presented in the last part.

II. The sample

The present paper is based on a field survey of one hundred small manufacturing enterprises belonging to the three fast-growing industry-groups viz; Electrical and Electronics (EE), Engineering (ENGG), and Chemicals including Drugs and Pharmaceuticals (CDP). The field study undertaken during......... covers the three districts of Telangana region in Andhra Pradesh, Viz; Hyderabad, Ranga Reddy and Medak.

The combined share of the three groups selected in the aggregated net value added was about 31 per cent (Table 2.1) at the All India level. At the state level, these three groups occupy first, fourth and fifth ranks respectively contributing little less than on-third of the total net value-added by manufacture. Further, these three groups are functioning in rapidly changing technological environments. Perhaps, that is one of the reasons that foreign collaboration agreements, imports of technology, research and development activities, utilisation of consultancy services etc. are found in large measure in these industries at the global, national as well as the regional level.

Coming to the three districts selected, it is found that there is high concentration of these industries and the districts are experiencing rapid industrial growth in these non-agro-based industries.

The selected units have a wide products rage, which includes import substitutes, exportable goods, making use of sophisticated and modern technologies and are competing with large-scale industries and even multi-national companies.

Another significant feature of the sample units is the educational background of the entrepreneurs. Majority of them (sixty five per cent) are qualified technocrats. Some of them are doctorate degree holders. Only eight per cent on the entrepreneurs had no prior experience before setting up their units, while the rest have either worked in public sector organisations or National laboratories and Multi-National companies. Further, a few of the entrepreneurs and their employees had undergone special technical training abroad in their respective fields as per the terms and conditions of their foreign collaboration agreements.

These aspects such as education, training etc., assume importance because, it is believed that technological capabilities is a matter of building-up skills in the work-force. Perhaps training of work-force is as important as the technology itself. Education, training and experience of the entrepreneurs and work-force can in fact be used as significant measures of their technological capabilities.

III. Sources of Technological Development

For the purpose of presentation, the various sources (Chart 1) have been first classified into formal and informal sources, within the formal channel are the internal sources viz; National Laboratories, Public sector undertakings and In House research and Development. Foreign collaborations, imports of technology, plant and equipment are the external formal sources. Obtaining information through foreign visits by the entrepreneurs, participation/visiting trade fairs and exhibitions, contacts with overseas customers and suppliers etc. Constitute the informal sources. Industry wise details are presented in table 3.1.

As can be observed form the data presented in table 3.1, the most prevalent internal source of technology in the selected units is In House and R & D. Contrary to the traditional view, this phenomenon signifies the self-dependent attitude of the small manufacturing enterprises. It also indicated the entrepreneurs' commitment to systematic technical effort as well as some measure of their technical capability, no matter how rudimentary.

It is significant to note that among the units who reported R& D activities, Nine Units have recognised R& D departments'. Under this scheme, some incentives are offered by the government to those industries having separate facilities for R&D.

---

1 . (Recognition is given by the Department of Scientific and Industrial Research Government of India (DSIR).

Among the external sources foreign collaborations and among the informal sources, visits to foreign countries by the entrepreneurs are prominent.

Another source of importance is perhaps foreign collaborations. Out of sixteen sample units, which reported foreign collaborations, majority of the collaboration agreements relate to supply of technical know-how, drawings and designs in EE and ENGG groups while in CDP groups collaborations are exclusively for marketing tie-ups. A few of the units have financial collaborations in the form of Equity participation. Imports of technology, plant and machinery, spares and component are relatively few and are not found in the CDP group.

Participation in fairs and trade exhibitions, discussions which overseas manufacturers, suppliers and custcmers are I perceived to the of great use by the entrepreneurs who view them as an economical way of obtaining latest technological developments be it new models, new designs, new processes etc.

Thus, the sample units are found to be depending on more than one source at times, according to their needs, in pursuit of technological excellence. The various sources are therefore not mutually exclusive. To what extent the sample units have succeeded in achieving technological excellence can be examined by the nature of technological development taking place in these units, which aspect is covered in section V.

IV. Entrepreneurial Perceptions and Practices

The Issue of technology acquisition whatever may be the source and strengthening the technology base at the firm level is of course a matter generally decided by the entrepreneur himself. This may be decided by him in the tight of cost, market and competitive conditions prevailing in the environment in which he is operating. In this context the perceptions of the entrepreneurs on various related issued assume importance. Implicitly, the practices they follow are likely to be influenced by and large by their Perceptions. The entrepreneurs reactions were not only sharp but also revealing specially on issues such as technology transfers, foreign collaborations, modernisation/

upgradation, role of various institutional infrastructure, Government policies etc.

Majority of the entrepreneurs strongly felt that the national laboratories lack adequate interaction with the industry to find out their research needs. Further, no market surveys are undertaken to find out the commercial viability of their research output. As a matter of fact, one of the premier national laboratories had to redesign the machinery, which was found unsuitable to the requirements of the industry concerned only after demonstration. This obviously results in wastage of time and scarce productive resources. Some of the entrepreneurs who received technology felt that the technologies developed in the National laboratories are not upto the mark. Thay also feel that the project reports supplied are mostly outdated.

Commenting on the working of the national level organisations and also the national laboratories functioning in the state, the entrepreneurs feel that they are ill equipped, lack awareness of developments in other organisations and necessary expertise. The technologies developed in these laboratories do not reflect the latest scientific knowledge of the scientists' inspite of their access to the well-equipped libraries. Implicitly, personal considerations over-ride the institutional interests. It is considerations over-ride the institutional interests. It is reported that some of the scientists working in the national laboratories and public sector undertakings are cashing in on the knowledge acquired with the national laboratories by rendering consultancy services to private industries.

The entrepreneurs pointed out that there is lack of coordination among the Organisation among the organisations working in the related areas; they are ignorant of the developments in other organisations and laboratories. One of the promoters complained that the public sector undertakings due to vested interests prefer to import certain components instead of purchasing the same indigenously produced, from the small units inspite of cost advantage and a matching quality.

Some of the promoters who are also the NRDC licensees observed that a few national laboratories are very cooperative in solving the technical problems arising out of technology transfers by providing the needed support facilities. However, it was pointed out that a few of them have not been able to devote the needed attention. Delays at various stages of processing of requests at the NRDC was also pointed out by the entrepreneurs. The popular opinion of the entrepreneurs in this context was that the flow of comprehensive literature about the know-how available for the release and product profiles giving the latest picture of these processes has been found to be inadequate.

To sum-ups, what comes out prominently is the low profile of the national research laboratories and other organisations functioning in the state, in terms of transfer of technologies to small scale sector and necessary back-up services compared to the huge investments and vast infrastructural facilities created. Lack of effective

VI. Concluding Observations

What comes out strikingly from the analysis made in the foregoing parts is that technological development in one form or the other is taking place in the small manufacturing enterprises. The entrepreneurs have realized the imperative need for acquiring and upgrading the technical base of their units. Evidences also show the conscious and rigorous efforts made by the entrepreneurs to this effect, inspite of many constraints. This is more conspicuous in units run by technocrats.

The policy initiatives announced by the Government form time to time have no doubt helped the process of technological development in the small-scale sector though not to the extent desired. Even though, a large number of national laboratories and other institutions which are well equipped and well staffed, are working for technological development, their impact on industry in general and small scale sector in particular has been extremely limited. The low utilization of the research efforts and services of these institutions by the selected small manufacturing enterprises is a testimony to this phenomenon. Further, lack of effective linkage between the laboratories and the industry on one hand, poor coordinated effort among the national laboratories and institutes on the other hand and absence of interface between the Government and the industry has created wide communication gap between the generators of technology and its users.

What is therefore required is strengthening and full utilization of the existing and available infrastructural facilities and resources for pre-determined requirements of the industry, more specifically the Small Scale Sector. This goes without saying that there is no need for creating new institutions.

The need of the hour is to render timely and efficient service to the small entrepreneur to enable his to competed not only in the domestic markets, but also internationally.

Finance should not become a bottleneck for acquiring technical know-how. As merged form the study, most of the R&D efforts and technology development strategies adopted by the selected units are self-financed. If only, finances were adequate, the entrepreneurs would have achieved better technological capabilities.

The funding agencies should realize the importance of this vital aspect and come forward generously to help all the deserving cases. Towards this end, commercial banks and other financial institutions should strengthen their evaluation system and credit rating cells, which will go along way in promoting technological development in this priority sector.

Above all, there should be an attitudinal change in the bureaucracy, Government, and the bank officials towards the small manufacturer. What the entrepreneur needs is the minimum interference by the Government simplified procedures and formalities.

On the part of the entrepreneur, continuous efforts have to be directed towards product designing, rather than reverse engineering or import-substitution production. Identification of new materials, new products and innovation of new processes is the order of the day. It is necessary for them to realize the fact that technological development is not a one-shot affair. It is a continuous process and demands conscious efforts. More importantly, manufacturing technologies when widely developed and used, enable the manufacturing firms to compete better through reduced costs, increased quality, reduced manufacturing lead time, reduced time to market and increased product variety.

Taking advantage of the present liberal policy environment the small entrepreneur should face the challenges posed by the opening up of the Indian economy to the multinationals and foreign investors both internally and externally.

Appendix A
About the Special Assistance Programme (SAP)

The Department of Commerce and Management Studies came into existence in 1934. It has a creditable record of imparting Commerce education for more than six-and-half decades at the under graduate and post graduate levels and thus has been contributing for promotion of Commerce education not only in Andhra Pradesh but also in the entire country. The department has the unique distinction of having pioneered management education right from 1957 by being first in India and has produced talented executives for four-and-half decades who have been occupying coveted positions in India and abroad. It has strong faculty who have carried out extensive research in the areas of Commerce and Management including small-scale industry. The department has been offering research facilities leading to M.Phil and Ph.D degrees. It has produced so far 130 Ph.Ds, around 100 M.Phils., 100 research reports, 50 text and reference books and hundreds of research papers published in reputed national and international journals. The faculty make a perennial effort to improve, add and achieve new heights of academic distinction and to serve the needs of industry and society.

The University Grants Commission has selected the Department of Commerce and Management Studies and accordingly sanctioned Special Assistance Programme (SAP),Phase-I for a period of 5 years(1988-93) and the thrust area was "Problems of Local Industry". In continuation, Phase-II of SAP was also sanctioned for a further period of 5 years

(1994-99) and the thrust area was "Regional Industry Development".

Having satisfied with the progress of the work done under Phase-II, the UGC has sanctioned **Phase-III** of Special Assistance Programme for a further period of 5 years from 1999 to 2004 with a financial assistance of Rs.32.25 lakhs. The Thrust area identified under Phase-III is "Industrialization of North and East Coastal Districts of Andhra Pradesh with Special Reference to Development of Small Industries".

During the past three and half years of Phase-III, Special Assistance Programme many activities were successfully carried out in fulfillment of the objectives of the project to a large extent. On the research front survey was conducted in two spells on the evaluation of the performance of 475 small enterprises in the four North Coastal Districts of Andhra Pradesh viz., Srikakulam, Vizianagaram, Visakhapatnam and East Godavari . Two national seminars, a regional workshop and a symposium were organized in the thrust area of the project. Entrepreneurship development programmes, one in each of the four years was organized for the students of Commerce and Management of the department and other affiliated colleges. 500 books in the field of Commerce and Management particularly in the thrust area were acquired for the library of the department while subscribing to 15 professional journals.

Work is under progress for development of Computer Lab which provides working facility for 45 students at a time. State of the art computer lab is being developed to enable them to acquire skills and access information for career building with quality perspective.

Appendix B

National Seminar on

"WTO – Challenges and Opportunities for Small Industry Development in India"

PROCEEDINGS

With the advent of WTO in the year 1995, the Indian industries are faced with the challenges that they have to manage themselves in line with the best of the world by raising their levels of efficiency and competitiveness to meet competition both in the domestic and international markets. The products of MNCs have the advantage of global branding, latest technology, quality and cost advantage and are offered at highly competitive prices. The Indian products, especially from SSI sector, are currently facing keen competition due to dumping of foreign goods in domestic markets at lower import duties. The Indian small and medium enterprises are gradually loosing the protection and facing greater competition from imports. This segment lacks awareness and market information. A lot of information and technology gap is created. Phasing out of competitive restrictions and bringing more and more products under Open General License (OGL) have posed a threat to SSI units. The SME entrepreneurs lack international exposure and knowledge of various provisions of WTO. The issues relating to labour standard also will effect the growth of exports of certain commodities. It is against this background, a National Seminar on **"WTO – Challenges and Opportunities for Small Industry Development in India"** was organized with the following objectives :

- To discuss the implications of WTO on Indian industry with particular reference to SSI sector;

- To review the government's policy initiatives to enable the SSI sector to meet the post-WTO environment;
- To deliberate upon the impact of tariff and trade regulations in creating opportunities for export promotion of SSIs;
- To focus on the extent of restructuring, upgradation and absorption of new technology in order to increase quality and productivity of SSI sector; and
- To evolve suitable strategies to increase competitiveness of SSI sector in the domestic as well as international markets.

The two-day seminar was organized under the sub-themes as :

- Trade environment, imports and exports, industrial tariffs;
- Government policy and role of government institutions;
- Technology upgradation and restructuring, R & D consultancy;
- Small and medium industry linkages, strategies for competitive advantage;
- Marketing, finance, HRD, and production – issues and challenges.

The seminar was attended by as many as 72 delegates, representing a cross-section like academicians, researchers, entrepreneurs, members of SSI Associations, Chamber of Commerce & officials of NIRD, NISIET, VEPZ, DICs, SIDBI, Small Industry Service Institutes, APSFC, Commercial Banks, KVIC, Department of Industries, Government of India and Andhra Pradesh.

Inaugural Session : The seminar was inaugurated by Sri Kotagiri Vidyadher Rao, Hon'ble Minister for Major Industries & Commerce, Government of Andhra Pradesh and was presided over by Prof. C. Suryanarayana, Co-ordinator, UGC Special Assistance Programme and Seminar Director. Sri K. Hari Babu, Hon'ble MLA of Visakhapatnam. Prof. J.M. Naidu, Registrar of

Andhra University, Prof. B. Parvathiswara Rao, Head of the Department of Commerce and Management Studies were Guests of Honour.

The Chief Guest and also Hon'ble Minister mentioned that the elected representatives of the people need to educate and prepare entrepreneurs, farmers and others about WTO and discuss on the issues as to how to face the challenges. The industries, big or small, should convert the threats into opportunities and improve their competitiveness. The present economic setbacks are only initial troubles of development. WTO provisions contain in-built protective measures and there is no harm to Indian farmers and entrepreneurs under the WTO regime. He was of the view that the government has the responsibility to conduct market survey about certain products and services and also about other factors like skills, technology and competencies required for small-scale industries to face the challenges and become more and more competitive. The academicians are required to take up research in 1 or 2 thrust areas and come out with appropriate suggestions, he added.

Sri K. Hari Babu, MLA stressed on the need to study the impact of WTO on the 2 major sectors of the country, namely, agriculture and small-scale industry, because 70 to 80 per cent of the population are depending on agriculture and on SSI sector.

Major Recommendations : The seminar made the following recommendations :

1. The definition of SSIs may be made compatible with the WTO agreements.
2. A separate law for SSIs may be formulated as suggested by the Abid Hussain Committee.
3. The law enforcement machinery need to be made simple to facilitate the State Govt. to implement Central Acts with state rules.
4. The powers tariff structure for SSI of both Central & State Governments should be such that it will not be disadvantage to the SSI sector.
5. The ceiling of 75 HP fixed under Low tension (LT)

category for SSIs may be increased to 150 HP in line with the neighboring states.

6. The Government of Andhra Pradesh must provide infrastructural facilities to SSIs at reasonable costs.
7. The critical balancing infrastructure fund may be spent more on rejuvenation of existing industrial estates rather than on promotion of new ones.
8. The State Government may create a 'market promotion fund' and make it available to the units engaged in exports. This may be done on the lines of Singapore Trade Promotion Board, which enables small exporters to bid in international markets.
9. The DICs may be renamed as 'District Entrepreneurship Councils' to enable them to perform the functions of not only promotions, but also development and monitoring of grounded units.
10. The research laboratories may be set up at the 'landing sites', (i.e., *sea ports and airports*) in India, in order to facilitate quality checks of goods being imported into India.
11. The trade-related property rights must be reviewed and implemented in view of possible hike in the prices of life-saving drugs.
12. A 'Comprehensive Competition Policy' may be evolved at the national level consistent with WTO, which would give due consideration to consumer interest and which would not be 'size-neutral', i.e., differential competition policy for different sizes is required *(on the lines of the US Anti Trust Law).*

Appendix C

National Seminar on

"District Industries Centres - Role Dynamics and strategies for Small Industrial Development in the changing global economic scenario"

PROCEEDINGS

The District Industries Centres ever since their establishment in 1978 have been functioning as the nodal agencies for industrial development of the districts, particularly by promoting small scale and cottage industries. Eventhough, the DICs have played a crucial role in this respect they were criticized for their ineffective functioning. It is pointed out that they are acting merely as industry registration departments. The needed linkage and coordination between DICs and other promoting agencies is found to be very weak and distressing. They have not been able to play a decisive role in entrepreneurship development, providing market intelligence, new technologies and innovative strategies for product development and diversification. The staff are found to be lacking professionalism that is essential in the context of the changing global market scenario.

In the light of the above shortcomings of the DICs a National Seminar is organised on "The District Industries Centres: The Role Dynamics and Strategies for Small Industry Development in the changing global economic scenario", with the following objectives:

- *To review the DICs' role in Industrial development of the region specific and the problems thereof.*
- *To identify the challenges of DICs consequent to New Industrial Policy and the responses of DICs.*

- *To find out the need and feasibility of restructuring DICs in the contemporary environment; and*
- *To suggest necessary policy initiatives and strategies to make DICs more dynamic and efficient in the changed global scenario.*

About 80 delegates participated representing a cross section from DICs, Bankers, SIDBI, APSFC, Entrepreneurs and Small Industry Associations like FAPSSIA, Department of Industries and a galaxy of academicians from universities and post graduate colleges and professional institutions.

The seminar was organized in three technical sessions:1) Changing Business Environment- Policy initiatives and responses of DICs and other SSI promoting agencies 2) Restructuring and Redesigning of DICs for competitive advantage and 3) Interface of DICs with other promoting agencies and entrepreneurs.

Inaugural Session: The Seminar was inaugurated by Sri B. Gopala Krishna Reddy, Hon'ble Minister for Small Industries, Government of Andhra Pradesh, while it was presided over by Prof. G. Subrahmanyam, Principal of Colleges of Arts and Commerce, Andhra University. Sri Sunil Sarma, I.A.S, District Collector and Magistrate, Visakhapatnam delivered the key note address. Prof. C. Suryanarayana, Director of the Seminar welcomed the dignitaries and delegates and briefed the relevance and significance of the seminar in the post WTO environment.

In his key-note address Sri Sunil Sarma emphasized that the Small entrepreneurs need to be given training by the DICs. The role of DICs should be changed in tune with the changes taking place in the domestic and international industry and business scenario and the challenges posed by SSI sector. The problems being faced by SSI sector should be critically examined and to ensure proper coordination among different agencies, a FORUM at the district level need to be set up, he added.

In his inaugural address, the Minister, Sri Gopalakrishna Reddy emphasized that the development of SSI sector has been receiving the attention of policy makers right from the 1956, by way of incentives, infrastructure facilities, subsidies, special reservations etc. Poverty alleviation and employment generations are inter linked and making profit is not the only objective of any industry, said the minister. The success of DWACRA should serve as a lesson in development of entrepreneurial skills, management and marketing practices of SSI sector. The Government of Andhra Pradesh is planning to start a virtual university as a part of its effort to develop human resource through Information Technology Enabled Services. The ITES has a potential to generate about four lakhs jobs in next three years. Further the Minister mentioned that there are plans to provide technical education and training to youth through Universities in developing entrepreneurial skills to enable them to secure gainful employment. Technology Training and Development Centres need to be established in each of the assembly segments to train the youth. The plan are also anvil to develop an Apparel Park at Visakhapatnam to generate employment opportunities and also to promote exports from SSI sector.

Major Recommendations: The deliberations of various technical sessions and the panel discussions resulted in some major recommendations to the policy makers.These include that 1) in the context of economic reforms and competitive business environment especially in the WTO era, the DICs functions should be revised through restructuring and redesigning the roles of different functionaries. 2) Single window system has been observed to be ineffective as the DICs have not been able to act as a powerful agency to coordinate with other SSI promoting Governmental and Non-Governmental agencies. It has been strongly felt that the DICs should be vested with more powers without usurping the interests of other promoting agencies. The heads of the other SSI promoting agencies need to be more positive in their outlook and approach, and work with a mission. 3) It has been observed that some of the key functionaries in DICs have been discharging stereo typed functions, some times with bureaucratic approach. The top and middle level functionaries of DICs need to be trained for skill upgradation, application of information technology, managerial skills with professionalism, knowledge of global business environment. 3) the DICs should give the leadership in the district as industry promoting agency. It should identify the training needs of entrepreneurs (both existing and prospective) and accordingly design and conduct training programmes periodically. 4) the DICs should also take up the responsibility of monitoring the performance of the SSI units and render necessary timely counsel. 5) the DICs documentation centres need to be updated with latest information about the availability of technologies, global market intelligence and use of information technology for product development and diversification etc.

Index

A

Abid Hussain Committee, 31, 51, 80, 82, 89, 251, 324

Acquisition of Land for,

Agenda for the Millennium, 5

APIIC – Telangana Area, 321-22

Agriculture, 153

Ancillary Unit, 42-44

Andhra Pradesh, 24-25
  Industrial development of, 310 11

Anne Krueger, Dr., 145

Anti Dumping, 161

Appa Rao, Dr. P.B., 41, 194

Appa Rao, Prof. B., 66

APIIC, 309, 337
  as Local Authority, 339-40
  ambiguity in allocation of duties, 346
  delegation of powers of UDAs, 343
  formation of Industrial Services Society, 341-42
    functions of, 318-19
    objections of, 317-18
    officials training, 341
    physical achievements, 319-20
  powers & functions as Local Authority, 340
  regionwise Analysis, 320-21
  sharing of property tax, 342
  status of Local Authority, 343-44

Artisans,
  assistance of, 198

Associations,
  role of, 171

Automobiles, 152

B

Balajiprasad, P., 351

Balance of Payments, 57, 127

BEVUN Murthy, Prof., 259, 330

Bhagwtgita, M.S., 102

Brettonwoods Conference, 95

C

Characteristics of SSI, 1-2

Chandrasekhara, Prof. M., 151, 351

Chandrasekhara Prasad Dr. J., 277

Cluster approach for focused development, 33-34

Competition from China, 155
Complexity of laws,
as regards Legislative Powers, 22
Conceptual Issues, 16-17
Coping with emerging environment, 83-84
Consultancy for Entrepreneurship, 334
Contribution of SSI,
to manufacturing sector, 5-6
Co-ordination from departments,
for speedy clearances, 293-94
Core Competency, 169
Credit assistance, 197
Credit Managers, 254

D

Definition on SMIs, 17-18
Deregulation and liberalization, 56-59
Dereservation of Items, 51-54
Dhar & Lydall,
Justification for SSI of, 352
District Enterprise Promotion Agency (DEPA), 255-56
District Industries Centres (DIC), 183-92, 195-96, 299-330
changing role of, 248-58
functions of, 184-85
Godavari District, role DIC, 277-85
Kakinada, 281-82
Nellore district, a case study of, 259-68
objectives, 184
organization structure, 187
outlook, 286-92
Promotional, 250
Recommendatory, 250
Regulatory function, 250
Vishakapatnam, a case study, 297-306, 300-301
weakest link, 252

E

EDII, 332
East Godavari district, 279-80
Economic liberalization, 113
Economic profile, 19
Electronics, 152
Emerging Trends, 82-83
Employment, 353-54
a study on managerial aspect, 352-53
Godavari district of, 281
methodology, 353
Employment Generation, 197
Employment in Small and Tiny Units, 213-20 (T-24, 239)
agro-based, 213-14 (T-25, 240)
chemical based, 214-15 (T-26, 241)
engineering based, 215-16 (T-27, 242)
forest based, 216-17 (T-28, 243)
livestock based, 217-18 (T-29, 244)
mineral based, 218-19 (T-30, 245)
miscellaneous, 219-20 (T-32, 247)
textiles, 219- (T-31, 246)
Enforcement laws, 22-23
Exim policy, 134
Expert Group (1997), 255

Export Obligation,
sustainability of, 163
Export Oriented Units, 44-46
Exports,
growth of, 115-16
Export promotion, 38-39, 170
Evaluation of Policy for SSI, 76-77
Evaluation Study, 254-55

F

Fair Competition, 98
Field Survey on,
manufacturing enterprises, 374-75
Frame-work for SMEs, 14
Finance, 19-20
Ford Foundation, 41-42
Functional Industrial Estate, 260
Future Outlook on Industrial Policy, 26-27

G

GATT, 95, 105, 124-25
Implications of, 125-26
GDP growth, 66-71
Global Economy, 92
Globalisation, 92, 93, 102, 110
challenges of, 116-18
Government Procurement, 162-63
Guidelines for reforms, 60-63
Gujarat, 25-26
Gupta, Dr. S.P., 31, 251, 267-68

H

H.R.D. Training, 12

I

IIMA, 331-32
Indian Institute of Management, (study), 191
Initiatives for development of Industries, 278
Industrial Development districts, 196
Industrial Estates Programme, 315-16
in Andhra Pradesh, 317
funding pattern, 316
objectives of, 316
Industrial Policy Resolutions, 1948-56, 2-46
Industrial Policy Resolutions, 1977-1991, 3, 44, 47, 49
Institutional Support to SSIs, 175
Internal Planning Team, 112
Investment,
Godavari district of, 281
Investment in Tiny Units, 207 (T-14, 230)
agro-based, 208 (T-15, 231)
chemical based, 208-09 (T-16, 232)
engineering based, 209 (T-17, 233)
forest based, 209-10 (T-18, 234)
livestock based, 210 (T-19, 235)
mineral based, 211 (T-20, 236)
miscellaneous, 212-13 (T-22, 238)
textiles, 212 (T-21, 237)
Israel Raju Vuram, Mr., 159

K

Kama Raju, Dr. T., 119

Kapur Committee, 1998, 324

Kapur, S.L., 31

Karl Marx, 86-87

Karve Committee, 111

KIADB, 323

KSSIDC, 323

Krishna Mohan, Dr. V., 138, 165

L

Labour laws, 90-91

Largesh Employer, 79-80

Large and Medium Scale Industries,
    growth of, 311-12

Legal frame work SMEs, 14

Lavanyalatha, K., 259

Laxman, study on Issues of Cottage and SSIs, 352

Liberalization, 66

Liberalization Period, 31

Limited Partnership Act, 13

M

MFN-Treatment, 96-97

MIDC, 322-23

Macro Economic Parameters, 56-59

Madhavi, Dr. A.D., 76

Maintenance of Industrial Estates,
    role of Industrial association, 337-50

Managerial aspect of SSIs,
    a study in Rayalseema & Nellore district, 351-60

Marketing Problems, 132-33
    assistance, 294-95
    orientation, 163
    strategy, 163

Marrakesh agreement, 96
    declaration, 102

Matthai, 1976, 332

Measures from RBI, 58

Measures for Promotion of SSIs, 368-69

McClelland, 332

McClellands Report 1996, 332

Measures to prevent sickness, 367-68

Meher Karuna, M. Mrs., 297

Mindset of Entrepreneur, 171

Minhas, B.S., 111

Multi National Corporations, 117-18

Murthy, 1982
    Study of, 333

Muthyala Naidu, Dr. M., 86

N

NRDC, 377-78

NABARD, 328

NISIET,
    study group, 270-71

Nagayya, D., 248

Nagaiah, Dr. D., 31, 55

Nageswara Rao, K., 277

National Treatment, 97

Nayak Committee 1991, 7-8

Nehru, 1

New approach to regulation, 23-24

New Economic Policy 1991, 373

New generation – Small
Industries, 28
New measures, 130
Nodal Agency, 276
Notified Area Service Societies,
344-45

O

Open general licence (OGL), 35
Outlook on,
development of SSIs, 179-82

P

Package on SSIs,
as announced by P.M.,
369-70
Parliamentary Standing
Committee, 53
Pathak, 1968, 1975, 333
Perceptions and Practices,
entrepreneurial, 376-78
Performance of SSI Sector, 78
Planning Innovativeness, 169-
70
Policy framework, 18, 19, 77
initiatives, 2 ,175
interventions, 167
measures on linkage, 28, 29
for reservation of items, 78
statements 1977, 77
1980, 77-78
1985, 78
1991, 78
Prabhakar Reddy, S., 174
Prabhu, V., 144
Predictability, 97
Present Scenario, 6
Prime Ministers Rozgar Yojana,
252-62
performance of, 301-03
Proceedings for SSIs, 22
Promotion of Entrepreneurship,
strategies of, 330-35
of new units, 197
Prospects and outlook, 6-7
Pulla Reddy, Dr. S.V., 86

Q

Quantative Restrictions, 89,
120-21, 126, 144-45
in India, 145
likely impact, 146
Quality Consciousness, 170

R

Rao, B. Appa, 66
Rao, K.V., 31, 122
Rao, Dr. T.V., 270
Rao and Moulik 1976, 331
Rajkot Estate, 260
Ramachandra Reddy, Dr. B.,
362
Reforms in Industrial Sector, 55
Regulatory Framework, 20, 22
Regulatory Laws, 10-11
Regional trade exceptions, 97
Registration implication, 63, 64
Registered Units in Godavari
district, 280-81
Reservation,
of policy, 35-36
of products, 100
for small sector, 50-54, 161
Resilient SSIs, 261-62
Revatty, Dr. J., 122
Revitalizing of DICs, 255-58
Revitalizing of Sick SSI Units,
role of government, 362-71

Review of literature, 352
Role of DICs,
  in changing scenario, 293-96
Rural Industries Projects
  Programme (RIPP), 194-95

S

SMEs, 14, 16, 98, 102, 107-09
SBUs, 122-23
SSIs, 86, 110, 116, 119, 138, 154-55
  agrobased, Nellore, Ananthapur, 356
  industry based, Chittor, Kumul, 356
  service based, Nellore, Guddapah, 356
  productivity investment, 357
  resilient, 261-262
SIDBI, 34, 35, 328
SEEUY Program, 271-72
SC & ST Entrepreneurs, 198-99
Sarah Varakki, Mrs., 14
Salt Cultivation, 280
Safeguards in W.T.O. rules, 37
Sathguru Merchant
  Consultants, 27
Seoul Declaration, 14-15
Seshaiah, Prof. K., 362
Sharma, A.P., 351
Shivaji Rao, H., 286
Shukla, Dr. A.V., 144
Single Window Clearance, 24, 295-96
  of service, 251
Single legislation, 32, 33
Sick Unit,
  definition of, 363
Sickness,
  factors responsible of, 366-67
Sickness position in states, 365
Simptoms of sickness, 363-64
Soft Drinks, 152
Small enterprises,
  definition of, 363
  in India, 166-67
Small Scale Industries,
  growth of, 312-14
Small Scale Sector,
  characteristics of, 1
  contribution of, 5
  growth of, 298-99
State Intervention in SMEs, 15
State level Co-ordination
  Committee, 254
Strategic thinking, 168-69
Strengthening Infrastructure,
  suggestions of, 325-28
Study of APIC, 309-28
Study on Development of Small
  Enterprise, 8-10
Subsidies, 126
Suresh Babu, B., 293
Suresh Kumar, Dr. T., 194
Suryanarayana, Prof. C., 55, 110, 138, 144, 297

T

T.N.C.s, 92-94
TRIMS, 127, 161-62
TRIPS, 84, 162
Tafford Park Estate Limited, 259
Tamilnadu, 26
Technical Barriers Trade, 133

Technological Development,
in manufacturing enterprises of, 372-80
sources of, 375-76

Technology management, 170

Textiles, 153

Tiny Estate, Hadapsar, 260

Tiny Units, 199-200 (T-3)
agro based, 200 (T-4)
chemical based, 201 (T-5)
engineering based, 201 (T-6)
forest based, 202 (T-7)
livestock based, 203 (T-8)
mineral based, 204 (T-9)
miscellaneous, 205 (T-10)
textiles, 206 (T-21, 211)

Topsy Turvey Policy, 86

Threats to Indian Companies, 151

Trade Policy, 36, 37, 162

Trends of Macro Economic indicators, 69-71

Tulasi Rao, Dr. G., 119

U

Udyog Sadan, 327

Unfair trade,
exceptions of, 97

Unfair practices, 126

Uruguay Round, 95, 102

Usha, Dr. M., 372

V

Varkky, Sarah (Mrs.), 14

Varum, Israel Raju, 159

Varshney, V., 144

Venkateswara Rad, Ch., 309, 337

Venugopala Reddy, 194

Vijayalaxmi, Dr. M., 76

Vijayaraju, Dr. S., 70

Village Small Scale Industries, 72

Voluntary bodies,
role of, 171

W

WTO, 95, 102, 103, 105, 114, 119
of agreement, 159, 177
of compatibility, 36-37
emergence, 160
first and second birth of, 95
genesis, 102
impact, 106, 107, 108, 141-43
implications, 106, 176
Indian industry, 127
rules to govern trade, 37
scenario, 138-43, 178
small scale industry, 128-30, 151, 160
trade, 94, 95, 104
trading system, 96
uniform law, 94

Winds of change, 167-68

World scenario, 92-94

World Trade agreement, 100

World War II, 95

Women entrepreneurs, 13

Y

Yerram Raju, Dr. B., 14

□□□